SHOW TIME

The American Political Circus
and the Race for the White House

ROGER SIMON

TIMES BOOKS

RANDOM HOUSE

Library of Congress Cataloging-in-Publication Data
Simon, Roger
Show time: the American political circus and the race for the White House
Roger Simon.
p.   cm.
Includes index.
ISBN 0-8129-2963-2 (hardcover)
1. Presidents—United States—Election—1996. 2. United States—Politics and
government—1993– . I. Title.
E888.S56   1998
324.973'0929—dc21   97-29268

Random House website address: www.randomhouse.com

Design by Robert Bull Design

Manufactured in the United States of America

9   8   7   6   5   4   3   2

First Edition

To Marcia's parents,
Anne and Martin Kramer,
and to my parents,
Pauline and Sheldon Simon

"Contrary to popular belief, Barnum's great discovery was not how easy it was to deceive the public, but rather how much the public enjoyed being deceived. Especially if they could see how it was being done. They were flattered that anyone would use such ingenuity to entertain them."

—Daniel J. Boorstin, *The Image: A Guide to Pseudo-Events in America*, 1981

CONTENTS

PREFACE

THE CURTAIN RISES

THE NEW YORK TIMES MADE IT OFFICIAL: "AS A MATter of fact, there hasn't been a duller national campaign in the last quarter of a century." The *Times* bemoaned the fact that even political workers were "pinching themselves to see whether they are really awake or dreaming. They seem scarcely able to realize that a national campaign actually is in progress and under full swing."

It hadn't always been like this, the *Times* griped. In past campaigns there had been spellbinding speakers and interesting campaign "stunts." Alas, those were now missing, and that contributed to the "dullness" of the campaign.

The date of the *Times* report was October 12, 1908. William Howard Taft was running against William Jennings Bryan, and the *Times* was unspeakably bored.

So even 90 years ago, the media felt that politicians had an obligation to be entertaining.

Historians of today see the 1908 race much differently than did journalists of the time. Looking back on it, the race was both exciting and highly significant. The nation's first public relations firm had been founded three years earlier, and Taft and Bryan were outdoing each other in trying to demonstrate their "common touch."

The Republican National Convention ballyhooed the claim that Taft was the "best-natured" candidate and "knows how to hold a baby." (In 1996, Bob Dole made the improbable claim that people would rather leave their children with him than Bill Clinton. Clinton responded: "Let's say that you were going on vacation for a couple of weeks. Who do you trust to water your plants? Bob Dole or Bill Clinton?")

"The 1908 campaign marked a milestone in campaign history,"

wrote modern-day campaign historian Gil Troy. "For the first time, both major party candidates stumped actively and openly. . . . In America's consumer culture, ambition was no longer a dirty word, and was in fact required."

T HE PRESS IN 1996 WAS ALMOST UNANIMOUS IN CONDEMN- ing the presidential campaign for being inexpressibly dull. A post-election analysis of the race by the Freedom Forum was titled: "Lethargy '96: How the Media Covered a Listless Campaign." Politicians, the press felt, still had an obligation to captivate their audience, to be engaging, interesting, and, whenever possible, funny (whether on purpose or by accident).

One way to be interesting was to be irresponsible. Nobody complained that the presidential campaign of 1988 was listless. It was decided on such "issues" as Willie Horton, flag factories, the Pledge of Allegiance, and tank rides. It was vitriolic, reckless, and trivial. The press loved it. But 1996 was a different campaign. Both sides decided that the press existed to be manipulated, not entertained. And both sides used vastly different methods, with different degrees of success, to achieve their goals. Neither side cared, however, whether the press was enthralled or not. "When you're an incumbent and the economy is doing well," Clinton aide George Stephanopoulos said, "boring is good."

But Stephanopoulos meant that the press would be bored, not the public. The entertainment, or at least the captivation, of the public was what the White House spent an enormous amount of time worrying about and working on. From the first day to the last, the campaign was viewed as a performance.

"This is the first campaign I know of," presidential spokesman Mike McCurry told me, "where we really beat the other side by a country mile on *stagecraft*."

T HOSE OUTSIDE THE WHITE HOUSE, EVEN DEMOCRATS, WERE slow to understand this essential fact. Clinton looked so weak going into the 1996 campaign (in April 1995, he had to assert during a press conference that he was "relevant" because it said so in the Constitution) that Chris Dodd, co-chairman of the Democratic Party, invited David Letterman's producer, advertising executives, and film producers to a breakfast to come up with a snazzy new image for Clinton and the Democrats. "[Dodd] was interested in a magic formula to hypnotize people and make them follow," one advertising executive told Rick Berke of *The New York Times.*

The meeting was a flop, but Dodd needn't have worried. Bill Clinton already had his magic formula: He knew that politics was a stage play, a show. You didn't have to hypnotize people. You just had to beguile them.

JOSH KING LIVED TO MAKE SURE THAT WHAT HE CALLED "THE OP-tics and theatrics" of each Bill Clinton event was perfect. In June 1996, in France for an economic summit, King had set up an outdoor event that was picture-perfect except for one thing: Clouds of gnats boiled up from nowhere, swirled around the presidential head, and threatened to fly up the presidential nose. The day before, King had gone out to the speech site at the time the speech was to take place to check on the position of the sun. (King always wanted the sun basking the president in its glow to show off his handsome features, but King also always added artificial lighting to take away any shadows.) He had also checked the sound for a solid two hours (there was no worse sin in the Clinton White House than a bad sound system) and no gnats had appeared. But on the appointed day at the appointed hour, millions of Gallic gnats treated Clinton like a slice of French pastry. And though it made for a funny TV picture (Clinton ducking and waving his hand in front of his face) nobody in the White House was amused. The gnat attack was treated with the utmost seriousness.

"We always want to associate the president with a pretty picture," King said, which is why he had picked a pretty outdoor site. "But it backfired."

"What the fuck was up with the gnats?" King's boss, Don Baer, had said to him afterward.

"It did not put the president in a position of commanding authority," White House Chief of Staff Leon Panetta had said.

"It was tough out there," the commander in chief had said.

Josh King was the White House Director of Production for Presidential Events, and it was his job to worry about gnats. And now he does. All the time. (It is not known whether the Secret Service has orders to shoot them.) Just as he worries about what words to put on the "armor."

Few know about the armor, even White House reporters who have seen it thousands of times without realizing it. Flanking each side of the presidential lectern is a panel about two feet high and four feet long. The panels are made of thick steel, and past White House advance teams have covered them up with plants or blue cloth to make them look less ugly. Their purpose, never talked about, is to protect the president should someone rise out of the audience and start shooting at him. The Secret Service wants those steel panels, which they refer to as the armor, at each speech so they can throw the president behind them should gunfire break out.

Josh King never saw the armor as mere protection, however. He saw it as a billboard. And he took away the plants and the cloth and started pasting signs on the armor like "Meeting America's Challenges" on the left and "Protecting America's Values" on the right. In Oklahoma City, in April 1995, Clinton had gone to memorialize the 168 people killed in the bombing of the Federal Building there. As at all presidential appearances, the "optics" and "theatrics" were carefully planned. (King had nothing to do with what the president said. He was in charge of what people *saw* when the president said it.) And a sign of how seriously the White House took this was the considerable power that King had. He noticed in Oklahoma City that the armor's usual position flanking the lectern (where it was most likely to save the president's life should it be needed) would spoil the TV shot of the victims' families, who were arrayed behind Clinton. "It was so goddamn frustrating," King said. Solution? Move the families? Naw. Move the armor. And after King made a "special plea" to the Secret Service, the armor was moved from in front of Clinton to behind him. The picture was that important.

"We've achieved as close as we could to perfection during the campaign," King said. And perfection, the White House believed, was made up of a thousand tiny things that had to be pursued with an almost maniacal attention to detail. The Clinton campaign distributed Mylar ribbons attached to balloon sticks to the crowds so that people could wave them, making a nice blur of color for the TV cameras. But King made sure the color was the right color. "We made sure the colors were *pride inspiring*," he said. "Orange for Arizona, green and orange for Florida, green for Oregon."

The Reagan administration had gotten a great deal of publicity for the simple act of making sure the president stood in front of pretty or awe-inspiring backgrounds when he spoke. But the Clinton White House did real pioneering work that it wanted no publicity for. ("Process pieces are bad because they make people more cynical than they are already," White House advance man Jim Loftus told me.) The White House analyzed the picture structure of television stories: Almost every TV story began with a wide shot to set the scene (Clinton comes to Chicago), a medium shot to show who Clinton was with onstage (Mayor Daley is standing next to him on the podium), a cutaway shot to show the audience (people applauding, laughing, cheering), and then the tight shot of Clinton's face during the speech (the president actually speaks words). The White House analysis showed that the tight shot lasted the longest, since the viewers had to hear what Clinton was saying. So it was the most important shot, but it was also ignored by other post-Reagan campaigners who were concentrating on the background, which was visible for only a few seconds in the wide shot.

Josh King set about to use the tight shot. But what could you do, considering the president's head filled so much of it? Well, there was some space to the left and the right of the head that was always visible. And if you displayed banners in exactly the right location to stay in focus, you could put messages that people would see on TV while the president spoke. So King cooked up a computer program that displayed the presidential lectern and a six-foot two-inch gray blob to represent the president and then wrote in banners on each side of the blob to see what worked. And pretty soon, whenever a voter was watching the president speak on TV, there would be these banners on each side of his head saying, "Stronger American Families" and "Stronger American Communities."

Nobody at the White House believed these would mesmerize voters (or even that viewers paid a lot of attention to them). But every detail contributed to the whole. And the whole was a picture-perfect presentation by a great showman, where the stage was always four feet high (so people could wave their signs in the crowd and not block the TV cameras) and where the people behind Clinton on the stage were carefully out of focus so they would not distract from the president.

King popped a tape into a professional tape-editing machine for me one day in his spacious Old Executive Office Building office next to the White House. The tape was network TV coverage of a Bob Dole speech, where the stage was crowded with young kids. (The crowded stage had also been a Ronald Reagan invention.) But while Dole spoke, the kids onstage grew fidgety and you could see one girl staring off into space and one boy scratching his head. "You see that and you'd go with the incumbent," King said. And he made sure kids were not visible in Bill Clinton's tight shot.

King made sure there was "podium discipline" so people didn't just barge around when Clinton was onstage (as they always did when Dole was onstage) and way before Chico, California, where Dole fell off the stage because a decorative banister had not been secured, the rule of the White House advance staff was: "If it's going on the stage, stick a nail through it." The arrival of *Air Force One* was pure ballet, with the press always grouped under the wing of the plane and the president standing at the top of the steps and waving to the crowd—whether a crowd existed or not.

Each event was a small play, a small theatrical performance, designed to convey the power, majesty, sensitivity (it changed from stop to stop) of the man in the White House. And just before the president took the stage at each event, he would walk over to Josh King, and King would say, "You go out and wave from the little X on the stage." And the president would do it.

Josh King was 31. But the president of the United States listened to him because he agreed, as everyone in power at the White House agreed, with what TV producer and presidential adviser Harry Thomason would tell me: "TV shows and movies and political events are *all the same.* They are all designed to move people."

Practically everyone in politics knows that instinctively. So when Josh King found himself one day giving orders to President Hosni Mubarak of Egypt and King Hussein of Jordan as to where to stand, he knew they would not be offended. "They didn't object," King said. "They watch CNN and know what we are trying to do."

And they did. Every politician across the globe knew about the show, the picture, the performance. Which made it even more astonishing that Bob Dole did not.

It wasn't that the picture or the color of the Mylar or words in the tight shot was enough. It was not. But neither were positions and policy enough. If you took a stand, developed a policy, implemented a program, and you couldn't communicate that to the public, it was truly a tree falling in a forest with no one around to hear it.

While press critics bemoaned the fact that too much of campaign journalism was devoted to the election process (instead of those oh-so-fascinating issues) the process is what elects people. And though the campaign of 1996 was criticized for being dull, it was actually one of the greatest shows on earth.

Just ask Bill Clinton: Before each stop, just before he exited *Air Force One,* he would square his shoulders, suck in his gut, turn to Harold Ickes, his deputy chief of staff, and say, "Okay. *Show time!*"

ROPE LINE

★

"He wanted to win the voters one by one. He would have gone to all 250 million of them if we could have figured out a way to do it."

—Mike McCurry, White House spokesman, to author, December 3, 1996

THE LONG BLACK ANACONDA THAT IS THE PRESIDEN-tial motorcade glides down the darkened streets of Universal City outside Los Angeles. The motorcade is an awesome thing, some forty cars and vans carrying Bill Clinton, his staff, honored guests, aides, hangers-on, technicians, reporters, Secret Service agents, and enough automatic weapons to end (or start) a small war. The president rides in a black Cadillac limousine, his flag of office whipping from the front bumper. (There are two identical limousines, in fact, and they travel one behind the other. Nobody is supposed to know which one the president is riding in. In tunnels they often switch positions to throw off potential assassins.) The motorcade radiates power. It is not just the massive length of the thing or the high speeds at which it travels, but its ability to ignore the laws that control mere mortals. The motorcade does not stop for stop signs or stoplights. It does not yield. All traffic stops for it. Whether it is winding its way down side streets or hurtling down interstate highways, all traffic is halted for the motorcade, even though the disruption can be enormous.

Here in California, motorcycle police, lights flashing on their giant Harley-Davidsons, halt traffic at each intersection and entrance ramp. As soon as the motorcade whooshes by, the police officer starts his cycle with a roar and hurtles forward, passing the motorcade to take up a position in front to block a new intersection. It is a motorized ballet, the dance that accompanies the unstoppable force that is a president on the move.

It is a cool October night, and only the occasional street light reflects from the flashing black shapes of the motorcade. Bill Clinton is on his twenty-eighth trip to California since becoming president, a fact that reflects two things: First, California has many wealthy people who like to give money to political causes (especially if those causes will provide them with a night in the Lincoln Bedroom), and second, it has 54 electoral votes, one-fifth of what a candidate needs to win the presidency. Think of it another way: If you deny California to your opponent, he has to win a lot of other states to make up for it. And Clinton intends to deny California to Bob Dole.

Clinton has been campaigning without letup, no matter how far ahead the polls show him. He has very much bought into the campaign strategy articulated, if that is the word for it, by his campaign manager, Peter Knight: "We wanted to be rolling over [the Dole campaign] every time they stuck their heads up. We didn't want to let them off the mat. We feared the race would tighten up. So we felt we had to keep their necks pinned to the ground." That all the metaphors used by Knight were ones of physical violence was no accident. The strategy was not just to stay in Dole's face, but to suck up his air supply. Bill Clinton was 15 points ahead in California? Send him back there. Why shouldn't he be 25 points ahead? Why not 55? Why not 155? Roll over them. Don't let them off the mat. Stand on their necks.

The Dole people approached the election with a totally different outlook, one that would handcuff their thinking throughout the campaign: Bill Clinton was a man of bad character and a bad president. He was a liar and a cheat and a scoundrel. He was motivated by naked ambition, personal greed, and sexual lust. The Dole people saw this clearly and felt it keenly, just as *anyone*, they believed, should be able to see it and feel it. So all the Dole campaign really had to do was wait for the public to wake up and smell the rot. So what if Bob Dole was not the silver-tongued campaigner that Bill Clinton was? When the people finally saw through Bill Clinton's pathetic act, they would turn to Bob Dole in droves. The Clinton people had no such blinders on their thinking. To them the campaign was not about morals or values or character. It was about reelecting Bill Clinton. The Clinton campaign staff knew that fundamentally Bob Dole was a competent and decent man. And that is why he had to be destroyed.

THE MOTORCADE ENTERS THE BACK LOT OF UNIVERSAL STUDIOS, where movies and TV shows are made. Slowing down only slightly, we whip past life-size streets: New York in the Gay Nineties, *Leave It to Beaver* suburbia, the cobblestones of a European town square, an ancient Roman plaza where Spartacus fought, the Victorian horror house from *Psycho*, and the Bates Motel next to it. As we begin to slow down, we come upon a beached boat. "The *Minnow*," a photographer in the press van whispers in awe. "*Gilligan's Island*." The ride is spooky and disconcerting. Where are we really? *When* are we really? The cars squeal to a halt and we pile out. The still photographers, cameras bouncing off their chests and hips, lead the way. We lope up a darkened side street, turn a corner . . . and burst into blinding light.

We are in a town square, a real town square with green grass and a gigantic spreading oak tree. The square is packed with thousands of people lit from above and behind by harsh klieg lights. There are buildings around the square: a movie house, a variety store, a gas station. I go up to one building and touch it to see if it is merely painted wood, but it is solid brick and real. Everything seems hauntingly familiar, but we cannot put a name to this place. And then we see the large stage that has been built for Clinton. It thrusts out from the steps of a grand courthouse, a massive building of red brick, fronted by four enormous fluted stone columns holding up a pediment that contains an ornate clock, with what look like stone mountain lions on each side. On top of the clock is a lightning rod. The hands of the clock are stopped at five minutes to six.

"Jesus H. Christ," a reporter says. "It's *Back to the Future!*"

Joe Lockhart, Clinton's campaign press secretary, turns around and beams at us. "Hill Valley," he says, a huge smile on his face. Hill Valley is the mythical town where Michael J. Fox kept going back and forth in his Delorean time machine. More important to the Hollywood glitterati standing now in the town square, *Back to the Future* did $210 million domestic gross and spawned two popular sequels. Bob Dole recently gave a speech praising *Independence Day* for its emphasis on American values. (Dole, who had never seen the movie, was unaware that the Capitol, the White House, and Los Angeles are blown to smithereens during the film. His critique was delivered in typical Dole-speak: "We won. The end. Leadership. America. Good over evil.") But this is a very nifty piece of stagecraft.

Bill Clinton is building a bridge to the twenty-first century, a bridge to the future (get it?), and his campaign has come *back to the future* (do you get it now?) to talk about it. The Dole campaign, whose typical speech site is a gymnasium, has never come up with a gimmick like this one. "We only do these events after Dole's bedtime," Lockhart says and laughs. "This is a campaign of *ideas.*"

The crowd is enormous, maybe 5,000 people packing the square and making numerous trips to the bars set up on the periphery of the lawn. They carry beer bottles and plastic cups of amber liquid. A jazz band plays off to the right on a small stage.

The air is crisp. Hanging in the sky is a sliver of moon so perfect you expect to see a man climbing down from a ladder after painting it on a backdrop. At this and two similar events, Bill Clinton will raise $10 million for the Democratic Party. Money is the fuel that makes the campaign engine run, and the Clinton engine has a voracious appetite. Huge banks of lights illuminate the stage, where legendary movie executive Lew Wasserman stands next to Michael Douglas. Off to one side is House Minority Leader Dick Gephardt, Senate Minority Leader Tom Daschle, Senator Chris Dodd, the cochairman of the Democratic Party, San Francisco Mayor Willie Brown, and Jesse Jackson.

Clinton walks out onto the stage and the crowd bursts into wild applause. He is late (he is always late). But as usual, the crowd is uncomplaining. Clinton's routine is to scan the crowd and then look piercingly at certain individuals, making eye contact, holding them in his gaze. It is his lifelong trademark. His boyhood friend David Leopoulos recounts that day when a 9-year-old Clinton walked into the playground of his elementary school, stuck out his hand, and fixed him with that penetrating blue-eyed stare. "Hi, I'm Billy Clinton," Clinton said. Years later, Leopoulos said, "There's just this *presence*. He'd look you in the eye and get to know you." Tonight, however, Clinton looks about him, directing a quizzical gaze around the square. Then he turns around and looks up at the clock. He does an enormous double take that can be seen all the way to the back row of the crowd (he is a born performer) and the crowd roars again.

Clinton walks over to Michael Douglas and points up at the clock. *"Back to the Future!"* the president says to him, a delighted, boyish look on his face.

Douglas looks a little puzzled. Yeah, right, they made the movie here. That's why they call it a back lot. So what's the point? Clinton then walks over to Jesse Jackson and whirls him around and points up at the clock, tossing his head back and laughing. *Back to the Future! Get it? Get it?*

Finally, his mirth subsiding, Clinton takes his place in line with the other dignitaries and begins the ritual: While he waits to speak, half listening to his introductions, he scans the crowd, making eye contact. He nods, shoots out a finger to point to a person, or mouths a little "hello." With the possible exception of Richard Simmons, he is also the only public figure in America who can get away with blowing the occasional kiss. Naturally, in large crowds nobody can be sure who the president is actually pointing to, but that only increases the effect: one nod can give a golden glow to 50 people.

"Hi," Clinton mouths silently as the dignitaries continue speaking about him. "Hah, there. H'ar you? Hah."

Michael Douglas steps up behind the lectern from which the presidential seal will be hung as soon as it is Clinton's turn to speak. The lectern is known as the Blue Goose; it travels in the same military cargo plane that transports the limousines and other presidential paraphernalia and is armored. It is also tall, and Douglas is dwarfed behind it.

"Stand on the box!" somebody shouts, and Douglas learns there is a little step that slides out from the back of the Blue Goose for people not as tall as the president. Douglas pulls it out and climbs upon it. Height notwithstanding, it is perfect casting. Douglas played Democratic President Andrew Shepherd in the movie *The American President*. He was a lonely widower who got to sleep with Annette Bening on their third date. (Clinton liked the movie a lot.) Considered a pro-Clinton movie—the president's archenemy was an older senator from Kansas played by Richard Dreyfuss—it contained the memorable lines uttered by a White House aide: "People want leadership, Mr. President, and in the absence of genuine leadership, they'll listen to anyone who steps up to the microphone. They're thirsty for it. They'll crawl through the desert toward a mirage, and when they discover there's no water, they'll drink the sand." The movie did a domestic gross of $60 million.

Clinton loves Hollywood in a star-struck, small-town way and he is unabashed about it. On September 16, 1992, Clinton had appeared before a crowd of Hollywood stars and said, "I've always wanted to be in the cultural elite!" This year, contributions from Hollywood to the presidential campaigns have been running seven to one in Clinton's favor. And Clinton has already had Barbra Streisand, Chevy Chase, Richard Dreyfuss, and Tom Hanks "over to the house" in Washington. Bob Dole? Campaign records show that Bob Dole received $1,000 each from Chuck Norris and Bob Hope.

Earlier on this day, Clinton had helicoptered over to the ten-acre Mediterranean-style Beverly Hills estate of Ron Burkle, chairman of the Ralph's supermarket holding company, where about 200 guests, including boxing promoter Don King, had coughed up big dough for the Democratic Party. Clinton was wowed by the home, especially when he learned that some scenes from *The Godfather* had been shot there. Though Clinton does not ask for money himself at such public gatherings—his fund-raising speeches are usually indiscernible from his daily campaign speeches—he is relentless in raising the dough. It is one of the many things that politics and moviemaking have in common: they are both obscenely expensive. In 1996, Clinton would attend at least 90 fund-raisers, including 23 in the month of September alone. And he personally recommended increasing the number of dinners for $10,000 donors. You get just 100 of those people in a room, or in a Beverly Hills mansion, and you've got yourself $1 million. Easy money. Besides, it was $1 million of Hollywood money that wouldn't disappear up people's noses. So you could look at what Clinton was doing as a public service. He did.

"I do know the difference between make-believe and reality," Douglas was saying to the crowd. "And while I was working on *An American President* I would think about the real president. I would think about his stamina and his incredible knowledge about so many subjects. And I just want to say . . ." And here Douglas turns and looks back to Clinton, 5,000 pairs of eyes following him. "And I just want to say: Mr. President, I'm a fan. I enjoy your work."

The crowd squeals with delight. "I'm a fan; I enjoy your work" is what every autograph seeker says when going up to a star. And here Michael Douglas, the playacting president, was saying it to Bill Clinton, the real president, and, well, it just worked. It bordered on too cute, but it worked. And though he did not say it, Douglas also was very familiar with another similarity between movies and politics: a slavish devotion to public opinion. In the original ending of *Fatal Attraction*, Glenn Close's character committed suicide. Focus groups hated it, however, and the ending was changed to let Michael Douglas's wife kill her.

Douglas walks back from the lectern and Clinton shakes his hand. Then Douglas turns and leaves the stage. He walks over to a waiting limousine and roars off. In Washington this would have been a terrible gaffe, bordering on deadly insult. Nobody leaves a podium before the president of the United States is finished speaking. But in Hollywood nobody gives it a second thought. Hey, Michael Douglas is a busy man. He is box office. What did *Clinton's* last film gross?

At 8:10 P.M., with a cold breeze now beginning to blow, Clinton begins his speech. As always, he begins with his thank-yous, which come out sounding like "thang-kyew" in his soft Arkansas drawl, a drawl that thickens when he travels to the South, but never disappears no matter where he is. This night there are thang-kyews for Lew Wasserman, Michael Douglas, the UCLA Marching Band, "Conrad Janus and the Beverly Hills Unlisted Jazz Band," and on and on. The press sometimes makes fun of this, but Clinton knows the effectiveness of it. It changes the dynamic of the event. The crowd is no longer faceless, but made up of individuals, some of whom have worked hard for their president and deserve to be thanked. And, by implication, those who work hard for their president in the future—or give him large sums of money—will be publicly thanked in the future. Bob Dole ends every speech (when he remembers) by saying, "God bless America." Bill Clinton ends every speech by saying, "God bless you." The difference is both simple and profound. Dole sees the country as

an institution: America. Clinton sees the country as a collection of individuals: You. You out there. All of you. Thang-kyew!

Clinton speaks slowly and easily for the next twenty-five minutes.
Like most of his speeches, there is nothing particularly memorable
about it. Except on extraordinary occasions, his speeches do not soar.
They are more like easy listening. But they are always, like the man
himself, engaging. "And I suppose even here on the set of *Back to the
Future*," Clinton says with a dip of his head and a chuckle, "I can say
we should be thinking about tomorrow."

When he is done, the people roar, some waving their beer bottles at
him, and the band starts up with Michael Bolton now singing "Georgia
on My Mind," which apparently is as close as they can come to
Arkansas. Clinton waves from the lectern and then slowly walks to the
side of the stage and down the stairs. A Secret Service detail flanks him
as he moves up to the rope line, which is stretched along the front row
of the crowd. After every speech, no matter how late, no matter if it is
blazing sun or pouring rain, Bill Clinton works the rope line. The rope
line is what he lives for.

Sometimes it is a real rope stretched between stanchions. More
often it is interlocked pieces of fencing with vertical bars, called bicycle stands by the advance staff, which are low enough for people to
easily see over but too high to hurdle easily. Sometimes, at outdoor
barbecues or picnic events, the rope line is made up of hay bales. The
Secret Service would like at least fifteen feet between the crowd and
the president during his speeches (though they are often argued down
to ten), but the distance becomes immaterial when Clinton works the
rope line. Here is where he reaches out into the crowd, touching and
being touched. Here is where he forges his link to the people.

Speeches are fine, but people can see the speeches on C-SPAN.
What you cannot get on C-SPAN (or on the Internet or in the newspapers or on radio) is the rope line. You can get that only by showing up
at the event. Ironically, TV helped create the rope line. For most of
American history, voters saw their presidents from afar, if at all. Unless
you were in the front rows of a political rally, the president was but
a speck on the stage. (In the only existing photograph of Lincoln at
Gettysburg, Lincoln is a tiny blob, recognizable only because of his tall
stovepipe hat.) But TV changed this. TV gave us not just the picture but
the close-up picture. And the close-up brought the president to us in an
extremely intimate way. We could examine every pore on his face, see
every twitch of his mouth, every tick of his eyelid, every welling of a
tear. The close-up was so powerful it created a bond. We felt we knew
the president "up close and personal." And now when Americans went

out to see him in the flesh, they wanted to see him as closely as they saw him on TV. They wanted to touch him and be touched back. And Bill Clinton loved to oblige.

His campaign days lasted as long as they did (often more than twelve hours) in no small measure because of the time he spent slowly and methodically working the rope line. It was not uncommon for Clinton's rope line time to last longer than his speech. "It's the only campaign I've ever been on where the candidate goes home after the crowd," Doug Sosnik, the White House political director, said. It was literally true. Working the rope line constantly made Clinton late, but he did not care. Late for *what*? The rope line *was* the campaign to him.

Clinton's favorite rope line technique scared the hell out of the Secret Service. He loved to reach both arms forward, spread out his fingers, rise up on his toes, and thrust his hands into the second, third, or fourth row of the crowd so people back there could touch him, too. It was an extremely vulnerable thing to do. When he spread his arms, it opened up his body. The Secret Service could only watch in horror. "The Secret Service does not decide what he can do," Jim Loftus, one of Clinton's advance men, told me. "*He* decides what he can do." People would clutch at his hands, his arms, his shoulders. They would immobilize him. They did not want to let go. In Chicago he had to slip off his wedding band and put it in his pocket because all the grasping hands made it tear into his flesh. And after working the rope line, Clinton would climb back in the limousine, take out a can of an antibacterial foam, and lather the stuff on his hands to kill the germs he might very well have picked up after touching hundreds of hands.

In September, late at night in Monterey, California, Clinton climbed a steep hill to a fence topped with barbed wire and thrust his arms between the strands, jagged metal inches from his flesh, in order to shake more hands. In late October a bizarre story circulated that there was a "groupie" flesh cult following Clinton that operated out of Hollywood and liked to collect the skin of famous people under their fingernails. Clinton aides never believed the story, and Clinton was never intentionally scratched that he knew of. The only real problem came from people trying to grab his presidential cuff links. (The cuff links were traditionally distributed by presidents as gifts, but Clinton liked them well enough to wear a pair himself.) In Seattle, when Secret Service agents found a live bullet outside the rope line area, they held up a portable Kevlar barrier in front of Clinton as he moved along the line. It was covered in dark blue nylon to make it look more elegant, but there was no disguising what it was. The agents would have been far happier if Clinton had skipped the rope line, but he was not about to. A bullet? Big deal. No bullet was going to keep him from touching and being touched.

And sometimes he would rescue people. At a rally in Philadelphia when Marion Hill, 65, gray-haired and arthritic, had sagged to the ground when the crowd surged forward to touch Clinton, he reached over the barricade, grabbed her by both arms, and tried to lift her to her feet. "I'm holding you," he said to her as the crowd clutched wildly at him. A Secret Service agent threw his arms around Clinton's waist to keep him from toppling over the fencing. It was a stalemate, but Clinton would not let go of Marion Hill. Finally, security guards moved the crowd back. (At a Fourth of July parade outside Chicago, a man thrust his small child into Dole's one good arm. Dole's knees buckled and he nearly dropped the child before a Secret Service agent rushed over to help. "I'm not supposed to lift anything real heavy with my left arm," Dole said. "I don't even do suitcases or things like that." Dole, too, worked rope lines, though not nearly as often nor as long nor with the same enthusiasm. "I kind of like to visit with them afterward, but you always have two rows of kids and can never get back to the taxpayers," Dole once grumped about the rope line. What he didn't understand was that by being nice to kids, by spending time with them, it not only got on television, but they went home and told their taxpaying parents about it, as Bill Clinton would later prove with spectacular results.)

The other thing people noticed about Clinton on the rope line was the utter concentration he brought to the job. His upper lip often curled over his lower one as he made eye contact with person after person, reaching out to them, lasering them with his baby blues. He once kept the leaders of Japan, Italy, France, Germany, Canada, and Great Britain waiting while he stood for five minutes on the tarmac in Nova Scotia, talking about Bosnia with a skeptical 16-year-old Canadian girl. In late October, in Miami, a young girl in a wheelchair had got near the rope line, but as the crowd pushed forward to touch Clinton she became frightened and began to cry. "Back up! Back up, please!" Clinton shouted. And as the crowd backed up, he reached down and wiped the tears from the frightened girl's cheeks with his hand. You can't teach that kind of stagecraft to a candidate. Candidates can be coached and rehearsed and choreographed and prepped for special events like speeches and debates. But certain parts of a campaign defy rehearsal. Which is where Clinton did his best work. "He is like an improvisational actor," Michael Sheehan, his speech and debate coach and a graduate of the Yale Drama School, said. An improvisational actor immerses himself in his role, becomes his role. "You feel the part, and you see what comes out," Sheehan said.

So Bill Clinton never had to worry about appearing caring or sincere. It was a role he had immersed himself in for a very long time. And he had it down pat.

And after each rope line, when he had gotten back in the limousine or climbed back aboard Air Force One, it was always the same. Clinton would tell rope line stories to his aides: how much the crowd liked him, how much they praised him. The stories were often so self-serving that the staff was reluctant to pass them along to reporters. But they realized he repeated them not to boost his own ego (which was considerable), but because he needed the constant reinforcement. He had his staff, which contained the usual number of toadies and sycophants. But they were the hired help. These people, the voters, as he constantly reminded everyone, employed him. "Did you hear that guy?" Clinton said after working a rope line at Ohio State University and meeting David Mitchell, 49, a Coast Guard veteran. "He said, 'When I came here I was voting for Dole, but I changed my mind.' Did you hear him say it? Did you hear him?" Later, stopping the motorcade to meet some elementary school children, Clinton was delighted to learn that his name had been on their morning spelling test. "I was on their *spelling test!*" he told his aides aboard *Air Force One*, the glee bubbling over in his voice. "Can you believe it?" They believed it.

Though some of them did not believe it was very important. Some thought it was a waste of time. Okay, give the rope line 10 or 15 minutes like Dole did, so the cameras could show you working the rope line, but then get the hell out of there and on to the next speech (or home). Even his advance staff often missed the point. Jim Loftus told him in 1992 that spending a lot of time on the rope line was a waste. "You can't shake enough hands to win the presidency," Loftus said. Clinton gave him a sad, sour look. Loftus just didn't get it. Unless you had been a candidate, you could not get it.

The roar of the crowd was great. It got you up. And you could learn from crowds—what lines they liked, what they didn't. After the campaign, disgraced presidential adviser Dick Morris said Clinton was a "little weird" in that he was able to measure public opinion by watching the crowd as he spoke. He has "a skin which can sort of absorb" what people were thinking, Morris said. But the speeches were not enough. Watching the crowd and listening to the crowd were not enough for Clinton. *He needed their flesh.* He needed to touch them and feel them and have them touch and feel him. He needed not just their protestations of love, but a physical manifestation of it. It sustained and strengthened him. In Greek mythology, Antaeus, a giant, almost defeated Hercules in a wrestling match. Every time Hercules threw Antaeus to the ground, Antaeus would draw strength from the earth and come back stronger. Only when Hercules lifted Antaeus above his head was he able to slay him. The crowds were Bill Clinton's ground. They were the source of his strength. But they could not be just a sea of faces. They had to be individual people.

On October 24, 1996, the ultimate rope line event occurred. It was after a speech at Lake Charles, Louisiana, and Clinton had been working the rope line for several minutes. Because the space between the rope line and the stage was narrow, the TV pool had a hard time getting a boom microphone over to him. But cameras captured the scene beautifully: Mary Ellen Savoie, a teenager from Sulphur, Louisiana, waited patiently for Clinton and then told him she was "very pro-life." She asked him he could take the life of innocent babies with the terrible procedure she called partial birth abortion. It was one of Bob Dole's key issues: While polls showed most of the country approved of choice when it came to abortion, something like 70 percent of the population opposed third-trimester abortions, in which the skull of the fetus had to be crushed to remove it from the birth canal. Congress had banned it, but Clinton had vetoed the ban. This was exactly the kind of issue, Dole and his campaign believed, that would expose Clinton as the left-liberal he was and open up a gulf between him and the voters.

Clinton was not unused to hecklers. And he knew it was sometimes best to simply keep walking when confronted by one. But he also knew he had the magic. He turned away from the rest of the crowd and settled his gaze upon Mary Ellen Savoie. He put his large hands on her slender shoulders. And for the next five minutes, she and Bill Clinton were the only two people in the world.

He wanted to sign that bill banning those abortions, Clinton told Savoie. He had signed a similar bill in Arkansas, when he was governor. But then he found out that a few hundred women every year were faced with the agonizing situation of giving birth to a horribly deformed child, who would soon die. Before vetoing the ban, he had met with six such women and learned that they could not have further babies "unless the enormous size of the baby's head" was reduced before it was extracted from their bodies, Clinton told her. And how could he tell these women that they could never have another baby? "I know there are just a few hundred of them, and I know that all the votes were on the other side," Clinton would say later. "And I'm just telling you— Hillary and I, we only had one child. And I just cannot look at a woman who's in a situation where the baby she is bearing against all her wishes and prayers is going to die anyway, and tell her that I am signing a law which will prevent her from ever having another child. I'm not going to do it."

Mary Ellen Savoie looked up at the president of the United States.

Tears streamed down her young face. She threw her arms around him. She hugged him to her. And Bill Clinton, tears welling up in his eyes, hugged her back. She still strongly opposed abortion, Savoie said, but now she could go home and tell her mom it was okay to vote for Bill Clinton.

"He's a nice man," Mary Ellen Savoie said later.

The news clip ran on the nightly news all across America. Because the TV crews could not get their boom mikes over to Clinton, it ran without words. Which made it even more powerful. In America today, one social scientist has noted, "eloquence is visual, not verbal." Visual images are more quickly comprehended by the human mind than verbal ones. Audiences (especially the ones sitting at home, far away from the event) are far more likely to remember what they *saw* than what they *heard*. And Clinton was a master of the visual image. So America saw him standing at the rope line, his hands on Mary Ellen Savoie's shoulders, speaking to her quietly, patiently, and then her hugging him and him putting his cheek on top of her head and hugging her back. It brought tears to the eyes of many who saw it, *even though they had no idea what the two were talking about.*

Television was the perfect medium for the transmission of emotion. Ideas were much harder to convey on television. It was not for nothing that the chief question asked by TV reporters has always been, "How do you *feel* about that?" TV commercials, in fact, whether for products or politicians, are not about words or pictures. They are about the feelings evoked by the pictures. When Coca-Cola ran an ad featuring a bunch of puppies licking a little boy's face, the company was not saying that Coke attracts puppies. It was evoking the warm emotional response that viewers got from watching the scene. When you can do that, the consumer doesn't care what you are saying.

What Clinton said at his Lake Charles speech was forgotten almost as soon as the words left his mouth. But the scene of him hugging that girl and the feelings it evoked—warmth, caring, protectiveness—lasted and lasted in people's minds.

"So many people have said to Clinton, 'You took the *time* with that little girl,' " Mike McCurry told me weeks later. "Jim Miklaszewski (of NBC News) told me, 'You couldn't have ordered it from Central Casting.' "

The Democrats didn't need anybody from Central Casting. They had Bill Clinton.

Also campaigning in Louisiana that day, Bob Dole was wondering what was going on. He was stressing issues like a 15 percent tax cut and he was dying in the polls. Didn't people see through Bill Clinton? Didn't they see it was all show?

"I wonder sometimes what people are thinking about," Dole said. "Or if people are thinking at all. Wake up, America!"

IT IS SERIOUSLY CHILLY NOW, BUT BILL CLINTON CONTINUES to work the rope line on the set of *Back to the Future*. The crowd has all but disappeared. The honored guests have gone. The band has packed up. The bars are closed. The small group of reporters in the press pool is invited up on the empty stage so they can look down and see Clinton work the crowd. I walk up to the lectern, the Blue Goose, to get a closer look at it. The top has foam pads on the sides covered in blue leather, because Clinton likes to rest his arms there and grab the front of the lectern with both hands. I look out into the blindingly bright lights. From here, the people can be sensed better than they can be seen. You cannot see individual faces, I notice. I look out at the small knot of people still waiting to shake Clinton's hand, but all I can make out is a blue-white nimbus of light bursting around the black outlines of their heads. A thought occurs to me, and I walk back up-stage to where Clinton had waited to be introduced before he spoke. I look out again and see the same bright lights. So how could Clinton have seen the people in the crowd? As Clinton stood on the stage and gazed out at people, fixed them with his stare, winked and nodded and mouthed hello to them, how could he have known to whom he was waving?

No matter. All good love affairs begin with a seduction, and this was Clinton's seduction: the wink, the wave, the nod, the stare, the speech, and then the consummation: the meeting of flesh on the rope line. And if part of it was an illusion, well, what part of presidential campaigning was not?

ABOARD *AIR FORCE ONE*, IN THE LARGE CONFERENCE ROOM next to Clinton's office, his campaign team gathered around the long, paper-strewn table, which was cleared only when the president came in to play hearts. Now, a more important matter was under discussion. The schedule had been heavy, the president looked tired, and his voice was always at risk. He was far ahead in the polls and so perhaps, somebody suggested, they should lighten up on the scheduling. Did the president really need to do four or five events a day?

Harold Ickes, the deputy chief of staff, went in to see Clinton and asked if he might want to cut back a little.

"Look," Clinton told him, "this is my last campaign. Don't worry about it."

DOLEFUL

★

Dole: [In] all the focus groups, a lot of people know that I'm a senator and in Washington, but they don't know much else.
Reporter: What is the single most important thing for them to know about you?
Dole: Beats me.

—Bob Dole, aboard his campaign plane, May 31, 1996

THE GREAT, SWIRLING MEDIA MOB SWEEPS ALONG THE aisles of Philadelphia's Reading Terminal Market with Bob Dole at its center. It is an elbow event, an event when the people crush up against the candidate and a path must be cleared by the elbows, forearms, and hips of the Secret Service agents. The agents loathe elbow events. Letting people reach out and touch a candidate is the same as letting them try to stick a knife in him. It is stupid and unnecessary, especially by the year 1996, when the whole campaign could be done from a nice, safe TV studio. Except that TV is a medium that exists for good pictures, and elbow events make for that: the people jammed up tight against the candidate, making it look like they really want to see him (while in fact they often can't escape from him).

The agents keep a tight perimeter around Dole, some facing him, some facing the crowd, eyes always moving, watching the hands of the people. If trouble is going to come, it is going to come from their hands. Nobody has ever kicked a presidential candidate to death.

"What's that?" an agent screams at a gray-haired man, who is beginning to take a long leather wallet out from beneath his jacket.

"A wallet," the man screams back, scared witless, trying to step away from the agent, who is now a few inches off his nose. "It's just a wallet! I wanted an autograph! On a piece of paper!" The agent looks at him and looks away. Harmless.

Bob Dole doesn't do many elbow events. For one thing, he doesn't like to be jostled, doesn't really like being touched, and people always touch you at these events, as if to confirm you are real and not just a TV picture. For another thing, elbow events usually depend on a certain amount of crowd enthusiasm, and his campaign has enough trouble generating crowds, let alone ones with discernible emotions.

But the media monster has to be fed. And so an elbow event was called for. In this case, luckily, the campaign didn't even have to assemble it. The Reading Terminal Market, an old Philadelphia railroad station converted into a city market, is always crowded at lunchtime, its air thick with the smells of fresh produce—fish, meat, sausages, hoagies, pretzels, and cheese steaks. The crowd had not come to see Bob Dole; they weren't here for a political event, they were here to get lunch or buy something for their evening meal. They didn't know Dole was appearing here until his small motorcade pulled up outside, disgorged him, and he was immediately surrounded by his media/security swirl.

Dole never lacked for media coverage. As the Republican challenger, he was accorded the full complement of more than a hundred traveling press: print, radio, TV, and still photographers. And each wanted but one thing: to be right on top of the candidate. Within the narrow aisles of the market, gridlock was instantaneous. Dole found himself in the center of the media mob, cameras thrust in his face, tape recorders held up to his lips. And somewhere outside it, pressed back against the food stalls, were voters. It was sometimes hard to see them, but Dole knew they were out there someplace.

The more determined ones reach out a hand for a handshake or a piece of paper for an autograph. Because of his war wound, Dole must shake left-handed, which most people grasp awkwardly with their own right hands. Dole once praised Richard Nixon for being the only man who always offered his own left hand to Dole. Even though Dole has great difficulty writing (he essentially draws his name), he never refuses to give an autograph. When George Bush ran for reelection in 1992, he had an aide hand out preprinted autographs on little cards, each adorned with a presidential seal. People hated them. What, the guy couldn't take the time to sign an autograph? Like he was busy being leader of the Free World or something? Even *Madonna* signs autographs. Who did he think he was? (Bush lost in 1992.)

So Dole signs autographs. But it is an arduous task and requires the aid of his assistant, Mike Glassner, who now steadies the piece of paper on a clipboard and Dole bends over it, drawing painstakingly. "Make it to Dora Shermer," a woman yells in Dole's ear. "S-H-E-R-M-E, not A! E-R. OK, now say with best wishes . . ." And Dole grimaces and complies.

Frankly, Dole is better at giving autographs than making conversation. Platitudes are not really his thing. Campaigning is not really his thing. He hadn't had to do serious campaigning for decades, not since cadres of fresh-faced "Dolls for Dole" handed out cans of Dole pineapple slices in his hometown of Russell, Kansas, to remind people of his name.

But things would be different now. "In focus groups, 80 percent of people don't know who Bob Dole is," he has said. "They know I'm a senator and in Washington and that's probably what you *don't* want them to know." But now he is liberated. He is no longer going to be known as a senator from Washington, he is sure of that. Instead, he is going to be known as . . . well, that was the problem. What *is* he?

"They have a right to know who Bob Dole really is, what his agenda is, his so-called vision for America," he says. *So-called* vision for America. That's how Dole viewed it, viewed campaigning. Campaigns were for presenting crap like vision. They weren't about important things like legislating and solving problems. Well, he would go along with it. It's what his staff wanted, and they had the focus group reports to tell them it is what the people wanted. The public didn't want to know what the vote total was on S-1028 or how the conference committee report would come out. They wanted to know how he would lead the country. So give them what they want, right? Isn't that what campaigning was all about?

But watching Bob Dole try to persuade voters to vote for him was often like watching Darth Vader try to persuade Luke Skywalker to come over to the dark side.

"Good to *see* ya," Dole says to the people crushed on each side of the aisle. "*Good* to see ya. Good to see *ya.*" On occasion, he would sometimes add "Where you from?" to his conversational repertoire, and if the person came from across the Mississippi from where the two were then standing, Dole would throw in, "You're a long way from home!" (Otherwise, he would just nod.)

By happy coincidence, the Thunderbolts, World War II aviators who flew P-47 fighter planes, were holding a national convention in Philadelphia, and scores of them were in the market this day. They were, like Dole, in their seventies. But seeing them shrunken, bent, their collars gaping at the neck, shuffling with canes, one realizes how *good* Dole looks at 72. His campaign has got it all wrong: At his speeches, his handlers crowd the stage with teenagers to make Dole look young and fresh. Instead, they should crowd the stage with these old coots. They *really* make him look young and fresh. And Dole loves talking to the vets. He understands the vets.

Dole stops in front of a man wearing the words 507th FTR GP/465th SQDN on his baseball cap, indicating the number of his Fighter Group and Squadron from World War II. "Have a good time," Dole says seriously to him. "You *deserve* it." The man swells up with pride. When is the last time anybody told a vet he deserved anything for having served?

"You gonna win Pennsylvania?" the man asks Dole.

"Why not?" Dole shoots back and then goes into his staccato shorthand speaking style, his own personal Morse code. "Leave Washington. Leave the Senate. Give up something for America. Like you guys did."

Dole is feeling pretty good now. Seeing the vets has buoyed him.

And though the Secret Service is near him, they are not tugging at him—he hates being tugged at—and the smells of the sausages, the onions, the frying cheese steaks fill the air and give the market a homey feel. So even though Dole doesn't like being in crowds, he is getting some energy from this one, some feedback, some positive reinforcement—and that, of course, is when it happens. And he is reminded of why he hates all this campaign bull.

Tony Lambert, 54, a Philadelphia investment consultant with a salt-and-pepper beard and wearing an open-neck dress shirt, steps forward. Dole smiles to greet him, expecting to give an autograph.

"You defended Richard Nixon!" Lambert yells at him. "And he was the biggest crook to ever sit in the White House!"

Dole is rocked. He is not used to being heckled. People might not *love* Bob Dole, they might not *know* Bob Dole, they may not be *voting* for Bob Dole, but hardly anybody *hates* Bob Dole. With the possible exception, it appears, of Tony Lambert.

"You defended Rich-*ard Nix*-on!" Lambert yells again, turning up the volume as if Dole, standing a foot away, might not have heard him.

"Well, I wasn't his *lawyer* or anything," Dole says, giving a lawyerly answer. In fact, as chairman of the Republican Party under Nixon, Dole was one of his staunchest defenders.

"What about your first wife!" Lambert screams at Dole, moving even closer. "Bill Clinton is still married to *his* first wife!"

Jim-in-*ny*! Where the hell did this come from? The character issue was supposed to work *for* Dole, not *against* him. Where did this divorce stuff come from? How come the focus groups hadn't turned *this* up?

Bob Dole is a master of the put-down, the sharp retort, the devastating quip, and handling this idiot should be no problem for him. (Dole is the author of perhaps the funniest political joke ever told. Commenting on a meeting of the then-three-living ex-presidents, Carter, Ford, and Nixon, Dole said it was a meeting of "Hear no evil, see no evil . . . and evil." That he actually *liked* Richard Nixon and would later weep copiously and sincerely at his funeral was not a sign of any internal conflict on Dole's part. A joke was a joke. He had learned all about joking, he said, when he stood around jerking sodas at Dawson's Drug Store in Russell, Kansas. Jokes were just *words*. They didn't *mean* anything.) But his handlers have tried to drum one thing into his head: Words mean *everything* on a presidential campaign; his least utterance would be picked up, put on TV, and printed in a hundred papers. And so he must never show meanness. No more lines about "Democrat wars" or "Stop lying about my record." That was the old Bob Dole. The new

Bob Dole must be sweet and likable. And Dole is under strict orders to keep his true nature, and sense of humor, in check.

So Dole turns from Tony Lambert, who is now red-faced with anger, a vein pulsing on his forehead, and a Secret Service agent steps in front of Lambert and plants himself there. Technically speaking, the Secret Service is not empowered to interfere with citizens in their lawful expression of free speech, but as a practical matter agents often invite hecklers to take a few steps back—like into New Jersey—when they get too close, too loud, or become too much of a pain in the ass.

"I have a right to ask a question!" Lambert yells. But the candidate and the press are already surging away from him. "Bill Clinton is still married to *his* first wife!"

Dole sees a group of black people sitting at a table, eating lunch, seemingly very happy to be outside the mad crush of media, aides, and agents. So Dole goes over to them, taking the crush with him.

"Where ya from?" he asks.

"Denver," one of them says.

Which is on the opposite side of the Mississippi from Philadelphia.

"You're a long way from home!" Dole crows.

Then he turns and moves on. Okay. That's over. Did the black thing.

At Lynette Chen's Tea Leaf booth, Dole orders a green tea bag—"That's the way I'm going to run my administration: green!" he chortles—and dips the tea bag into a paper cup of hot water about two dozen times. He picks up the cup with his left hand and, with his pinkie extended, sips it delicately.

"It's good for preventing cancer," Chen, 31, a Dole supporter, tells him. Dole, of course, has already *had* cancer, and the reporters wince when they hear the word. Dole takes it well, however.

"Does it help your brain?" he asks. "Does it make you vote Republican?" Everybody laughs. Nelson Warfield, Dole's press secretary, stands at the edge of the crush and nods approvingly. This kind of humor is acceptable.

Dole pushes his way down to where Garrett Schanck, 72, greets him. Schanck tells Dole he flew over France in World War II.

"Have a good time while you're in town," Dole says, instantly serious in the presence of a veteran. "And don't forget the infantry."

"You didn't forget us," Schanck says, equally serious.

"Yeah, but you guys got clean sheets and showers every night," Dole says, smiling now.

"Like hell we did!" Schanck says, a grin on his wrinkled face.

It is a nice little scene, though perhaps two old warhorses remembering the good times of a half century ago is not exactly the image Dole should be striving for. But you take what you can get. At least Dole didn't ask Schanck if he was a long way from home.

The crush moves on and I linger to ask Schanck if he's going to vote for Dole.

"I haven't made up my mind," he says.

Which means no.

Dole is now supposed to turn to his right and walk a few yards to where he is going to eat a Philadelphia cheese steak for the TV cameras. But he sees an exit door to his left and heads for it. Black thing, did that. Green thing, did that. Quip thing. Veteran thing. Can't he go home now?

But a young, junior aide, really just a kid, notices that Dole has turned the wrong way and shouts into his walkie-talkie, "He's going the wrong way!" And then he shouts at Dole: "No, no, no!"

A senior aide grabs the kid. "You don't *yell* at the senator," she hisses at him. "You never *yell* at the senator." It is easy to make the mistake, to forget that the candidate is not just an actor to whom one must constantly be giving stage directions, but a former member of the U.S. Senate with a distinguished history of service.

Dole turns around. Every time he tries to get away, they suck him back in. And now he heads to his right, plunging through the aisles, where people grab his good left arm and pump it and slap his back. One woman taps him on his bad right shoulder to get his attention, and he flinches. A large part of the shoulder is gone, there is just scar tissue left behind, and he wears specially padded clothes to disguise this. Just how much pain Dole is in at any given moment is not known, but some discomfort always seems to be there.

Dole makes it to Rick's Cheese Steak and gets handed a cheese steak on a paper plate. He puts it on the counter and stands staring at it. The gooey mass of meat and melted cheese spills out of the long, soft bun. He cannot possibly eat this thing. He only has one hand. Don't they know that? Can't they see that? If he picks this thing up with one hand, half of it is going to spill out onto his shoetops. And won't TV like to get a shot of *that* for the evening news? An aide quickly steps forward with another plate. On it, a cheese steak has been cut into bite-size bits. Dole picks one up and eats it. "Mmmmm-mmm, good," he says for the cameras.

Then he motions to the counter girl for a Coke, holding his fingers a couple of inches apart to signal for a half-cup. He always orders half-cups, and the reason is immediately apparent as his hand visibly trembles bringing the cup to his lips. If he had a full cup, it would splash all over him. Also, he holds the paper cup so hard, it buckles in the middle. Dole has little feeling in his "good" left hand and has a hard time telling how hard he is gripping anything.

A man with a badge that says JUROR—the Reading Terminal Market is not far from the municipal courts—approaches him and says, "I hope you win!" This is the first expression of support Dole has received all day.

Oddly, the news seems to depress him. "I'll try," Dole says sadly.

Others wish to meet him, to greet him, to press his flesh, which is what these things are supposed to be about, but having invested some ten minutes in the event, Dole wants to move on. "I have to get on a plane soon," he tells the people.

Actually, he doesn't. There are no other events scheduled this day and it is just lunchtime. But Dole does not like long campaign days. He is always antsy to get back home to his three-room ground-floor condominium at the Watergate, where he can put his feet up, watch C-SPAN, and be asleep by 10 P.M. Earlier in the day, Dole had appeared before a meeting of Catholic journalists in Philadelphia, in the same hotel where two months before he had told members of the Republican National Committee that he realized they were "yearning for another Ronald Reagan. So I'm willing to be another Ronald Reagan if that's what you want. I'll be another Ronald Reagan."

The committee members were stunned by the comment. It is hard to imagine a candidate less like the sunny, optimistic, photo-op-loving Reagan, who during his first winning run for the presidency held press conference after press conference. Even though Reagan said all sorts of outrageous things, including how trees caused pollution, he never feared the press. He was confident he could communicate his message through the press and to the people, and that the people would love him for it. (And he was right.) But even though Dole this day was giving his speech to a press association and everyone in the audience was a reporter or editor, he once again refused to take any questions. "Unfortunately, the senator is on a very tight schedule," the reporters were told. Yeah, Dole had to go over to the Reading Terminal Market and eat a cheese steak.

In reality, Dole's handlers live in mortal fear that anyone will see too much of, learn too much about, or talk too much to Bob Dole. They have determined early on to keep him "in the box" and away from reporters' questions as much as possible. Dole, they believe, is capable of saying anything. He might screw up the whole campaign. He might show his "meanness." That this policy also keeps people from learning about Dole, knowing him, or getting to like him never occurs to them. There are few seasoned pros on Dole's campaign staff. Scott Reed, 36, the campaign manager, has never been a campaign manager on a presidential campaign. Nelson Warfield, 36, the press secretary, has never been a press secretary on a presidential campaign. Though Dole always looks like he is surrounded by talent—expensive talent—in fact, he is alone. Which is the way he wants it. He doesn't want anybody to run him. But now he is alone and afraid. He has been beat up relentlessly in the past for micromanaging his campaign, and now he has put his fate in the hands of people he barely knows but is reluctant to criticize, lest he give the appearance that his campaign is in chaos.

Dole gulps a few more pieces of cheese steak and looks for the nearest exit. As he does so, Joseph Daniels, 31, steps forward out of the crowd. Daniels looks exactly like what he is: homeless. His clothes are gray, his skin is gray, his face is greasy with dirt. He moves toward Dole, and immediately a Secret Service agent blocks his path.

It is no crime to be homeless in America, but it might as well be.

"Hey, Bob Dole! Hey, Bob Dole!" Daniels yells at the candidate.

Dole turns and looks at him. Perfect. This was the perfect opportunity for Bob Dole to meet one of the people he was trying to represent: one of society's miserable, a man who had "felt the pain" of Bill Clinton's America. Ask this man if he is better off than four years ago! Ask this man if America's economy is good! It's the economy, stupid, but this time the economy is hurting people like Joseph Daniels. What a perfect opportunity for Bob Dole to make his point!

Dole glances at Daniels, turns away, and heads out the exit like a burglar leaving the scene of a crime.

One Secret Service agent beckons to another. "Keep an eye on him," he says, motioning at Daniels.

Daniels has no harm in mind. All he has on his mind, in fact, is exactly what these events are supposed to be about: a chance to speak with the candidate.

"I got AIDS," Daniels tells Jodi Enda of *The Philadelphia Inquirer* afterwards. "I want to ask him something about my life. I live on the streets. I want to know what he's going to do about people like me. Who can't read. I wanted to find out."

And is he disappointed at not meeting Dole? Enda asks.

"Yeah," Daniels says. "I never met a *celebrity*."

ON BOB DOLE'S BAD DAYS, HE LOOKED LIKE GRANDPA MUNSTER. On his really bad days, he sounded like him. Reporters had great difficulty quoting him exactly. When they did, editors assumed they were making fun of him. *The New York Times* did a real public service, however, by printing word for word the beginning of a Bob Dole speech delivered in Bakersfield, California, on June 18, 1996:

My wife was here six days last week, and she'll be back next week, and she does an outstanding job and when I'm elected, she will not be in charge of health care. Don't worry about it. Or in charge of anything else. I didn't say that. It did sort of go through my mind. But she may have a little blood bank in the White House. But that's all right. We need it. It doesn't cost you anything. These days, it's not all you gave at the White House—your blood. You have to give your file. I keep wondering if mine's down there. Or my dog. I got a dog named Leader. I'm not certain they got a file on Leader. He's a schnauzer. I think he's been cleared. We've had him checked by the vet, but not by the FBI or the White House. He may be suspect, but in any event, we'll get into that later. Animal rights or something of that kind. But this is a very serious election.

"How many are gonna vote for Bob Dole?" he asked a crowd in Santa Barbara one day. Then, without warning, he clutched his chest and staggered backwards, feigning a heart attack. "This is the big one!" he shouted. "Any of you remember *Sanford and Son*? This is the big one!" Which is a routine that Redd Foxx used to do in his sitcom. Which maybe a few people in Santa Barbara still remembered. But probably a lot more just figured that Dole was undergoing a real cardiac arrest. (Contrary to what some audience members must have believed, Dole was not a drinker. When he did drink, he usually had just one vodka and onion juice, which apparently was as close as he could come to piss and vinegar.)

In March his handlers started taping "talking points" to his lectern to persuade him to include some actual issues in his presentations. Later, he would start using a TelePrompTer and then abandon it. It didn't make much difference. He gave the speech he wanted to give no matter what. And why shouldn't he? He had served four terms in the House of Representatives and been elected to four terms in the Senate. Hadn't he made speeches in all those races?

Well, yes, he had. But he was well known in Kansas (though more for what he had done for the state than his powers of oratory). And he hadn't faced a tough reelection campaign in 22 years. His former presidential outings had all been disasters. (In 1980, in the New Hampshire primary, Ronald Reagan got 72,000 votes. Bob Dole got 607.) Now, there was a horror-show quality to Dole's speeches. They began with a nervous tic at the corner of his mouth, followed by a false start. Visiting a rehabilitation hospital in Battle Creek, Michigan, in May, in what was planned as a moving evocation of Dole's own arduous struggle to rebuild his war-shattered body, he was supposed to begin by saying: "A lot of brave men and women came here after World War II, and some of them never left. Those of us who did leave became much stronger individuals. We've been tested by fire and tested under fire, and we've made it."

This is how Dole actually began: "Can you hear me? Can you hear me on the right? Well, I want to thank you for the Dole pineapple and the Dole bananas. Let me say that, as many of you know, Battle Creek has a lot of special memories. I sort of recovered in Battle Creek. It took a long time."

Reporters also did story after story on his use of the word "whatever," which he used as an excuse to stop thinking about what he was saying: "I accept your nomination and whatever." "I'm going to wait until I'm the nominee before I start making judgments on running mates or whatever." "They were all shouting, 'Viva, Viva Bob Dole, viva, viva, whatever.' " "I must say I woke up a lot of nights wondering what I did wrong in New Hampshire. Or what the pollsters did wrong or whatever."

Often he would have no ending to his speeches, especially during the primaries. And his speeches also lacked applause lines. Speakers need applause lines to build their own confidence, to pump them up. Without getting a little positive reinforcement from the audience, there are few things more terrifying or depressing than giving a clunker of a speech in public. And Bob Dole had to do it several times a day. Dole knew he could be a dud on the stump. "I gave a fireside chat the other night," he once said, "and the fire went out."

In February in Iowa, I went to hear one of his early speeches. He spoke at the Memorial Union at Iowa State University in Ames, an easy venue because there were 19,000 kids on campus, some of whom might be grateful to skip a class and hear a famous man. A few days earlier, Hillary Clinton had drawn 450 people to a large room in the same building, at which point the fire marshal ordered the doors closed, leaving hundreds of people waiting outside in the subzero cold. Now, for Dole, it was a relatively balmy 19 degrees. Dole spoke in a smaller room than Hillary had—the smallest room his campaign could find—but there were no more than 65 people there, including the campaign workers planted to ask friendly questions. ("Steve Forbes says he's trying to phase out ethanol. What do you think, Senator?")

Dole began his speech 10 minutes early (he was frequently impatient to get the day over with), leaving some audience members and reporters still in the rest rooms or cafeteria. He walked to the lectern, his mouth a grim slash. As always, he wore a gray suit and dazzling white shirt, and this day a black and gold tie. He stooped over the lectern, shoulders hunched. "Elizabeth was just here, but she left for Garner and Northwood," he began, mumbling into the microphone, head down. "She's been in 77 of the 99 counties, and she wants to make them all." Dole loved numbers. He knew that he had cast 13,836 votes in Congress and loved telling people that. (People *hated* Congress.) Numbers were solid, numbers were real. They weren't like campaigning, which was all show and fakery.

In a slow, halting voice he tried out the "vision" and "warmth" lines his staff had written for him. "If you grew up in the Midwest like I have," he said, "if you keep a grain elevator on the horizon, you're never far from home." The audience made no response, and Dole abandoned his notes and took off oratorically for parts unknown. "Saturday at one o'clock was called Discipline Day in our house," he said. "I didn't think much of it at the time, but it probably was a good idea." And you could just see the other kids in Russell, Kansas, playing baseball or hopscotch or tag on Saturday afternoons, but at the Dole house he and his brother and sisters were lined up waiting to get strapped or spanked or . . . whatever.

And it made you realize that for Dole, the campaign *was* Discipline Day. It was punishment. It was the necessary evil you needed to hold office. Instead of reveling in the campaign, enjoying it, making the most of it, Dole endured it. And that came through in speech after speech.

Dole looked up at the crowd in Ames and decided to advance the time line of his speech from his childhood to at least the 1950s. "My military hero is Dwight David Eisenhower," Dole declared. "He took us on a tour of the Gettysburg battlefield. I thought I'd died and gone to heaven. I visited him in Walter Reed Hospital." The audience sat in utter silence. Who could blame them? What were they to make of this stream of nostalgia? It was beyond dull. It was your high school chemistry teacher explaining the Periodic Chart of Elements. But it had the capacity to get worse.

Dole began blowing the lines that had been carefully prepared for him: "President Clinton was a governor. Maybe he knows why we don't trust governors!" Uh-oh, mistake. Dole had based his whole campaign strategy on lining up the endorsement of governors. "*We* trust governors," he quickly said, correcting himself. "Why *he* doesn't trust governors." At the end of his address, Dole tried to give a reason for electing him to the highest office in the land. "Maybe something will happen the day after the inaugural," he said. "Maybe foreign policy or something else." Then he looked around. "I'll take some questions." He had even forgotten to include his last line, a line you'd think he could not forget: "God bless America!" So there was no applause at the end of his speech.

He did this time after time, speech after speech. He would bark out disconnected words and phrases. It was the Tourette's Syndrome Campaign: "Grain elevators . . . Discipline Day . . . Ike . . . argh . . . governors . . . foreign policy . . . whatever . . . argh!"

Afterwards, a student reporter came up to Dole and asked: "How come there were only a few students here?"

"Maybe they were in classes," Dole said and turned away.

What struck me, however, was how much worse Dole had become since his 1988 race for president. In those days he was not known as a great orator, but there were no stories about his inability to deliver a coherent (let alone compelling) speech. In eight years, he had simply aged. Physically he was fine and he wasn't slower mentally, but he was less flexible, more set in his ways, less willing to work at things he didn't like, such as practicing his speeches.

His handlers, all too young to remember what he used to be like, thought his reputed "meanness" was what they had to guard against, which is why they kept him away from the press. (Dole had appeared more times than any other guest on *Meet the Press* and *Larry King Live*, a considerable accomplishment. But this hurt him. The public knew him only as a legislator, a Washington fixture, the consummate insider at a time in American history when being an insider was a huge minus.) The handlers were so afraid he would say something mean—as he had in the past, like "Get back in your cage!" to a college student who asked him about nuclear war—that they came to grips too late with the real problem: Dole had difficulty saying anything at all, or at least anything anybody wanted to hear from a presidential candidate. His handlers begged and pleaded. They wrote him memos and hired a speech coach. They used shabby tricks like anonymously criticizing him to reporters so that he would read their criticisms in print the next day and be shamed into changing. But nothing worked. Dole was set in his ways, set like an iron bar in concrete.

"I probably won't change," he said. "I probably can't change."

From the beginning of the campaign to the end, people said they did not know why Bob Dole was running for president, so his handlers gave Dole lines to read that were supposed to answer that question. But it didn't matter what they wrote down. Dole delivered what he wanted to deliver.

"I'm running for president of the United States," he said in the last week of the campaign, "because I believe that with strong leadership, America's days will always lie ahead of us, just as they lie ahead of us now."

OK, so he was no Demosthenes, no William Jennings Bryan, no Jesse Jackson. So what? Why should it matter so much? It mattered because to the American people, the presidency is like no other office. Electing a president is not the same as electing a governor or a senator. In electing a president, they want someone to inspire them, to embody American ideals or American myths. They want a president who has a clear vision of what America's aspirations should be, and they want him to give a reasonable (if not totally believable) blueprint of how to get there. They want a few speeches with vision.

Dole hated the vision thing. "I know some of these people, the dreamers, sit out there and they fantasize what a vision is," Dole told a group of newspaper editors in March. "You know, it's like something *misty*. They don't know what it is, but I don't have it. Well, I hope not. I don't *want* it. I want to be real. I'm a real candidate. I want to get things *done*. To me, that's a vision—getting things done."

But contempt for the process is a dangerous thing in a candidate. Seeing through the game is not the same thing as winning it. "My vision for America is to have a better America," Dole said one day in New York. Then in Hershey, Pennsylvania, he criticized "liberals and the media" for pushing him to come up with "some touchy-feely thing." But Americans wanted a little touchy-feely. They weren't electing a wheeler-dealer in chief or a deal maker in chief. They wanted someone who shared their hopes and dreams, someone who would lead and comfort them.

They also wanted something else. People had plenty of harsh reality in their lives. They also wanted a little happiness, a little simple delight. They knew they had mountains to climb—some climbed them every day—but they wanted their next president to tell them what they would find when they got to the mountaintop.

"He just doesn't elicit *joy*," Stanley Greenberg, a Democratic pollster, said of Dole. "It makes it hard to articulate a vision when he does not seem to bring out in people some sense of happiness."

While despairing in private, the supporters of Bob Dole tried their best to defend him in public. "This is not a country that elects an entertainer in chief," Newt Gingrich said.

Oh, yeah? Since *when*?

THE MAN WHO WOULD BE KING

★

Q: So your success is because your taste is in sync with a majority of the American people?
A: Or they're in sync with me.

—Larry King to author,
February 19, 1996

BILLY BLYTHE WAS A "TALKATIVE, SENSITIVE, CHUBBY little boy. The only blue jeans that fit him at the waist were so long that he had to roll them up halfway to his knees," his biographer, David Maraniss, wrote. He loved to dress in an all-black Hopalong Cassidy outfit, including a big black hat. Some kids called him a sissy, but he was a very popular kid. He lit up when other kids were around. Once, when he broke his leg and had to wear a cast, the other kids noticed how much he liked the attention. Being the object of attention made him feel special, excited, alive, welcome. After he became a success, he told his friend Susan McDougal: "This is fun. Women are throwing themselves at me. All the while I was growing up, I was the fat boy in the Big Boy jeans." Billy Blythe took the name Bill Clinton, and he knew from a very early age that he wanted to make people love him.

Bobby Joe Dole was a high school sports star who loved to hear the roar of the crowd. He was handsome and popular, and the girls of his high school voted him "Ideal Boy." He dreamed of becoming a doctor. After he came back from the war, however, his body was so shattered that he was convinced he would spend the rest of his life selling pencils on a street corner. But when, through enormous mental and physical effort, he recovered enough to begin a political career, he knew he could hear the roar of the crowd again by working twice—three times! five times!—as hard as anyone else. He knew he could make people admire and respect him.

Lawrence Harvey Zeiger was "an acne-faced, overweight, Jewish kid whose father died, who was on welfare, whose mother spoiled him, and then, in the course of his life, in his mid-twenties, he became Larry King." That is Larry King talking years later, telling a reporter how he created himself out of nothing. How, as a kid nicknamed the Mouthpiece, he would stand on a Brooklyn street corner and do imaginary radio commentary on the passing traffic. "Here comes a Dodge, now, folks. A *big* Dodge with whitewalls, New York plates, man in a suit at the wheel and a woman with a hat beside him, yes!" Lawrence Zeiger knew, even as a poor, unattractive kid that someday he could make people listen to him.

* * *

L ARRY KING WAS GOING TO HOST A DEBATE IF IT KILLED HIM. THE primary debates were not so much about informing the public about important issues as they were advertising vehicles for the media. Newspapers and TV stations would sponsor debates, slap their corporate logos all over the set, put their star reporters or anchors in as the moderators, and then get some national publicity. If you hosted a debate, you were somebody. CNN, which in its early years had been known as Chicken Noodle News because it was such a pathetic, low-rent operation, was now a major player and was willing to spend big bucks to have its stars associated with the 1996 election. So a November 1995 Republican debate would have to be moderated by Larry King, the network's superstar. And there was no doubt from the very beginning, at least in the mind of King and the network, that he would be bigger than the candidates.

"This is *not* a debate," King tells me when we first meet at the debate site. "This is *Larry King Live*." That, he believes, is an improvement. Whatever it is, it will cap an event called Presidency III, a Republican straw poll to be held in Orlando, Florida. In August the Republican Party had held a straw poll in Ames, Iowa, that everyone recognized in advance would have no meaning whatsoever. It was strictly a fund-raising event. Anybody with $25 could vote for the Republican presidential candidate of his choice. You didn't have to be from Iowa. You didn't have to be a Republican. You didn't even have to be a U.S. citizen. All you had to do was have a ticket and vote. And you didn't have to buy your own ticket. The tickets were purchased by the candidates and handed out to supporters. So the only real contest was which candidate could squander the most money on a contest so cynically devised.

Bob Dole and Phil Gramm tied.

The press knew this had no real significance. But we couldn't help ourselves. So we wrote all sorts of stories and analyses about Dole's weakness and Gramm's strength, even though deep down we knew the straw poll signified no such thing at all. But state party after state party (each of which was interested in the same thing: money) held straw poll after straw poll, and the press trudged along willingly. By the time Florida rolled around, it had become a case of "stop us before we write again." The rules for the Orlando straw poll were stricter than the Iowa rules: You actually had to be a Republican from Florida in order to vote. But the candidates—especially Bob Dole—campaigned for votes in the same tried and true way: with bribes. Delegates to the convention got free Godiva chocolates, bath oil, fruit baskets, hotel rooms, booze, food, and dance lessons, all courtesy of the Dole campaign. Having been embarrassed in Iowa (even though it was a meaningless embarrassment, Dole was determined not to be embarrassed again. And so he spent around $2 million campaigning for an event that would elect not a single delegate to the Republican National Convention in 1996. And although he would later bitterly complain about running out of money during the primaries, his spending was now profligate. He rented the entire seventh floor of the swanky Peabody Court hotel and hired scores of staff. His video featuring his terrible war wound was running 24 hours a day on the hotel's closed-circuit TV channel. He spent $20,000 to rent a parking lot across the street that he called "Camp Bob," where there were live bands, games for the kids, free food, and a man on stilts juggling Indian clubs. In the food tent 10 TV sets were set up running his war-wound video as people ate barbecued pork sandwiches and corn on the cob. Everything was very high-tech. All of Dole's staff was beepered, cell-phoned, laptopped, wired, and hooked-up.

Back in the real world, a large chunk of the federal government was shut down because the White House and Congress could not agree on a budget. As majority leader of the Senate, Dole should have been playing a critical role. He knew the shutdown was a disaster for the Republicans. The White House was able to direct public opinion to its side because it had a single focus: Make Bill Clinton look good. Congress had no such unity of vision. It had warring factions with different goals and ideologies. Speaker of the House Newt Gingrich saw the shutdown of government as a good thing, a lesson to the president and the American people. Who needed government, anyway?

Bob Dole, who could read the polls, saw his life flashing before his eyes. Bill Clinton's approval rating had jumped to 52 percent, the highest in 18 months. And when asked who was more to blame for the government shutdown, Clinton or GOP leaders, the public blamed GOP leaders by 47 to 25 percent. So what was Congress doing? It was passing meaningless balanced-budget bills, all of which Clinton had said in advance he would veto. And the polls showed that the public wanted Clinton to veto those bills if they cut spending on Medicare and Medicaid. The public was furious, the Republicans were being blamed, and Dole wanted a solution. But every time he tried to push Gingrich to a compromise with Clinton, Phil Gramm would jump up and bash Dole for "cutting deals" with Clinton that could "lead to $1 trillion more in federal spending." The White House was giddy with delight: the government shutdown was a triumph, and Dole looked trapped.

The Dole primary campaign strategy was the same as always: Slog on. Dole is the inevitable nominee. Nobody can beat him. Only Dole can beat Dole. So keep Dole under wraps, out of uncontrolled situations like debates, and away from unfriendly reporters. A Larry King debate? No, forget it. The Senate (meaning Bob Dole) had scheduled a vote on a balanced budget bill for Friday, November 17, the same night as King's debate. And Dole was going to stay in Washington and vote, not fly off to Orlando. Besides, if Dole pulled out, the Dole staff figured, CNN would pull the plug on the debate. Who would watch a debate without the front-runner?

CNN was furious. Larry King had always provided a friendly venue for Dole, and now Larry King needed Dole. So wouldn't Dole make an exception and show up at the debate? After all, this would be the last big campaign event of 1995 and CNN wanted to establish its political supremacy and enter the new year with a bang.

The Dole campaign told CNN to shove it. Larry King? Fuck Larry King. Larry King was a big deal *last* election. Just cancel the debate, and maybe Dole would show up for a later one. Maybe. Give us a call. Or better yet, send us a fax. CNN management huddled, discussed, and refused. Dole didn't want to appear? He was prepared to look like a coward? Fine. Fuck Bob Dole. Here's how it would work: Senators Phil Gramm, Arlen Specter, and Richard Lugar would stay in Washington and vote on the balanced-budget bill. Then, joined by Representative Bob Dornan, they would go to a Washington studio and be hooked up by satellite to Orlando, where Larry King would have Lamar Alexander, Pat Buchanan, and Alan Keyes on the set with him. (Morry Taylor had been barred from Presidency III because he had voted for Ross Perot in 1992 and was therefore not considered a pure enough Republican to join the others.) Steve Forbes said he would not debate if Bob Dole did not debate.

King might not know the intricacies of a balanced budget, but he knew lousy TV when he heard it, and this was lousy TV. A seven-way debate from two cities? King thought it would be unfair. The candidates with him on the set would get to bask in his glow. Their conversation would be directed by him and shaped by his mastery. That would give them an unfair advantage over the group in Washington. King had an idea: He would go to a neutral third city and appear on a bare set and would direct the two other groups by satellite. Jeb Bush, chairman of Presidency III, was horrified. Why would anybody come to Orlando just to see a petting zoo of candidates? "You're the *draw*, Larry," Bush told him.

★   ★   ★

PAT BUCHANAN HAD WON THE PRE-DEBATE LOTTERY AND COULD
pick any seat he wanted for the Larry King debate. Naturally, he
took the seat closest to Larry King. "For us, this is a glorified *Cross-fire*," his press secretary Greg Mueller says, speaking of the popular
CNN show that had been cohosted by Buchanan. To Buchanan, host-
ing a TV show as a journalist was no different from appearing on one as
a candidate. It was all TV. It was all about being a celebrity. In America,
anyone who got on TV a lot was automatically a celebrity, and it was
this status and not the job they held that counted. This is why it was so
easy for Buchanan to move from politics to journalism and back to
politics. Switching back and forth was all the rage. You could turn on
CNN and see John Sununu, former governor of New Hampshire and
former chief of staff for George Bush, now hosting *Crossfire* as a journalist, opposite Geraldine Ferraro, now a journalist, though she was
once a Democratic candidate for vice president. While some journalists
howled about this, the public took it in stride. If you were on TV, you
were a famous face. Journalist, politician, or both, it didn't matter.
Everyone was an entertainer.

Now, a few hours before show time, Buchanan had come to the
enormous Orange County Convention Center to view the debate set.
Unfortunately, the vast, echoing hall was far better suited to boat shows
than TV shows, and the King staff was struggling to create a decent-
looking stage upon which to place the participants.

"Your cameras are going to be there," Mueller says to Buchanan,
pointing. "Not to the far right, but to the left of the one on the right."

"Not to the right, but the one to the left of the right?" Buchanan asks.

"*Not* the one to the right," Mueller says. "One left of right."

"Will there be water?"

"Pitchers of ice water."

"The ice will melt under the lights," Buchanan observes. Mueller
knows no way of preventing the laws of physics from occurring and remains silent.

"Will there be little Johnny-on-the-Spots I can use during the commercial breaks?" Buchanan asks. "I tend to drink a lot of water."

"We'll put a catheter in you," Mueller says.

Buchanan cranes his neck to look around the huge, dim cavern of
the debate hall. "They're going to get 3,000 people here when they can
watch it on TV?" he asks doubtfully.

"The delegates are very, very excited," Mueller says.

"But they can watch it on TV," Buchanan says. Which is exactly
what the press will be doing. Reporters fly hundreds, sometimes thousands, of miles to cover these events, and then sit in the press room

and watch them on TV. Which they could do from home. (Though you can't put a dateline on your story if you stay at home. And, more important, you can't get frequent-flier miles.)

Mueller changes the subject. "You going to use your own IFB?" An IFB is an interruptible feedback device, used with an earpiece, over which you can hear prompts from the director and the like. Pros have their own IFBs, cast in the shape of their ear canal.

"You bet I'm using my own," Buchanan says. "I'm Fast Eddie. I travel with my own pool cue."

THE MOST STRIKING PARALLEL BETWEEN THE DOLE STAFF AND the Larry King staff is their protective attitude toward their star. Just as the Dole staff (mistakenly, as it turned out) feels Dole will suffer if people learn his true nature, so some on the Larry King staff seem to live in dire fear that a reporter will actually get close enough to King to learn his true nature, which turns out to be strikingly similar to his TV nature: affable, friendly, egocentric, and risqué. The fear comes from both staffs because the stakes are so high: the presidency in the case of Dole, and a multimillion-dollar career in the case of King. But the protectiveness also comes from the staffs' sense of self-preservation. If the staffs can keep the celebrity to themselves, their power is increased. The celebrity can access the public and press only through the staffs. The staffs claim to shape the popularity of the celebrity, and so the celebrity becomes their slave and not their master.

Juli Mortz, 28, King's publicist, is dark haired, very pretty, and new on the job. In Orlando she tells me that Disney World is going to have a Larry King Day, in which he will ride through the streets of the theme park on a float. I ask if I can attend.

"No," she says.

Why not? I ask.

"It's a personal moment," she says. "He's taking his daughter."

Oh, I say. How old is the kid?

"Twenty-seven," she says.

King is in the bedroom of his hotel suite getting dressed a few hours before the debate. Mortz and I are standing in the living room, and I ask her the purpose of tonight's debate.

"First and foremost to be entertaining," she says and then pauses. "And informative."

Yep, mustn't forget that.

King is on the phone with Wendy Walker Whitworth, the show's senior executive producer for just over two years. She does not travel with the show and will oversee things from Washington, where the show is headquartered. Since this is a CNN debate, it will be interrupted by commercials (*The Miami Herald* will estimate about one-fourth of the two-hour debate is devoted to commercials), but King is on the phone telling Whitworth he doesn't want to interrupt the candidates for commercial breaks if the candidates are really cooking.

"Don't let time interrupt quality," King says. "I will *never* let time interrupt quality. I won't interrupt Buchanan saying, 'I think Dole should be shot.' "

Which is an interesting concept of "quality." King comes out into the living room and puts on a blue houndstooth jacket over his dark blue shirt. On the air, he never wears a jacket. ("Only once did I ever wear a jacket on the air, and it was for Yitzhak Rabin's funeral," King says. "Out of respect.") Being jacketless is supposed to make him look friendly and down-home on the air, and it is also a holdover from his radio days. His first senior executive producer, Tammy Haddad, engineered his transformation from radio to TV and tried to make things comfortable for him. King was used to bending over a microphone, which is why his TV show still has an old-fashioned microphone on the desk in front of him. And, since leaning over made his shirt balloon out from his chest, Haddad first put him in sweater vests and then switched him to suspenders, which are now his trademark.

King, Mortz, and I go down a few floors in the hotel to where Time Warner Cable has set up a hospitality suite. Time Warner has just purchased CNN and wants to show off its superstar, Larry King. The room is cramped, hot, and humid and smells of cooked shrimp and overripe cheese. There are about thirty people crowding the room, all of whom are too intimidated at first to approach King. For a man so friendly on TV, King is not a mixer. He is quite capable of going to a party and standing in a corner, speaking only when spoken to. His body language tonight is all defensive: his feet are spread, his arms are crossed, he has a grim smile on his face. A fifty-something woman finally barges up to him and shrieks: "I want to tell my mother I met him!" King grimaces. He puts his arm around her, and a photographer hired for the evening steps forward and snaps the picture.

After this, King is summoned to the small wet bar in the corner, where a phone sits on the countertop. Juli Mortz tells him he will be doing a live telephone interview with a reporter named Jeff for radio station WDBO. As soon as King picks up the phone, his attitude changes. His voice brightens. He smiles. He is on the air and happy.

"Good evening, Jeff," King chirps into the phone. "Would you like me to do the stock report? I could do the weather. The weather in

Florida is party cloudy. I am glad this debate will be on DBO, one of my favorite stations." King does a little more shtick and hangs up the phone.

A man comes over to King with a copy of one of King's books. He hands it to King. "I'm Frank," he says.

King looks at him.

"I'm the attorney for Time Warner," Frank says.

King takes the book and signs it: "For Frank."

Another Time Warner executive comes up and begins an excruciatingly dull discussion of interactive TV. King burps in his face. King doesn't say excuse me. King never says excuse me, though he burps all the time.

The executive moves on. King makes no attempt to mingle with the guests.

"How will Perot do this time?" he asks me.

He'll get less than 19 percent, I say, repeating the conventional wisdom. In 1992, Perot got 19 percent of the vote, but he was hot then. He is old news now, and since the NAFTA debate with Al Gore in November 1993 (brought to America courtesy of *Larry King Live*) Perot looks like just a wealthy nut.

King is protective of Perot, however. Nobody has been better for the King show than Perot, who announced his candidacy on the show and returned often. In 1992, Perot helped make King into a kingmaker, but America can change dramatically in just four years. And few people care what Perot now has to say, on *Larry King Live* or off.

"He won't do *much* less than 19 percent," King says defensively. (Perot will end up with 8 percent of the vote.) "If there were a Powell-Kennedy ticket or a Powell-Bradley ticket and they were appearing in Detroit and you had a choice of seeing them or Dole or Clinton, where would you go?"

Dazzled by that array of choices, I am still trying to figure out an answer when King goes on: "Arthur Godfrey told me: 'Tonight, nine o'clock will become eleven o'clock. This is not brain surgery. The clock will move. Be glib and curious.' I don't think a lot about what I am doing. One of my secrets is not to take it too seriously."

King quotes Arthur Godfrey all the time and likes to be compared to him, even though Godfrey is a man not all that many people still remember. (When, in 1997, King gets a gold star on Hollywood's Walk of Fame, it will be placed next to Godfrey's.) Godfrey also specialized in entertainers. There were no presidential debates when he was on the air. And today a presidential debate should be taken seriously, at least by the moderator, should it not?

King is now in full gallop, talking about his past triumphs, how he started out on Miami radio as a 25-year-old. He quotes Jackie Gleason and Barbra Streisand and speaks of his performance as Puck in *A Midsummer Night's Dream*. *"Miami Herald,"* he says, quoting. " 'Shakespeare has begun to spin and he's still spinning!' "

There is a certain purity to King's ego. He knows the evening, the debate, the cocktail party, even my presence here, are all about him. So why pretend otherwise? "I'm like Segovia with a violin," he says and yawns in my face. He doesn't say excuse me.

"I got a deal, one week every month, I can go to California," King says. "There, I can get off at seven P.M., go to dinner, go to a ball game. I like the parties. I like the people." King has wanted to move permanently to Los Angeles for a long time, but CNN won't let him. He could insist, but close associates say he hates fights, hates scenes, and is too easily pushed around.

Juli Mortz comes over to him and says, "I got a guy from *The New York Times* on the phone. Don't say anything to him about the format tonight. Don't say anything to him about us having a camera outside the Senate." She doesn't explain why.

King takes the phone, listens for a moment and says: "We got a camera outside the Senate!"

Juli hits him hard on the arm.

When King gets off the phone, he is furious. "Why would you do that!" he shouts at her. "Why would you do that when I am on the phone?"

"I told you not to tell him!" she says. It is an odd scene. Juli Mortz is barely more than a child; Larry King is a superstar. But she can yell at him. She is a handler. She is just like Scott Reed, Bob Dole's campaign manager, who brags to reporters that he yells at Bob Dole.

"He asked me a question," King says, defensively, backing down. "I've got to answer his question!"

The argument peters out and King says, "Are we going?"

"You've got to say thank you to your hosts," Mortz says.

King says his good-byes, goes downstairs, and gets into a huge stretch limousine. The convention hall is next door, about a three-minute ride away. "I got a very nice letter from John Kennedy Junior," King says on the way. "He was raised well. Smart. A great combination from his mother and father: Looks and personality."

We pull up outside the convention hall, and King sees a middle-aged woman waiting by the side of the building, anxiously looking down the drive for somebody she is supposed to meet.

"A hooker!" King shouts as he gets out of the limo. "A hooker for guys over fifty! A courtesy of Phil Gramm! If this was only Vegas."

His energy level is up now. He is getting nearer to air time. He strides into the building. He is pumped. You can hear it in his voice. He is all shtick now, shouting, mugging, singing Cole Porter and Frank Sinatra medleys. He goes into the nearby CNN workspace, which is overflowing with equipment. In the workspace, the on-air CNN stars—Gene Randall, Bruce Morton, Bill Schneider, and Judy Woodruff—who will be reporting on Presidency III and other political events, are all crowded together while the Larry King staff gets its own area. The two groups do not mix and the resentment in the room is palpable. The CNN news stars view themselves as journalists, but what is King? Well, extremely popular, that's what. But King greets the CNN reporters warmly and then walks over to his area, sits down, and takes a new pair of shoes out of a box. "Onstage, you don't want dirty soles when you cross your legs," he says. "It looks terrible."

You know all the tricks, I say.

"I could announce for office tonight," he says. "I could run on Ross Perot's ticket."

And why shouldn't King run for president or vice president? He has the skills: He is amiable, good on TV, popular, able to take direction. And he knows the tricks like the one about shoe soles. So why shouldn't he go after the White House?

At 8:03 P.M. he is called to the phone. It is Wendy Walker Whitworth, his senior executive producer. He listens for a moment and puts down the phone. "Dole is doing it!" he says. Dole has changed his mind. He will debate after all. He doesn't want to look like a coward. Now the show is big time again. Now people might actually watch it.

King walks into the makeup room, where a woman takes a sponge and applies heavy makeup to his face, erasing a road map of wrinkles. She leans over to touch up a spot on his forehead and King belches loudly in her face.

"You know the good thing about burping?" he asks. "It makes you feel better."

He stands. "I have to go to the bathroom," he says.

I have to go too, and we stand at adjoining urinals. He keeps tapping me on the shoulder as he speaks. King is always touching you when he talks to you. He is always putting his hand on your arm or poking a friendly finger in your chest. It is a little disconcerting at a urinal, however.

"I'm gonna be tough on Lugar," he says playfully, picking one of the nicest candidates in the race. "Something about him pisses . . . me . . . off!" He adopts a prosecutorial tone. "Isn't it true, Senator

Lugar, that you not only were *in* the car accident, but were the *driver* of the car!" He pauses. "More of Jenny Jones in a minute."

We walk back to the workspace and King starts drinking coffee. Courage can be defined as a man who starts drinking coffee half an hour before a live two-hour TV show.

Bay Buchanan, Pat's sister and campaign manager, walks in and asks about the 90-second opening statement. Pat has worked very hard on it and she wants to be sure it is still 90 seconds long, since they have timed theirs to the second.

"There is no ninety-second opening statement," King says. "I ask a question instead."

Bay looks stunned. "Oh," she says. "Okay."

When she leaves, King shouts, "I love this shit! I love the weirdness!"

The show begins and, just as Arthur Godfrey said, 9 P.M. eventually becomes 11 P.M. In between, however, the show is a qualified disaster. The audience in the hall can barely hear because the sound is terrible. The lighting is also very bad and, predictably, King has difficulty controlling the debaters in Washington. He has trouble cutting off their answers as they ramble on and on. Also, because the Senate vote goes late, none of the candidates in Washington is ready by 9 P.M. So King has to start with the candidates in Orlando while the candidates in Washington straggle in. Dole is the last to show up.

In the workspace, some CNN staffers are watching the debate on monitors, and they seem delighted with the chaos. Every time King makes a mistake, they hoot with glee. At one point, King interrupts the debate to announce, "By the way, we just learned the Senate has passed the balanced budget amendment, 51 to 44."

In the workspace, Bill Schneider shouts, "It's not an *amendment!*"

Then, to make matters worse, King says, "The vote was, the vote was 61 to 44." And on the air, Alan Keyes—Little Mr. Perfectionist— points out you can't have a vote of 61 to 44 in the Senate, since there are only 100 senators, forcing King to say sheepishly, "I've got extra guys in the Senate."

In the workspace, the CNN staffers are laughing so hard they can barely stay in their chairs. Haven't they said all along that a real journalist should be doing this, and not Larry King?

Coming back from a commercial break, King says, "Welcome back to *Larry King Live,* where the Senate tonight has passed the balanced-budget concept by a vote of 51 to 44."

"Concept!" Schneider shouts, and everybody begins laughing again.

Juli Mortz observes me observing them and goes over and talks to the reporters, and they immediately shut up and stop making fun of King. One word from Larry, and all of them could end up doing the weather in Pocatello, Idaho.

When the show is over, King comes bursting into the workspace. He is up, high, bubbling with energy. "This was *work* tonight," he says. "Normally it is not work, but this was *work.*"

Bill Schneider is the first to rush up to him. "*Great* job tonight, Larry," he says. "*Really* great job."

IT IS FEBRUARY 1996 IN DES MOINES, IOWA. IT IS 2 DEGREE outside and the wind is blowing snowdrifts across highways, cutting off whole towns. Roofs are collapsing; schools and businesses are closed. The state police are advising all motorists to travel with survival kits in their trunks. Tomorrow the temperature is going down to 9 below. CNN is broadcasting from the semi-restored Old Historical Building near the state capitol. There is peeling paint, half-demolished walls, and the smell of dry rot everywhere. A fierce wind whistles through the building. The Larry King set, placed in the middle of this mess, looks beautiful, however. Landscape paintings are hung on fake walls, some dried flowers are stuffed in a vase, there are bookcases and an oriental rug. It looks like Daniel Webster's study. Not exactly Iowa, but homey and historic.

It is a few minutes before show time, and everything is ready except for the host, who seems to be missing. "Where's Larry?" The shout travels up and down the dismal hallways. King appears and with his usual infectious sense of excitement begins tells everyone about his near-death experience.

"It's a wind-shear landing at the airport," he says. "On the plane, Brokaw, me, Bob Woodward, Hal Bruno (political director of ABC), and Cyndy Garvey (former wife of Los Angeles Dodger Steve Garvey). What's the headline if we crash?"

I shake my head.

"King, Brokaw Die; Woodward Also Lost!" King says.

Mark Merritt, press secretary for Lamar Alexander, is standing nearby and has a different suggestion. "How about: 'Good News for Country'?" he whispers to me.

King sees Cyndy Garvey, his blond and beautiful girlfriend, walks up to her and puts his arms around her. "I love you, Cyndy Garvey," he says.

"I love you, Larry King," she says.

King turns to me. "She's on first base, but she's heading home with a King."

I pretend to know what he is talking about.

"Anybody can take a woman to Bermuda," King shouts. "I take them to *Iowa*! She's half Czech and half Jewish. The Czech is in the mail! Hey, I'm on the Academy Awards. I'm doing the rules. They want me to do it Brooklyn style. 'Hey, here's duh rules.' Hey, I got a joke for you: Guy's arrested for fucking a goat and he hires the best jury-selection expert in the business. The guy is great. 'I'll get you a great jury,' the expert tells him. 'Don't worry about a thing.' Okay, first witness gets up and says, 'Yeah, I saw him fuck this goat up the ass. He really pounds it into the goat and then pulls it out and the goat licks the stuff off his dick.' And one juror turns to the other and says, 'A good goat will do that.' "

King roars with laughter.

Someone suggests that maybe he would like to do a TV show and he walks into the studio, strides onto the set and sits on the adjustable office chair they have provided for him, and promptly sinks to the floor. His mood instantly changes. "We can't have this happen!" King shouts. "This is bad news."

"Your leg hit the lever," somebody yells back at him.

Cyndy turns to me and says, "He's gonna be mad."

We are told we can't be on the set because it is a special show involving a quick change of guests: first a group of political campaign handlers and then Steve Forbes and his entire family. The change between the two segments must take place in a matter of seconds, there are a lot of people to switch around, and no outsiders will be allowed on the set. Cyndy listens intently, nods, grabs my sleeve, and takes me onto the set, where we take two seats behind the cameras. "Larry and I have been friends for seventeen years," she says without any prompting. "We don't know whether to take it into romance. We don't want to ruin it. But what else is there?"

She moves her chair a foot to the left. "I don't want to be in Larry's eyeline," she says. "When I was married to Steve Garvey, I never sat where he could see me. I didn't want him hit in the head with a ball. I don't even like to *come* to these shows. Larry insists."

Cyndy is warm, engaging, friendly, and compulsively likable. When I see her the next night at a group dinner, she startles me by kissing me on the lips. Months later in May I read that Cyndy, now using the name Cyndy Truhan, has six criminal charges pending against her for lying to the Santa Monica, California, police about being stalked. A former boyfriend has obtained a restraining order against her, alleging she stalked and threatened him. Steve Garvey has obtained a restraining order against her after she allegedly threatened his current wife. A month after that, I read in *The Washington Post* that Cyndy has entered a guilty plea on filing false police reports and "admitted sending weird notes to herself, defacing her door with an X, and pretending that an attacker had bitten off her ear." Four other charges against her are dropped and she is placed on "nonsupervised probation."

The show begins, and Cyndy notices that Larry has tucked his left foot behind his right ankle, which is about an inch away from the little lever that lowers the chair.

At the first commercial break, Cyndy screams: "Larry! Put your foot down!"

He looks at her, but doesn't understand what she is saying.

He comes back live and is talking to his guest when he accidentally kicks the lever and sinks to the floor. Luckily the camera is on the guest at the time. King shakes his head, gets up, and grimly drags the seat back to the right height.

At the next commercial break, Cyndy, who is hungry, wonders aloud what would have happened if Larry's plane had gone down in the storm, they all survived, were trapped, ran out of food, and had to revert to cannibalism. Who would be eaten first?

"The photographers first," she finally says. "They just take pictures. Then the print guys. Then the TV people last." It seems to be something she has thought about.

In the back of the studio and off-camera, Steve Forbes, his wife, Sabina, and their daughters walk in. This is a coup. Nobody can get Forbes and his family, and Larry King has got them. Just like the old days! Though fabulously wealthy, they appear to be very ordinary people. Sabina is large and plain and friendly looking, the daughters are all beautiful. On the air, they giggle and laugh at each other's stories and seem to like one another a lot. Afterwards, in the Green Room, they are the same: Forbes puts his hand on one daughter's back and rubs it. The other daughters hug each other. They seem like an all-American family. An all-American family in which the father has gone a little nuts and decided to run for president.

S TEVE FORBES SITS IN THE SMALL SOUND STUDIO AT THE RADIO station, wearing yellow foam earphones and taking softball questions from the host. Asked to explain why he had once stated his favorite song was "Stars and Stripes Forever" but another time had stated it was Aretha Franklin's "Respect," Forbes's Howdy Doody face breaks into a grin. "My favorite song is Aretha Franklin *singing* 'Stars and Stripes Forever,'" he says, and the host laughs.

Outside, in the cafeteria, where his staff people are listening to the show, there is an almost audible sigh of relief. Forbes has done it. He has carried off that rarest of political feats: an actual ad lib.

At the first commercial break, Forbes wipes the grin off his face and silently motions to the host that he would like to see the copy of *The Wall Street Journal* that is sitting at the host's elbow. On the front page of the first section is a story with a picture of Steve Forbes and a subheadline: A LOOK AT HIS PAST INDICATES HE IS LARGELY UNTESTED IN MAKING BIG DECISIONS.

As if that were not bad enough, the story also reveals that his father, the late Malcolm Forbes, reportedly "was propositioning male staffers" at *Forbes* magazine, where Steve worked. So naturally, Steve Forbes might want to peruse this story a bit. But when the host hands him the front section, Forbes tosses it aside and motions for the third section, the serious section, the one called "Money & Investing."

When he gets his hands on it, Forbes immediately turns to page C16 and begins scanning the Futures Prices section, which lists how soybeans, oats, copper, cattle, cocoa, coffee, crude oil, gasoline, the yen, the deutsche mark, and the dollar are doing. And as he pores over the columns of densely packed figures, Steve Forbes seems for the first time to be truly relaxed and happy. This is a world he understands. A world where figures are what they are and where things mean what they say. A world, in other words, very different from politics.

Not that Forbes is doing badly at his new profession. On the contrary, if one believes the current polls, he is the Republican front-runner in New Hampshire and in second place in Iowa. Why? Well, there are the millions he has spent on attack ads, his championing of the flat tax, and his buoyant sense of optimism. But more than that, Forbes passes the "person like me" test. With his unassuming manner, his not-cut-from-granite face, still bearing the scars of teenage acne, his ill-fitting suits (the sleeves are so long that he curls his fingers around the cuffs, looking like a nervous kid in his First Communion suit), Forbes gives the voters the impression that he is nobody special, that he is a person just like them.

He is not, of course. Not unless they grew up in a mansion named Timberfield, own a yacht, a jet, a helicopter, a château in France, and a private island in Fiji. But in politics, this does not necessarily matter. Image is what counts. And while the average American may dislike the wealthy as a class, he does not dislike wealthy people as individuals, just as long as they claim to share his pain. The Kennedys, the Rockefellers, and the Roosevelts have all proved that. And when Forbes promises that his flat tax will give all Americans more money, which means more control over their lives, he gets a big response. His delivery is smooth (though robotic) and he has his applause lines down pat. Give him something to memorize, and he will memorize it—but in states like Iowa and New Hampshire, where a tradition of "retail" politics means you have to answer questions, he sometimes falters.

In the tiny town of Earlham, west of Des Moines, Forbes stood on the step of a bright red fire engine and took questions from a small but enthusiastic crowd. He got the usual questions about his flat tax proposal, which he easily dealt with. But then he got a high, hard one.

"The breakdown of the marriage-based family is the primary cause of our social ills today," a well-dressed man asked from the back of the crowd. "Does your definition of a family include same-sex marriages?"

Forbes looked rocked. "Uhm, it, uhm, I'm, I'm afraid I'm hopelessly conventional," he says. "At uh, so I believe, uh, I, I, uhm, the answer, the answer would, uh, if you want to live together, that's fine. If you want to have a life together, fine. But all I can say is, compassion is not approval. And, uh, that's, that's, that's the heart of where I'm coming from."

A few minutes later, another verbal bomb was lobbed his way. "Mr. Forbes, is homosexuality morally acceptable?" a reporter asked.

Which is not exactly the kind of issue Forbes thought he would be dealing with on the campaign trail. These questions, after all, have nothing to do with elevating the economic well-being of the American people, which is what Steve Forbes really wants to talk about.

"I think that, uh, as I said, compassion is not approval," Forbes said about whether he thinks homosexuality is morally acceptable. "There should be special rights for none; equal rights for all."

Which did not really answer the reporter's question. Which meant Steve Forbes was learning.

The main purpose of his TV ads, into which he has poured millions of his family fortune, is to beat up the front-runner, Bob Dole. And the polls show Forbes's popularity rising. But the polls aren't really measuring anything important (a common problem with polls) and miss the fact that Forbes has made a fatal mistake: Because Forbes is so rich, he is paying for the campaign himself. In Iowa, the voting system for the caucuses is supremely goofy. It is not a secret ballot with votes cast throughout the day. Instead, people gather together at one time on one evening, in thousands of church basements, lodge halls, and living rooms. Those people for Bob Dole stand by the sofa, and those who want Pat Buchanan stand by the rocker, and those who want Steve Forbes stand under the moosehead, and then the votes are counted. It takes hours. And those people who bother to show up for this arcane ritual (and very few Iowans bother to show up) are usually those who have contributed five or ten or twenty dollars to a candidate. In Iowa, if you contribute money, you show up to protect your investment.

But Forbes has not asked for their dollars, and so few feel any attachment to him. He will finish a disappointing fourth. It is one of the few times in political history when a candidate has had too much money.

L ARRY KING SITS AT A LONG TABLE AT A PRICEY RESTAURANT in downtown Des Moines that specializes in slabs of meat too large for any normal person to desire. Though two network anchormen are also dining here tonight at separate tables—Peter Jennings of ABC and Tom Brokaw of NBC—and two presidential candidates—Steve Forbes and Pat Buchanan—King is the center of attention. (The legendary Johnny Apple of *The New York Times* is also here, but print reporters are not noticed in public unless they appear on TV a great deal.)

People, strangers, come up to King and do the same thing: they touch him. They put an arm on his shoulder, pat him, grasp him, make contact as if they actually knew him. He is a celebrity, but he belongs to them. He is their creation. "It doesn't bother me anymore," he tells me later. "You come into their homes, they figure they know you. And they always call you Larry. Always."

Earlier in the day he had gone to a movie (since he never prepares for the show, he has nothing to do during the day) and had set off a frenzy of people rushing up to him for autographs. "They weren't prepared for a celebrity at the movie," he says. "The place went crazy."

As usual, he is talking about his favorite subject: himself. "When I was hired [by CNN] in 1985, I had a three-year deal: $200,000, $225,000, $250,000, but either one of us could cancel after each year. Now I get $3 million," he says.

"Oh, Larry," a staffer says, "you do not."

"Two point seven million," King says, "but it goes to three at the end of the year. And we're renegotiating. Even though I've got four years to go on my contract, we're renegotiating. They're very fair. Murdoch offered me $6 million to go to Fox."

"What does Barbara Walters get?" somebody asks.

"Nine million," King says instantly.

Barbara Walters gets nine million dollars? For asking people what kind of trees they'd like to be? And how many times a week is she on the air? Once. King is on six nights a week. It is not fair, simply not fair.

"Sixty thousand a speech!" King says. "That's what I get!" (The figures, like all figures that come from King's mouth, are subject to change.) And then he laments how much time it takes to fly around the country to make all these speeches.

So why do it? I ask. You don't need the money.

He shrugs. "I get out, I get to meet people."

Bob Woodward of *The Washington Post* passes by, and King shouts out: "Bobby!" which absolutely nobody calls Bob Woodward, and Woodward comes over and they exchange pleasantries. Then Jennings comes by the table, then Tim Russert of *Meet the Press,* and then Pat Buchanan. They all come by Larry's table to kiss his ring and then depart.

"Hey," King says. "Topless woman goes into a bar and a hobo goes into a bar. Topless woman goes into a bar and a hobo goes into a bar. Topless woman goes in and three hoboes go in. What's that called? 'William Tell Overture.' *Titi bum, titi bum, titi bum, bum, bum.* I've been telling that since the eighth grade." He looks around as if he expected someone to disagree.

"Guy's arrested for fucking a goat," King says, "and he hires the best defense attorney money can buy. 'I'll get you a great jury,' the defense lawyer tells him. 'Don't worry about a thing.' . . ." He goes on with the joke and finishes with the punch line: "A good goat will do that!"

Cyndy Garvey, who has been eating quietly next to him, looks up at the punch line and repeats, "A good goat will do that!" They roar together.

King doesn't drink, has stopped smoking since his heart surgery, and almost always orders the same thing in restaurants: a piece of dry swordfish cooked well done. When it comes, he eats a few bites, messes up the side dishes, and leaves the rest. When the check comes, he pays for the entire table, leaving a 20 percent tip.

"Marlon Brando said I could act," he says. "I was driving around with Marlon Brando, and he said acting is easy, anybody could do it, and he said, 'Okay, look, I'm picking up the phone and someone tells me your sister has died.' And so he picks up the phone and listens for a second and turns to me and says, 'Larry, your sister has died.' And I said: 'What! How? Where?' And he said I was great."

More people come by King's table, ordinary diners who ignore the candidates and media stars in the room. For all his ego and self-obsession, King never turns down a request for an autograph, a picture, a chat. On the contrary, like Bill Clinton, he seems to feed on the attention. And it doesn't seem to matter whether the attention is good or bad. Maureen Dowd, a columnist for *The New York Times,* has just written a slashing satire of the column King writes for *USA Today:* "Questions, questions, questions: Why do they call it the Heartland? Don't the rest of us have heart? . . . I'm outta here . . ."

As we start to go, King says to the table, "Did you see the Maureen Orth column on me? The whole column on me. My name in the headline. Dot, dot, dot. Iowa, I'm outta here. Maureen Orth."

No, that was Maureen Dowd, I say to him. Maureen Dowd writes for *The New York Times.* Maureen Orth writes for *Vanity Fair.*

"Yeah," King says. "My name in the headline."

I⁣T IS MONDAY, FEBRUARY 19, AND LARRY KING IS SITTING IN A grim hotel suite a few miles south of Manchester, New Hampshire. He is wearing a casual shirt and black denim pants. It is late morning, he has gone to breakfast, he has read the papers (he actually keeps up on current events), it is something like ten hours before his show, and he has nothing to do. No, it is worse than that. He has nothing to do and he has no show. Pat Buchanan is the big story in New Hampshire, but the show can't get Pat Buchanan. This didn't used to happen. Being on Larry King was a big, big deal, and candidates would disembowel themselves to do it. But a strange new dynamic seems to be developing, and King does not like it: Candidates are stiffing the show. They are organizing their own media events, events they can strictly control. While King is often criticized for asking softball questions, candidates don't even want softballs these days. During the 1996 campaign Bob Dole will organize his own "town hall" meetings, where friendly audience members will ask friendly questions. It is the Larry King show without Larry King.

I tell King there is a Buchanan event just a minute's drive away if he wants to go see Buchanan.

"I've never been to a political event," King says, startled by my offer.

Never? I say. Never ever? In your whole life?

"No, never," he says. "Never been to one."

Let's go, I say. I've got a car. Let's go.

King looks dubious. "I don't know," he says.

Look, you could ask Buchanan to be on your show, I say. How could he say no?

Now King is interested. He climbs into his coat and I go get the car and we are off. As we drive, I realize how audacious this is: It's like taking the *Mona Lisa* out into the sunlight.

We drive over the snow-clogged streets until we get to downtown

Elm Street in Manchester. There is a huge crowd on the sidewalk outside Buchanan headquarters.

"Park here! Park here!" King says, pointing to an open space in
front of a fire hydrant.

It's illegal, I say. I'll get towed.

"Park illegal!" he says. "This city can't afford a tow truck!"

I continue to look for a legal space as King starts doing shtick. "The
sun peeks through the clouds in Manchester—I'm doing radio," he
says. "The hubbub of campaign disquiet is interrupted by a quiet that
is almost sleepy."

We finally park and walk over to Buchanan headquarters. Like the
Red Sea responding to Moses, the crowd outside parts for King without
his having to ask. Buchanan headquarters are up a narrow, long interior
staircase. Every step is filled with reporters and camera people trying to
get inside the second-floor office. But the Buchanan people have locked
the doors because there is no more room. There is really no room to
move up the staircase, but people look over their shoulders at us, ignoring me and fixing on King. "Hey, Larry," the hard-bitten reporters say,
flattening against the staircase wall. "Come on up."

We walk up and get to the glass office door. The gatekeeper inside
is staring out sullenly, and when I knock on the glass he starts to shake
his head and then sees King. He unlocks the door, throws it open, and
King enters the packed room. Buchanan has already begun his speech,
and about thirty TV cameras, arrayed on a riser, are trained on him.

As soon as Buchanan sees King, he stops the speech. "The overnight polls must be looking good if Larry King is here!" Buchanan
crows.

All the cameras on the riser swivel away from Buchanan and lock
on to King. A newsman like Tom Brokaw would be horrified at this; an
entertainer like King is electrified.

"Bay called last night and said they needed a Jewish person," King
shouts and holds up his hands for silence. "First, we need you on our
program at nine o'clock . . ."

"I can't do it," Buchanan says. "I'm hopping around . . ."

"And second, if you are elected will you still do *Crossfire*?"
King asks.

The crowd erupts in laughter.

"I'll do it every other week from Camp David!" Buchanan shouts.

Buchanan abandons his speech as people crowd around King, who
now wisely retreats downstairs. A protester on the sidewalk goes up to
King and says, "He's a racist, Mr. King. Buchanan's an anti-Semite."

"I've been a friend of his a long time and I've never seen it," King
replies. "I'm Jewish, and some things he's said over the years have

bothered me. I've talked to him about it. He is a complex man, but I've never seen it."

King walks a few steps farther, but now he is crowded by reporters shouting questions at him, wanting to get a Larry King angle in their stories. "I've never been to a campaign event!" King says, shouting out lines to them. "It must have been like this for Rabin in the streets of Tel Aviv! I really wanted to see this in action! Get a rabbi up there!"

Gene Randall of CNN goes up to him and says, "Larry, I'm going to be with Buchanan all day, and if you want me to reinforce your request, I'd be glad to."

"Call Wendy," King says. "She wants to know why he's not doing it. I can't figure it out." But by 1996 even the Larry King show was dangerous. King could skewer you without meaning to, or a caller could. Or some other candidate's press secretary could call up and ask you an embarrassing question. Why risk that? Besides, Buchanan had a different strategy, and it was working.

P AT BUCHANAN COULD NOT BELIEVE IT. HE PUT DOWN THE phone and shook his head and was silent for a moment before his face split into a huge grin. "Guy says I've got to get rid of my diabolical chuckle after I tell a joke," Buchanan says. And then he gives a chuckle worthy of Lucifer himself.

There are not many people with the nerve to give Pat Buchanan advice. Not these days. In his quest for the Republican nomination for president, he has won in Alaska and Louisiana, has come in second in Iowa, and is poised to win New Hampshire.

I sit in his hotel room for ninety minutes, watching him make call after call to radio station after radio station. He has been making the calls for hours, sitting on the hard-backed chair at a desk. His shirt, always a luminescent white, is now bunched and wrinkled. The room on the seventh floor of the downtown Holiday Inn smells of sweat, aftershave, and old pizza. A plundered gift basket lies in the corner, only the bottle of white wine and a raw fig untouched. The king-size bed is rumpled from where Buchanan spent a few minutes between calls trying to relax. He sits now with the phone at his ear, nervously tapping his feet on the floor, looking at pink note cards for the first names of the radio hosts he is talking to and dropping their names into the conversation to make it look as if they were old pals. Buchanan knows what it takes to make a radio host like you.

"You know, Dan, this has been a good campaign, an honest campaign, aboveboard, fair, and tough," Buchanan says into the phone. He falls silent for a moment as he listens to a caller. "I appreciate it," he says. "I hope those other Gramm folks will come our way. Phil repre-sented a lot of the things that I do. Some we disagreed on."

I would imagine they disagreed—for instance, over how Buchanan operatives in Louisiana called voters and informed them that Phil Gramm had divorced his "white" wife for an "Asiatic" one.

"But, look," Buchanan says into the phone, "this is basically a fight now between a genuine, authentic conservative and the establishment heir, Robert Dole. I think the campaign he has conducted is unworthy of him with these attack ads."

Greg Mueller, Buchanan's press secretary, walks into the room and clamps his hands on my shoulders. "Twenty-nine radio shows," he whispers in my ear.

This is the new math of politics in 1996. This is the new Buchanan way. Before each of his victories and his second-place finish in Iowa, Buchanan has worked the phones while the other candidates were out pressing the flesh or trying to get a few minutes on TV.

To Buchanan, radio is the new retail politics, electronic retail, where people can call in and ask you questions and feel as if you were in their living rooms with them. "We're headed for South Carolina and up to the Dakotas," Buchanan says into the phone. "Then to Colorado and Arizona. We're going to stay right in there to San Diego, my friend!"

The day before, Tim Russert, moderator of *Meet the Press*, had left the NBC set, which is located in the same hotel where Buchanan was staying, and walked over to the elevators. On NBC, Newt Gingrich had declared that if Buchanan won the Republican nomination, Bill Clinton would be reelected president and the Democrats would retake Congress.

"I walked out of the studio and down to the lobby of the hotel, and Pat Buchanan was getting out of the elevator," Russert said.

Buchanan stepped out of the elevator, stopped in front of Russert and fixed him with that beady stare of his.

"Hey," Buchanan said. "You tell Newt: '*Deal* with it!' "

I DRIVE LARRY KING BACK TO HIS HOTEL SUITE AND HE CHANGES his cashmere socks and stretches out on the couch, from where he calls his senior executive producer. "Wendy, I went in and the cameras *turned*," he says, bubbly with enthusiasm.

Yeah, but will Buchanan go on the show? As it turns out, he won't. He has radio calls to make. Each radio listener is a voter in New Hamp-shire. King reaches all the way around the world, which is a waste for Buchanan.

Hours later, on the set of his show, King is clearly peeved and talking about the renewed charges in the press that Buchanan is an anti-Semite. "You know what it is with Buchanan?" King says to me. "It's a Catholic thing. He believes my ancestors killed his Lord. It's *that* kind of anti-Semitism, but he wouldn't keep a Jew from moving into his neighborhood. But if he was president when Hitler was rising, he'd say, 'Forget it. Let Europe take care of its own problems.' "

Instead of Buchanan, King gets Lamar Alexander and his wife, Honey, and Steve Forbes and his wife, Sabina, for the show. But the air has rushed out of Forbes's balloon. He is no longer a big story. Larry King does not need him now, but Forbes needs Larry King. Pretty soon, Forbes will have to hold up a 7-Eleven to make news.

When the show is over, King talks about how he is soon going to appear on David Letterman. "You know, after his show, Letterman watches a tape and critiques it!" King says, as if that is the most outrageous and bizarre thing he has ever heard.

Don't you do that? I ask. Don't you ever critique your own performance?

King looks at me as if I had asked him if he ever looked up his own nose. "Me?" King says. "No."

You've never seen your show? Not once?

He thinks. "A couple of times," he says. "Maybe."

Later we go to a gourmet Asian restaurant, the kind that has shark fin on the menu, and King orders chow mein, which is definitely not on the menu. But the kitchen gladly makes it for him. King puts the noodles on this plate, a huge portion of chow mein on top of that, and then a huge portion of white rice on top of the chow mein. He doesn't offer to share. "I got a joke for you," he says. "This guy's arrested for fucking a goat and he hires O.J.'s jury consultant . . ."

I've heard it, I tell him.

"You know who I told that joke to?" he says.

I try to think. Mamie Eisenhower? Mother Teresa? The pope?

"Denise Brown!" he says.

You told Denise Brown, sister of Nicole Simpson, a joke about O.J.'s jury consultant?

"She *loved* it," he says.

IT IS TUESDAY, PRIMARY DAY IN NEW HAMPSHIRE, AND KING HAS neither Buchanan nor Dole scheduled for this evening. It is unbelievable, unimaginable. Though King's show is a mix of newsmakers and Hollywood types, the newsmaker shows always do better in the ratings. (CNN's audience is more public-affairs oriented than general TV audiences are). And King's reputation is at stake. He is the guy who is supposed to get the guests that nobody else can get. And so, along with some staff members, King has gone to another political event, this time a visit by Bob Dole to a restaurant in Nashua, New Hampshire, to grab Dole for the show.

Again the crowd goes crazy and begins to chant, "Lar-ry King! Lar-ry King!" King goes up to Dole and Dole, startled—he is not used to seeing King when the sun is out—says, "What can I do for you?"

"You can come on the show!" King says.

"I'll do it if I win," Dole says. "Or maybe if I lose."

"Then come on Friday night," King beseeches him. "It will be Neil Diamond and you. A Kansan and a Jew!"

That night, King walks into the CNN workspace, which is a series of offices just vacated by a TV station and is pretty shabby. His staff has been squeezed into a small and cheerless cubbyhole. King looks at it and looks at the much larger workspace where John Sununu, former governor of New Hampshire and now a CNN star, is standing.

"Sununu has a better room! Why?" King asks. "He's a Republican, that's why. No, he's an Arab! The Arabs always get the better deal."

King walks over to his staff. "So what have we got here, girls, ladies, whatever? Dole, if he wins, is he coming?"

The staff looks at him bleakly. Yeah. Right.

King changes the subject. "I saw a piece where Brokaw says people hate the media," he says. "They like me." He looks genuinely baffled.

He turns to Carrie Stevenson, his floor director, the person who tells him what to do while the show is going on. "Where's my Coke, Carrie?" he asks.

"Right there," she says, pointing to the can, not looking up. She is typing background information on Christopher Reeve, who will be on the show in a few days. She is also busy getting plates of pasta and salad and Cokes for Larry King. TV work is *so* romantic.

"She's so *officious*!" King says. "I'll never lose her. I'll marry her or I'll adopt her. Which do you want? Marriage or adoption?"

"Huh?" Stevenson says, still bent over the computer terminal, doing six things at once.

King, with nothing to do, starts walking around, shmoozing with people who have plenty to do. He walks over to Judy Woodruff, who is preparing to go on the air. "You're a fashion plate," he says to her.

"I don't know how to take that," she says.

He bends down. "We've got Vannatter and Lange," he says. Maybe the politicians are stiffing him, but the police detectives from the O.J. trial are still interested.

King wanders over to the makeup room, which is ratty looking, with holes punched in the walls, broken ceiling tiles on the floor, and abandoned, ripped-out lockers leaning up against the walls. The makeup person is Sharon "Dede" Slingerland, who owns a salon in Amherst, New Hampshire, and has been hired by CNN for nine days. She is a pretty, gum-chewing blonde and King starts his usual, though harmless, banter with her as she makes him up.

"I fantasized about you last night," he says. "You were great."

"I hear you're engaged," Dede says.

"No. I don't want to be married. Monogamy is hard. Your lipstick gave me a bump on the lip, by the way," he says, raising a fist.

"Don't hit me!" she says in mock terror.

"I'd never hit a woman," King says. "I'm Jewish; I'm a Scorpio. We run. I have never lifted a hand to a woman. I've cursed, I've ridiculed, I've embarrassed, I've yelled, but I've never hit. Never even thought of it."

Dede keeps working on his face, bending low over him.

"I could have tremendous desire for you," he says. "You are beautiful."

"You lied to me," she says. "You said you were married three times."

"Three times to four women," King says. "No. Wait. Four times to three women."

"What was your first wife?" Dede asks.

"German-Irish Catholic," he says. "I never turned my back on her. I never took a shower in her presence."

"Tom Brokaw was here," Dede says. "He didn't do anything for us charismatically."

King beams through the makeup. "I hear you're dating a contractor," he says. "What do you talk about, bricks?"

Dede finishes with him and starts packing away her little swabs and sponges. "Is Lamar Alexander coming?" she asks. "I've got to get rid of his orange face."

Bob Squier, who is doing the television commercials for the Clinton campaign and who is also a CNN commentator, comes into the makeup room and King says to him, "C'mere. I've got a joke. This guy's arrested for fucking a goat . . ." He goes through the whole joke and ends with, "A good goat will do that!"

Squier roars. "That's great!" he says. "Great!"

Encouraged, King says, "You write a book on jury consulting, and you could call it, 'A Good Goat Will Do That!'"

Squier roars again. He is practically slapping his thighs. This is a guy who knows how to keep a star—Clinton or King—happy.

At 8:24 P.M. Woodruff goes on the air and says, "CNN is now able to predict that Pat Buchanan will be the winner in New Hampshire."

But will Pat Buchanan be live on *Larry King Live* tonight? No. How about Bob Dole? No. Instead, King gets Alexander (again) and Steve Forbes (again), who nobody cares about anymore. It is a real low point for the show. So King decides to see if he can humiliate Dole into coming on.

"I saw Senator Dole today," King says on the air, "and he said he'd be with us this Friday night on *Larry King Live*. Four years ago tonight, Ross Perot got in the race on *Larry King Live*." And what a difference four years makes.

"Friday night, Bob Dole and Neil Diamond!" King says later in the show. Then, once again, when they cut away to Dole's concession speech, King says, "He will be with me Friday night!"

The next day, at a brief airport press conference (it will be one of only two press conferences Dole has during his entire campaign), Dole says, "We stayed up until eleven o'clock. Pretty late for me, eleven o'clock. This is a fight between the mainstream and the extreme, between hope . . . and fear. It's about freedom and intolerance. Hang on to your seats. Hang on to your seat belts. Whatever. The ride has just begun." Then Dole says, "I can't get up and you push a button and you get a message. I mean, I am what I am."

Which is exactly what his staff fears. Dole then gets on a plane and takes off on a campaign trip to Fargo, North Dakota; Sioux Falls, South Dakota; and Denver. On the leg between Sioux Falls and Denver, Dole walks back to talk to reporters (he will later severely cut down on this) and stops by the seat of Jodi Enda of *The Philadelphia Inquirer*. "I did find a penny leaving the hotel today," he says. "I think it was heads." Then he reaches into his left pocket and brings out the entire contents—a penny and a black tube of Chapstick—and proudly shows them to her.

Is this guy your grandfather or what?

King flies down to New York that night to appear on David Letterman. On the air, King tells the story about being on the plane in Iowa with the wind-shear landing. "So it's Cyndy Garvey, Tom Brokaw, Bob Woodward, me on the plane," King says. "We go down, what's the headline?"

"Well," Letterman says, "Cyndy Garvey and then everyone else."

"Friday, we got Bob Dole," King says.

FRIDAY COMES AND LARRY KING DOES NOT GET BOB DOLE. INstead, Larry King gets Neil Diamond and Dr. Stephen Gullo, nutrition expert and author of *Thin Tastes Better*.

Bob Dole will do Larry King's show in 1996, but only twice, one of which is a disastrous appearance for him in which Elizabeth continually corrects, silences, and upstages him. After that, the Dole campaign people decide Larry King is no longer their kind of show. King tries to get Bill Clinton.

"You're employed by the people," King argues. "A movie star does not *have* to do the show. But *you* work for *us*. You are the president!" Bill Clinton does not appear on Larry King's show in 1996.

"It's not an audience that gravitates toward Clinton," Mike McCurry tells me after the election. "It's disproportionately elderly, upscale, and anti-Clinton. And we were not big on high-profile TV interviews in 1996." King would have settled for Al Gore, but his attempts there fail, too.

"Gore didn't go on in 1996," King says. "He said he would, and he didn't. And he's an old friend!"

King falls briefly silent. "They were scared," he says. "Scared. But wait, in four years, in 2000, you'll see. It will be Al Gore versus Colin Powell. And we'll have them on ten times! *You'll* see!"

ARM AND THE MAN

★

"You got shot; I think we can get you elected."

—Party official to Bob Dole
following World War II

As BOB DOLE STEPPED CAREFULLY OVER THE LOW HEDGE that separated the walkway from the grave of Richard M. Nixon, it occurred to him that maybe this was not such a good idea after all. The press was already calling this his "All-Death-Tour." It was March 1996, and this was his first trip to California as a candidate for president. Clinton already had been here twenty-three times in the last three years, which was more times than Ronald Reagan had been to California in his entire first term, and Reagan had a *home* here. So Dole's first trip had to be good, it had to click, it had to make him look like a winner. So what did they do? They put the planning in the hands of California's governor, Pete Wilson, who is not the sharpest knife in the drawer.

And the first thing Wilson does is take Dole to San Quentin to visit death row. Gee, that ought to help change Dole's dark image. There are 424 men on death row, all facing lethal injection, and Dole's handlers take Dole inside the prison so he can stare at them. What else was Dole going to do with them? Ask them how they felt about a flat tax? So Dole looks through this double row of bars at them and they look back through the double row of bars at him and then, well, what's he supposed to say now? "I hope you get dead soon?" Which is the point of Dole's speech. We ought to speed up the death penalty to kill these guys quicker.

It is not a bad issue; it has tested well in the opinion polls. But coming out to San Quentin to see the condemned men in their cells with their steel bunks and toilets without seats and getting right up in their faces to wish them a speedy death seems a little undignified, a little too *political,* if there is such a thing in America by 1996. And, as it turns out—just Dole's luck—there is. Even conservative Republicans find the event a mistake and say so. "A trip to San Quentin is not a way to show your concern for crime," Lyn Nofziger, White House aide to Ronald Reagan, tells reporters. "Going up there and looking at a bunch of people in cages."

But what is Dole supposed to do? He is going where Pete Wilson tells him to go. And so he finds himself standing outside at a lectern with the looming prison wall just over his shoulder and the prisoners

staring out the windows of their cages at him while Dole reads from
his speech and laments the fact that in recent years more death row in-
mates have died of old age (14) than have been executed (3). Actually,
since they end up dead either way, what difference does it make? And
even Dole seems a little ambiguous about the whole thing. "It kind of
makes you wonder," he says. "Is this America?" Whatever the hell
that's supposed to mean.

And where do they take Dole next? Well, just to shake off the
blues, they take him to visit Richard Nixon's grave. Jim-in-ny! It's not
that Dole didn't like Nixon; he did. Sure, Nixon screwed him by kick-
ing him out as chairman of the Republican Party and installing George
Bush, but who didn't Nixon screw? That's just the way he was. Above
all, Dole tells reporters later in the day, Nixon was a guy who knew
how to *win.* And Dole sounds very wistful as he says it.

So now Dole is in Yorba Linda, stepping over a little hedge and
standing in front of Nixon's grave, where brilliant sunshine reflects off
the polished black granite marker. Dole whispers for Elizabeth to kneel
and place a plastic-wrapped bouquet of flowers on the grave. Dole
would do it himself, but holding the flowers in his one good hand and
kneeling and trying to get back up again is not something he wants to
try in front of twenty TV cameras. So Elizabeth dips down on one knee
and put the flowers on the black granite and gets back up and puts her
arm around Dole's waist in one fluid motion. God, she is good. Every
move a perfect picture. She never misses a trick. Now if she could just
pass that instinct on to her husband.

But Dole is, as always, impatient, wanting to get on with
the speech and get the heck out of here, so he does a quick silent
count of three at the grave—one Mississippi, two Mississippi, three
Mississippi—and then whirls and walks across the bright green lawn to
the podium.

About two hundred well-dressed, well-coiffed, well-heeled Republicans are sitting on little folding chairs on the lawn in front of him,
staring at him as if to say: "Okay, you've got the nomination wrapped
up, now how are you going to beat Bill Clinton?" Which is a question
Dole has been asking himself.

"Some people think Bob Dole was born in a suit and doesn't have a
town," Dole begins in his trademark speaking style of fluent non se-
quitur. "I grew up in Russell, Kansas, my hometown, where I was born
a long time ago. Like others I was wounded on the fourteenth of April,
1945." Dole likes peppering his speeches with phrases such as "like
others" and "like all of you." He feels it makes him sound less like a
big shot, less removed from the people. Not a bad thought, but like

many of Dole's thoughts, when it gets filtered through his mouth any-thing can happen. Like the day he told a crowd in New Hampshire, "Like everyone else here, I was born." Or that day in Bakersfield, when he said, "Like a lot of people in this audience, the war came." Which he followed up with, "I was born like everybody else here, in Russell, Kansas."

The press giggles over this kind of stuff. But Dole likes the theory behind what he is trying to say, even if he often can't say it. Being above people is not the way to get elected. You learn that growing up in Kansas. You never want people to envy you. It is much better if they like you. Or, even better, pity you.

"Nothing is easy," Dole tells the crowd at Nixon's grave. "I haven't found it so in my lifetime. Blood clots in my lungs. Guinea pig for streptomycin. Learned to feed myself, dress myself, go to the bath-room." The crowd sits silently. "I believe you're going to elect some-one who knows a little about sacrifice." Sacrifice? To this crowd sacrifice means letting the maid go home early because she has the flu. "Thank you for letting me speak in this hallowed place," Dole says, "and God bless America." The crowd applauds weakly.

Some reporters make a mad dash for the gift shop where for $17.95 they can buy T-shirts that say "Nixon in '96. He's tanned, rested and ready." (In Dole's Capitol Hill office there is a sign that reads: "Dole '96. Tougher, Meaner—Kinder, Gentler." Nobody can explain what it means.) Dole climbs back into his car and wonders who ever decided to listen to Pete Wilson. First the prison thing with the killers staring at him, and now the grave thing with the fat cats staring at him. What next, the county morgue? Maybe they can get some actual *corpses* and tie them into chairs so *they* can stare at him. Jim-in-ny! Can it get worse? Of course it can. This is the Dole campaign.

Dole's seventeen-vehicle motorcade rockets down the freeway, all traffic stopped, all exits and entrances blocked off. There are no Dole signs on any of his vehicles, so angry motorists, stacked up twenty deep at the entrance ramps, will not know whom to blame. The motor-cade exits the freeway and enters a neighborhood of modest one-story, mostly stucco homes with red-tile roofs and small storefront busi-nesses with names like Doan Trang Immigration Service and Do Nhu Muu, D.D.S. This is the Little Saigon section of Orange County and all the faces on the street are Asian.

The motorcade squeals to a halt in front of the two-story Asia Gar-den Mall, where many of the signs are solely in Vietnamese. Six months ago to the day, Dole had warned against the evils of such "eth-nic separatism" and called for making English the official language of

America. "We need the glue of language to help hold us together," Dole told the American Legion.

Today, however, glue is not what Dole will talk about. Today Dole will endorse the controversial California Civil Rights Initiative (CCRI), which would end affirmative action in state hiring and college admissions. In a rare move, the Dole campaign has actually told reporters ahead of time what the speech will be about (they suspect reporters are the major leaks to the Clinton campaign and therefore keep things from them) and have even handed out a press release. Getting handed a press release on the Dole campaign is like getting handed a moon rock, and the reporters are in an advanced state of awe. The release is highly detailed and the reporters are told to expect a major address.

Also, an actual crowd has been assembled for Dole, some 2,000 screaming people in a too-small space, which is perfect for the TV pictures. Finally the Dole campaign has gotten its act together. The crowd is pumped up. There are dragon dancers and men beating drums and banging cymbals together. The crowd is 99 percent Asian, and while a number of people will later admit they don't speak or understand English—"If he had really wanted to reach us, he should have had an interpreter," Thanh Nguyen, 74, says afterward in Vietnamese. "I heard him, but I didn't understand anything"—they cheer madly throughout. These voters do not like affirmative action, because they are afraid it will be used to keep their kids *out* of college. Their kids are home studying every night and getting twin 800s on their SATs. These parents see "diversity" as a code word for "keep Asians out."

So Dole can expect a good response to his attack on affirmative action. True, he has long been a supporter of affirmative action and in 1986 was one of twenty-three Republican senators to ask Ronald Reagan not to overturn federal set-asides for minority contractors. But polls show public opinion in California 2–1 in favor of CCRI, and Dole needs a bandwagon to jump on. (CCRI will be approved on Election Day by 54 percent of the vote, but will be put on hold by the courts.) A speech has been carefully written out for Dole, and as with all his speeches, each page is encased in clear plastic so he can turn the pages by swiping across them with his "good" left hand, a hand that lacks sufficient sensitivity to feel a piece of paper.

Pete Wilson tries to make up for San Quentin and Nixon's grave by giving Dole a rousing introduction. "You struggled to come to these shores," Wilson tells the crowd and then points to Dole. "He fought for freedom in Italy and he bears the scars of it today. You can be all you can be. That is what Little Saigon is all about!" The crowd roars, the drums beat, the cymbals clash, and Dole walks up to the lectern, his face beaming. Finally a crowd of actual living people! Not like those dried-out old WASPs in Yorba Linda. "Only in America could a meeting like this take place!" Dole begins, and the little stand holding up the microphone promptly falls over onto the lectern.

To any other speaker this would be a small embarrassment. To Dole, it is a disaster. He keeps picking up the mike stand with his left hand, but every time he takes his hand away from the pages of his speech, they threaten to fall off the slanted top of the lectern. There is a little lip on the lectern to keep the pages from slipping off, but it is not big enough to hold the thick, plastic-covered pages. And how can Dole turn the pages if he has to hold up the microphone? He only has one hand, goddammit! Hasn't anybody noticed that? True, if he had gone over this speech, a major speech, in advance or rehearsed it or even knew much about it contents, he could deliver it off the top of his head. But Dole hates rehearsing speeches and often doesn't see them until a few moments before he arrives at the site.

Elizabeth, seeing his predicament, jumps up from her seat and walks over to the side of the lectern and, smiling brightly, takes hold of the mike stand for Bob. He continues speaking. "I'll not rest until we have human rights and democracy in Hanoi!" Dole says, and the crowd roars approval. "Had Bob Dole been president, I would not have normalized relations with Vietnam!" Now to the meat of the speech. "We ought to do away with preferences! It ought to be based on merit!" Dole says. Then, irritated with Elizabeth, who is still standing there holding the microphone, he rudely takes the mike stand from her and tells her to sit down. "I have to pay her overtime," he says and nobody laughs. "We have a good mike system; we just don't know who's in charge of it." There are oohs from the reporters. All candidates complain from time to time, but few do it in front of 2,000 people.

Now, with nobody to hold the mike so he can turn the pages of his speech, Dole simply drops any further mention of CCRI or affirmative action and falls back on the one subject he can deliver from memory: World War II. "I'm from the World War II generation, and we had to train with broomsticks!" he says. The people cheer madly, especially, one assumes, those who do not understand English. "He [Clinton] has been out here twenty-three times dropping off little bags of money. But little bags of money won't do it. The people of California want leadership! Okay, I'll wrap it up. God bless America." And he sits down. The band swings into "Way Down Upon the Swannee River," apparently believing that it flows through Kansas. Bob Dole has spoken for exactly ten minutes. True, he has said very little that the press can make fun of (in about three months, he will tell an ethnic audience in Los Angeles,

"We are the boiling pot; we have open arms"), but he has also failed to mention CCRI after his aides have distributed a press release titled "DOLE ENDORSES CCRI." He has not even specifically mentioned affirmative action, which was the point of the event. He does not care, however. He stalks furiously from the stage, as angry as anyone has seen him in public. Who was responsible for the damn microphone? Why didn't they have a better lectern? Why did Elizabeth embarrass him like that in front of all these people?

On the buses heading for the airport, reporters ask aides why Dole is so angry with this small boo-boo. "It exposed his handicap," an aide replies. Which is an odd complaint, considering Dole talks about his handicap in nearly every speech and there are few subjects he has exposed more. But what Dole wishes to sell to the public is his triumph over his handicap and how warm and sensitive it has made him.

Now, hours later on his campaign plane on the way to Seattle, Dole is still fuming over the incident. He doesn't care that he has blown a major speech. He is still angry over that damn mike stand and lectern. "You get hold of Scott Reed and you tell him I want the podium right!" he yells at an aide. Reed, his campaign manager, is supposed to be worrying about things like Bill Clinton's 58–37 lead in the California polls. Now Reed has to worry about podiums, lecterns, and mike stands.

But the next day dawns bright and clear, and Dole appears to be in a better mood. He is flying home to Russell, Kansas, a place that always makes him happy. He comes back from the front of the plane and talks to the press, laughing and joking. Dole reports that there are high winds in Russell and, turning to the TV reporters, makes spritzing gestures with his fingers. "Put plenty of that stuff on," he says. "Hair spray. Fall down and your hair breaks. I'll be using it." The reporters laugh. Dole has no embarrassment talking about the hair spray or hair dye that he uses. Now Dole starts talking about Main Street in Russell. "After five o'clock you could shoot a cannonball down there and it wouldn't disturb anybody!" he laughs. Then a reporter asks him about the event at Little Saigon and the mike stand and the lectern.

Dole's face immediately darkens, his brows knit, and a shadow falls across his deep-set eyes. It is like a thunderstorm sweeping across a prairie. "Somebody's going to get *reamed* when I get back," Dole says.

HOW BAD IS BOB DOLE'S WOUND? SO BAD THAT TO THIS DAY HE will not look at it. When he stands in front of the mirror every morning to shave, and that is the *only* time he stands in front of the mirror, he drapes a towel over his right shoulder, over his *missing* right shoulder. People do not understand this. He has come so far, done so much, in spite of a shattered right shoulder and useless right arm. He can dress himself and tie his own tie and drive a car (though he rarely does). True, he could never pick up his daughter in his arms when she was a child—she would stand on a chair to hug him—but that was a long time ago. He is, after all, still a big and strapping man, 6 feet 1 and 175 pounds, and handsome to boot. So what is the big deal with the arm? Why can't he bear to look at it?

Because he remembers what used to be there. He is one of the few still alive who does. He knows what the shoulder looked like, the shoulder that is now gone, the shoulder that was blown away and the right arm, the right arm now two and a half inches shorter than the left, reattached with muscles from his thigh. He remembers what it was like to dribble a basketball and throw a football and hit a baseball. In his dreams, a dream he still has, he is playing basketball. He is standing at the free-throw line. "That's where I'd fire from in my dreams," he told Laura Blumenfeld of *The Washington Post*. In the dream, he shoots and he never misses. "And I'd always wake and wonder: Did I dream using my right arm, my right hand? I must have."

And that is why he will not look at this shattered part of his body. Because in his dreams he is whole and in reality he is not. Don't get it? Can't quite understand it? Can't feel what Bob Dole feels? Cut off your arm and try again. "A wall of fire," is the way he described it to me in 1988. Every day of rehabilitation after his wound, he would walk through the wall of fire. At the worst, at the very lowest, when he thought he would be sitting in a wheelchair in front of Dawson Drugs on Main Street in Russell selling pencils, he would think, "Why me? What have I done wrong? What did I do to deserve this?" There was never an answer. There never is an answer. Why him? Why *not* him? That is the only answer there is.

"Suffering," Somerset Maugham wrote, "does not ennoble; it embitters." And Dole was embittered by his wound. It contributed, he was sure, to his loss to George Bush in the New Hampshire primary in 1988. Dole had begun his second attempt for the presidency by beating Bush the week before in the Iowa caucuses and if Dole could win New Hampshire, too, Bush would be finished. But Lee Atwater and Roger Ailes and John Sununu had masterfully reinvented Bush in that week and had changed his image from "wimp" to "good old boy." And now Bush was driving semitrailer trucks and shoveling walks and having snowball fights with reporters. While Bob Dole sat and watched him on TV. "He was out there shoveling snow for the TV cameras," Dole told me bitterly, months after he had lost. Bob Dole cannot shovel snow. Or even make, let alone throw, a snowball. And that, he was sure, contributed to his defeat. He had been beaten not by a better man, but by a man with a better arm. "For the first time in his public life, he has forced himself to speak openly about the horrible war wound that turned a strapping, athletic youth into an emaciated, bedridden hospital patient," *The Washington Post* reported in 1988. "The experience left him bitter and disillusioned, Dole has told audiences this year."

Eight years later, however, "bitter and disillusioned" was not what his wound had made him. On the contrary, now his wound had made him more sensitive, more warm, more human, more caring, and better able to understand people. And as for 1988 being "the first time in his public life" that Dole "forced himself" to speak about the wound? Well, that is what the press kept writing because it was a good story, and that is what the Dole campaign kept selling them. But it simply was not true. Bob Dole had spoken about his wound, used his wound to gain sympathy from the voters, for decades.

In 1974, for instance, in his first Senate reelection campaign, Dole just happened to mention his wound to journalist Lou Cannon, though once again Dole appeared to have to force himself to do so. "He was not comfortable with war talk," Cannon wrote in a column, "and even less with discussion of his long recovery." This time, Dole said that his wound was the reason he used such biting one-liners to respond to people. Dole was facing a tough reelection in 1974. He had been chairman of the Republican National Committee from 1971 to 1973 and a great defender of Richard Nixon throughout Watergate. Voters remembered that, and they also remembered Dole's sharp tongue. When Cannon asked Dole what Nixon could do to help his reelection, Dole said, "Stage a flyover of Kansas." Then Dole begged Cannon not to use the joke. It was his war wound that made him say stuff like that, Dole said. "You see things in the war and in the hospital, and you think about them," Dole said. "Sometimes you have to deal with them by joking."

But one easily could find Dole talking about his wound even before 1974, though the press continued to be amazed anew each time he did it. In 1964 the *Chicago Tribune* ran a very long story on Dole with the six-column headline: REP. DOLE TRIUMPHS OVER HIS WAR WOUND. The story was highly detailed about the wound and the recovery, and the reporter interviewed Dole at length. (It also included a line that Dole would later drop from his life story. He enlisted in the army, he said, only because "the draft would have got me.")

In 1996, thirty-two years later almost to the day, the *Chicago Tribune* again ran a long story on Bob Dole's war wound. This time it appeared on the front page and was headlined: SHARING HIS PAIN: NEVER BEFORE HAS BOB DOLE DISCUSSED HIS WAR INJURIES IN PUBLIC.

"Never before in his public career," the story said, "has Dole been as open and candid about the personal struggles that accompanied the injury. . . . The revelations are not therapeutic for Dole, an intensely private man." The wound, Dole said, had made him more sensitive. "I've never talked about it much in politics," Dole told the *Tribune* reporter. "I always thought it might appear to be self-serving or seem that way." And then he added, "People tell me to do it."

But they must have been telling him to do it for a very long time—all the way back to 1953, in fact, when he first ran for county attorney in Russell, Kansas. Though reporters always loved to think Dole was opening up to them "for the first time," it was hard to find an election when Dole did *not* exploit his wound. And for much of his career, it made sense. Dole *was* a severely injured war veteran, and for decades in America that would still count for something.

"You got shot; I think we can get you elected," a party official told Dole when he got out of the hospital and returned to Kansas. And it was Bob Dole himself who told that story. As Richard Ben Cramer points out in his book on the 1988 presidential race, the people of Russell and the surrounding county who elected Dole county attorney did so in no small part because they felt that county attorney was a job a guy with a shattered body could handle. They didn't want to see Bob Dole selling pencils on the streets either. And Dole had always recognized the political value of his wound. Writing about his race for county attorney in his autobiography, Dole says, "I scored a narrow win over Dean Ostrum, a Yale-educated lawyer whose professional credentials probably counted less than the local voters' sympathy for a banged-up veteran."

A few reporters did bother to delve, however gingerly, into Dole's use of his war injury, though the references often came deep in stories about the heroic wound itself. In December 1995, Stephen Braun of the *Los Angeles Times* interviewed former Dole aide Jim French, a florist and Republican state committeeman, who drove Dole through 58 counties in his 1966 congressional race. "Few gatherings passed without a tactful mention of his military service in Italy and the frozen right arm. It hit home with the veterans . . ." French said. And "if a meeting wasn't going good, sometimes I'd have a guy in the back of the room ask him about the war wound." And in his 1974 Senate race, Dole "distributed flyers detailing his recovery—down to the blood clots and bone transplants—with a close-up snapshot of his hand," reported Laura Blumenfeld in *The Washington Post*.

Yet the media loved the story of the stoic Dole, biting back the bitter memories, refusing to talk about his wound until it was dragged out of him. *The Philadelphia Inquirer* reported on April 10, 1995, that Dole "has refused to talk about his war record or his crippling injury in the past." Jack Shafer of *Slate,* an electronic magazine, wrote an exposé titled "The Wound" in August 1996, quoting newspaper story after newspaper story claiming that Dole was "reluctant," "reticent," "loath," and "uncomfortable" to talk about his wound, "because to do so," wrote *Newsday,* "would unearth the demons that he has lived with—and mostly hidden from the public—for the majority of his 73 years."

The record plainly shows, however, that far from hiding the wound from the public, Dole recognized its political value from the beginning. On May 19, 1996, Elizabeth Kolbert of *The New York Times* did a very lengthy front-page story on Dole and his hometown of Russell. Unlike many upbeat pieces about the honest, down-home, prairie goodness of Russell, Kolbert emphasized a bleaker and darker side (an "unlovely town" now even "sleepier and perhaps shabbier" than when Dole lived there, she wrote), but more important, she showed a bleaker and darker side of Dole's campaign tactics. Townspeople in Russell recall, she wrote, "a campaigner who ran what were, by the standards of the place and time, some memorably rough races. And they recall a man who, from his earliest campaigns, was already relying heavily on his biography." Biography being a code word for his wartime injury.

"He's always been able to get great mileage out of his injury," said John Woelk, the Russell attorney who encouraged Dole to get into politics. "He learned to do a very good job of drawing sympathy." So when Dole began his first race for Congress in 1960 and faced a very tough Republican primary, he knew what button to push. He distributed little cards that showed a picture of a wheel and the slogan "Roll with Dole." Along the spokes of the wheel were phrases like "Russell native" and "Twice-wounded vet."

The claim of "twice-wounded vet" was especially ironic. Dole had indeed been wounded twice in fierce fighting in Italy. But his first wound was self-inflicted. At Monte Belvedere on February 25, 1945, Dole had been sent out to find some German snipers holed up in a farmhouse. Dole approached the location, there was an exchange of gunfire, and Dole took a grenade from his belt, pulled the pin, and tossed it at the farmhouse. The grenade struck a tree, however, bounced off and exploded near Dole, sending a sliver of metal into his leg. Back at an aid station, the sliver was removed, Dole got swabbed with some Mercurochrome, marked down for a Purple Heart, and sent back to the front lines. How do we know this? Dole lays it all out in his autobiography, published in 1988.

The other part of the wound story that the press loved involved

Castel d'Aiano, 25 miles southeast of Bologna, which a number of reporters visited and wrote about during the 1996 campaign. It is a mountain village of 1,700 kindly souls in the Apennine mountain range of central Italy. It has a main street that trails down a mountainside, a town square, a bell tower, flowers on the balconies, lemon trees, the works. Dole political operatives had been flogging the story of Castel d'Aiano for years. Dole first went there in 1962, when he was a congressman, and returned five more times over the years, often trailing TV crews. On the day of his presidential nomination in August 1996, the town rolled vintage World War II tanks through the streets, a Dixieland band played, and parachutists fell from the skies. A giant pasta dinner was served in the town square, where a large screen beamed Dole's speech from San Diego. In October in a speech in Toms River, New Jersey, Dole spoke of "my" town, where he had recuperated from his wounds. "If things don't work out here," he said, "I might go over there; could be an opening for mayor." Could be. The village displayed "Bob Dole for President" signs in every shop window, reporters pointed out. And the town had erected a plaque on the spot where Dole was wounded, with a citation stating that people of Castel d'Aiano had done so as a "token of their eternal gratitude" because Dole was "seriously wounded while fighting for the freedom of our town."

In fact, however, the town was liberated more than a month before Dole was wounded. And though the townspeople claimed to have nursed Dole there after his crippling injury, in reality Dole was never brought to the town, but taken to a military hospital 35 miles away. So what was the connection between Castel d'Aiano and Bob Dole, aside from the fact that reporters found it a perfect setting from which to retell the Wound Saga? In 1962, on his first visit back to the site of his wounding, Dole stopped his Cadillac in the town and asked for directions. And that was the sole connection between the town and Bob Dole. But the Dole story was good for business. Tourists, both Italian and foreign, came to see the place where the famous American candidate had recovered. And on election night 1996, 33 townspeople flew to Washington for Dole's victory party. Their trip was not a total loss, however. Afterward they went on to Disney World.

AFTER DOLE LOST THE 1996 NEW HAMPSHIRE PRIMARY, THE CAMpaign went into full Wound Mode. And his writers began inserting a new line into Dole's speeches in which he was supposed to say: "President Clinton may *feel* your pain, but I *share* your pain." Which Dole mangled in any number of ways. In April in Houston, Dole said:

"President Clinton says, 'I share your pain.' I can say 'I feel your pain.' Or whatever." Dole did still feel pain on a daily basis from the wound, though he said it was only "a little uncomfortable." Dole still carries shrapnel in his back from the wound and sleeps each night holding a gauze-covered block in his bad right hand to keep the fingers from cramping. He also carries a black felt-tip pen in that hand to keep people from trying to shake it.

The news media enjoyed the wound stories, as long as they were accompanied by a Gary Cooper–like stoicism. Dole always had to appear reluctant to talk about the wound, or the wound wouldn't work. "In recent days," the New York *Daily News* wrote in March 1996, "Dole has forced himself to open up more about his dogged fight after World War II to gain a normal life and body." And also in March, Dole began visiting rehabilitation hospitals to emphasize the story of his wound. First, he went to Battle Creek, Michigan, where he had been treated 50 years earlier. After the hospital visit, Reuters reported that Dole had been "reluctant" to talk about his wound in the past. *The Washington Post* noted that "the laconic Kansan, who for more than three decades in Congress has been reluctant to draw attention to his wounds," was now doing so. "It's about character . . . about making a little sacrifice for America," Dole said. Dole aides flogged the wound story relentlessly to the press, emphasizing to reporters how this visit was "very emotional" for Dole. The only trouble was that Dole showed virtually no emotion during the hospital visits. And for good reason: He *hated* this kind of crap. Sure, he had always *used* it, but that didn't mean he *enjoyed* it. It was the kind of thing you had to do to win, to beat the other guy, who might be more photogenic or richer (or, as in the case of his first opponent for county attorney, better qualified).

And so the campaign began scheduling Dole for more rehabilitation hospitals, because the TV pictures were so good and the wound story "humanized" Dole. His handlers barely noticed that Dole was becoming increasingly more uncomfortable with each visit. Three days after Battle Creek, Dole went to River Grove, Illinois, to visit with the widow of Hampar Kelikian, the surgeon who had reattached his right arm to his shoulder. "I spent thirty-nine months learning how to feed myself and dress myself, doing things that people take for granted," Dole said. "I know about sacrifice." Was this, a reporter asked him, a clever way of raising the issue of Bill Clinton's failure to sacrifice by avoiding service in Vietnam? "I don't talk about President Clinton," Dole replied. "But I think they should know who Bob Dole is, and I don't think I have to hide the fact I was a veteran or that I spent time in a hospital." And now he was spending a lot more time in hospitals. He went to a rehab hospital in Washington, D.C., and then 11 days later to yet another one in Sacramento. But by now some reporters were getting uncomfortable with the story too. Using the wound as a prop was one thing, but using the shattered bodies of patients in hospitals was another. And when Dole came upon an 88-year-old patient who seemed to think Dole was Bill Clinton, or at least the incumbent president, the reporters grew disgusted. "After that, we just got sick of it," one said. In June, when in Winston-Salem, North Carolina, a 9-year-old dwarf was trotted out onto the airport tarmac to sing all the verses of "Getting to Know You" to Dole, "the candidate looked decidedly uncomfortable," the *Los Angeles Times* reported. Four days later Dole visited an artist who had broken his neck in 1949 and now painted with his teeth. A few days after that, Dole began a pretty good speech that had the members of the audience laughing and then plunged them into five minutes of silence as he talked about The Wound: "And I learned a lot. How to walk. How to dress myself. How to write left-handed . . . And that's what America is all about," Dole said.

AT THE WHITE HOUSE, DOLE'S TACTIC DID NOT GO UN-noticed. Just as there was no question that Dole would use his wound to his advantage, there was also no question that Clinton would use the wound against him. And the image makers at the White House knew just how to do it:

Bill Clinton stepped out of the presidential limousine wearing a blue work shirt, baggy khaki work pants, and clunky brown outdoor shoes. His sleeves were rolled up on his muscular forearms, and his shirt was unbuttoned to the second button, exposing his bare chest beneath. (Not since Clark Gable peeled off his shirt and exposed his bare chest in *It Happened One Night* had there been such a blow to America's undershirt industry.)

Al Gore followed Clinton from the limo. He was wearing a blue golf shirt, blue jeans, and black leather boots. The two had motorcaded out to Great Falls in Maryland, about half an hour's drive west of the White House, on Earth Day, to show their concern for what winter floods had done to the C&O Canal National Historic Park. About 250 high school kids, congressional notables, and members of the National Park Service had been assembled to hear the president and vice president speak. But what the two said was entirely beside the point. It was the pictures that counted.

And the pictures were gorgeous: A warm breeze ruffled Clinton's full head of hair. Two bald eagles circled lazily overhead. Kayakers bobbed in the Potomac River below. And instead of "Hail to the Chief," the advance crew played Vivaldi's "Spring" over the loudspeakers. Then came the best part of all: Bill and Al pulled on heavy yellow-leather work gloves and started cleaning up the canal by tossing around these gigantic logs. It was symbolic, the president said, of all the good work being done across America that day.

But as he and Gore lifted an enormous shattered tree trunk, easily two feet in diameter, Gore said: "Whoa! That's a pretty heavy symbol!" And Clinton put back his head and laughed and laughed. Then the people around them put back their heads and laughed and laughed. And they clapped their hands. A pretty heavy symbol! That Al Gore! What a scamp! What an absolute scamp! And the cameras recorded every moment as the two men—the two healthy, fit, strapping men—tossed the big log into a ravine, the muscles knotting and unknotting in their healthy, fit, and strapping arms. ("We spent a lot of time on pictures, on what things looked like," Doug Sosnik, the White House political director, said after the campaign. "That's why on Earth Day we had the president throwing logs around." Sosnik shook his head. "Dole was always surrounded by men with dark suits.")

At the very moment Bill Clinton and Al Gore were throwing logs around, Bob Dole was giving a speech on the Senate floor. He wore a dark suit, a white shirt, and a dark tie. He read head down from a prepared text, mumbling into the microphone. "Years ago we wrote on typewriters," Dole said. "Today we use computers. Were we rolling back our desire to communicate efficiently by moving from typewriters to computers? I think not. Let's take the same approach on the environment."

Out at Great Falls the president and the vice president were tossing more timber around. They bent their knees—always lift from the knees, not from the back—slapped their gloved hands together, and wrestled the fallen logs out of the way. "A true champion of the environment, not just on Earth Day but every day!" Gore said of Clinton. Clinton, hands on hips, wind in his hair, sun bouncing off his tanned face, looked appropriately modest.

On the Senate floor, Bob Dole went on to other business.

The month before, Bill Clinton and Al Gore had gone out to California for a visit to Ygnacio Valley High School in Concord, east of San Francisco. When Clinton arrived, he stripped off his blue blazer, revealing a blue sports shirt beneath, pulled on electrician's gloves, and with his similarly attired vice president, grabbed a huge spool of heavy cable and took off down a long corridor with it.

The Clinton-Gore team was wiring the high school for a computer hookup for NetDay96, an idea fostered by Gore, who, Bill Clinton reminded the crowd, had coined the phrase "information superhighway" 20 years earlier. When the pink, white, and blue cable was unspooled, the president jumped up on a ladder and began feeding it into a ceiling crawl space while the vice president in a nearby classroom stepped off his ladder onto a sink top, reached up into the crawl space, and began hauling it down.

It was boring, sweaty, "grunt" work, but the two men—and the many camera crews present—loved it. Later, in a demonstration of how the computer connection would work, Clinton was asked for the White House's zip code but had to admit that he did not know it. Neither did Gore.

"We don't mail ourselves a lot of letters!" Gore said, and the crowd roared with laughter. Then Gore rattled off the White House's World Wide Web address and the crowd applauded. Bruce Springsteen's "Born to Run" was piped in over the loudspeakers.

Bob Dole does not use a computer. Because of his wound, he has difficulty not only typing but even writing. Taking notes is such a laborious process for him that instead he depends on a prodigious memory. His mind is extremely sharp. But minds do not photograph well on TV. What does photograph well is Bill Clinton tossing logs around and running down hallways with big spools of multi-colored wire. What does photograph well is a 50-year-old man in the prime of his life doing vigorous things, even if those vigorous things are merely playing golf or going down a river on a raft.

Bob Dole has no hobbies. None. (Unless you count watching C-SPAN as a hobby. "Sometimes he'll come up to you and say, 'I saw you on C-SPAN last night,' and you'd think, 'Oh, God. Get a life!' " one aide said.) He does not golf or swim or play tennis (though one-armed people can do all those things). Unlike the Clinton family on vacation, he and Elizabeth do not ride horses or camp out or go white-water rafting or host celebrities at dinner parties. Unlike George Bush, Dole does not pitch horseshoes or ride around in speedboats. What Bob Dole likes to do is lie around in the sun like a lizard. "Give me the sun and I'm a cheap date," he says. On vacation in Florida in April, he was stopped by a reporter while leaving a Miami Beach restaurant and asked what he did that day. "Read a book on Washington," Dole said. "Took a nap. Went out in the sun. And came here tonight. Can't beat that." And dinner, of course, is the early bird dinner, usually at 6:30 P.M. Bob Dole is in bed by 10:00 P.M.

He once asked himself how, if he were elected president, he would toss out the first pitch to begin the baseball season. "I guess I'd have to toss it underhand with my left hand," he said. And wouldn't *that* make a lovely picture?

Dan Balz, the national political writer of *The Washington Post*, flies to New Hampshire in February and attends a focus group conducted by Frank Luntz, a Republican pollster.

"Which candidate would you *not* want to be trapped in an elevator with?" Luntz asks the group.

Dole wins easily.

"People say he's cold," one member of the group says.

"I'd have nothing to say to him," says another.

And then a man says, "He couldn't push me up through the trap door because he's only got one good arm."

THERE WAS ONE WONDERFUL ANECDOTE ABOUT THE ARM THAT revealed the true Bob Dole. Senator Daniel Inouye, Democrat from Hawaii, was a fellow patient with Dole at the Percy Jones Army Medical Center in Battle Creek, Michigan, after the war. Inouye had lost an arm, and both men were fighting to survive their wounds. "We in the hospital could be very dark and cruel at times," Inouye said. "And one of the amputees pointed at (Dole's) hopeless right arm and said, 'Bob, why don't you cut that damned thing off?' He turned right around and said, 'Obviously you're jealous.' "

Which was the real Bob Dole. The dark, funny, sardonic, and honest Bob Dole. The Bob Dole the campaign was terrified that people would see.

A few in the Dole campaign were nervous about using the arm as the central metaphor for the campaign. Steve Merrill, the national chairman, thought it was a loser from day one. "They think it *works,*" he told me with a sigh in the middle of the campaign, "but I never thought it would work. Reminding people of World War II is like reminding them of the Civil War." Even before Dole had announced his candidacy for president, Merrill was listening to Dole's speeches and cringing every time Dole talked about going to the fiftieth anniversary of D-day or deciding he had "one more mission to perform for my country." Merrill was a veteran, but he was also just 50 years old and he knew that while a few people in the audience might hear Dole ramble on about D-day and think "war hero," far more were likely to think "old fart."

And Merrill was right. David Letterman began running a series of phony but realistic-sounding Dole ads. "Some candidates for president lived through Vietnam and World War II," the announcer said in a serious baritone voice. "But only one candidate lived through the Civil War and the Declaration of Independence. Vote for Bob Dole! *He's a thousand years old!*"

On the day that Bill Clinton went in and got a clean bill of health in his annual physical, Dave Letterman said, "And in a related move, Bob Dole went in today for his annual autopsy." And Letterman continued: "Bob Dole is so old, his Social Security number is 2. He's so old that when he was a teenager, his cologne was New Spice. He's so old, his Secret Service code name is The Clapper."

Merrill called Scott Reed and begged him to get Dole to drop the "one more mission" line from his speeches. It just reminded everyone of how long ago Dole's first mission had begun. And as a sop to Merrill, whose support they badly wanted, the line was removed from his speech when Dole announced officially for president. Scott Reed called Merrill shortly afterward. "That was because of you," Reed said. (Typically, the line was soon reinserted in all Dole's speeches.)

"They believe it is the best way to humanize Bob Dole," Merrill said of the use of the war and wound imagery in the Dole campaign. "I flew to New York to preview 'An American Hero' (the Dole campaign videocassette, which was distributed by the hundreds of thousands), and I said, 'There's too much of the *war* stuff, too much of the *injury*.' And they were shocked. Because I'm a romantic."

Merrill had his own theory about how to package Bob Dole: Tell the American people exactly what they would know if they got a chance to meet Bob Dole in person. "We should have told the American people how *nice* he is, how *smart* he is, how *principled* he is," Merrill said. Instead, the campaign spent a lot of time and effort telling people Bob Dole had a bum right arm he got in a 50-year-old war. "We did the best Dole we could do," Merrill lamented. "But that was not good enough. We needed to do a new Bob Dole. A Bob Dole for the nineties. And no one was capable of urging him to go there."

Ignoring Merrill's advice, the campaign cut a 60-second commercial totally devoted to The Wound and aired it in the crucial New Hampshire primary (which Dole promptly lost). It featured Elizabeth Dole speaking about Bob's wound. It began in color, with them walking hand in hand in a flower garden and then cut to black-and-white pictures of a plane in the sky, a sailor at a deck gun, and Bob Dole in uniform.

A narrator says: "On a hillside in Italy, he was severely wounded saving a fellow soldier." (In reality, Bob Dole did not save a fellow soldier. "From where I crouched I could see my platoon's radio man go down," Dole wrote in his autobiography. "After pulling his lifeless form into the foxhole, I scrambled back out again. As I did, I felt a sharp sting in my upper right back." Over the years, reporters—including me—constantly got this wrong, writing how Bob Dole had crawled out of a foxhole under gunfire to successfully save the life of his radio man. Dole didn't bother to correct these stories, just as he didn't bother to correct his own TV ad. But he never hid the truth when writing about it himself.)

Then Elizabeth comes on and says: "Bob was paralyzed for a year." And there is a picture of an emaciated Dole lying in bed in bandages. "Some said he'd never get out of bed," Elizabeth says, "but they, the experts, didn't understand what a man like Bob Dole was made of."

Then there are "feel good" pictures of Dole in front of a church, Dole shaking hands with people, an American flag, a child with a parent pointing a small American flag at the Vietnam Veterans Memorial, and a fadeout on Bob and Elizabeth.

The campaign especially liked the Vietnam Veterans Memorial thing. Screwed Bill Clinton with that one, they thought. Merrill found the commercial depressing. And he thought painting Clinton as a draft dodger was stupid. "It didn't work in '92," Merrill told the Dole staff. "Don't waste your money on it." Nobody listened. Merrill felt the wound strategy had an even bigger problem: It kept reminding people just how old Dole was, as if they needed to be reminded.

If Dole won the presidency, he would take office at age 73. The average age of an American president at inauguration is 55. Dwight Eisenhower was younger when he *left* his second term (70) than Dole would be upon entering office. Visualize George Bush. Now visualize Bob Dole. Bush is only a year younger than Dole, but his image was that of a considerably younger man. (John Glenn is two years older than Dole, but when people think of him they think of the grinning, crew-cut astronaut. In politics, image is everything.) But age was the issue that defined Bob Dole, and all the talk of The Wound and World War II drummed that into every audience Dole spoke to. The late-night comics didn't help matters. Dole was very funny when he went on Letterman to begin his campaign, but if Dole thought he could charm Letterman, he didn't know Letterman. "Dole made an appearance at a retirement home, but the orderlies wouldn't let him out," Letterman said later.

Jokes about Dole's age were everywhere. "Dole was asked the one thing it would take to get this country moving again," one went. "He said, 'Metamucil!' " (Which, in real life, Dole took every day for his diverticulosis, *Time* reported in a cover story headlined "Is Dole Too Old for the Job?")

At the beginning of the campaign, a polling firm asked respondents what words they would select to describe Bob Dole. The three most frequent answers were "old," "conservative," and "too old."

Which should have been a wake-up call. Any smart campaign would know it could not survive "old" and "too old" as images when running against a 50-year-old incumbent. And any smart campaign would have set about working on correcting that image by emphasizing what good health Dole was actually in (and his medical reports indicated just that) and by emphasizing Dole's vigor in ads, personal appearances, and speeches. If image makers had once made George Bush seem like a good old boy, they certainly could make Bob Dole look vigorous. It was all in the packaging. Everything had to fit together, each part had to support the whole. And in a way, Dole's campaign did just that. But the ads, personal appearances, and speeches all seemed to emphasize Dole's age. Age became the filter through which the entire campaign was viewed. When Dole made an innocent slip, calling the Los Angeles Dodgers the Brooklyn Dodgers, it was not dismissed the way Bill Clinton's slips were (Clinton once confused the Gettysburg Address with the Declaration of Independence). No, it was a sign of Dole's age, a sign the guy was out of it. And this was a problem not just on small things like slips of the tongue. "The tobacco issue played to our weakness," Tony Fabrizio, the chief Dole pollster, said after the campaign. "What does a female voter think when she sees Bob Dole saying, 'Tobacco is not addictive'? She thinks: 'What planet is he on?' She thinks the guy just doesn't get it. That he doesn't understand what it is like to try to raise a kid today. That he is just too darn old."

Which made Bob Dole the ideal candidate for Bill Clinton to face. After all, Bill Clinton was born when Harry Truman was president, and Bob Dole was born when Warren G. Harding was president. (Dole and Clinton are literally a generation apart: Clinton's mother, Virginia, was born the same year as Dole: 1923.) And long before Dole had locked up the nomination, the White House had already decided on its strategic vision. "We decided that the entire campaign should be about the future versus the past," Mike McCurry, the presidential spokesman, said. "Dole was emblematic of the past. Clinton was the guy with the V-chip, the supercomputer, rats growing their tails back or whatever he used to talk about. Clinton created an excitement and curiosity about the future." And what were Dole's speeches full of? Franklin Roosevelt. Dwight Eisenhower. D-day. Gettysburg. The Wound. The war. The past. Relentlessly, ceaselessly, the past.

So where Dole went wrong in exploiting The Wound one more time was not in the act of exploitation, but in choosing what to exploit. America no longer cared about war injuries or the heroism that produced them. Time moved faster now. Nobody dwelled on the past. "What have you done for me lately?" was the ethos of the age. All of which was brought home starkly in a story by Adam Nagourney in *The New York Times,* in a classic "goober" story (i.e., a story that interviews voters) in California. Nagourney was in the Republican counties around Los Angeles, interviewing people who had voted against Bill Clinton in 1992. It was just March 1996, but Nagourney found the signs already were not good for Dole and that his supporters "are neither plentiful nor particularly enthusiastic." Nagourney also found something else: "Even his attempts over the last two months to flesh out his public image by reminding voters of the crippling war injuries he suffered in World War II may not be having the effect Mr. Dole and his advisers have intended."

"This is tacky to say, I guess," Jane Shirkey, a retired oil company worker from Houston now living in Riverside, told Nagourney, "but I'm tired of him going through that bit that he has a lame arm. I know that's terrible. I'm sorry. I'm sorry about that. But good grief. That was fifty-odd years ago. Get over it."

Get over it. Keep moving. The past is no good to us. Seize the day. Never look back. That is what the '90s were about. World War II? Which countries fought in that one anyway?

IT HAS BEEN A GOOD DAY IN RUSSELL, KANSAS. DOLE FLEW IN from Seattle and all his old friends came and packed the high school gymnasium. The lectern was not slanted, and the mike stand was firm. The campaign had made sure of that. An earthquake could hit, a hurricane, a volcano, and all of Russell would be destroyed, but that mike stand would be standing up straight and tall from the rubble. "At this moment I wanted to be home and see all my friends," Dole said, reading from a text, choking up. "I was helped here." Everybody in the audience knew the story: The townspeople putting their nickles and dimes into a cigar box—a cigar box Dole still has and shows people—to pay his hospital bills. "It shaped my values and showed what compassion is all about, trying to restore me to health. Some debts can never be repaid. But I have come to Russell to try to repay mine. I will never forget. I am one of you. I consider that one of the real privileges of my life." It was one of Dole's best speeches, neither too spare nor too flowery, and it was delivered from the heart.

Now, at the end of the day, flying back to Washington, my request for an interview is granted and I make my way forward from the press section into first class. The first row of seats is turned around to face backward and Dole sits in the aisle seat. I climb over him and sit in the window seat. I put down my tape recorder and punch the record button. We chat a little about his past campaigns, and then I ask him if he feels he has to become a better public performer in order to win this time.

"Well, I'm not much of a public performer," he replies. "So if that's the case, I'll be lost. But, uh, uh, what I've been trying to tell people, it's not easy to, to, because I don't like to talk about it, but the arm. And I wasn't born in this suit and tie or the majority leader or ya-da-ya-da. Well, people tell me afterwards they appreciate that. In fact, I had a black guy tell me last time, 'Boy, that's powerful, keep telling that story. That's America.' You know blacks have had it tough and others have had it tough, so they don't think of Bob Dole . . . or, you know, it's not just Bob Dole. So I don't know whether you can tell the story enough or whether you should tell the story enough. I think it also breaks down the, you know, that you've lost touch and you're surrounded by yes people, and they drive you to work and drive you home and suit you up and spin you up and off you go."

I ask him if, initially, it was difficult for him to make the arm a "campaign thing."

"I never made it a campaign . . ." he says, shaking his head. "I think, in fact, thinking back, I remember reading letters to the editor after I had run for the Senate a couple of times, people were pretty [upset] that I wouldn't shake hands with my right hand, that I wouldn't extend my right hand to them. So they didn't know about my disability and I didn't wear a sling around or anything."

Dole had, in fact, made his wound and his arm a well-known story long before he "had run for the Senate a couple of times," but it seemed like a good moment to raise Adam Nagourney's story, which Dole said he had not read. I tell him about the story and ask him about Jane Shirkey telling him to get over it.

"Well, I'm over it," Dole says and falls silent.

Are you finding, with interviews like this, that there is a downside in talking about the arm? I ask.

"Well, I think you're going to find somebody out there like that, I guess," Dole says. "*I've* gotten over it, but I want her to know, maybe she doesn't listen, that it changed my life for the better. . . . It's not that I get up every morning and say 'I'm gonna go out and tell somebody I got wounded.' " Then he goes on talking about how the wound has "humanized" him. But Shirkey's quote continues to eat at him. And when he brings up his prostate cancer surgery, he unloads on her.

"Maybe *that* would make her happier," he says bitterly. "That was only *five* years ago!"

*   *   *

BOB DOLE STANDS BENEATH A HAZY BLUE SKY UNDER TOWERING palm trees in San Diego's Balboa Park, waiting to make his speech. Bo Derek stands just a few feet away. Derek, whose 1979 film made double digits famous, is chicly dressed unchicly. She wears a blue blazer, blue work shirt, faded blue jeans, white tennis shoes, and dark sunglasses. Her blonde hair is pulled back from her face and she is wearing a minimum of makeup. All those stories about how Hollywood beauties aren't really that beautiful in person turn out to be untrue in her case. She can still stop traffic.

Which, in a certain sense she is doing, since a good part of Bob Dole's traveling press corps immediately rushes over to her before Dole begins to speak. Actually, nobody is quite sure what Bob Dole is doing here anyway. Dole has arrived in San Diego on Sunday of the opening week of the Republican Convention even though he has nothing to do until he makes his acceptance speech on Thursday. Nothing to do except rehearse his speech, that is, which he refuses to do, at least all the way through. He doesn't like the speech and rehearsals bore him. So the campaign has decided to throw together an event just to give him something to do. The event, naturally, emphasizes his "humanizing" war injury.

(In Chicago, Bill Daley, Democratic Convention cochairman, has won his battle to keep Clinton away from the convention until the night before his speech. "Roosevelt didn't even *come* in forty-four," Daley tells me. "It was in California, and they dumped his vice president and put Truman in. Eleanor gave the acceptance speech. I told Clinton that, and I think Clinton thought I was implying he shouldn't come at all! But if he comes, what does he do? Sit around the hotel room? Play golf? Let people picket him? Let people come and ask him for favors?")

But Bob Dole has come and come early, and maybe the campaign can squeeze one last news story out of his arm. And so they set up on Tuesday what is being billed as the Crippled Dog event. Given the fact there is nothing else to cover, a large press contingent shows up . . . and makes a beeline for Bo Derek.

"Why are you here?" a reporter asks her.

"Gee," she says, "I heard about it on television this morning and I did everything I could to get here. My stepson is a quadriplegic, and he trained his own Doberman."

The event is hosted by a group called Canine Companions for Independence, which trains dogs to aid the disabled. Today the dogs are on a small plaza in the lush park, surrounded by TV cameras and ringed by people in wheelchairs.

"The dogs have to be big enough to pull a man in a wheelchair and reach a light switch, but small enough to go on airplanes," Diane Johnson, an instructor with the group, tells us.

During a brief demonstration, with Dole watching patiently, the dogs pull people in wheelchairs around the plaza, pick up objects, take phones off their cradles, and watch impassively as the instructors roll balls at them. (The dogs are not supposed to be distracted by playthings like balls.) When the demonstration is over, Dole takes the microphone.

"Mainstream," he says. "Independence. How important those words are. Let me confess that when I was young and had no disabilities, I didn't really appreciate people who were having difficulties, trying to make it up the curb, up the whatever. Suddenly you become a member of that community, you understand, you are more sensitive."

(In a few weeks, Dole will prove the axiom that anything worth doing in politics is worth overdoing. He will fly to Nashville and try to persuade the National Association of Black Journalists that his bad arm has made him an honorary black person. When he was wounded, Dole tells the crowd, "I became a member of a minority group called the disabled. And I gained an understanding of hardship." Yeah, right, but he was still a white male. And a few weeks later, Dole will imply to the international convention of the B'ni B'rith that his wound made him an honorary Jew. "Nor have I forgotten that I'm sort of a member of a special group—with a disability—and what would happen to those of us with disabilities if we discriminated in America," Dole says. "You don't face any risks in a Dole administration. I know what it's all about.")

After his remarks in Balboa Park, Dole spends half an hour talking to the people in the wheelchairs. It is not an easy crowd. They have a lot of complaints: How the government is not doing enough to give them access, how the Americans with Disabilities Act, which Dole sponsored, is not really delivering on its promises. And then there is Bonnie Hough, an alto in the San Diego Interfaith Gospel Choir, which is going to perform at the Republican Convention Wednesday night. Hough, a former family physician, was severely injured in a plane crash in 1979, lacks feeling in the lower half of her body, and uses a wheelchair. On Monday the bus from the convention comes by to pick up the choir for a rehearsal, but it is not wheelchair-accessible and Hough cannot board it. "They just left me in the parking lot and went," she says.

But Hough is tenacious, as the disabled find they have to be. I'll drive my own van to the convention, she tells the convention officials.

No, she is told, there are no parking passes available.

Well, she says, a friend will drop me off and I'll just roll inside.

No, she is told. No way.

So Hough tells Dole her story. A disabled person denied access to the same convention he is about to address! What a perfect issue for Dole! What a way to show how sensitive his arm has made him! Dole listens to Bonnie Hough and nods and has an aide take down her story, her name, her phone number.

"Don't worry," Dole tells her. He will have somebody take care of it. And, he quotes Winston Churchill to the people in the wheelchairs: "Never give up," he tells them. "Never give up. Never give up." Dole turns to the reporters. "This will be one of the highlights of my week in San Diego," he says.

It is Tuesday, and Hough's choir is to perform Wednesday. She waits by the phone. But nobody contacts her. Not Dole, not the convention people, not anybody. And so she never gets to sing with the choir, all because she is disabled. Five months later, in January 1997, I call her.

"I made a point of not watching it on TV when the choir sang," Hough says. "About a month later, I got a nice autographed picture of Dole and his wife. It was color, eight by ten. There was a form note, thanking me for my involvement in their campaign. You know, life is pretty good for me here. I guess I have gotten to expect things to work. I can take care of my needs and I forget what the real world can be like. I guess I should not have trusted anyone."

In the park that day, Dole had ended his speech with one clear message: "I hope I can stand here today," he said, "without somebody saying, 'Well, there's a politician trying to exploit the disabled.' I have never done that. That is not my bag."

WEIRD AND INCONSEQUENTIAL

★

"The kind of person who is attracted to the job is power-driven, ego-driven. You watch some of these guys—you really get the impression they would kill to get it."

—Ross Perot on the kind of person who would run for president

THE REAL PROBLEM FOR ROSS PEROT WAS NOT THAT he was too rich to be president—Americans had previously chosen seriously rich people like John F. Kennedy as their president—or that Perot spoke with a funny accent (it was no funnier than Lyndon Johnson's) or even that he had never held public office (neither had Dwight D. Eisenhower). No, the real barrier between Ross Perot and the presidency was that he was loony.

And while at first that seemed refreshing to some people—weren't all presidential candidates a bit loony; didn't you have to be a little bit loony to go through what these guys went through?—Americans are capable of simultaneously disdaining those who become president and cherishing the office of the presidency. We might despair over the election of a particular president, but we also want to think that the system works well enough to elect reasonable, sound, and at least minimally sane people to the highest office in the land.

Ross Perot seemed to fail that test. It was not as if he were a danger to himself or others or that he fit some clinical definition of insanity, but the man did seem to have some major problems. And if Americans had any doubts about that, Ross Perot was quick to dispel them.

Take the third presidential debate in 1992, the one between George Bush, Bill Clinton, and Ross Perot. George Bush was trying to defend his presidency, Bill Clinton was promising a middle-class tax cut, and Ross Perot was talking about the night his dog rounded up a group of Black Panthers who had been hired by the North Vietnamese to kill him.

"The Vietnamese had sent people into Canada to make arrangements to have me and my family killed," Perot said, in a voice that sounded like a piece of barbed wire twanging in a Texas windstorm. "The most significant effort they had one night is five people coming across my front yard with rifles." This attempted hit was allegedly taking place in 1969, and the reason the North Vietnamese had hired the Black Panthers to kill Perot is that Perot was trying to get our POWs out of Vietnam. So it's night on the Perot estate in Dallas, and the five Panther-ninja-assassins come crawling onto the grounds, and what does Perot do? Call the police? No, he does not. That's what *you* would do, but you are not Ross Perot, not by a long shot. No, Perot sics his dog on them and the dog *chases them away.* "He worked them like a sheep dog," Perot said. But don't think that Perot let the attempted killers off easy. His dog took a chunk out of the butt of one of the Panthers. Take that, Ho Chi Minh. And just because Paul McCaghren, chief of police intelligence operations in Dallas in 1969, says this entire incident was a product of Perot's fevered mind—"It didn't happen. It did not happen," McCaghren told ABC News— that doesn't mean anything. Listen to Ross Perot's explanation to re- porters as to why he could provide no confirmation on the North Vietnam/Panther/doggie story. "I'm not going to get into that with you because it's none of your business," Perot said. "I'm not going to—hey, look, I don't have to prove anything to you people to start with."

And he didn't. Nor did he have to give any evidence that there really was a plan by the Republicans to disrupt his daughter's wedding. It is 1992 and Perot is running for president and is at something like 26 percent in the polls and is telling people his candidacy is going to throw the election into the House of Representatives, and then on July 16 he pulls out of the race. Had no choice. Later, he goes on *60 Minutes* (Perot seems to favor large venues to demonstrate his lu- nacy) and says he dropped out because the Republicans were going to publish fake photographs of his daughter to disrupt her August wed- ding. "I found myself in a situation where I had three reports that the Republican Party intended to publish a false photograph of my daugh- ter," he said in a later speech. The photograph was the kind where they put a "head on another body" and was going to be given to the super- market tabloids. "This is one of the most important days of her life," Perot explained, "and I love her too much to have her hurt." (Nor was this the first time that Perot used his children as an excuse for his be- havior. In 1992, Larry King managed to pin Perot down as to why he be- longed to a country club that excluded Jews and blacks. "It's a good safe place for the children to swim, that sort of thing," Perot said, though he did not explain why his children, the youngest of whom was then a college senior, would not be safe at a club that allowed blacks and Jews in the water. King later said Perot's answer was "explainable, but inexcusable.")

Because Perot had made a serious accusation in the middle of a presidential campaign against the Republican Party—and by implica- tion, George Bush—the charge was investigated not only by the media but also by the FBI. Nobody could find a shred of evidence to support the story, however, and Bush dismissed Perot's accusation as "loony."

And though Perot later would reenter the race, his pullout helped brand him not only as a head case but also as a quitter. "The Yellow Ross of Texas" is how local papers began referring to him. That bothered him more than being called crazy.

Then there was the time Perot described to *Washington Post* reporter David Remnick "a conspiracy inside the Pentagon" to cover up sightings of American POWs in Vietnam. Perot opened his office safe and showed a snapshot to Remnick of a defense official and a young Asian woman. It was a photograph, Perot insisted darkly, that "completely compromised" the Pentagon. Remnick didn't know what the hell Perot was talking about. But Remnick said he had not seen such a smile of self-assurance on anyone's face "until recently, and it belonged to Oliver Stone."

And then there was the famed NAFTA debate. Some people might have thought NAFTA was a rather complicated piece of trade legislation notable mainly for the odd coalition its opponents formed. (Ross Perot, Jesse Jackson, and Pat Buchanan were all virulently anti-NAFTA. The only other thing they had in common was their disdain for one another. Buchanan called the group the "Halloween Coalition.") But, Perot said, a "Mafia-like" group had hired six Cuban assassins to kill him in order to get the treaty passed. The treaty did pass, but it wasn't the Mafia that did in Perot, but Al Gore. In a debate on national TV, Gore soundly beat Perot. Any person less self-absorbed than Perot might have asked himself what Jack Kemp later asked himself: How the hell does anyone lose a debate to Al Gore? But that question never crossed Ross Perot's mind. He knew why he lost: Gore was wearing a secret metallic earphone in his left ear and was getting tips from the White House during the debate! "Watch the debate, and you will see that thing twinkle," Perot said. "They cheated. All I know is that you can see it twinkle. It was right at the bottom of the ear."

Lorraine Voles, Gore's spokeswoman, denied the accusation, saying, "Yeah, then Scotty beamed him up to the Starship *Enterprise*."

ALL THIS TOOK A TOLL, AND GIVEN PEROT'S DIMINISHED STATUS by 1995, there was only one thing for him to do: He demanded that all the leading national politicians in America come down to Dallas in mid-August to grovel before him and his supporters. He called the gathering "the political event of the century." (Perot seemed to feel that so little about his life was modest that he could do away with modesty entirely.) All nine Republican candidates for president immediately accepted. It would be the first time they had ever appeared in front of the same audience, and hundreds of reporters flew in to cover the event. (Perot had been accused numerous times in the past of hiring private detectives to gather information on people, including his own children and their friends, and the organizers of the event now demanded the Social Security numbers of reporters wishing to cover the three-day convention. Only the White House requires such information from reporters so that the Secret Service can run the numbers through its computers in order to safeguard the president and vice president. Since Ross Perot had no access to the Secret Service computers, why did he need the information? Most reporters provided the information to Perot without thinking about it, but John King, the chief political writer of the Associated Press, refused. "The president is not going to be there," he said. "There is no reason for them to have my Social Security number so they can find out everything about me." Perot's people told King that if he refused to provide the information, he would be denied a press pass. "Fine," King said. "I'll stay home." They issued King a pass.)

But why, if Perot was such a lunatic and laughingstock, would all the Republicans troop before him to kiss his mistletoe? Because Perot did pretty well in 1992, lunatic or not. "This man had 26 percent in the polls, dropped out and made a fool of himself," David Garth, a political consultant, said. "Came back in with a very sad vice president candidate, admiral something-or-other, and he still got 19 percent of the vote." Perot was not saying whether he would run again in 1996, but the Republicans were scared stiff that he would. They figured he would help split the anti-Clinton vote and help ensure Clinton's reelection. Even Clinton seemed worried. Among Perot's followers were a number of "populist" and "reform" types that normally might be expected to vote for Clinton. So maybe if both parties massaged Perot's ego a little, the little geek might just stay home this time and fondle his billions. And so if he wanted the nation's top politicians to troop down to Dallas, they would do it. Yes, they would crawl. Because why else did God give politicians bellies?

And Perot felt humiliating the candidates was only right. Who were they anyway? Bunch of legislators, lawmakers, gridlock boys. Phooey on them. Had any of them ever turned a $1,000 investment into a billion-dollar computer services company? Any of them ever rent two Boeing 707s, paint them red and green, and then send them to Southeast Asia to try to take Christmas packages to American POWs in North Vietnam? Any of them ever rescue two employees from an Iranian jail by launching a commando raid that was the subject of a best-selling book and a TV miniseries? Naw. Never. They never even thought of it. They were too busy campaigning for votes and kissing babies and passing NAFTA. Bunch a sissies. Enough to make you puke. Perot's philosophy of what a politician should be was (like all of his philosophies) simple. Listen up now, and we'll be dancin' like Fred and Ginger in no time: "If you want the system to work again, you have to go back and make it work with the people of the country being the owners and the elected officials being the servants."

That's what these people were: servants! Not senators, not majority leaders, not representatives, not incumbent presidents. They were the *hired help!* And everybody knows that the only thing to do when the help gets uppity is to rub their nose in their own doo-doo. Even the president. In a press conference held just a few days before Perot's conference began, President Clinton had said: "The things that Ross Perot and Bill Clinton advocated in 1992 had a lot of overlap, and we have made significant progress in implementing 80 percent of the things that Ross Perot campaigned for."

You catch that billing? "Ross Perot and Bill Clinton." Whose name came first? You betcha. And that's as it should be. According to Ross Perot, Perot would have been elected president in 1992 if it weren't for all the low-down dirty tricks that were played against him. "The exit polls showed that if everybody who had wanted to vote for me had voted for me and had not been affected by all the propaganda—'Don't waste your vote on Perot'—I would have won," Perot said. "Those are the facts." But the system is broke, see? The mudslingers and their hired guns have busted it. Probably can't be fixed. And so when Larry King asked Perot if he liked America's two-party system, Perot shook his head. "No." Perot said. "What we want is a system that works."

He did not specifically rule out a monarchy.

R OSS PEROT WATCHES FROM BACKSTAGE AS THE ARENA SLOWLY fills. Or, more accurately, he watches from backstage as the arena slowly fails to fill. "We've got to fill up the auditorium—that's eight thousand," he has told people. "We've got a backup auditorium, that's seven thousand." A week before the conference, with only about 2,500 tickets sold, Perot decided to paper the hall. Even though the executive director of his organization, United We Stand America, has held a press conference announcing that "every person is paying their own way" into the arena, in fact Perot is picking up the tab for firefighters, police officers, nurses, teachers, professors, college students, and anyone over 65. Even with that, he cannot fill up more than half the hall. And forget about the backup hall. Though Perot got 20 million votes in 1992, the bloom definitely seems to be off the rose, at least judging by the poor turnout in the hall. The people who voted for him in 1992 viewed him as a way of getting even with the system. They didn't want just to *elect* Perot, but to *inflict* him on Washington. They wanted Perot to bring down the pillars of the temple, to make life hell for Congress and the federal bureaucracy and the media and for everyone else who has lived fat and smug for so long. Their vote for Ross Perot was not an act of affirmation; it was an act of revenge. Now, however, Perot seems no longer to be what they are looking for. His quirkiness and the fact he dropped out in 1992 have profoundly disappointed those who supported him. Hurting him even more, however, is the fact he is no longer a novelty.

Yet he remains hopeful that disgust with the system will rally people to his cause one more time. Frank Luntz, who did polling for Perot in 1992, now conducts a focus group of Generation X-ers to see how they feel about the current state of politics in America.

"Give me one word to describe government," Luntz asks one kid.

"Bad," the kid replies.

"OK, then, give me three words," Luntz asks.

"Really, really, bad," the kid says.

"I AM NOT A LEGEND," PEROT LIKES TO TELL PEOPLE, "BUT I AM a myth." And nobody gets to shape that myth but him. As one reporter observed, he is the "curator of his own image." Some of the stories about him have been repeated so often, they have taken on the hard veneer of truth, and the repeater is often Perot. "He gets to the point where he believes every word he says," said Richard Shlakman, a longtime associate and then competitor of Perot's. "A part of his genius is that he can be self-delusional when most of us are only hypocritical." There is the story, for instance, of how as a youth Perot delivered newspapers from horseback (others say he rode a bicycle), becoming the first white paperboy with the nerve to enter a tough black neighborhood (others say a white kid had the route before him), and how he grew up in a poor home. In fact, Perot's father was a cotton buyer and a horse trader and was able to send Ross and his sister to a private grammar school and give Ross accordion lessons and afford membership in a country club, where as a teenager Ross used to hang around the pool. (Although some media continue to call him H. Ross Perot, he never uses the H. That was an invention of *Fortune* magazine in 1968. At birth he was named Henry Ray Perot and was called Ray up until the fifth grade, when his parents changed his name to Henry Ross Perot. His brother, Gabriel Ross Perot Jr., named for his father, died of spinal meningitis three years before Perot was born, and his parents decided they wanted another namesake for Perot's father. Armchair psychologists can make what they want of this; Perot doesn't make anything at all of it.)

To this day the legend continues that Perot leads a life of Lincolnesque simplicity. And though he does drive a 1984 Oldsmobile, he loves buying expensive jewelry and cars for his wife, Margot, and their daughters. He also buys very expensive racing boats for himself, and owns two homes in the Dallas area, one on a 22-acre estate, in a neighborhood where the property sells for $500,000 an acre. So when Perot talks about fat cats, he knows whereof he speaks.

But unlike George Bush, he was not born on third base and thinks he hit a triple. No, Perot knows exactly how he came up in the world. After graduating from Annapolis and serving a hitch in the navy, he was working at IBM, very successful mind you, but not liking it much, and one day he gets a haircut and picks up a *Reader's Digest*. His eye falls on a filler quote at the bottom of the page. It is from Thoreau's *Walden* and it goes: "The mass of men lead lives of quiet desperation." And Perot finds that so wise, so deep, so very, very moving, that he goes home and sits down at his kitchen table and draws up plans for Electronic Data Systems (EDS), one of the first computer services companies in the nation, the company that would make him a billionaire. That *Reader's Digest* is now kept in a glass case in his office, an office filled with Norman Rockwell originals, Gilbert Stuart's *Washington* (the model for the $1 bill), A. M. Willard's *Spirit of '76*, Remington bronzes, and the Walther PPK pistol that was carried in the commando raid in Iran that preceded the freeing of his employees from prison. Which just happens to be the proudest moment of Perot's life. John Kennedy had his PT-109 and Ross Perot has his commando raid.

To hear Perot tell it, two of his employees were jailed on trumped-up charges by the revolutionary government that overthrew the Shah. The government demanded a multimillion-dollar "ransom." Others tell a slightly different story. According to Sidney Blumenthal in *The New Republic*, "EDS had refused to fulfill its obligation to the Iranian social security administration, and the hostages were held for a ransom equal to the amount stipulated in the broken contract." There is no dispute over what happened next, however: Perot went out and hired himself a mercenary, Colonel Arthur "Bull" Simons, an ex–Green Beret and leader of the failed 1970 rescue mission to the Son Tay prisoner-of-war camp in Vietnam. While others thought Simons blew that mission, Perot threw him a lavish party at which Clint Eastwood and John Wayne showed up. According to Ken Follett, who wrote Perot's story in a book called *On Wings of Eagles* (Perot had approval rights over every word), "Wayne shook Simons' hand with tears in his eyes and said: 'You are the man I play in the movies.' " As often happens with such stories, this one was quickly corrupted. On April 3, 1986, in a Barbara Walters *20/20* profile of Perot, Richard Crenna, the actor who played Perot in the TV miniseries, said: "John Wayne when he first met Perot said: 'You are the man that I always play in the movies.' " This made no sense. Perot was a businessman, a former computer salesman. John Wayne played combat soldiers, rough-and-tumble cowboys, and other brawling figures. But Barbara Walters let the Crenna anecdote pass without comment, and to this day Perot supporters believe that John Wayne went to his grave wishing he were Ross Perot.

In any case, Bull Simons needed a combat team, and Perot recruited them from his own computer company, EDS. They trained for a month, with Simons showing them the best techniques of silent killing (a knife to the kidneys) and then they were off to Tehran in sort of a "Revenge of the Nerds" kind of rescue raid. It was a mess. Their plan to scale the prison walls was foiled when it turned out that the prison had the wrong kind of walls, and then the prisoners were moved to a different prison. (The British publication *The Guardian* would later call the plan "a regressive wet-dream for frustrated, desk-bound pen-pushers.") Finally, on a weekend when mobs took to the streets after they heard the news that the Ayatollah Khomeini was about to return to Iran, an EDS employee named Rashid led a mob attack on the prison and, in the confusion, the two Perot employees (and 11,000 others) escaped. While Perot would claim that Simons had planted the idea in Rashid's mind, in *On Wings of Eagles* the truth is admitted: "There was a fair-sized mob in the square already [Rashid] realized; probably the prison would be stormed today without his help." Henry Precht, the State Department Director for Iranian Affairs at the time, was a little more blunt. "Pure bullshit," he said of the raid. "Anybody who was in jail at the time walked out. Things just fell apart that weekend." Yet the media and the public prefer exciting myths to mundane realities, and so Barbara Walters breathlessly contributed her part to the legend: "The jailbreak worked. All the men came home safe. But Perot is much more than just a short-term hero. First and foremost, he is a Texan." Whatever that was supposed to mean. But Perot does not take attacks on his myth lightly. When *The New York Times* questioned how much Perot really could take credit for the jailbreak, Perot never forgot. In 1981, when a reporter from the *Times* asked Perot to write his own epitaph, he said: "Made more money faster. Lost more money in one day. Led the biggest jailbreak in history. He died. Footnote: *The New York Times* questioned whether he did the jailbreak or not."

There are some, however, who do give Perot credit for making history. According to a CNN report, Perot's rescue mission exacerbated tensions between the United States and Iran and contributed to the seizure of the U.S. embassy hostages, an act that humiliated America before the world, strengthened the hand of the Muslim fundamentalists, and brought down the presidency of Jimmy Carter.

"I wanted to be a beautiful pearl," Perot likes to say, "but I looked in the mirror and decided that wasn't in the cards. And then I said, 'Oh, well, maybe I can be an oyster because the oyster makes the beautiful pearl.' And that never did work out either. Now, unfortunately, my lot in life is that of the grain of sand that irritates the oyster."

T HE CROWD SLOWLY SHUFFLES PAST THE SECURITY GUARDS and into the arena inside the Dallas Convention Center. A huge staff of friendly, smiling people—some of them armed to the teeth— has been hired to control them. Up to 100 extra Dallas police officers have been assigned to the convention center, with Perot's group footing the estimated $75,000 in overtime pay for them. The convention center's general manager, Oscar McGasky, Jr., has perfectly captured the spirit of the event. "We will pay extra attention in light of what happened in Oklahoma City," he announces.

Ross Perot likes that kind of talk. To be a big man is to have big enemies, and Perot has the biggest. After all, haven't entire nations tried to kill Ross Perot? "There is a risk involved in all we were doing," Perot once told a crowd at an anti-NAFTA rally. "I am willing to stand up here like a clay pigeon in public." Some might say that Perot's paranoia is fueled by his desire to be more important than he actually is. But Ross Perot knows the truth: Even paranoids have enemies. And though the crowd entering the arena is small, it immediately backs up because every person must be checked by a security guard with a hand-wand. Every time a person wants to enter the arena, he must stand in front of the guards, thrust his arms out and be wanded up his front side, then turn around and be wanded again down his back side. The Perot crowd is not used to such intimacy from strangers. "Whose rules are these?" one elderly gentleman complains as he is searched for weapons and explosives. "The arena's? Or Perot's?"

"Mr. Perot's," the guard replies.

The gentleman shrugs and gets wanded. This is not really a crowd that complains much, even though they are in a constant state of irritation. They feel as Perot feels: "I bought a front-row ticket to utopia, and the show didn't hit the road." Life has not been that tough on them—most of them are solidly middle class or better economically—but life was never what they thought it was going to be. They never reached the heights they imagined or realized the goals they dreamed of. Now—judging by the ones who showed up for this event, anyway—they are old and carrying a few extra pounds. They favor brightly colored clothes of "miracle" fabrics that can be washed out in the hotel sink at night and hung up on those little elastic clotheslines that stretch across the bathtub. Their children have grown and don't visit as much as they should. They don't see their grandchildren enough. Their lives have been painfully ordinary. But now they are doing something extraordinary. They are backing a man who is neither a Republican nor a Democrat. Which makes them feel like revolutionaries, even though all they have found is a rich father figure, a company executive, exactly the kind of man they have taken orders from all their lives.

"If Ross Perot decided he wanted to go to Egypt and didn't have a canteen of water, I'd be right behind him," Bert Keith of North Potomac, Maryland, says. "The guy's a little quirky, but who isn't?" But there are also a number of people in the crowd who like Perot's message—the system is broke and ordinary politicians are the problem and not the solution—more than they like the messenger. Sharon Struse, sixty-something, her mouth a thin gash of dark red lipstick and her hair a violent henna color, has traded up. "Do you know what really happened in Oklahoma?" she asks. "All the agents they wanted to kill in the Federal Building were out of the building. None were there when the bomb went off. What does that tell you? And minutes before, they saw a black helicopter overhead taking pictures. There was no truckful of explosives. It's just like Hitler: He went after the militias and then the talk shows. The media is the enemy. I read in this book that Bush and Bill Clinton sold arms to Nicaragua and got planeloads of dope and laundered cash. I went with Perot before, but now I'm for Buchanan. I've given him money from the beginning. He's ahead in New Hampshire and is leading in every poll. Everybody hates him but the people. Send Pat money. He needs you. Here, take this." She places a glossy pamphlet in my hand. I assume it is a Buchanan pamphlet, until I look at it later and find it is titled "Someone Cares for You" and says: "Rest—real rest—from the burdens of life, is what

Jesus Christ offers you. Rest from fear and guilt, from worry and frustration, from loneliness and disappointment." Which is what some of the people in Dallas are looking for, not from Jesus but from a presidential candidate."

IN THE GLOOMY ARENA THE CROWD SITS QUIETLY. THERE IS NO milling around, no clogging the aisles, no waving of signs or popping of balloons or anything else associated with political conventions. People barely speak to one another, even though they are as homogeneous a crowd as any political event has ever drawn, with the possible exception of a George Wallace rally. The crowd is overwhelmingly white. It could be a hockey crowd. If effective political organizing is about reaching out and embracing different kinds of people, inviting the participation of the many and not the few, this is not an effectively organized political party. In fact, it is not a real political party at all. These people are empty vessels. They are the vacuum called disaffection from the process. And they wait patiently, silently, for someone to fill them up.

A recording of "This Is My Country" begins, and the audience rises even though nobody has asked them to. Boy Scouts, dressed in khaki shorts, march into the arena, poking their way through the press corps with lowered flagstaffs. On stage, Lee Ann Rimes, flanked by two signers for the deaf, sings a country version of the song. ("Land thay-ut I luvvvvvvvv!") About twenty-five reporters have wandered into the arena for the spectacle, the rest remaining in the cavernous press room, watching on TV monitors. Uniformed Dallas police officers, sidearms on their belts, constantly roam the aisles, eyeing the crowd, eyeing the press.

Perot bounds across the stage and into a spotlight. Only the stage is well lit. In the rest of the arena, the lights are kept down so low that the hall takes on an undersea quality. Camera crews are strictly forbidden from turning on their portable lights, so there are few camera shots of the crowd or the thousands of empty seats. But there are plenty of camera shots of Perot, who now stands behind a lectern that is low enough not to cover him up. (At 5 foot 6 inches, he is 2 inches taller than our shortest president, James Madison. Napoleon was 5 feet 2 inches.) Perot reaches out a hand to the singer. "I want to bring this young lady out here to remind you why we're here for three days!" he shouts into the microphone. His hair, which was worn in a crew cut before, is now a little longer and slicked back. Maureen Dowd of *The New York Times* calls it the "wet-otter" look. The singer stands at

Perot's side as the crowd leans forward to learn why they are spending three days here. "The doctor told her parents there was no way they were going to have a child, and they prayed hard and they had this young lady!" Perot says. The crowd bursts into applause. "She has never had a voice lesson!" Perot says quite credibly. "Isn't that incredible? Keep that in your thoughts. No matter what it takes, we'll do it for you!" What this means is not clear. Is he offering to pray so that people can have children or so they can have natural singing voices? In any case, he is soon off religion and into more comfortable territory: the glorification of the military. "Everyone who died for this country is looking down today and smiling," Perot says. "True patriots are alive and well today in Dallas." More applause. Perot, who never saw action when he was in the navy, has a serious case of combat envy. But that is how the crowd sees itself: Patriots. Minutemen. John Waynes. Sergeant Rocks. Eat death, Washington! "This is a country where ordinary people can do extraordinary things," Perot says, motioning with his palms up. "Everybody in this country can achieve their dreams. They are limited only by their willingness to work."

"It is easy to blame elected government," Perot goes on, and there is huge applause. "But we elected them, so let's blame ourselves." The applause is much more subdued this time. The crowd does not like to face the fact that in a democracy your public servants serve you right. If our elected officials are all bums, who put them there? Well, we must have been fooled. We must have had the wool pulled over our eyes by their clever media handlers and mesmerizing commercials. Or else we elect good people (because we are not stupid) but once they get across the Potomac they sell out and turn bad. "I'll sum up with Thomas Jefferson," Perot says. " 'Whenever people are well-informed, they can be trusted with self-government.' Can you do it? Yes! Will we do it? Of course we will." In reality, however, the crowd does not trust self-government, not completely. Which is why they are such strong supporters of term limits. They want some of their power removed, such as the power to endlessly reelect members of Congress. They want the old scoundrels thrown out automatically (in order to make way for the new scoundrels) without any heavy lifting on their part. The great appeal of Perot, at least in the beginning, was that he promised an end to the nasty little by-products of representative government: debate, discussion, and a need for consensus. You didn't need those things in business, and Perot, like many businessmen, believed that government simply was a gigantic business and could be run exactly the same way. "Business is rational," he is fond of saying. "Politics is irrational." So Perot came up with a quick fix: the Electronic Town Hall.

It was the way in which Perot intended to return the country to its rightful owners. And it had the appeal of simplicity: Instead of the wrangling, gridlock, and venality of Congress, we would have direct voting by the citizens. TV shows would be broadcast, emulating the New England town meetings of old. Our tax system would be revised first. Think scrapping the old tax system and getting a new one would be complicated? Naw. "Number one, it's got to be fair," Perot says of whatever the new tax system will be. "Number two, it's got to raise revenues. And number three, let's make it as paperless as we can. Then run all the different models, go back to the Town Hall, explain it to the American people and say, 'Okay, here are our recommendations'. . . [present] the various options, build a consensus, and then put it in. See, now isn't that better than being in gridlock all year like we are right now? Build a consensus and move, move, move. Act, act, act!"

And sitting in their La-Z-Boys and Barcaloungers, watching experts discuss tax policy for 10 or 12 hours (how to keep people from switching channels to *Baywatch* is a problem that Perot has not yet solved), citizens would then "view the various options" on their TV sets and press a button on their remote control devices (we will have to wire the entire nation for interactive TV, of course, and provide access to such sets for those who do not own TVs and also somehow deal with those 23,000 American families who live in homes without electricity, but this is small potatoes). The votes will be recorded by congressional district, a direct instruction to one's representative in Congress as to how to vote. But even a dimwit would soon see that Congress is an unnecessary step and could be done away with. A small constitutional change is all that is required, and Perot is perhaps the first candidate in decades to openly disdain the Constitution. In 1991 in an interview with Charles Gibson on *Good Morning America*, Perot explained why America was losing the economic world war. "Let's look at who's winning and who's losing," he said. "Germany and Japan are winning. Why are they winning? They got new constitutions in 1945. We gave them to them. This was at a time when the Industrial Revolution had occurred. Our Constitution was written 200 years ago, before it occurred." Which was a really big drawback, because our Constitution has all these safeguards and rights and liberties that can get in the way of a smooth, efficient business. A few minutes later Perot described the kind of government he'd like to see. "Decide what you want to do and do it." Without any of that crummy democracy stuff getting in the way, apparently. But even with his Electronic Town Hall, a few possible glitches can be imagined: Can anyone make such a complicated subject as the tax system understandable to the average voter? As Perot once lamented: "Twenty-five percent of college seniors in Texas can't name the country on Texas' southern border. That's scary."

No, what's really scary is that these same people would be voting on our new tax system.

"This is the way the framers of our Constitution envisioned our country would work!" Perot said. "We started out with town halls and citizen participation. Our problem today, and the reason half our people don't even vote, is they feel they no longer have a voice." But is the town hall what the framers of the Constitution really envisioned? If so, why did they choose a representative form of government to make the laws? Historian and author Garry Wills said: "The town meeting was only a New England form of government, and James Madison argued that you didn't want the unfiltered opinions of the people. In his writings he called for a select body to refine these opinions through debate." But did town halls ever work, even in Colonial New England? "Actually, when everybody talked, nothing happened," Wills said. "So caucuses, held in secret before the meetings, were invented as a way to rig the town meeting ahead of time." In reality, Ross Perot's faith in the Electronic Town Hall may not really be based on a faith in the innate wisdom of the people, though he preaches this constantly. Instead it may be based on Perot's faith in his ability to persuade (some would say manipulate) people into believing what Perot wants them to believe. He probably envisions a gigantic shareholders meeting where the CEO talks and shareholders listen and nod and endorse his plans to solve the problems of America. And problems we have. Speaker after speaker would come before the audience in Dallas to talk about the problems of taxes, health care, political corruption, trade imbalances, and the sinking state of American industry.

"But if you listen to these speeches and get depressed, just remember that song from *Annie*," Perot says from behind the lectern. "Tomorrow. Tomorrow. It's only a day away."

The crowd roars.

ROSS PEROT IS THE AUTHOR OF ONE OF THE LEAST FELICITOUS phrases in modern political history: the "giant sucking sound." This was the sound, Perot said, of jobs being sucked out of America and into Mexico because of NAFTA. But the metaphorical sucking sound heard most often at his convention is the sound of reporters sucking their thumbs and trying to figure out just what this is all about. In speech after speech, 12-hour day after 12-hour day, nothing new was being said. Pete Domenici still wanted a balanced budget, Sam Nunn still wanted a strong military, Phil Gramm still loved his "Maw-ma," and Dick Armey still got laughs with the same jokes: "The American Dream is not just owning your own home, but getting your children out of it!" But then, at the end of the first day, an interesting phenomenon was noted: Jesse Jackson stood up and gave his standard left-of-center speech ("You can't thrive in the suburbs as the cities die!") and got one of the two standing ovations of the day. Newt Gingrich got up and gave his standard right-of-center speech ("Welcome, my fellow revolutionaries!") and got the other. This demonstrated something about the ideology of the crowd: It didn't have one. What these people really liked was polarizing figures, politicians who were "pure" in their own ideologies, no matter what those ideologies are. This was not a crowd that wanted to hear about political compromises, or trade-offs, or logrolling, or taking half a loaf when that was the political reality. So when Pat Buchanan showed up on the second day, he knocked them out.

Buchanan was an "agin-er" just like they were. They were against many different things and they couldn't agree on what they were against, but they knew that if it represented incumbency or the status quo or what went before, they were against it. (Sam Brownback, a Republican congressman from Kansas, summed it up nicely: "If we always do what we've always done, we'll always get what we've always got.") By 1995, long-term incumbency was well on its way to being a negative. Spending your life actually doing something for the public was becoming a minus. To have done nothing, or in the case of Pat Buchanan, to have spent much of his life criticizing those who had done something, was a new qualification for office. It had the added benefit of establishing no record. And if you had no record to defend, you were darn near unassailable. Bob Dole had more than 13,000 votes in Congress to defend. Pat Buchanan had none. Bob Dole knew what it took to actually get controversial legislation through both houses of Congress. Pat Buchanan had no doubts. Bob Dole was the whore; Buchanan was the virgin.

Illegal immigrants? Pat Buchanan was agin 'em. "I will build a security fence, and we will seal the borders of this country cold, and we will stop the illegal immigration in its tracks if I'm elected. You have my word on it!" he told the crowd. And the crowd awakened from its slumber and was up on its feet, with people throwing their fists into the air and yelling, "Yeee-haaa!" And you know those federal judges? Those federal judges who keep yapping about the law and constitutional rights and thwarting the will of the ordinary people, the real owners of this country? Buchanan was agin them, too. "I've got a solution for these federal judges!" he bellowed into the microphone. "We're going to impose term limits on every federal judge we have!" And the people were on their feet again and roaring as Buchanan brought them down the home stretch. "I'm here to tell you now, our time is coming! Our time is coming!" he said. "We will take America back to the things we believe in!" And, yeee-haaa, these folks really liked that. Taking America back—back from their enemies, real or imagined—is what they were here for.

And then Bob Dole came to the lectern and gave a moderate speech and in return got a moderate response. No yeee-haaa's. No interruptions by standing ovations. Most of the audience sank back into the gloom. And that is because Dole tried to tell the crowd what it did not want to hear: that life is not all poles apart, not all rushing to the barricades, not all simple extremes. "Yes, the federal government is big, but the federal government does a lot of *good* things," Dole told the Perot people. "I got to go to college on the GI Bill of Rights." And many of those in the audience were getting Social Security and Medicare and were able to deduct their home mortgage interest from their taxes and all sorts of other benefits that the government gave to people. But Dole's mistake was to believe these people saw those things as good things the government did for them. They did not. They believed (mistakenly) that they had paid for all the Social Security they got and the Medicare and every single other benefit. They felt they were getting only what they deserved, and so they had no reason to be grateful to government or the lawmakers or other public servants who struggled to make government work. They had *bought* their ticket to utopia, hadn't they? And what did they get for it? Not enough. Not nearly enough.

And when it came to an issue they loved, an issue that really hit the politicians where they lived—campaign finance reform—Dole tried to be reasonable. He said he would work to come up with a new system. "Then we'll have a good campaign reform system that will get rid of the special interests as far as we can," Dole said. *As far as we can?* What the hell kind of qualifier was that? These people did not want qualifiers. They did not want to hear about political realities. They much preferred political fantasies. Which is why they had a certain fondness for Ross Perot.

PEROT WOULD, IN THE END, RUN FOR PRESIDENT AGAIN, BUT "run" may be too strong a word. For months he made few public appearances and held no press conferences. He depended largely on 30-minute infomercials, which few people watched. And when he was barred from participating in the presidential debates because the commission in charge of them determined he had no real chance of becoming president, his campaign seemed over. Only one thing saved him from a 3 or 4 percent finish, which is where his poll numbers were heading: the quixotic trip of Bob Dole's campaign manager, Scott Reed, in the waning days of the race to urge Perot to drop out so that Dole could win. Dole had insisted that Perot be barred from the debates and Perot now hated Dole as much as he hated Clinton, so the trip was doomed before it began. And the next day Perot flew to Washington, spoke to the National Press Club, and denounced Dole's attempt as "weird and inconsequential" (which psychologists might call projection, since "weird and inconsequential" pretty well summed up the Perot candidacy). But the failed Dole rescue mission had a startling effect: It put Perot's name back in the news, it made him seem important, and it convinced some people that if Dole wanted him out of the race, he couldn't be all that bad. (Scott Reed took such a beating over the mission, he felt the need to defend himself. "We were trailing, losing," he said after the campaign was over. "So I flew down and met Perot in an airplane hangar. I wasn't going to not try. I didn't know it was going to get out. I didn't know he was giving a Press Club speech the next day. I'd do it again, but I'd do it a little slicker." Like maybe by fax.)

Perot ended up with 8 percent of the vote, down 11 percentage points from his 1992 finish. In 1992, Perot had bragged: "I'm spending my money on this campaign; the two (other) parties are spending your money, taxpayer money. I put my wallet on the table for you and your children." But this time Perot had taken his wallet off the table and took $29 million from the taxpayers in matching funds to finance his campaign. If Ross Perot was a joke, he was becoming an expensive one.

Gerald Posner, author of the 1996 biography *Citizen Perot*, had said early on that Perot "wants to be a sort of climate-controlled candidate," and Posner had laid out Perot's strategy: "If he buys enough airtime this fall, just on the infomercials, and sticks to friendly live television à la Larry King, he thinks he can get his message out and people will say, 'You know what? He doesn't seem so wacky to me.'"

But it didn't work. Americans won't accept campaigns that are based solely on commercials or appearances on friendly TV shows. Voters want to believe they know the candidates, can see, hear, touch, and feel them, even while at the same time knowing the candidates carefully package those things. It was as P.T. Barnum said: People loved illusions. They just wanted the candidates to come before them and show them how it was done.

Ed Rollins, who briefly managed Perot's campaign in 1992, described Perot as the "the ultimate control freak." But, Rollins said, "politics is a world full of things you can't control; what you have to do is manage them." It was the lesson that the Dole campaign was struggling to learn and the Clinton campaign was well on its way to mastering.

ROLLING
THE DICE

★

"I have friends outside the Senate, but I must say not many."

—Bob Dole on C-SPAN,
July 21, 1996

L IKE A MOTHER GOOSE LEADING HER GOSLINGS TO water, Tom Korologos led the U.S. senators through the thicket of reporters. "Pardon us! Pardon us! Pardon us!" Korologos chanted as he shoved his way through the press.

"Hey," Arlen Specter said brightly from behind him, "that's what Nixon kept saying!" Nobody laughed. This was a day of utmost seriousness (and nobody was surprised that Arlen Specter didn't get it). Bob Dole was quitting the U.S. Senate. He was jump-starting his campaign. He was throwing a Hail Mary pass. He was going from old to bold. Pick your cliché. And whether it was desperation or necessity or desperation born of necessity didn't matter now.

"I'm rolling the dice," Dole kept saying. Why? Because he was losing badly. Losing the election was a possibility that had occurred to him before (like every night around 2 A.M.), but there was a difference between losing and losing badly. If you lost badly, history did not record any of the good things you had done. It recorded only that you had ended your career with a "humiliating loss." Lose narrowly, and you were Hubert Humphrey or Gerald Ford. Get stomped, and you were Barry Goldwater or George McGovern.

And even though it was still six months until Election Day, Dole had every reason to believe he was about to get handed a one-way ticket to Palookaville.

On May 2 the Gallup Organization sent out its latest poll with a shocking headline: IF HISTORY IS ANY GUIDE, CLINTON IS ALMOST CERTAIN TO WIN REELECTION. Clinton had an approval rating of 56 percent and a 21-point lead over Bob Dole, the poll noted, and no president with a lead like that had ever blown it. "Polling over the last six decades," Gallup declared, "suggests that for Bob Dole to overcome Clinton's popularity and current lead in the polls would be unprecedented."

But those were only polls, snapshots; they were not carved in stone. And though Dole's pessimistic side made him believe in polls that were bad and distrust in those that were good, the other vital signs of his campaign were not all flat-lined: Voters were volatile in America in the '90s, swinging back and forth between the parties like weathervanes whirling in a windstorm. Because what, after all, did they owe the parties? When is the last time a political party had done anything for any average citizen except ask for money?

Besides, if you put Dole and Clinton on a political spectrum, they were both closer to the middle than they were to the extremes. Sure, there was an ideological gulf between them, but ordinary citizens saw things much less ideologically than the politicians did and were capable of choosing either Clinton or Dole regardless of party label.

In addition, Dole had certain arrows in his quiver: He had lined up the support of numerous governors—George Bush had beat him in the primaries in 1988 partly by securing the support of governors, he believed—and for the first time in U.S. history there were 31 Republican governors in office, including in 8 of the nation's 10 most populous states.

Dole also had an historical anachronism going for him, the Electoral College. The Founding Fathers were revolutionaries, but they feared the masses as much as they wanted to liberate them. And so to keep the people from electing presidents who appealed to their self-interest and emotions, they established a system whereby the people would elect state legislatures, the legislatures would choose electors, and the electors would choose presidents. The electors, it was assumed, would be men of standing, property, and cool reason. Men, in other words, like the Founders themselves. And though the system broke down under democratic pressures and was replaced with a system in which the electors were chosen by popular vote, the Electoral College had survived as the law of the land. And certain peculiarities that the Founders could not anticipate—a lot of Republicans spread over those square-shaped states in the West, while many Democrats were bunched cheek-to-jowl in a few Eastern states—gave Republican candidates an edge in the Electoral College.

Then there was the issue of character. Dole felt he had one and Clinton did not. Dole looked clean. If he, like the president, had affairs, that was long ago and his personal business. Besides, would any man have the nerve to cheat on Elizabeth, a woman who could turn bread to toast with one glance? Elizabeth was the kind of woman who would have asked Lorena Bobbitt why she threw away the wrong piece. No, if Dole had stepped out on his wife, everyone was sure it was in the distant past.

Then there were the more mysterious signs that pointed to a Dole victory: Bill Clinton was one of only five left-handed presidents in history, and none had ever won reelection. When hemlines head downward in an election year, Republicans win, and hemlines were heading south in 1996. And Dole was pulling like hell for the Yankees to win the World Series: in years the American League won, the Republicans usually did, too.

Dole had no shortage of advice on how to turn the tide: The newspapers and magazines were filled with exact blueprints of what he should do. *The Wall Street Journal* presented a detailed one on May 3. It instructed Dole to do a better job telling his life story, to define Clinton as a liberal and hit him hard on taxes, crime, national security, and welfare, and to then go after Clinton on character and moral leadership. There were, according to the paper, two stumbling blocks, however: Dole's image "was closely tied to that of the new Republican Congress" and Dole was a "thoroughly uninspiring" campaigner.

Oh, well, was *that* all?

But something clearly would have to be done. The old Bob Dole (the *very* old Bob Dole, some would say) was not working. So old Bob Dole would have to be scrapped. And a new Bob Bold would have to be invented. Bob Dole would have to leave the U.S. Senate.

ALTHOUGH THERE ARE MANY LOCATIONS WITHIN THE CAPItol from which Dole can make the Speech (the campaign had already started to think of it in capital letters), his staff chose the top floor of the Hart Office Building, across the street from the Senate. The modern, institutional Hart lacks any grandeur or sense of history, but up on the little-used ninth floor, there is a drop-dead gorgeous view of the Capitol dome through the windows. So instead of Dole giving his speech *inside* the Capitol (like a Capitol "insider") he will be *outside* the Capitol (like an outsider), which will be evident when the dome shows up behind his head.

Scores of red chairs have been set up in front of the floor-to-ceiling windows, and the press has been carefully penned off from the "real" people, all of whom are either dignitaries or staffers. The talk in the press pen is about the embarrassing stories that have appeared in the morning papers, all of them reporting that Dole would resign as majority leader of the Senate, none of them reporting he would resign from the Senate itself.

By keeping the secret from the press, Dole has assured himself the phrase "stunning announcement" in newspaper lead after newspaper lead. (When a reporter is surprised by an event, it automatically becomes "stunning," whether the public would have been stunned by it or not.)

Now the reporters discuss whether the Dole staff lied to them or really didn't know Dole was going to go all the way. As it turns out, the

story that was to run in *The New York Times* this morning had specu-
lation from one source that Dole might resign his seat, but it was taken
out by an editor who thought it was patently ridiculous.

In front of the windows the usual lectern has been set up, but now
there are two glass TelePrompTer panels flanking it. Dole will be able
to read his speech on the glass panels, turning his head from side to
side, instead of reading the speech head down, as he usually does. The
invention is not new—Lyndon Johnson was the first president to use
one—but this is a first for Dole.

All the press seats fill up and the reporters jam the aisles. Soon all
the aisle space is filled. ABC's Sam Donaldson, not seen at a political
event since Colin Powell announced he was not running, comes in late
and sits in the front row of the press seats, the spot having been reserved for him earlier in the day by an ABC staffer. While the press has
been waiting, Dole has been meeting with senators in his magnificent
suite of offices in the Capitol and, in telling them the news of his resignation, he breaks down and sobs repeatedly.

(Though Dole's reputation is for taciturnity, in fact he has cried in
public time and again: He cried when he went back to his hometown
as the vice presidential nominee in 1976, he cried at Richard Nixon's
funeral, at the Eisenhower museum, on *60 Minutes*, at a Senate party
honoring George Bush, on a radio show when the host played "You'll
Never Walk Alone," when congratulating Phil Gramm on dropping out
of the race, speaking at Russell High in March 1996, and when recall-
ing his late mother's phone number.)

His chief of staff, Sheila Burke, is so overcome during the private
meeting that she cries through several tissues and switches to a
terry-cloth towel. Some senators cry also. To them it is an almost
unimaginable moment, akin to the death of FDR.

Members of the public seem somewhat less moved when questioned about it later, however. What's so strange about a 72-year-old
guy with a $147,000 a year pension retiring, especially when he has a
condo in Florida? This is something to cry about? And, hey, he might
actually win and end up in the White House, right? So what's with all
the tears?

But Bob Dole is leaving the world he knows and loves, and he
seems shattered by it. He is cutting the umbilical cord that has nour-
ished him for more than 35 years. He feels adrift and alone and he is
wondering where will he go each morning and whether Leader, his dog,
who comes to the Capitol each morning with him, will like his new offices a few blocks away in an office building near Union Station.

While the Speech is supposed to be a launching pad to victory, Dole keeps viewing it as his Farewell to the Troops. He has practiced it several times now in front of a voice coach, and each time he has broken down crying. His staff is beginning to worry. Moist eyes, fine. A little choked up, swell. But tears running down cheeks accompanied by racking sobs is not quite what most voters have in mind when they visualize a president announcing a tough decision. But, look, Bob Dole is a guy who has faced machine-gun nests. So he could take on a TV camera for a few minutes, right? Right. They hoped.

The room atop the Hart Building fills and then overfills. People are crushed up against one another. Then the elevators open and the Republican senators who have been meeting with Dole saunter out. They see the packed room and hesitate. There is no aisle for them. These are men and women who are used to doors being held open and chairs being pulled out for them, and now they are confronted by a sea of people that does not seem to be parting before them.

So Tom Korologos begins leading the senators through the press pen. The reporters, who are facing forward, feel a push and find Al D'Amato or Nancy Kassebaum shoved up against their backsides or Alan Simpson, Phil Gramm, or John McCain stepping on their feet.

"Pardon us, pardon us, pardon us," Korologos keeps chanting. Although he rarely gets his pictures in the papers, nearly everybody in the room knows Korologos. A lobbyist, he goes back a long way with Dole and has free access to Dole's Senate office, sometimes even calling his clients from there. Korologos's nickname is "The 101st Senator."

People use Korologos to convey messages directly to Dole, and some of those people are Korologos's clients: the National Rifle Association, Monsanto, and the Union Pacific Corporation. Korologos helped Dole become majority leader, lobbying behind the scenes when Dole defeated Ted Stevens of Alaska in 1984. This year Korologos has worked for Dole in New Hampshire and South Carolina and went with Dole to California, when Dole endorsed the purchase of twenty more B-2 stealth bombers at a cost of $30 billion.

The B-2 made by Northrop Grumman, which—wouldn't you know it?—just happens to be a Korologos client. Not that there is any connection. (Though Dole knows how clout and influence work. When his only child, Robin, fell in love with Paul McCartney as a teenager, Dole wrote the British Embassy asking it to arrange for the Beatles to play for her and her classmates at Jeb Stuart High School in Falls Church, Virginia. Unfortunately, the Beatles were busy that day.) But when Korologos boards the campaign plane on the same day Dole is endorsing the B-2 deal, a deal that would net Korologos's client several billion dollars, some say that he has crossed the line of good taste. Korologos shrugs. He doesn't have to lobby Dole on the campaign plane, he points out.

"I lobby him *every day* about expanding the B-2," Korologos says.

And while corporations are forbidden by law from giving money to presidential campaigns, Northrop Grumman has given $100,000 to the Better America Campaign, a think tank created by Dole that he is later forced to disband following complaints that the organization served as a front for his presidential campaign.

It is all very Washington. Bill Clinton has similar conflicts. Surveys show that voters hate it and want reform, but in 1996, campaign finance reform has as much chance of being enacted into law as Robin Dole had of becoming Mrs. Paul McCartney.

After the Republican senators push their way through the throng, the Democratic lawmakers enter the room: Tom Harkin, Bill Bradley, even the highly partisan Tom Daschle, the Senate minority leader. At the White House, Clinton aides are watching this on TV, and they are upset. By attending, the Democrats have made this an affair of state, rather than a political affair.

Though the Speech will be carried live on all four major networks, the Dole staff exercises a discipline heretofore unseen in the campaign: It refuses to allow scores of camera crews and still photographers into the room. The campaign limits access to one camera crew, which will share its pictures with everyone. When CBS hears the news, the producers hit the roof. One camera crew? So how do they get reaction shots from the crowd when the sole camera has to stay on Dole? It is so amateurish that CBS can't believe it. Hasn't anybody in the Dole campaign ever *watched* television?

"You want it to look like he's running for fucking county sheriff!" a senior CBS staffer yells at Nelson Warfield, Dole's press secretary.

Warfield quickly relents and allows one other crew to "roam." But, because of the crowd, there is no roaming room and the second crew is pinned down at the right side of the podium.

At 3:06 P.M. Dole enters and the staffers take up the chant: "Dole! Dole! Dole!" (Nobody ever chants "Bob! Bob! Bob!")

Dole is accompanied by Robin, dressed in shocking pink, and Elizabeth, dressed in canary yellow. He is in uniform: blue suit, dazzling white shirt, red tie. He looks left and right into the glass TelePrompTer panels, makes sure he also has a copy of the Speech on the lectern, and begins. Mentally, he keeps telling himself not to look directly at the faces of the people in the audience, because that will make him cry. That is why he cried in Russell. "It's not easy," he said in Dole-speak. "When you've got all your friends there. As long as you don't look at them directly."

Dole begins with no false starts, no asides, no jokes, no numbers.

"My time to leave this office has come," he says, his voice thick with emotion. "I will seek the presidency with nothing to fall back on but the judgment of the people of the United States, and nowhere to go but the White House or home."

This is the line that will electrify the press and be repeated again and again on the news. Home to Dole, most people assume, is the windswept streets of Russell, Kansas. But except for campaign appearances, Dole almost never goes to Russell anymore. And Elizabeth would not live there if you named the town after her and put in a Starbucks and a Talbots. To the Doles, home is their Watergate condominium in Washington and has been for a long, long time.

"I will stand before you without office or authority, a private citizen, a Kansan, an American, just a man," Dole goes on. He looks left, right, and down. He avoids looking into the faces of the people. His tongue darts out and moistens his lips.

"I trust in the hard way," he says, "for little has come to me except in the hard way. . . . I am content that my fate and my story are for the American people to decide. . . . I say thank you and farewell to the Senate. As the summer nears and as the campaign begins, my heart is buoyant."

He looks about as buoyant as lead, but the speech has been a triumph. Dole's eyes are moist, but he has not cried. Robin, who remembers when she used to break off pieces of French bread for her father because he couldn't do it one-handed and when, as a 5-year-old, she campaigned for him in a homemade skirt with writing on it that said "I'm for my daddy, are you?" now blinks back tears.

Elizabeth's Miss America smile has not wavered a millimeter.

And while Dole will go around saying how he has "rolled the dice," another sporting metaphor now occurs to him: He has hit a home run. Unused to being interrupted by applause, Dole this day has been interrupted five times in seven minutes. (He is not able to handle such success, however, barking "thank you" and hurrying on with the speech rather than letting the applause run its course.)

The speech has been lyrical, emotional, and beautiful. It has been both measured and passionate, sad and triumphant. It has been the phoniest speech Bob Dole has ever given in his entire life.

It has been unlike all his previous speeches in tone, diction, pace, language, and imagery. It was a pure creation, pure invention, a pure fiction, almost totally divorced from the man himself. It was a naked attempt to fashion a different, more emotional, more appealing human being at the price of anything like realism, candor, or sincerity.

The public loved it.

The one flaw in the staging of the speech, however, and it was noted in a number of accounts, was the senators and congressmen who crowded behind Dole, ruining the background. Alan Simpson of Wyoming, a senator with a well-deserved reputation for nastiness, manages to neatly block the Capitol dome with his own bald dome in every shot. And Newt Gingrich, from whom Dole was supposed to be distancing himself, has attached himself to Dole like a limpet mine on a battleship. Asked later why Gingrich was allowed in the TV shot at all, Dole will say: "I like Newt. He's been very supportive." Dole can't turn his back on anyone.

Tom Korologos will have a different criticism of the speech. It was too gracious. "You should have stood up and said, 'Now you won't have Bob Dole to kick around anymore,' " he says.

"I thought of that," Dole replies. "But it was probably going a little bit too far."

After basking in the final applause for exactly two minutes, Dole pushes his way out of the crowd. He will take no questions. Nothing will spoil the moment.

"I have a question! I have a question!" Sam Donaldson shouts at Dole's retreating back.

Dole keeps walking, but another reporter asks Donaldson what he would have asked.

"I was going to ask him if this is a sign of desperation," Donaldson says.

No story the next day will upbraid Dole for not taking questions. The reporters understand stagecraft.

Dole's national chairman, Steve Merrill, governor of New Hampshire, is not exactly exulting, however. Merrill had not been told about Dole's decision to resign until he showed up at Dole headquarters that morning. ("I guess I'm not in the inner circle," Merrill says, though after his failure to carry his home state for Dole in the Republican primary, it is hard to imagine him being placed there.) Dole will later say he has told almost nobody about his decision in order to build the drama, and campaign aides improbably report that if the secret had leaked, Dole would not have resigned.

But there seems something more at work than tactics: Dole just couldn't bring himself to tell people that he was leaving the body he loved so much. He has not even told his sisters, who live in Russell, of his decision. And when reporters call to ask them for their reaction, his sister Gloria Nelson says: "He would have *told* me if he was going to resign. He would have *called* me!"

"It's a roll of the dice," Merrill tells reporters in what has become the operative phrase of the day. Will the roll work? Merrill will not say. After New Hampshire, Merrill is staying out of the prediction business.

"He's unshackled," Alan Simpson says. "The leg irons are off. The hood is off the falcon."

But will the bird fly?

THE FIRST THING EVERYBODY WANTED TO KNOW WAS WHO wrote the Speech. And although Dole will tell reporters he wrote it with the "help" of a friend, nobody believes that Dole has contributed so much as a line.

The author remained a mystery for about twelve hours and then his identity was revealed: Mark Helprin, a writer of mystical, often beautiful, though densely layered novels. Helprin was perfect as a speechwriter in at least one sense: Even when he was supposed to be dealing in reality, he liked to make things up.

Helprin once told a reporter that his father did not allow him to eat supper until he stood at attention and told an original story. On another occasion, Helprin allegedly told a reporter that his mother had been sold into slavery. (In fact, his mother was a Broadway actress and his father a former movie-studio head. In June 1996, Helprin went on Charlie Rose's TV show and said he had told the reporter that his mother had been sold into slavery, but then had backtracked by explaining that she had been contracted out to a theater company when she was a little girl and "was not free to leave." "Well, I make my living by telling stories and I—I often speak figuratively," Helprin said. After the Speech, Helprin told reporters how he and Dole met. In movie terms, they "met cute."

Helprin said he was in the Senate dining room in 1990 or 1991, stuffing free candies into his pocket, when Dole saw what he was doing. Their eyes locked. Helprin looked sheepish. But Dole "smiled a beneficent smile" and "the bond formed and grew." Helprin said the meeting "was imprinted" in Dole's mind and Helprin "kept running into him in the Senate for years later."

Dole's version of events was slightly different: He had never laid eyes on Helprin before 1996. After Helprin wrote an article for *The Wall Street Journal* headlined LET DOLE LEAD in February, Dole wrote him a note and they met. "I had never met him personally," before that date, Dole told reporters on his campaign plane.

Oh, well, what difference did it make? Wasn't Helprin's version better, more visual, more fun? Who cares whether it happened or not? Helprin would also claim that he told Dole to quit the Senate. He was meeting with Dole on April 22, out on Dole's Capitol terrace, which Dole calls his beach, and Dole was staring, Helprin remembers vividly, "into the space between the Washington Monument and the Smithsonian." Helprin later gave no fewer than three versions of what happened next: He told *The Washington Post* that Dole "gave his reasons" to Helprin for stepping down. In the *Newsweek* version, which Helprin wrote, Dole merely implied that he would step down. "If I'm going to be president, I'm going to run for president," Helprin quotes Dole as saying and "what was left unsaid but fully understood were the words 'and do nothing else, and rely on nothing else, and give all, and risk all, as once I did before.' " Which is a lot to fully understand from a Bob Dole silence.

But *The New Yorker* version is the best of all. In this, Helprin gives Dole the idea of resigning. "I must have arrived at the right time in his thinking," Helprin tells a reporter, "because when I suggested that he resign from the Senate, he was in full agreement."

Newsweek appropriately headlined Helprin's essay, which was filled with sycophantic babble, A SPINNER OF MYTHS.

Dole's version was more straightforward. And, of course, less lyrical. "I had already been, remember we were down in Florida, it's been so long ago, six weeks. I had made up my mind then that it's best to get out." Weeks later, when he met with Helprin, "It just happened we were talking and he said 'You ought to leave the Senate,' and I think I said to him, 'You ought to pull up a chair, I've been thinking about that.' " (Helprin's version leaves Dole's final comment out of it, giving all the credit to Helprin.)

While speechwriters like Peggy Noonan became famous for writing speeches that matched Ronald Reagan's speech patterns, Helprin became famous for creating speech patterns that never existed before. The campaign was not overjoyed at all the publicity that Helprin was getting and tried to get him to shut up. But Helprin couldn't help himself.

The Speech was an instant hit, but it also was an instant problem: Sure, Dole needed a jump start, but Helprin's speech was like Doctor Frankenstein running a lightning bolt through a corpse and shouting, "It's alive!" Modern campaigning is not about dramatic jump starts. It is about solid repetition. It's about distilling and driving home your message again and again and again in media market after media market.

Unlike the players in the game (the candidates, the staffs, the media), the public is not tuning in to the campaign on a daily or even weekly basis. People catch a glimpse here, a phrase there. And for anything to register, campaigns believe, it must be repeated relentlessly. This is why campaign speeches rarely change. Though listening to the same speech five times a day drives the traveling press corps batty, the traveling press corps is not the target audience.

"You sell the image by *repetition*," said David Axelrod, a Democratic political consultant. "Here is the rule we follow with our clients: When the campaign staff and the reporters become *physically ill* over the repetition of the message, only then have you *begun* to penetrate the public consciousness."

But how could Dole deliver the Speech again and again? How could he hit those high notes? As it turned out, he couldn't. As it turned out, he didn't even try.

THE NEXT DAY DOLE WAKES UP, PUTS ON HIS NAVY BLUE SUIT, white shirt, and regulation tie and, on this, his first day of personal liberation, he goes to . . . the Senate.

Though he is still a senator, this is probably not the best move in the world. (Couldn't he go out and buy a cappuccino somewhere and schmooze with human beings? How about a nice jog in the park for the TV cameras? How about doing something normal for a change?) But Dole can't help himself. He must go back to the Senate. It is totally unnecessary, but it is what he wants to do. He *likes* the Senate. It's the *campaign* he doesn't like.

So he goes and, as he has for decades, he listens to the opening prayer. It is given by the Reverend Lloyd Ogilvie, who thanks God for Bob Dole: "Quite apart from presidential politics, we want to thank You for the way that You have used him here in the Senate through the years." The prayer surprises Dole. He has almost forgotten he is leaving the joint.

Dole stands at his little desk on the Senate floor and does what he always does: He mumbles his way through the opening business, announcing some Senate resolution on setting a budget ceiling for 1997. Somebody must have forgotten to tell him that he is unshackled, that the hood is off the falcon. It looks like the old bird has gone to roost. Eventually, he is reminded he has a plane to catch and he turns to Senator Slade Gorton, Republican of Washington, and says: "I'm outta here. I'm headed for Chicago." And the falcon takes wing.

With him on the plane are 58 reporters, a larger number than on any trip since Dole announced back in April 1995, a fact that buoys his campaign to no end. The staff has begun to associate the number of reporters with how their candidate is doing, a very unsound measuring stick. Fifty-eight reporters can just as easily cream you as help you. Once the plane is in the air, Dole goes into the little forward washroom and changes into more casual pants, an operation that would be difficult for any man in such close quarters, but for a one-armed man is a real struggle. Dole has often complained that the inside waist button on pants drives him crazy because it is so hard to do up one-handed. But doing it in an airplane lavatory with the added danger of falling into the toilet and coming out bright blue? That is a real challenge.

"Not easy changing clothes . . . bumpin' all over the place," Dole will admit later. But changing pants was worth it, he decides. "Loosen up a little," he says. "Lighten up a little." Which becomes the order of the day.

When Dole lands at Chicago's Midway Airport, the press exits the rear of the plane and then runs around to the front to watch Dole exit. And they get their first real shock: Dole has taken off his necktie! He is wearing the same heavily starched white shirt with French cuffs and cuff links, but the shirt is open at the neck. A collective "Whoa!" goes up from the press corps. It's like seeing your father naked. You want to avert your eyes. Ronald Reagan's campaign leaflets used to feature him in an open-neck shirt, but that was a western shirt with the sleeves rolled up and the shirt open to the third button. Reagan looked like exactly what he was: a relaxed ex–movie actor. Dole looks like a senator who has taken off his tie because he wants to get in touch with the Woodstock generation. And the coat! Dole has abandoned his suit coat and is now wearing some kind of blueish sports coat that nobody has ever seen before, some kind of coat that a Florida geezer would wear to attend a Single-Mingle dance in his nursing home rec room.

The reporters, knowledgeable to every nuance of politics, are baffled as to fashion, however. Not since Ed Muskie either did or did not cry during the 1972 New Hampshire primary have so many reporters seen the same thing and disagreed: *The Dallas Morning News* calls the color of Dole's sports jacket "dusty blue." *The New York Times* says "powder blue." The *Chicago Tribune, Los Angeles Times* and Reuters insist on "pale blue," the Associated Press "light blue," and *The Washington Post* "blue-gray." They all agree it is not navy. It seems as if Dole has picked a transitional color, as if he is dipping a toe in the water, before he commits to, say, plaid.

That it is chilly and drizzling in Chicago, not exactly beachwear and open-neck shirt weather, does not matter to the Dole campaign.

Dole has a film crew with him shooting campaign commercials and he has changed clothes for it. Jim Edgar, governor of Illinois, is there to greet Dole, and he, too, takes off his tie.

The campaign has been unable put together a real crowd on such short notice, so Dole goes to a ballroom in the Conrad Hilton Hotel to speak to a few hundred supporters. This will be the first speech he gives since the Speech. The press waits anxiously. What will the second act bring?

Not much, as it turns out. Helprin has written only one speech, and it is all used up. Dole reads from his notes, head down, ignoring the TelePrompTer, gobbling the words just like in the old days.

"I've been coming to Chicago for a long, long time," Dole growls. "Probably before many of you were born." (That's right, remind everyone how old you are.) "I came here for Dr. Kelikian, who operated on me seven times and never took a dime." (That's right, try to get age and infirmity into the same paragraph.) Dole then lapses back into his old campaign speech. "It's about electing a president who's not attracted to the glories of office but to the *difficulties,*" he says. Not for nothing has Bob Dole been called the Nation's Undertaker. He is always talking about hard times, bad times, sacrifice, blood, sweat, tears, and pain, which is fine if your audience went through the Depression and World War II with you. But a considerable chunk of the electorate has no experience with any of those things and doesn't think pain is a strengthening experience. They think pain *hurts,* and given the choice, they would rather avoid it. Ronald Reagan never talked about pain. Pain is what the *other* guy gave you.

"I've done it the *hard* way," Dole goes on, "and I'll do it the hard way once again." He plunges on, flubbing the lines, reading mainly off the text, glancing nervously to the TelePrompTer panels on his left and right and adding his rhythm-killing and weird asides. "I'm not really very complicated—some would say I'm complicated," he tells the baffled crowd.

But the reporters still anxiously await Phase Two of Dole's liberation. Phase One was the bold sacrifice of leaving the Senate. But that was stylistic. Phase Two is what counts: Now Dole must separate himself from the Republican Senate, just as Clinton has separated himself from both the Republicans and Democrats in Congress. The reason is clear: While people may not feel that great about the presidential candidates, they loathe Congress. In a May survey by CBS and *The New York Times,* the public gave an approval/disapproval job rating of 51–37 to Clinton, 42–36 to Dole, 33–48 to Newt Gingrich and 19–71 to Congress as a whole.

A disapproval rating of 71 percent is practically enough to get

Congress deported. What's worse is that while Congress is loathed by Democrats and Independents, which one might expect considering it is a Republican Congress, 60 percent of all *Republicans* disapprove of Congress. So it is absolutely essential that Dole distance himself from it. If not, Bill Kristol, a Republican strategist, can predict the result: "Once we had a 73-year-old majority leader with no message. It won't work if in a month we just have a 73-year-old ex–majority leader with no message." Actually, Dole is still 72, but the point is a good one: The dramatic departure from the Senate must have some purpose.

The public doesn't really care that much about Dole giving up his job. He is well taken care of. (Aside from his pension, he is still collecting $18,300 a year in disability pay for his war wound and also qualifies for Social Security.) Distancing himself from Congress is what matters. Distancing himself from Newt Gingrich and gridlock is what matters.

Being part of the Senate was important to Bob Dole, but the Senate has almost never been a jumping-off point to the White House. John Kennedy in 1960 and Warren Harding in 1920 were the only two sitting senators ever to be elected president (compared with 6 incumbent governors, 9 sitting cabinet members, 9 vice presidents, and 10 generals). The job of a senator, especially the majority leader, is to cut deals. Consensus is what counts in the Senate, not charisma. As Allan Lichtman, a political scientist and historian, wrote, "Congress is America's house of ill repute, standing between the Cosa Nostra and the Ku Klux Klan in public esteem."

You got ahead in the Senate by giving and getting, logrolling, back-slapping, and, most of all, giving personal loyalty no matter what the merits of the issue. There was the famous story of Russell Long, who was elected to the Senate at age 30 in 1948 and served there until he retired in 1986. One day he lost the passage of one of his bills by a single vote and he grabbed a fellow senator as he came off the floor.

"You promised me your vote!" Long shouted at him.

"Yes," the senator said, "but it's a bad bill; you were wrong and I'll be with you when you're right."

"Fuck *that*!" Long roared. "I *need* you when I'm wrong."

And the problem in 1996 was not just that the Republicans had overreached and overpromised in their election victory of 1994. Congress has been loathed since the pollsters started keeping track. Since 1974, when Gallup began polling on it, the approval rating of Congress averaged 30 percent, while that of the president averaged 52 percent.

It was not always thus. For most of American history, Americans felt closer to their congressmen than to their president, and during that period Congress was the most powerful of the technically coequal branches of government. Why? People knew their congressman and senators. Early congressional campaigning was a endless string of speeches that one got to first by horseback, then by train, and then by motorcar. Candidates would give 8, 10, or 12 speeches a day. Voters expected them to show up in their town square or town hall or down at the depot. A president, campaigning nationally, could not possibly provide the same saturation, and so presidents remained much more remote, much less well known than congressmen. But first radio and then TV changed all that.

Now, presidential candidates could reach the people directly over the airwaves (and reach them in the comfort of their living room). And the new medium demanded a new kind of style. Bombastic oratory had worked for more than a hundred years, but it did not suit the new media. A more intimate style was called for. While few would be able to remember what FDR said in his fireside chats, many could remember the feeling of confidence he projected. Once elected, presidents held televised news conferences, speeches, and special addresses to the nation. Professional handlers (who, not surprisingly, came from the advertising industry) came forward to package presidents as personalities who embodied certain American ideals: fortitude, courage, patriotism, and homespun goodness. Presidents had long been packaged that way, even before TV, but the visual medium had a new and powerful impact.

With mass media, the power of the presidency changed forever. It was now the presidential *personality* that dominated politics. Members of Congress haggled and argued and debated and horse-traded. Presidents could act swiftly and decisively. So swiftly and so decisively that one of the greatest powers given to Congress by the Constitution, the power to declare war, was taken over by the presidency. FDR was the last president to go to Congress to get a declaration of war. Truman didn't in Korea; Kennedy, Johnson, and Nixon didn't do it in Vietnam. Reagan didn't do it before sending troops to Lebanon or Grenada; Bush didn't do it before the Persian Gulf, Panama, or Somalia. And Clinton didn't do it for Haiti or Bosnia.

They were the president. They had the power. They had the juice. And they got it from their ability to go directly to the people and make their case. Presidents can have a clear, strong voice. Congress has a muddled roar akin to the Tower of Babel. So distancing himself from Congress was the only thing that made real sense for Bob Dole. And the reporters who traveled to Chicago with Dole waited for his dramatic announcement.

But it never came.

"I cannot predict how some might characterize my departure from the Senate," Dole said in Chicago. "But let me remind you this Congress was elected by the American people to reform, and reform we did!"

If Dole was expecting thunderous applause, he got only silence. Not even a crowd of Republicans was going to applaud that.

"We kept our promises!" Dole said. "Which is unusual in American politics!"

The speech ended. It had been meaningless and informationless and Candy Crowley of CNN got its exactly right when she said that night: "The lead is the pictures." Dole without the tie. Dole in that sports jacket. That was the whole story. The campaign had the perfect opportunity to have Dole actually say something. Instead, he said nothing and he didn't even say it very well.

After the speech, desperate actually to get Dole with some ordinary citizens, the campaign takes him to nearby Berghoff's Restaurant, a Chicago landmark where waiters still wear long white aprons over black suits. Perhaps liberated by his tielessness, Dole now plays the zany madcap, stealing a French fry from a woman's plate. People are loving this and when two guys drinking beer hold up their steins and shout, "Citizen Dole!" the press has its lead paragraph, its caption, its symbol.

On the flight back from Chicago, Dole chats with reporters. He is noticeably tired because the night before he had thrown caution to the winds and stayed up until midnight to watch himself on TV. And what will tomorrow bring?

"That's what all those quote 'experts' work on," Dole says, making fun of his staff.

Now that he has left the Senate, he is asked, does he feel free, liberated, unburdened?

"Oh, no," he replies seriously. "I missed some votes. So I am not totally unburdened."

Missed some votes? Has somebody clued this guy in that he is *leaving the Senate*? That this is the whole *point of the exercise.* Isn't he reading his own clippings? Here is a nice one from former adversary Phil Gramm on the impact of Dole's speech: "It's like when Cortez burned his ships when he went to Mexico. It sends a pretty clear message: victory or death."

Dole does not seem to be thinking about either, however. He is thinking about returning to the Senate and casting a few more votes.

You're planning to return to the Senate? the shocked reporters ask. When will you return to the Senate?

"Tomorrow," Dole says. "If I can find my tie."

Hey, no problem. Dole knows exactly where his tie is: In his pocket. And when he lands at National Airport in Washington, he takes it out and holds it up to his neck and grins for the photographers.

"Gotta put my tie back on," he says.

The old Bob is back.

D URING THE WEEK THAT BOB DOLE WAS BEING BORN AGAIN, President Clinton was busy being tough on crime. Though more Democrats were crime victims than Republicans (there were more Democrats who had low incomes or were minorities or women, all high on the crime victim list), the Democratic Party had ceded the issue to Republicans in 1968, when Richard Nixon had run on a law-and-order platform, painting the Democrats as "soft" on crime, just as they were supposedly soft on communism. The image stuck with the Democrats for more than two decades. But by 1992, Democratic presidential candidates realized they would never be elected if they allied themselves with criminals instead of those afraid of crime.

Willie Horton had not only participated in the killing of a garage mechanic, he killed the desire among most Democratic candidates to defend the "rights" of murderers. In 1992, Clinton was the standard bearer of the New Democrats, who were easily distinguished from the Old Democrats on the issue of the death penalty.

Old Democrats talked about societal ills, how poverty caused crime, how capital punishment failed to deter crime, how the death penalty was applied unfairly to minorities, and the value of mercy.

New Democrats said: Fry 'em.

And Clinton was such a New Democrat that in 1992 he rushed back to Arkansas from the New Hampshire primary, where he was fighting for his political life, to preside over the execution of a brain-damaged black man. (Clinton might have figured that no candidate ever lost many votes in New Hampshire by electrocuting a black man.)

The Old Democrats were best exemplified by Mario Cuomo, governor of New York, who kept vetoing death penalty laws until he was turned out of office in 1994. Being squishy-soft on crime was clearly a losing venture, and New Democrats wanted to be tough on crime.

So Clinton spent the best part of this week fighting crime: Monday, it was a new bill to fight juvenile crime. Wednesday, the day Citizen Dole was born, Clinton spoke at a memorial service for slain police officers. And here Clinton showed the cleverness of his crime position: While gun control had once been thought of as a liberal issue, Clinton now had redefined gun control as a moderate issue. Clinton didn't want to take guns away from hunters and decent folks, but away from crazed killers, wackos, nuts, militia members, and wife-beaters.

"The NRA has replaced the ACLU as the one special-interest group that has pulled a party over to the periphery on the issue of crime," Rahm Emanuel, a White House aide, said. And nobody wanted to be on the periphery. The votes were in the middle.

Clinton, speaking that Wednesday before a huge crowd of uniformed police officers and the survivors of those slain while on active duty, called for a ban on cop-killer bullets and also said he wanted to hand out more money to local police departments for community policing. Then on Friday, Clinton signed a law requiring communities to be notified when convicted sex offenders moved into their neighborhoods, after which he flew to Missouri to talk to high school students about drugs and violence. It was not flashy stuff. It did not compare to the high drama of Citizen Dole. But it was concrete. Maybe it was bite-sized policy, but at least you could bite into it. It was more than just air. And the White House publicity team made sure Clinton's actions got saturation coverage.

The White House pollsters waited anxiously to see how Citizen Dole would play versus Supercop Bill. Their anxiety faded quickly. Clinton's daily tracking polls showed him maintaining a rock-steady lead over Dole.

"In 1996, both candidates got a second look," Rahm Emanuel said after the campaign. "For Clinton it came after the government shut down. People took a second look at him. And we were prepared: We created a dialogue with the American people. We had legislation on education, crime, welfare, school uniforms. We were *ready*. Dole got his second look when he quit the Senate. People were willing to take a new look at him. But what happened? *Nothing* happened. He had *no* dialogue. He had no *campaign*."

And in politics, a second look comes only once.

CITIZEN DOLE'S NEXT MAJOR SPEECH CAME MAY 20. MAYBE the speech in Chicago had been an aberration. In Chicago, Dole had been tired and nervous and the campaign didn't have time to prepare. Okay, fine. So now Dole was going to speak to the American International Automobile Dealers Association. As soon as Dole began, however, it was like déjà vu all over again. Though Dole continued to travel with TelePrompTer screens, he also continued to ignore them. He kept his head down and began with a trademark false start.

"I'm thirty minutes late," he said. "But we had a little problem. Not a major problem. Just a little plane problem. In Charlotte. So I apologize for being late." He gazed out into the spotlights. "I can't see you out there. But many of you I know."

And then, amazingly, he attacked himself. He had read the good reviews for his Citizen Dole speech and the lousy reviews for his Chicago speech, and now Dole decided to make a startling admission: The lousy speech was the *real* Bob Dole. Take it or leave it. "I know it's not *poetry*," he said of his speaking style, "but I believe in America."

As if one justified the other.

And all that advice about distancing himself from the Congress? Forget it. Having attacked himself, Dole felt it was now time to attack the audience.

"I *like* public service," Dole said. "Some of you don't like public service."

And then he was off and running. One of Dole's few rhetorical techniques was to say the phrase "it's about" and attach something to it. The list could get quite long without ever adding up to anything.

"My campaign is not merely about attaining public office," he said. "It's about fundamental things. It's about consequential things. It's about things that are real."

And you wanted to shout: For the love of God, *name* one! Just *one*!

"It's about telling the truth," Dole said. "It's about doing what is right."

Give us an example!

"And it's about electing a president who's not attracted to the glories of office, but rather to its *difficulties*," Dole concluded.

Again with the difficulties. Dole may have promised to be another Ronald Reagan, but he was actually more like another Richard Nixon, the moody Richard Nixon, sitting in his office, brooding over Cambodia, Watergate, and those goddamn protesters across the street.

Dole had mouthed Helprin's speech once, but that was as far as he would go. The campaign aides had seen the pattern time and again. You could berate Dole, cajole Dole, beg Dole into doing something, and he would do it. Sort of. You could tell him he had to repeat the same speech five days in a row, and instead he would repeat the same *phrase* five times in one *speech*.

"So I've done it the *hard* way," Dole said. "You do things the *hard* way, just as you have done things the *hard* way, and I've done it the *hard* way and I'll do it the *hard* way once again."

There. They want repetition? He would give them repetition.

He simply would not read the daily speech as written by his

speechwriters. And he drove the TelePrompTer guy *crazy*. Dole's speeches were fed into the TelePrompTer and the operator (usually off to one side or sitting behind a curtain) listened to Dole speak and controlled the speed at which the words rolled down the glass panels. It was not that difficult a task. The operator followed the speaker, adapting to his rhythms. But Dole had no rhythms. And how was anybody supposed to follow this:

"And it also seems to me that it's about electing someone—and I don't have—this is true of anybody running for president—that once he takes office—as forty-two have in the past—that they will keep their perspective and remain in his deepest nature and inclination one of the people."

The simple rhythms that Helprin had scripted for him were so antithetical to his nature that he destroyed them without thinking about it when he tried to repeat them. Dole's love of numbers was so intense—from how many presidents America had elected to the exact vote count on thousands of bills that had come through the Senate—that when it came to throwing some numbers into a speech, even if it was just a date, Dole had to do it even if it destroyed the poetry that Helprin had crafted for him.

Here was the line as written and as delivered by Dole in his Citizen Dole speech: "I will stand before you without office or authority, a private citizen, (pause) a Kansan, (pause) an American, (pause) just a man."

It was a beautiful line. And, after hours of practice, Dole had managed to deliver it beautifully. But a campaigner must deliver the same line beautifully time after time after time, like an actor in a play summoning up the same energy night after night and again for the Wednesday and Saturday matinees.

Here, just five days later, was Helprin's line as Dole now delivered it for the auto dealers: "So it seems that I think on or before June 11—and probably before June 11—that I'll be standing before you without office or authority, a private citizen and Kansan, an American."

And you couldn't explain the difference to Dole. You couldn't tell him that by inserting "on or about June 11" or rushing through the ending without the pauses, he was wrecking the speech. It was like explaining to a caveman why he couldn't throw a rock and hit the sun. If you didn't get it, you just didn't get it.

Okay, so could he just read the speech off the little glass screens? No. He couldn't. He wouldn't. He would not let anybody control him, not even the TelePrompTer guy. He would not let *words* control him. When his campaign gurus picked what their polling revealed was the perfect issue for him—attacking Clinton for the appointment of liberal judges—Dole still could not deliver the message coherently. Take Judge Harold Baer.

Baer, a federal judge in New York, had ruled inadmissible as evidence 75 pounds of cocaine and 4 pounds of heroin that police had discovered in a car after a car chase. Why? Because Judge Baer found it reasonable for citizens to run from the police in New York because residents there regard the police as "corrupt."

It was a brain-dead decision and was criticized even by Clinton, who had appointed Baer to the bench (an appointment Dole had supported). And Baer later reversed himself. But in politics just about everything is fair game, and the Dole campaign thought the Baer case would show just how irresponsible Clinton really was when it came to controlling crime.

That was the message. But every message requires a messenger. And here was Bob Dole, the grating communicator, explaining Judge Baer to his audience: "Like Judge Baer of New York. Had this big cocaine bust. And he said it wasn't introduced because they fleed—when they fled from the cops they weren't—they didn't look suspicious. Or something."

Or something. Dole was aware that he was not going over. He was fascinated by focus groups and how little ordinary citizens seemed to know about him. For instance, almost nobody knew why Bob Dole wanted to become president (including, perhaps, Bob Dole). It was an important matter. Ever since Ted Kennedy had blown the reply when asked by Roger Mudd in 1980, every candidate who has ever run for any post higher than library commissioner has been prepared to answer the question: Why do you want the office?

The answer had to be clear and powerful. It had to be simple but memorable. It could not be mush. It had to be concrete.

"And people ask me," Dole told the auto dealers, " 'Why do you want to be president?' And I'll just say very quickly—and maybe it's not *poetry*—but I believe in America, just as you believe in America."

End of speech. Got that? He wants to be president because he believes in America. Concrete enough for you? Powerful enough for you? Or mushy enough for you? And keep in mind this was the *new* Bob Dole. This was Citizen Dole. This was the more articulate Bob Dole.

This was not going to work.

THE WASHINGTON POST AND ABC NEWS QUICKLY REPORTED THE results of a new poll. There was good news and bad news for

Dole. The good news was that while in January only 38 percent of the American people approved of the job he was doing as majority leader of the Senate, now 56 percent did.

The bad news was that he had just given up the job.

And the really bad news was that 80 percent of those polled said his resignation from the Senate made no difference to them whatsoever.

Of those 20 percent who said it did make a difference, half said it made them *less* likely to support him.

Bob Dole had given up something he was good at for something he was bad at. He had given up something he enjoyed for something he endured. He had abandoned service to the people for service to his ambition. And the voters were not impressed.

Bob Dole had rolled the dice all right. And thrown snake-eyes.

CLEARING
THE STAGE

★

"Ickes . . . forced the balloon man [at the 1992 Democratic Convention] to climb into the rafters to cut the netting with a large knife. The sight of an armed man climbing through the lights at Madison Square Garden drove Clinton's security detail to distraction. 'The Secret Service guys nearly shot the guy out of the rafters,' recalled a White House aide, 'all because of Harold.' "

—*Time*, January 23, 1995

POLITICAL CAMPAIGNS NEED A LEG BITER. THEY NEED a person who can put aside the notion that politics is about something grand and elevated, that it has something to do with the future of humankind or the possibility of a better life. Campaigns need a person grounded in the real world, who realizes that, at its most fundamental level, politics is about sinking your teeth into your opponent.

Harold Ickes once bit a man. And unlike most political operatives who would have tried to cover it up in the years that followed in order to present a more dignified image, Harold Ickes didn't bother. He didn't want a more dignified image. "I bit him," Ickes said. "It was a good, solid bite." Which is what Ickes cared about: If you are going to bite a man, don't do it halfway, don't be sloppy, don't miss the meaty part of the leg. If you are going to bite a man, make sure it is a good, solid bite. And that way, you can look back on it with pride.

It had something to do with a sound system. Ickes, like all the really top people in the Clinton-Gore '96 campaign, sweated the details of the performance. In fact, Ickes's role was less concerned with developing policy than with how the policy was conveyed to the people, how the picture looked, how the voice of Bill Clinton sounded. If the sound system went bad, if the volume dropped or squealed from feedback, Ickes treated it not only as a disaster but as a personal insult. In Longview, Texas, in September 1996, when the sound system failed, Ickes exploded, swearing at the sound man at such length and with such hostility that those within hearing range (which was nearly everybody) were stunned. Ickes's profanity was a performance in itself. "It was unbelievable," a friend said of one such episode. "It was more than just profanity, it was poetry—like the *Iliad* and the *Odyssey* rolled into one." Staffers referred to such outbursts by Ickes as "going DefCon 4," a reference to nuclear attack. And even though at the very next stop, the sound system was working fine, Ickes would later send out a memo that said, "Hello! Hello! Hello! Is anybody listening? You probably can't hear because of the sound system." A system that, Ickes continued, "resembled orange juice cans connected by strings." So he cared about sound systems. Which is why he bit a man in 1973. In that year, Ickes was working in the campaign of Bronx Borough President Herman Badillo, who was running for mayor of New York. "Somebody was bringing in a sound system to do an interview in our campaign headquarters," said Charles Kinsolving, an aide in the Badillo campaign. "I have no idea why [Ickes] got so excited about the sound system, but eventually he grabbed the equipment and swung it around and hit me and knocked me down. He was down on the floor with me, and the switchboard operator panicked and called the police." Ickes had Kinsolving's head in a scissors lock between his legs and was slowly crushing the life out of him. Why? Because the sound system sounded like orange juice cans! And if you can't hear the candidate, then what is the point of politics? Anyway, a guy named Jim Vlasto decided to play Good Samaritan and pull Ickes's legs away from Kinsolving's throat. "And [Ickes] then sunk his teeth into Jim's leg," Kinsolving said. "At that point, the cops started to come in the front door and [Ickes's] girlfriend didn't think that would be very helpful to the campaign and so she took him out the back door."

So what was the big deal? Bad sound, head lock, bit a guy, escaped the cops. What on earth was the big deal? "I don't know," Ickes said 21 years later. "But there is enormous anger [within me]. I don't know why or where it comes from, but it's still there." Which, actually, was fortunate. Because maybe it was anger that made Ickes sweat the details. Maybe he thought that if he missed one tiny detail (bad sound, balloons that didn't drop), it would cause his candidate to lose. And though Ickes had ample experience with losers, by 1992 he had finally hitched his wagon to a winner.

He had met and befriended Bill Clinton in 1967 when Clinton still was a liberal and when both men were working on something called Operation Pursestrings, an effort to end congressional funding of the Vietnam War. Twenty-five years later Ickes was running Clinton's New York primary campaign and then went on to oversee the Democratic Convention for him that year. And it was no accident that Clinton picked a tough guy to stage his convention. In the modern era, conventions are nothing more or less than TV shows, but they are elaborate TV shows that require attention to thousands of details. Take balloons. Ickes had a pathological fear of his balloons not dropping from the ceiling at big events. Jimmy Carter was humiliated at the Democratic Convention in 1980 when his balloons failed to release properly (and he lost the election that year). In 1996, Bob Dole would have the most embarrassing of balloon problems at one campaign stop: a premature release. Thousands of his helium-filled balloons took off early, interrupting his speech, though few in the audience seemed to care. Ickes was determined that no balloon would fail on his watch. His determination on the subject was almost creepy. The lawyer who wrote the balloon contract for the 1992 convention still remembers it. "The balloons had to go into the hall Saturday, before the convention opened," he said. "This raised the question, which Harold and Harold alone focused on: How many balloons would stay inflated until Thursday night? He instructed us to write into the contract exactly what percentage of balloons would stay inflated, or the vendor wouldn't be paid. I have never met anybody who could simultaneously focus on the big picture as well as the smallest detail the way Harold does."

Harold Ickes knew politics. Harold Ickes knew performance. And he knew that both required scrupulous attention to details large and small. Balloons were a small detail. Making sure that no Democrat would run against Bill Clinton in the Democratic primaries of 1996 was a large one. And Ickes devoted himself to making sure that before Bill Clinton began his run for reelection, there would be no other Democrat to hog his spotlight, no other star in the wings. The stage would be cleared for Bill Clinton. Harold Ickes guaranteed it. Which is why, starting in the long, hard winter of 1994, Ickes decided that Jesse Jackson had to be destroyed.

To MOST AMERICANS (OR AT LEAST THOSE WHO BOTHERED TO think about him at all) Jesse Jackson already was irrelevant politically by that time. He was the host of a low-rated cable talk show, an unpaid and ineffective lobbyist for making the District of Columbia our fifty-first state (tentatively to be called New Columbia, which would give it the same initials as North Carolina, the least of its problems), a loser in the fight over the North American Free Trade Agreement, and in danger of becoming a self-parody to those young African Americans who found more inspiration in the separatist exhortations of Louis Farrakhan than in the euphonious phrase-making ("Put hope in your brains, not dope in your veins") of Jesse Louis Jackson. He was older, grayer, and paunchier. He had considered running for senator from Illinois and had backed off. He had considered running for mayor of Washington and had backed off. He had considered running for executive director of the NAACP and had backed off. His options were limited. Which is exactly what the White House was afraid of. When he had nothing else to do, Jackson usually ran for president.

Having said in 1973 "I would not run for president of the United States because white people are incapable of appreciating me," Jackson felt by 1984 that their tastes had matured. He ran that year against

Walter Mondale in a campaign most often remembered for Jackson's "Hymietown" crack, and then ran again in 1988, coming in second to Michael Dukakis. When Jackson started the 1988 race, winning the presidency was immaterial. "Man, but there's so much else to win: the transformation of America is winning!" he said. Jackson believed that by running he was transforming America: each time someone who previously had harbored a racist thought—or suffered from "historical and cultural prejudices," as Jackson liked to put it—each time one of these people cast a ballot for Jackson, then that was a sign that America had become a redeemed nation. If you voted for Jackson, you washed away your sins and were saved.

"I carry not only the burden of this campaign, but the burden of history with me," he said. "By people concentrating on the blackness of Jesse Jackson, they do not concentrate on the Greekness of Dukakis or the Jewishness of his wife or the Italianness of [Mario] Cuomo." But while Jackson was playing the lightning rod, taking on all the burdens of race and religious prejudice in America (causing him to wear a bulletproof Kevlar-lined raincoat for some public appearances), a strange thing was happening: He was getting votes. When the Democratic primaries had ended, Dukakis had received about 9 million votes and Jackson had received about 7 million. And as soon as the primaries ended, Jackson wanted more than just the satisfaction of having made America a better place. He wanted a job, a good job. He understood there were certain problems. "Dukakis has got pressures," he told me. "White racist pressures. And Jews telling him that if he makes me secretary of state, they'll never vote for him, I understand that." Actually, Jesse Jackson did not want to be secretary of state, a job for which he felt overqualified. He wanted to be vice president. He had come in second, hadn't he? And that's what happened when you came in second, right? You got the second spot on the ticket, "It's not just presiding over the Senate," Jackson said about what his new duties would be. "The office of the vice president can carry out significant missions." He would carry out those significant missions and then, having shown the nation what he could do for two terms (which required two enormous assumptions: first, that Dukakis would pick him and, second, that Americans would pick Dukakis for eight years), Jackson would run for president in 1996.

But there was a problem. Dukakis had no more intention of putting Jesse Jackson on the ticket than of putting Jesse Helms on the ticket. Instead, Dukakis chose Lloyd Bentsen (who demonstrated his confidence in victory by promptly deciding he would run simultaneously for reelection as senator from Texas). Jackson got offered what Jackson usually got offered: a few Jackson aides on the Dukakis payroll, a plane for Jackson to fly around the country in so he could register Democratic voters and make speeches and show off his famed "charisma" on behalf of the Democratic Party. Jackson had heard it all before. *"Fuck* charisma," he told me. But he took it, because what else could he do? The years passed.

Now the 1996 campaign season was approaching, and it was not just Bill Clinton who was preparing for a Jesse Jackson candidacy. Bob Dole was practically counting on it. "My assumption in early 1995 was that Clinton was very weak and would have a primary challenger by May," Scott Reed, Dole's campaign manager, said after the election. "One of the smartest things [Clinton] did was avoiding a skirmish with Jesse Jackson."

Smart, yes. Easy, no. Clinton was so weak heading into 1995 that it was not clear how he was going to keep anybody out of the race. His presidency was a slowly leaking beach ball: The Democrats had lost both houses of Congress, there was Whitewater, Hillary's commodities trading, Travelgate, Troopergate, and Paula Jones. Labor unions were still furious over NAFTA, and some African Americans, the Democrats' most loyal voters, were still furious over a crime bill they felt victimized the black community and over Clinton's treatment of Lani Guinier (Clinton had withdrawn her 1993 nomination to head the Justice Department's Civil Rights Division after conservatives protested that she would favor racial quotas). Clinton could scare some Democrats away from running, but even one Democrat mounting a primary challenge could, the White House political operatives believed, prove fatal to his reelection. "Primaries are death for presidential incumbents facing reelection," Doug Sosnik, the White House political director, said. "Ask Bush, ask Carter, ask Ford, ask Johnson. All incumbent presidents; all faced primaries; none got reelected. The Democratic [congressional] debacle of 1994 was the wake-up call. We wanted to avoid a primary at all costs."

The point was not that Clinton could be beaten in a primary; he probably could not be. The point was that a primary could so weaken Bill Clinton that the Republican nominee, even a hapless one, could finish him off in a general election. "Primaries sap your resources, and you have to spend time talking to your base voters exclusively," Sosnik said. "You have to appeal to your activist wing." And those things you had to do to pander to your activist wing in the primaries could doom you with swing voters in the general election.

So the White House started keeping a careful eye not just on Jackson but also on a host of usual suspects: Senators Bill Bradley of

New Jersey and Bob Kerrey of Nebraska on the left, and former Pennsylvania Governor Bill Casey and Representative David McCurdy of Oklahoma on the right. And the decision was made that since Clinton was in no position to be tough, then at least he could look tough. It is what the White House called "body language." And the body language that the White House needed to scare off the opposition was that of a hard guy, a guy who sent the message that if you dared oppose Bill Clinton, he would knock your block off.

Or, perhaps, bite your leg.

HAROLD MCEWEN ICKES HAD WORKED FOR A LONG LINE OF liberal presidential candidates, which is to say he had worked for a long line of losers. He had served Eugene McCarthy, Ed Muskie, Morris Udall, Edward Kennedy, Walter Mondale, and, in 1988, Jesse Jackson. Ickes had impeccable liberal roots. His father had been a member of FDR's cabinet, and when young Harold graduated from Washington's Sidwell Friends prep school (where Chelsea Clinton would go several decades later), he became the only member of his class not to go to college. Instead he took to the road, striking out to see how "real" people lived by going West and becoming a working cowboy. Then, at the age of 25, Ickes went into Mississippi and Louisiana to register black voters. In Tallulah, Louisiana, while driving with two young black men in his truck, Ickes was stopped by four armed white men. "They ordered us out of our truck," Ickes said. "I told the black guys, 'You get out of here. They will really kill you. I don't think they'll kill me.' " The white guys beat Ickes savagely and left him for the sheriff, who arrested Ickes for disturbing the peace and threw him in jail. An ACLU lawyer bailed him out. Heading back north on a bus, Ickes felt an agonizing pain in his back, "fell off the bus in Roanoke, got a cab to the hospital, they gave me some painkillers, and I continued up to Washington to have my kidney out." He later attended Stanford University and Columbia Law School, graduating there at the age of 32.

Though Ickes had grown up in the Washington suburbs, he did not like the town. "You can't get a fucking cab and you can't find a fucking restaurant that stays open past nine P.M.," he once said. But there was another reason: When his father died, his mother had been treated badly by the Washington power structure. "Many people who she thought had been her friends turned out to be her friends only because of the person she was married to," Ickes, who was only 12 at the time, said. "That left a very marked impression on me. I came to expect that of Washington."

Ickes's father was the legendary Harold LeClair Ickes, a member of the Progressive movement, a founder of Theodore Roosevelt's Bull Moose Party, and Franklin Delano Roosevelt's Secretary of the Interior. And, as his son would proudly recount, "one of FDR's political hatchet men."

The acorn does not fall far from the tree.

Ickes's first goal was to show Clinton's would-be opponents the money. Though Clinton's massive fund-raising would later prove to be profligate and irresponsible, the idea was not merely to raise enough money for Clinton's needs, but to deny money for anyone else's needs. Raising money had a chilling effect. "The money came in much faster than we thought," Ickes said. "I don't think any president has ever raised money so fast. It surprised us. I think anybody who thought of running [against us] was given serious pause." Almost as valuable as gathering dollars was the gathering of intelligence. Through a national network of Democratic officeholders, party activists, and contributors, the White House kept careful track of what potential opponents were doing. When Bill Bradley started making calls to California to see what money was available to him, the White House got a call and Bradley found the big money had been buttoned up. But while Ickes knew locking up the money would scare off the logical candidates, he also knew that Jesse Jackson's campaigns were not based on logic. Jackson needed very little money to run; he lived off the land (one of his favorite techniques was to raise funds after each speech, announcing from the podium, "Anyone who can contribute or raise $500 please come forward! Anyone who can contribute or raise $100, please come forward!") and generated enormous media attention out of all proportion to his ability to win the nomination. Besides, there was the problem of Iowa.

The 1996 campaign year began with the Iowa caucuses, where Jackson had done relatively well in the past among the small number of liberal activists who dominated the arcane voting process. And neither Clinton nor Al Gore had ever organized in Iowa: Gore had skipped Iowa when he ran for president in 1988 in order to concentrate on the South, and Clinton had skipped it in 1992, because Iowa's favorite son, Senator Tom Harkin, was running that year. Neither Clinton nor Gore, therefore, had a political organization in place there. So Ickes poured nearly a million dollars into Iowa and half a million into New Hampshire, the next state on the political calendar, even though Clinton had no declared opposition and had not even announced for reelection himself. (As it turned out, Clinton would never announce for reelection; he decided it would look more presidential if he did not. He just ran.) And Ickes's preparations were not based on paranoia. From 1993 through 1995 nobody had been a tougher public critic of Bill Clinton than Jesse Jackson.

Jackson was so angry at Clinton that it pushed Jackson to new heights of alliteration: "Posturing and positioning supplant principles and policy. Polls dictate poses, poses define priorities." The way Jackson saw it, Clinton had betrayed labor, minorities, and city dwellers, and had forged a "DLC/Republican alliance" for cynical political purposes. (The centrist DLC, the Democratic Leadership Council, had been cofounded by Clinton in 1985 in part to reduce Jackson's influence on the party.) Jackson went so far as to revive the nickname he knew that Clinton loathed: Slick Willie. "Slick too often doesn't slide through," Jackson said. Jackson said he was so "sadly disappointed" with Clinton that he was seriously thinking about running in the Democratic primaries or as an independent candidate. To an outsider, it was hard to tell exactly why Jackson was so angry. After all, Clinton was the first Democrat elected since 1976 and after 12 years of Ronald Reagan and George Bush, wasn't that a change for the better? But people who looked at it logically tended to forget the personal side of the equation. They tended to forget all about Sister Souljah. Which was something Jesse Jackson had sworn he would never forget.

SISTER SOULJAH WAS NECESSARY. IF IT HADN'T BEEN HER, IT would have been somebody else. After the New Hampshire primary of 1992, Bill Clinton starts calling himself the "Comeback Kid" (and, more important, persuades the media to do likewise) for having come in second in the face of the draft evasion and Gennifer Flowers scandals. He is now trying to put together a winning strategy that will take him to the Democratic nomination. He faces 22 primaries in the next few weeks, mostly in the South, where he must show strength. Georgia, which comes next, is crucial to him.

But Tom Harkin, facing elimination from the race, has made an ad for black radio stations in Georgia saying "Bill Clinton did his own version of Willie Horton [by making] a big deal of going home to Arkansas to oversee the execution of Rickey Ray Rector, a brain-damaged man who didn't even know he was being executed. Bill Clinton used a black man's death to boost his campaign." Following Harkin's attack, another opponent, Senator Bob Kerrey, who lost a leg and won a Medal of Honor in Vietnam, begins attacking Clinton for having dodged the draft. Clinton's explanation is "baloney," Kerry says. "Had he wanted to go and serve his country, he could have." (This turns out to be a political mistake. Voters are sufficiently conflicted over Vietnam to want to forget the whole thing, and Kerrey will soon be forced to drop out of the race.)

Jesse Jackson decides to sit out 1992. Lose twice, and you are a bold risk-taker. Lose three times, and you are Harold Stassen, he figures. But Jackson finds that being a noncandidate is not much fun. No camera crews are following him around; no reporters are hanging on his every word. He has no plane, and he has no campaign funds to finance his travels. Jackson sorely misses the spotlight, and so he announces he will campaign at the side of any Democrat who wants him to. Harkin, nearly out of money, facing political extinction, and having already played the race card against Clinton, seizes the opportunity and takes Jackson up on his offer.

In an Arkansas TV studio, where Clinton is doing several satellite interviews with stations from around the country, he is told off-camera by a reporter from a South Carolina station (who gets it wrong) that Jackson has *endorsed* Harkin. Clinton explodes. His face is contorted by rage and he turns a bright red. He turns to a staff member and says, "It's an outrage! It's a dirty, double-crossing, back-stabbing thing to do! For him to do this to me, for me to hear it on this television program, is an act of absolute dishonor." What Clinton does not know is that a Phoenix TV crew, setting up for the next satellite interview with him, has its camera on and has captured the moment. CNN will show the videotape of the enraged Clinton ten times in the next nineteen hours, and NBC will put it on the *Nightly News*. Jackson reacts with anger to Clinton's anger. "I'm disappointed with his overreaction without verification," he tells CNN. "I'm disturbed by the tone of the blast at my integrity, my character." When Clinton learns that Jackson has not really endorsed Harkin, Clinton calls Jackson and the two men make a deal: In the future, if either has a problem with the other, neither will make a public statement until the two have had a chance to talk. Both men agree this is reasonable, fair, and just. Neither has the slightest intention of honoring it.

In March, Jackson's hopes for retaking the national stage rise slightly when Jerry Brown, the former governor of California, tries to exploit the unease between Jackson and Clinton by announcing during the New York primary that if Brown is nominated, he will select Jackson as his running mate. It is an odd piece of political timing. Jewish voters, who play a significant role in the New York Democratic primary, are still angry with Jackson over his "Hymietown" slur and his championing of Louis Farrakhan, and they turn against Brown and flock to Bill Clinton in droves. Jackson sees his hopes for a political future fading and decides to turn up the heat. In April he tells the New York *Daily News* that he sees himself "as a running mate for the Democratic Party." He adds: "If I am rejected this time, I am prepared to react."

Clinton, who by now has wrapped up the nomination, states publicly that, of course, Jackson is on his list of potential running mates. Privately, Clinton assures people that Jackson has about as much chance of landing on his ticket as he does of landing on the moon. But Clinton does have big plans for Jackson. Clinton has carefully studied the losing campaigns of Walter Mondale and Mike Dukakis. Both pandered to the traditional left-labor-minority elements within the Democratic Party, and both lost. Clinton will not make this mistake. Following Dukakis's 1988 loss, his onetime campaign manager, John Sasso, gave a speech in Boston listing all the reasons for the defeat (it was a long speech) and blamed Jesse Jackson. "In some ways, voters seem to judge the strength and skill and character of the Democratic candidate on how effectively he gets along with or copes with Jackson," Sasso said. "It becomes a litmus test." Clinton agrees. If Clinton were an ordinary campaigner, he would merely ignore Jackson. But Clinton sees the potential: If he publicly rebuffs Jackson, if he makes a performance out of it, it will drive home the point that he is not a captive of the left, not a captive of minorities, that he is a New Democrat, a moderate, a man whom swing voters can comfortably cast a ballot for. All Clinton needs is the right issue. Which a rap singer of no great fame (and even less voice) hands him on platter. Sister Souljah will be Bill Clinton's ticket to the political center.

In May, Sister Souljah raises a flurry of media interest by telling *The Washington Post* that blacks should kill whites as revenge for the Los Angeles riots. She expects some criticism for this, but, as one of her songs says, "America is always trying to strangle and silence black people." A month later Souljah joins a panel discussion at Jackson's National Rainbow Coalition meeting in Washington. The next morning, Clinton is to speak. Before he speaks, however, Clinton does two things: He alerts the media that he is going to make major news, and he meets privately with Jackson. But though the two have an agreement that they will talk about their differences privately before going public with them, Clinton mentions nothing to Jackson about Sister Souljah.

The morning session begins with Jackson, Clinton, and other dignitaries sitting behind a table on the podium. Jackson rises to introduce Clinton and mentions with pride the appearance of Souljah the night before. Clinton rises, walks to the lectern, and begins a routine speech about race relations, criticizing President Bush and Vice President Quayle for insensitivity. Then he switches gears. "You had a rap singer here last night named Sister Souljah," Clinton says. "Her comments before and after Los Angeles were filled with a kind of hatred that you do not honor today and tonight. Just listen to this, what she said: She told *The Washington Post* about a month ago, and I quote, 'If black people kill black people every day, why not have a week and kill white people? So if you're a gang member and you would normally be killing somebody, why not kill a white person?' If you took the words 'white' and 'black' and reversed them, you might think David Duke was giving that speech."

Jackson is floored. Clinton is upset with Sister Souljah? Then why didn't Clinton say something to him first? Jackson would have explained what she really meant. And he certainly would have explained to Clinton that black people, lacking the power to oppress, cannot be racist; it is impossible in Jackson's view. So the David Duke reference is totally unfair. Worse, however, is that Clinton has come into Jackson's house, as it were, to show disrespect for him. And what happened to that agreement that they had? Jackson is so angry that he doesn't see the yawning jaws of the trap that Clinton has set.

"I don't know what his intention was," Jackson tells reporters immediately after Clinton's speech. "I was totally surprised." Then, at a news conference a few hours later, the trap is sprung. "She [Souljah] represents the feelings and hopes of a whole generation of people," a furious Jackson says. *"She should receive an apology."*

An apology? Bill Clinton should apologize to a woman who advocates the murder of white people? Bill Clinton should apologize for attacking racism whether it is white or black? And Jesse Jackson, who has never asked Louis Farrakhan to apologize for his anti-Semitism or Yassir Arafat to apologize for his terrorism, wants Bill Clinton to apologize to Sister Souljah? The media go wild. News stories are followed by analyses, which are followed by media stories about the news stories and the analyses. At first, some political analysts are confused and wonder how Clinton could risk angering black voters. But Clinton knows that many black voters think Souljah is an extremist and also believe that Jackson is fine as an inspirational figure but not as a political one. Besides, who else are black people going to vote for if not Clinton? Far more important, Clinton knows his attacks on Souljah are being viewed with favor by so-called Bubba voters in the South and ethnic Joe Six-Pack voters in the North. Clinton is not only standing up to black racism, he is standing up to Jesse Jackson.

Jackson, still blinded by his anger, just makes things better for Clinton when he argues that Clinton's denunciation of Souljah is a rejection of Christ's teachings. "When Jesus was on the cross, he chose to reach out and forgive the robber and the thief and to renew them," Jackson says. "Equating black and white racism is another thing. Black people do not have the institutional power to be racist; we don't have the power to lock people out." Then Jackson says the whole incident "again exposed a character flaw" in Clinton.

Clinton is unruffled. "After I gave that speech, Jesse Jackson invited me to come back that night and play the saxophone," he says calmly. He also says that he "will not back down."

Jackson is asked by reporters why he is angrier now with Clinton than immediately after the speech. "At first we thought the Souljah example was innocent," Jackson says. "We later found it to be intentional, that many press people had already been alerted to it."

Duh. No kidding. Eventually Jackson will get it. He will realize that it was never about *Souljah.* It was about *him.* Clinton needed a way to put distance between himself and Jackson, to publicly rebuke Jackson, and Souljah was merely a convenient way of doing that. Jesse Jackson thought he knew something about showmanship and manipulation. He realized with a sinking stomach, however, that he had come up against a master.

CLINTON HAD USED AND HUMILIATED JACKSON. BUT IN POLITICS what goes around comes around, and now in the 1996 campaign season Jackson had a perfect chance for revenge: Clinton was weak and Jackson could weaken him further by beating him up in a series of early primaries. But it was not Clinton that Jackson was really up against. It was Ickes. And Ickes, having worked for Jackson, knew Jackson, how he thought, how he acted, and where he would go for his initial support. So Ickes decided to get there first. And he quietly began walling Jackson off from an important power base within the Democratic Party: the nation's African American mayors. These included Dennis Archer of Detroit, Marc Morial of New Orleans, William Campbell of Atlanta, Norm Rice of Seattle, Freeman Bosley of St. Louis, Kurt Schmoke of Baltimore, and Wellington Webb of Denver. (Two white mayors, Ed Rendell of Philadelphia and Richard M. Daley of Chicago, were also considered essential to Clinton's future.) And in the fall of 1995, Alexis Herman, the White House director of the Office of Public Liaison, held an informal gathering of black mayors in her home in Washington. Commerce Secretary Ron Brown was also there.

(The only white face in the room belonged to Doug Sosnik, and at the beginning of the meeting Brown put his arm around him and announced laughingly to the mayors, "He's one of us.") The mayors were told that they were the rising stars of the Democratic Party, its next generation of leaders. They would be listened to seriously by the White House because Bill Clinton liked mayors and he liked them because mayors actually did something for a living. Clinton shared their concern, felt their pain, and expected the mayors to support him and not Jesse Jackson if there was a contested Democratic primary.

At the same time that Herman was lending her house and talents to lining up opposition to Jackson, she also was working with Jackson to try to satisfy whatever political needs he had. "Alexis worked very hard with Jackson," a senior White House official said later. "Her being [nominated] as secretary of labor has something to do with that." (Jackson may not have known of Herman's role with the mayors or he may have accepted it as part of politics, because he publicly pushed very hard for her nomination as labor secretary when Clinton was wavering between her and Harris Wofford, the former senator from Pennsylvania.)

But while locking up the money and building a fire wall around Jackson were proceeding without a hitch, a major derailment of all plans loomed: Throughout 1995 there was violent disagreement within the White House staff over what to do about the budget battle with Congress and the possibility of a government shutdown. Shadowy Clinton adviser Dick Morris (whom Ickes loathed) and pollster Mark Penn were urging Clinton to sign a budget deal with the Republicans. Ickes and George Stephanopoulos, Clinton's senior adviser, were opposed. At issue was the protection of increases in spending on Medicare and Medicaid. Clinton leaned toward doing a budget deal on some days and leaned against it on others. But what really brought him around to Ickes's and Stephanopoulos's thinking was not the policy but the politics. The two men, joined by Al Gore, told Clinton that if he compromised on Medicare and Medicaid, Jesse Jackson as well as others from the left wing of the party would oppose him in the primaries. They would have no choice. Clinton would be seen as selling out the poor and elderly, and hard-core Democratic activists would never allow that. So Clinton hung tough through two government shutdowns, and though nobody knew at first how it would play with the public, it turned out to be a political triumph for him: The public blamed Newt Gingrich and the Congress for the paralysis, not Bill Clinton.

But Ickes continued to keep a careful eye on the campaign calendar. Meeting filing deadlines in the 50 states was a daunting challenge for any primary contender, and Ickes watched as deadline after deadline passed without a Democratic opponent announcing. Ickes made weekly reports to Clinton, telling him how many delegates had been locked up for him without opposition. But every time Ickes was convinced that nobody in his right mind would challenge Clinton, Jackson would remind him that you don't have to be in your right mind to run for president. Choosing the thirty-second anniversary of the Reverend Martin Luther King Jr.'s "I Have a Dream" speech, Jackson announced on August 28, 1995, that he was going to enter an urban straw poll called CityVote. If he did well, he might then challenge Clinton for the presidency.

Nobody, including Jackson, knew how serious he actually was about a race. He tended to decide these things at the last moment. But he was keeping his options open and as long as he did so, the White House had to take him seriously. So Ickes decided it was time to show Jackson what it was really like to screw with Bill Clinton.

CityVote had been endorsed by the U.S. Conference of Mayors, was funded by the Carnegie, Schumann, and Joyce foundations, and had the support of Walter Cronkite and former *Newsweek* editor Osborn Elliott. The idea was to shift some attention away from the rural voters of Iowa and New Hampshire and onto city dwellers, who would hear the candidates outline their views in nationally televised debates and then cast ballots in cities throughout America. It was a dream come true for Jesse Jackson. Cities were where most of his voters lived.

Ickes demolished CityVote. Clinton himself had noticed an early article about it in *The New York Times*, clipped it, and sent it to Ickes with the note, "We better keep an eye on this." Ickes did more than keep an eye on it, he kept both his feet on its windpipe. Using Don Fowler, the cochairman of the Democratic Party, to publicly denounce CityVote as a useless and harmful exercise, Ickes also made calls to mayors, encouraging them to drop out of the project. Mayors in Baltimore, Boston, Cleveland, and Rochester decided CityVote was not such a good idea after all. And in New York, the Board of Election Commissioners decided CityVote could not be placed on the ballot. Some of the nation's mayors complained. They had wanted to use CityVote to fine-tune their fund-raising and political operations. But Ickes and Fowler convinced them that this would be a very bad idea.

CityVote backers could not believe the White House would go to such lengths to destroy such an innocent event. And even in the White House, some thought the effort was overkill. "Some said, 'Where is it going? It's fun and games. Let them have their fun,' " Ickes said. "But we moved on it very concertedly." By the time CityVote was held, it had been beaten up so thoroughly that most of the media ignored it. "Ickes *crushed* CityVote," Rahm Emanuel, senior White House adviser, said. "He sucked the *oxygen* out of it. It was *stillborn.* Its best day was the day it was *announced.*" Presidential spokesman Mike McCurry agreed. "CityVote never reached critical mass, and that was due to the sheer tactical brilliance of Harold navigating us through this," he said.

But Ickes's real brilliance was avoiding the classic mistake of the political samurai. Having just whacked Jackson with a stick, Ickes didn't refuse to offer him a carrot. Ickes wanted to crush Jackson's candidacy, not Jackson. "Nobody is a more loyal Democrat or has registered more voters or supported more Democratic candidates," Ickes said. "Jesse Jackson can proudly wear the title Mr. Democrat." Which was typical of Ickes and why his "body language" was of such value to Clinton in scaring off enemies. Ickes *liked* Jackson and *respected* Jackson. So imagine what Ickes would do to someone he *didn't* like.

A fairly large group, including Ickes, Stephanopoulos, Herman, and McCurry, made themselves available to Jackson. Jackson wanted to be respected, which meant being listened to, not just on his own behalf, but on behalf of his constituents. Listening to him could mean a real investment of time, often at very late hours, but the group cooperated. And so did the president of the United States. Jackson visited the Oval Office nearly a dozen times, and the meetings between him and Clinton were as delicate and stylized as the mating of cranes. Jackson never mentioned his plans for the presidency and neither did Clinton. "But he knew we read the newspapers," Ickes said. "We knew what he was saying."

In the summer of 1995, when Clinton had to decide whether to continue his support for affirmative action, he called Jackson in to consult with him. "Did Jackson influence the president on affirmative action?" Ickes said. "Yes. How much, I can't tell you. It was way too subtle and much too profound." Well, perhaps not that subtle. "We should have a simple slogan," Clinton said in his speech on July 19. "Mend it, but don't end it." Which did not sound very much like Bill Clinton. (Clinton's usual homilies ran closer to lines like "Even a blind hog can find an acorn sometimes.") In fact, it sounded downright Jacksonian. So did Jesse Jackson author the line?

"It could well be," Ickes said. "It certainly *sounds* like Jesse."

Afterward, Jackson said Clinton's speech was "one of his finer hours as a leader of the country."

Then, in fall of 1995, just about the time when Jackson would have to make his final decision whether to get into the race, there was a piece of real luck for Bill Clinton: Mel Reynolds was going to prison. Reynolds, 43, resigned his House seat representing the South Side and south suburbs of Chicago on October 1, having been convicted of having sex with a 16-year-old campaign worker and obstructing the subsequent investigation. Jackson's son, Jesse Jackson Jr., 30, having never held elective office, having never held any job except in his father's Rainbow Coalition, decided he wanted the seat.

Anyone who knew Jackson knew that his pride in his children was enormous. The reporters who covered Jackson's 1988 campaign, in which Jesse Junior worked, saw the interaction between father and son and came to understand the strong bonds that bound the family together. While at age 54 it was growing clear to Jesse Senior that there might be mountaintops to which he could not climb, he saw no such limits on the future of his children.

The White House was prepared to exploit the moment. Jesse Junior would have to run in a special election in December 1995, and then, if he won, again in November 1996. So perhaps there was something the White House could do? Perhaps Jesse Junior would like a campaign visit by the vice president? Or by Democratic Party cochairman Chris Dodd? Both were arranged. Speaking on the Monday before the election in 1995, Al Gore, son of former senator Albert Gore Sr. of Tennessee, said: "I know what it's like to enter public service as the son of a famous man, admired by people who have heard his commitment to justice." Jesse Junior could wax eloquent himself. "I inherit my family's friends and my family's detractors," he said, "neither of which I have earned."

And then there was the matter of money. Money has always been helpful to an up-and-coming politician. When asked what money may have been offered to Jesse Junior, Ickes replied: "Certain Democratic fund-raisers close to the president gave money to Jackson for the Congress campaign." To put it mildly. Two contributions would later stand out: a $3,000 contribution from the Lippo Group and $1,000 each from Soroya and Arief Wiriadinata, whose $450,000 contribution to the Democratic National Committee was returned when the couple went back to Indonesia. The exact source of their largesse remains a mystery. Mr. Wiriadinata is a landscaper, though his wife is the daughter of a major investor in the Lippo Group, who when hospitalized received a hand-delivered get-well card from Bill Clinton.

Which is not to suggest that the donors did not have a deep and abiding interest in the welfare of the South Side of Chicago.

Jesse Jackson Sr. decided not to run for president in 1996. Jesse Junior was elected to Congress. And his swearing-in ceremony in Washington might have marked the first time in history when words failed his father. Attempting to describe to Laura Blumenfeld of *The Washington Post* just how much pride he felt, Jesse Senior became almost incoherent with joy. "Like, I feel elephant joy," he said. "Or dinosaur excitement."

Asked the same day by a reporter if he would have been elected if his name had been Jesse Jones, Jesse Junior replied, "Ask Patrick Kennedy."

At Clinton's second inaugural, Jackson was given a starring role. He was center stage at the prayer service preceding the swearing-in and knew exactly the right tone to take, now that Clinton was being subjected to new character attacks for his fund-raising. "Character is measured not by what we are but by what we stand for," Jackson said. "You can take a crooked stick and hit a straight lick." From the audience, Clinton beamed.

At the swearing-in, Jackson was given a prized aisle seat behind Clinton, which meant the president could stop and shake his hand on the way out. Jackson's daughter Santita sang the National Anthem to close the ceremony.

Still, all this was small potatoes. Jesse Jackson wanted to be somebody, and he wanted to be somebody in the Clinton administration. And if anyone thought Jackson was going to wait quietly for his reward, they were reminded in February 1997 of how easy it was for Jackson to make news. *Time* magazine reported that Jackson was unhappy with the Clinton administration and was considering a run for president in the next election. "I've never seen him so serious so soon about running," a source told *Time* (apparently with a straight face).

Though Jackson quickly denied the report, his wake-up call had been delivered. And he expects to hear from the White House just as soon as the political operatives there start thinking about how much Al Gore would like to avoid a primary in 2000.

A T ONLY ONE POINT DURING THE LONG NEGOTIATIONS WITH the White House did Jackson overreach. He asked to participate in the prep sessions for Clinton's two presidential debates. His request was refused. The White House had its standards: Jackson might be allowed to affect presidential policy, but not presidential stagecraft.

LOVE AFFAIR

★

"[Bob Dole] hasn't spurned me. He loves me. I think he loves me. He's like my dad. He is just like my dad: 'Well, I haven't told you I love you, but I told you at Christmas. Did you doubt me?' That's the whole generation: You're supposed to tell your kids you love them only at Christmas."

—New Hampshire Governor Steve Merrill,
to author, October 9,1996

THE SEDUCTION

THE GOVERNOR OF NEW HAMPSHIRE SITS IN THE DARK-
ened room of the lonely house. Donated to the state years
before for entertaining guests, the house resembles a hunting
lodge inside. There are exposed beams and a two-story stone fireplace.
An enormous moose head hangs from one wall. A 6-foot-tall grandfather clock morosely tick-tocks the seconds from one corner. In the
daytime the interior might be bright and pleasant, but it is dark now
and melancholy seems to seep from where the governor sits and gath-
ers in the shadows.

The governor, Stephen E. Merrill, whom everyone calls Steve, is
wearing blue jeans, a blue blazer, and a long-sleeved maroon knit shirt
buttoned to the throat. He is wearing moccasins. He stands, strips off
his blazer, and tosses it onto one of the two blond couches that are at
right angles to each other in front of the fireplace. On a coffee table
in front of the couches is a plate with crackers, cheese, and grapes.
There is a bowl of cheese-flavored popcorn. There is an open bottle of
chardonnay. He pours me a glass.

He turns to an aide and to his state trooper driver and dismisses
them both from the room. He walks over to the fireplace and in a few
practiced motions soon has a enormous crackling blaze going. On his
way back he turns off even more lights until the only lamp left on is
the one illuminating my notepad. I sit on one couch and he sits on the
other. The fire casts a dancing orange glow on his face.

He is a handsome man, balding, with light blond hair. He has dazzling blue eyes. But his face, which is often creased in smiles, is now
slack and somber. For a few moments he says nothing. There is only
the tick-tock of the grandfather clock and the soft burble from a TV set
in an adjoining room, where his driver is about to watch Al Gore and
Jack Kemp debate.

Finally, Merrill pours himself a glass of wine and brings it to his
lips by holding the base. He sips, sets the glass down, and hunches over.
He twiddles his thumbs slowly. The logs burn and fall into a heap. He

rises and puts another log on the fire and pokes it back to life. He comes back to the couch and sits down.

He is not exactly sure where to begin. He is a professional politician, yet he has done exactly what a professional politician is never supposed to do: He has given his heart away. He always respected Bob Dole, if not his politics. Merrill is much more conservative than Bob Dole. Merrill believes in conservatism as an ideology and normally would have little to do with the kind of political pragmatism and deal-making that has marked Dole's life. But Merrill has fallen in love with the man. He is not ashamed to use that word. Now, a month before Election Day, Merrill's heart has been broken. If it weren't so sad, it would be a B-movie cliché: Boy meets candidate, boy gets candidate, boy loses candidate.

H E REMEMBERS THE DAY HE FELL IN LOVE. WHO EVER FORGETS the first time? As the Republican governor of New Hampshire, which hosts the first primary in the nation, Merrill had been courted for months. Every presidential candidate had come to see him, some several times. Merrill was the most popular governor in New Hampshire history and possibly the most popular governor in the nation, with an approval rating of 70 percent. Every candidate wanted his endorsement. Would Merrill like to be attorney general of the United States, perhaps? Or vice president? It could be arranged. Anything could be arranged. At Halloween, Phil Gramm had gone trick-or-treating on the block where Merrill lived in the hope of getting just a few more minutes of Merrill's time. And seconds after leaving his wife's side after the birth of their second child, still walking down the hospital corridor, Merrill had received a call on his cell phone. It was Lamar Alexander congratulating him.

Bob Dole had simply come to the office.

It was Merrill's small office in the state capitol in Concord, a sunny, pretty room with a desk, a couch, and three armchairs. Impressionist watercolors hang from cream-colored walls. Merrill sat in an armchair and Dole sat on the couch. Merrill, 50, was nervous around Dole. "I was always worried that I would cross over the line with such a dignified man and ask him something that was inappropriate or rude," Merrill said.

Finally, Merrill gathered his courage. "Can I ask you a personal question?" he said.

"Sure," Dole said.

Merrill pulled his chair closer to the sofa. "Why are you doing this?" he asked, very seriously. Why bother? Dole had done so much already. And the campaign would be brutal. His age, his length of service in Congress. Those would be great if they were positives, but what if they were portrayed as negatives? Bob Dole's career, his reputation, his place in history were assured. Why risk it all for this?

Merrill remembers that Bob Dole looked him "right in the eye" and called him "Steve" before he answered, which surprised Merrill. Dole had always called him "Governor" before.

"Steve," Dole said, "do you know this is the first generation of Americans that isn't certain their kids are going to have a better future than they had?"

Merrill was going to say that he had read that somewhere, but Dole went on. "You know this country is based on optimism," Dole said. "Every generation believes that the next generation is going to have it better than they've had it, and that's what America's all about. It's our core.

"It was optimism that brought me off the farm," Dole continued, "and into the military, believing that I could make a difference. And it was optimism that brought me off the battlefield when they told me I wasn't going to live."

Merrill could think of nothing to say. Dole had never spoken to him that way before. Merrill had never heard Dole speak to *anyone* that way before.

"It was optimism that told me, that convinced me, I could not only live but walk again, and eventually run for office," Dole said. He paused. He did not list any of his accomplishments, and Merrill admired him for that.

"I wasn't going to run for president," Dole said. "But after the 1992 elections, a number of people came to me and said, 'Do you realize that you have become the standard-bearer of the party? Do you realize it is now you and Bill Clinton, whether you like it or not, Bob, it is you and Bill Clinton on the evening news every night?'" And then Dole told Merrill about how he beat Clinton on his $16 billion stimulus package and led the fight against Clinton's $265 billion tax increase. (Dole never could give up talking numbers completely.)

"And they saw me as a potential candidate before I even saw myself as a potential candidate," Dole told him. "But I can't sit idly by and let this generation of Americans believe that America won't be a better place for their children." And then Bob Dole stopped talking.

Merrill choked up. "I knew from that moment on," he said, "that I was going to support him."

The logs in the fireplace hissed and popped. Merrill took a sip of wine.

You *believed* this? I asked him. You thought Dole was *sincere*?

Merrill leaned forward. "Dole and I were as close as you and I are now," he said. "Two and a half, three feet away. And I am telling you, he was *overpowered* by the substance of what he was saying. He was *not* trying to convince me to support him. He wasn't even *looking* at me for probably half of his answer! He was so *taken* by the answer, so *captured* by the answer."

Merrill did not tell Dole that day he was going to support him. But that evening Merrill went home to Manchester to his wife, Heather, and told her he was going to endorse Bob Dole. He repeated what Dole had said, word for word. And then Merrill said, "We've got two small babies. And Bob Dole's sincerity and his concern with this generation convinces me that he will get the nomination, and that if he's elected he will be a great president."

Merrill leaned back on the couch. "And, to say, Roger," he said, "that it was like lightning striking is not unfair."

I said nothing, although I agreed it was like lightning striking. Though for a different reason. Never before had I heard of Bob Dole spinning such an effective line of crapola. Dole was supposed to be the candidate who was *incapable* of performing. But it turned out he was incapable of performing only in *public*. In private, he was a master. He would have to be to do so well in the back rooms of the Senate, where knowing a person's strengths and weaknesses, likes and dislikes, vulnerabilities and invulnerabilities, were so essential to cutting a deal. And Bob Dole knew the essential facts about Steve Merrill. He knew that Steve Merrill had held elective office for less than four years. He knew that Steve Merrill had a romantic streak a mile wide. He knew that in terms of national politics, Steve Merrill was a virgin. And he knew that he could pluck Steve Merrill's heartstrings like a banjo.

Optimism had brought Bob Dole off the farm? Bob Dole had never lived on a farm. When Bob Dole's father, Doran, came back to Russell, Kansas, from World War I, he opened up a café on Main Street. When it failed (not many people had money for restaurant meals in Russell in those years), Doran opened up an egg and cream station, which is what he was doing when Bob was born in 1923. Later, Doran would manage a grain elevator on Main Street. Bob Dole was a town boy all his life.

Optimism had brought Bob Dole into the military, believing that he could make a difference in World War II? Well, possibly. Except that it was a call-up notice that brought him into the military. Dole didn't enlist at the outbreak of World War II. He was in college at the time of Pearl Harbor and he wanted to stay there. Dole was having a heck of a good time. He ran track and played football and basketball and lived at his fraternity house. He joined the ROTC, because he knew the draft board would get him eventually, but he was in no hurry. In 1943 he was called up. He served honorably and bravely and was injured terribly. Optimism might have gotten him through his recovery, but what he talked about for years afterward was the rage and despair that he felt at being wounded, not the optimism.

No matter. It was a wonderful performance on Dole's part. It was certainly good enough, at any rate, to win over Steve Merrill and make him think about his two babies at home and how they needed Bob Dole to protect their future. No, there was nothing wrong with Dole's act. The only thing wrong was that Bob Dole could perform it only behind closed doors, where he would not be embarrassed by it. Some harmless bullshitting, one-on-one, no staff present, Dole was up to. But do that in public? In front of people? In front of voters? Naw. Couldn't do that. Wouldn't be right. Nope. Wrong. Phony. Whatever.

None of which Merrill knew at the time.

You were impressed by Dole's sincerity, I said to Merrill. And you assumed he would convey that sincerity to the American people?

"I felt that I was seeing a side of Bob Dole that I had never seen!" Merrill said. He was excited. And why not? It was like finding out that Old Dobbin, which you were about to put out to pasture after a lifetime of pulling a hay wagon, was really a lightning-fast thoroughbred with a Kentucky Derby win left in him. Bob Dole wasn't a dreary, disjointed, rambling speaker. No, he was sincere and compelling and, best of all, optimistic. "I thought it was a side that most Americans had not seen," Merrill said.

He picked up his glass of wine, put it back down and pushed it away. The light from the fire flickered on his face. "Let me tell you," Merrill said, "sadly, they still haven't."

IT STARTED GOING WRONG ALMOST IMMEDIATELY. AFTER MERRILL told Heather he was going to endorse Dole, she urged him to go up to a cabin in the woods with a group of old friends to hunt whitetailed deer for the weekend. Just to get away from it all and think things over. The cabin had no electricity and no phones. Dole's staff was trying to reach Merrill to lock up his support but had no way of getting through. Dole's staff knew that Dole was not a "closer." He was good at setting the hook, but the staff had to reel in the fish. And they were experienced in the black arts of Washington politics. So they leaked to the media the fact that Steve Merrill was about to endorse Bob Dole.

They didn't know it was true, but what could Merrill do? Get angry and deny it? That would hurt and embarrass Bob Dole. It was a standard box play, and Merrill was the guy who had just been boxed in. Merrill was learning how the big boys played. And it would not be his last lesson.

Time magazine, which came out the weekend that Merrill was unsuccessfully shooting at deer, ran the story, the wires picked it up, and Dole was asked about it on *Meet the Press* that Sunday. Dole said there would be an announcement in a few days. Merrill knew nothing about any of this. He didn't get back to civilization until Monday. When he got to a telephone, he called his staff and innocently asked them if anything was going on. His staff was aghast.

"You haven't talked to the *Union-Leader* yet!" an aide wailed into the phone. "You haven't talked to Joe McQuaid! They've done this to you! The Dole people have done this to you!"

Joe McQuaid, the editor in chief of the *Union-Leader*, lived across the street from Steve Merrill. Their two careers, their two lives, the lives of their families, had been intertwined for years. Steve Merrill and Joe McQuaid were very good friends.

And Steve Merrill knew that Joe McQuaid was going to be really, really pissed.

THEY WERE, IT COULD BE ARGUED, THE TWO MOST POWERFUL men in the state. One was the young and handsome governor, and the other was the young and handsome newspaper editor. Both were very conservative, both were very funny, both were natural-born storytellers.

"It was in Ronald Reagan's first term," Joe McQuaid is telling me, "and he was going to be in Massachusetts and he invited Mrs. Loeb to come down to visit him." Nackey Loeb is the publisher of the *Union-Leader*, having inherited the job when her husband died in 1981. She still writes the front-page editorials that he specialized in. And while she lacks her husband's vitriol-dipped pen (under William Loeb the paper called Gerald Ford a "jerk," Nelson Rockefeller a "wife-swapper," and questioned whether Henry Kissinger was a "kike"), she shares his deep conservatism, his general distrust of politicians, and his penchant for carrying a .38-caliber Charter Arms pistol.

"So she goes down and she has to go through a metal detector to see the president," McQuaid continues, "but she uses a wheelchair and that would set off the detector, so the Secret Service just waves her around the machine. She meets with President Reagan, she comes back out to her van, she gets in, she opens her handbag, takes out the pistol, and hands it to her driver saying, 'I don't need this anymore, put it away.' Now can you imagine that? She had a *gun* with her while talking to the president of the United States!"

The real question is why she felt she *needed* a gun while talking to the president of the United States, I say.

McQuaid shrugs. "I don't know why she carried it," he says. "Maybe she thought he'd say something she might disagree with."

Which is the funny side of Joe McQuaid. This is the other side of Joe McQuaid: It is 1980 and McQuaid gets a call from Ronald Reagan's advance man saying Reagan has a few empty hours in Manchester and could McQuaid arrange something.

So McQuaid calls his mother and she sets up a coffee in her home for Reagan. "The hour came for coffee, there are 150 people in my mother's living room and no Reagan," McQuaid says. An hour goes by, two hours, three hours. No Reagan. Finally, the advance man calls and says Reagan can't make it.

"You get him here," McQuaid says quietly into the phone.

"Can't do it," the advance man says. "But, tell you what. I will have him get on the phone with your mother *personally* and apologize. How about that?"

"I don't want him on the phone," McQuaid says, biting off each word. "I want him at my mother's house!"

Twenty minutes later, Ronald Reagan arrives at Joe McQuaid's mother's house. Smiling.

Joe McQuaid was 30 years old at the time. He likes that story. He smiles when he tells it. Now it is a month before Election Day 1996 and McQuaid, 46, is sitting in his office at the newspaper and the smile is gone. He is talking about Steve Merrill. The man who used to be his friend.

"We are both lifelong Granite Staters," McQuaid said. "That's unusual. Unlike all the other New England states, in New Hampshire, natives are a minority." But they both love the state; they both have devoted their lives to the state. McQuaid dropped out of the University of New Hampshire three times before leaving without a degree, and Merrill became the first governor of New Hampshire ever to graduate from there. Merrill went on to Georgetown Law School in Washington but returned to New Hampshire, where Governor John Sununu appointed him attorney general.

McQuaid was managing editor of the paper then but did not know much about Merrill. Then one day a man with the unlikely name of Glyde Earl Meek was accused of killing the parents of his girlfriend, setting their house on fire and fleeing. McQuaid called Merrill and asked for a picture of Meek for the paper.

"You can't have it," Merrill told him. "The case is under investigation."

"Moron," McQuaid replied. "You want to catch the guy, but you don't want to give us his picture?"

The friendship began there. McQuaid moved into a house across the street from Merrill's in Manchester's North End, an upscale neighborhood where the overseers of the mills used to build their homes. Merrill left public life in 1989 and went to work for one of the state's biggest law firms, but he was so bright and personable— and conservative—that there was talk of him running for Congress. The *Union-Leader* did not like the idea. "We suggested he not run," McQuaid said, "because he would have run against someone we liked. So Merrill didn't run, and I liked him even more."

There are few papers left in America willing to use that kind of muscle, but the *Union-Leader* is one of them. Every four years reporters come into the state and write about how the *Union-Leader*'s grip on politics in the state is slipping, how it has been supplanted by TV and other newspapers. But the *Union-Leader* will do one thing the other media will not: It will be relentless in its praise or attacks on people. The *Union-Leader* will run not just one or two editorials praising or damning, but editorial after editorial. What would be a crusade to an ordinary newspaper is daily journalism to the *Union-Leader*.

By 1992, with McQuaid now editor in chief, Merrill was ready to run for office. And he came in to the paper and said he wanted to run for Congress against a conservative congressman just completing his first term.

"We said he shouldn't run for Congress," McQuaid said. "We said he should run for governor. We liked Merrill. And he said he would think about it." By this time, McQuaid and his wife, Signe, and Merrill and Heather were great pals. Not just neighbors, they vacationed together in Miami and Key West. Signe bought shirts for Merrill. "He wears terrible clothes if you let him," McQuaid said.

Merrill decided he would run for governor, but he was by no means the favorite. He had never run for elective office, and he faced opponents who had a lot of money and considerable political support. Merrill had no money and no organization. But he had something better. He had Signe McQuaid, who was a gifted political organizer, putting together events for him and even buying him denim shirts so he could look like a man of the people. He also had several editorials of support in the *Union-Leader*. And Merrill did a little himself.

"He was young and handsome and had a great personality and was a good speaker," McQuaid said. "And he took The Pledge." The Pledge was a promise to veto any sales or income tax that ever crossed his desk. New Hampshire had no such taxes. Which meant New Hampshire had fewer services and higher property taxes than a lot of states, but income and sales taxes were a political third rail—instant death. Merrill was also the only pro-life candidate in the race, and the *Union-Leader* liked that too.

Merrill won in a huge landslide. Even though Bill Clinton did very well in New Hampshire that year, Merrill did fabulously well: He got more votes than any candidate in New Hampshire history. There is no real governor's mansion in New Hampshire (unless you want to live in a place that looks like a hunting lodge and has a moose head on the wall) and so Merrill continued to live across from the McQuaids. The friendship grew even stronger, though Merrill did have a few quirks. "He's a finicky guy," McQuaid said. "First he complained he was getting his newspaper too late and so we made sure his paper was delivered earlier. And then Merrill complained that when the paper delivery guy got out of his car to deliver the paper, the car made *bong-bong-bong* noises that woke him up."

Merrill somehow forgave this, and Joe and Signe and Steve and Heather had dinner together every Sunday night at the Merrills. A picture of the Merrills' first child, Ian, reading the *Union-Leader* still rests under the plastic protector on Joe's desktop at the paper. The *Union-Leader* backed Merrill for a second term in 1994, and again he won easily. Everybody liked Steve Merrill: Republicans, independents, even some Democrats, and of course, the *Union-Leader*.

Until the day Steve Merrill endorsed Bob Dole. And Joe McQuaid had to hear about it on the radio.

"He shocked the whole state," McQuaid said. "He shocked me. He was supposed to tell me first, so I could get it in the paper first."

To a newspaperman, there is no greater sin. Steve Merrill had not just betrayed Joe McQuaid, he had scooped him.

THE FIRE HAD BURNED DOWN TO EMBERS AND MERRILL LEFT IT alone. "There is a profound sadness to this race," Merrill said. "The profound sadness of this race is what has happened to my relationship with Joe and Signe. That's the saddest part of it."

The saddest part? Sadder than the likelihood of Bob Dole losing? Sadder than the likelihood of Bill Clinton winning?

"It's been terrible. *Terrible.*" Merrill said. "It's very sad. Joe is humorous and he's very bright and he thinks well and he writes well and . . . I miss that relationship. And it has affected us at all levels. Professionally and personally and politically." The grandfather clock tick-tocked in the corner for a while.

So, I said, you come back from this hunting trip to find out you had endorsed Bob Dole, or at least that is what the media rumors are.

"I had to go to New York," Merrill said, rising and walking over to revive the fire. "The Dole campaign told me I couldn't say anything, that everything would be handled from Washington." Merrill was to endorse Dole that Wednesday and Dole would name Merrill his general chairman, the person who would shape strategy and keep Dole "on message."

The *Union-Leader* had already endorsed Pat Buchanan, and Merrill knew McQuaid would not be happy with his choice of Dole, who was much too moderate for the *Union-Leader*. But now Merrill agreed not to call McQuaid and give him the official word that he was endorsing Dole. Which meant that Merrill's allegiances were already shifting from his old friends in New Hampshire to his new friends in the heady world of national politics. It meant that already, from the very first day, he was changing into a different person. But that is what love affairs do.

"The announcement was a blur," Merrill said. "I remember Bob Dole came in and we met at the Manchester airport. We went over to the Alpine Club, a workingman's club, a workingman's bar. The announcement was great, but there was Joe . . . I had no idea . . . I just . . ." Merrill stopped talking. "We ought to talk about whether this," and he motioned to my notepad and tape recorder, "will sink the relationship for the rest of my life. Which it may have already."

I don't get it, I told him. I had seen Joe and Signe just a few hours earlier in Manchester and the three of us had had dinner together. Many national reporters who troop up to New Hampshire every four years get to know one or both of them. At dinner they had been laughing and joking. They knew I was about to drive up to Concord to see Merrill, but they did not indicate anything was wrong.

Merrill looked at me. "He has not stepped foot inside my house since then, since I endorsed Dole," Merrill said, with an awful, deliberate slowness. "You have to understand we had dinner every Sunday evening, *every* Sunday evening we had dinner together. And now we don't."

Because you endorsed Bob Dole? Because you didn't tell Joe ahead of time?

"I go in to see him in his office the next day," Merrill said. "And Joe looks right into my eyes and he says, 'Well, if that's your decision, then I don't know you politically. And if I don't know you politically, then I don't know you professionally. And if I don't know you professionally, I don't know you personally.' And then he got up and walked away. Walked *away*. And that was that."

Merrill had tried to make Joe understand. "Joe," he said, "if Dole weren't a real conservative, he wouldn't be choosing someone like me!"

"You're just being used by this guy!" McQuaid had shouted back. "He's not a real conservative!"

"Look, he's not a conservative in the Pat Buchanan sense, but he's a real conservative, Joe," Merrill said.

"But look at him on abortion, look at him on balancing the budget!" McQuaid said.

Merrill had argued, but it had done no good. Now Merrill sat back on the couch and took a breath. "It was very sad," he said.

So when was the first time they missed dinner at your house? I asked. The first Sunday after this?

Merrill nodded. "We figured that was it."

The *Union-Leader* now had two targets: One had betrayed the cause of true conservatism, the other had betrayed the *Union-Leader*. "I knew Joe didn't like Bob Dole," Merrill said. "He's never liked Bob Dole. But now the paper wanted to beat Bob Dole *and* Steve Merrill. And they did. We probably would have lost New Hampshire anyway. But they certainly should take some credit for it."

JOE MCQUAID REMEMBERS BEING FULLY PREPARED TO LISTEN to Steve Merrill. Just in order to find out if Merrill had gone mildly nuts or completely nuts. "Merrill calls up and say he wants to come in and explain the endorsement to me," McQuaid said. "I was cold. I said, 'Yeah, come in.' I wanted to hear this."

Merrill came in and the two sat down across a table.

"Dole will come to me and we will chart out a conservative course," Merrill said to McQuaid. "And he won't be able to walk away from it because I will be there to make sure."

McQuaid laughed. "Come on, Merrill!" he said. "You believe that?" Bob Dole was a master politician, a man who had entered politics at about the time Steve Merrill was being toilet trained. Bob Dole *snacked* on guys like Steve Merrill. And now Merrill was claiming that he would control Dole? McQuaid did not buy one word of Merrill's explanation. He was convinced that Merrill was endorsing Dole because Dole was going to bring him to Washington and give him a fat job. And besides, there was that other problem. "I was not so much pissed off because he endorsed Bob Dole," McQuaid said. "I was pissed off because we lost our scoop."

Merrill did what he could to bring McQuaid around. He told him about Dole's answer that day in the governor's office. That dramatic account about the next generation of kids, about optimism leading him off the farm, optimism leading him into the army, optimism causing his recovery and . . .

"You are *kidding* me!" McQuaid said to Merrill. "Are you *kidding* me?" He could not believe this. Merrill was a bright, savvy guy. How could he have fallen for this . . . for this line of sheer crap?

"I thought it was sad," McQuaid told me. "I do not think Steve Merrill believed in Bob Dole. How could he? There was nothing to believe in."

And so you set out to ruin them? To ruin them both?

"We push our candidates and we bash all the others," McQuaid said.

And you stopped going over to his house for dinner.

"We stopped going over for dinner," McQuaid said. "We stopped being invited." He paused. "Look, I didn't even *want* Buchanan to run. I didn't think he could win. 'Get your column back in the newspaper,' I told him. But he was on a crusade. Dole? Dole doesn't have any core beliefs. He's too old. He stands up and says, 'One more mission.' That was fifty years ago! He's not from my *father's* generation; he's from my *grandfather's* generation.

"Merrill made a bad decision and it hurt Merrill. He was perceived as a political opportunist. And he was. I don't call him. Sometimes he calls me. I don't know what he'll do. I wish him luck."

THE AFFAIR

WHEN STEVE MERRILL LOOKS BACK ON THE DOLE PRIMARY campaign in New Hampshire, he remembers it as a freight train rushing out of control to its inevitable doom. Merrill knew New Hampshire; nobody knew it better. But he didn't know Bob Dole. Nobody did. "This was a level of stress, a level of anxiety, a level of combat that I . . . that I . . ." Merrill said and then his voice trailed off.

Why was it so bad? I asked.

"I haven't told you what it was like to try and get Bob Dole to be the real Bob Dole," Merrill said, leaning back against the couch cushions, expelling a sigh, shaking his head. "Bob Dole campaigning in

New Hampshire was Bob Dole the Senate majority leader. I'll tell you what it was like every day. He would fly in. He would get in a van, and we'd go off. And he'd say 'How you doin'? How's it goin'?' And then he'd reach for the phone. Or he'd say to [his aide] Michael Glassner, who traveled with us, 'Could you get Sheila, get Trent, I want to find out what's happening at the Senate.' He was *constantly* torn between two enormous tasks. I don't know if others could have done it, but he could not do it."

Dole would turn around from the front seat of the van—he liked the front seat so he could stretch out his legs—and with the phone in his ear he'd say to Merrill, "I know this event is important." And then he'd keep talking into the phone about this bill or that subcommittee or that conference report. And the van would pull into the parking lot of the event and they'd sit there until Dole eventually would hang up the phone and say to Merrill, "Now tell me about this event." And they'd have, oh, two minutes maybe. And then Dole would be onstage and he wouldn't really know where he was or what he was supposed to talk about. He'd have a speech in front of him, but he never had time to read it in advance. So he talked about what he knew best: the day Franklin Roosevelt died or what it was like to live in Russell, Kansas, or the time Dwight Eisenhower took him on a tour of Gettysburg, or some other flash from his past. And Merrill would stand in the wings and listen and know how awful it was. Merrill was a very good campaigner; he knew what it took to motivate an audience to vote for you. It wasn't rocket science. If it was rocket science, how could so many politicians learn how to do it?

"So now it's after the speech and he's in the front of the van and I'm in the back of the van," Merrill said, "and I say to him, 'Senator, you've got to *repeat* this theme five times today, because if you don't they will not understand that it is important to *you*. The press corps in New Hampshire is good, but you've got to repeat it over and over again for them to believe that you have a *commitment* to it.'

"And Dole turns around—I'll never forget this, Roger—he turns around and looks me right in the eye and he says, 'You know I really don't like to give a speech more than once. I think it's *intellectually dishonest*.'

"I almost had a heart attack!" Merrill said. "I said to myself: 'This is one of the most naïve men I've ever met.' And I *loved* him at that moment. And I wanted to jump out of the van at that moment."

And he couldn't get Dole to do it. Oh, maybe Dole would repeat a speech once so that Merrill wouldn't look at him with that crushed look on his face. But Merrill couldn't get Dole to play the game.

Soon reporters would notice that something was terribly stunted about Dole's campaign abilities, and they would begin writing stories speculating on whether Dole was to blame or his handlers were to blame. But as much as he loved Bob Dole, Merrill came to the only conclusion he could: it is *always* the candidate who is to blame. Although reporters had elevated handlers to cult status (the handlers were the only people who would talk to them), in reality, the handlers probably never determine the outcome of a race.

"There was no fire," Merrill said. "There has to be a fire generated by the candidate. And Bob Dole didn't ignite that fire in New Hampshire." It pained Merrill to say so; it tore his guts out to say so. He wanted to win New Hampshire so badly. And the media expected him to do it. Sure the *Union-Leader* had endorsed Buchanan, but Merrill was more important than a newspaper. Merrill was the most popular governor in history. Now if only he could do something about that lug running for president.

Dole flew into New Hampshire after a narrow victory over Pat Buchanan in Iowa and immediately did something a politician should never do: predict the future. "Whoever wins next Tuesday in New Hampshire will probably be the Republican nominee to run against President Clinton," Dole told a small group of firefighters in a suburb of Manchester. Most of Dole's crowds in New Hampshire were pathetic. While Buchanan was drawing large, enthusiastic throngs, the Dole campaign had to bus people in from out of state to swell his feeble audiences, not just for the candidate's morale but so the media wouldn't notice. Dole, however, began to recognize the same faces at speech after speech and complained to his staff. "He didn't like that," Merrill said. "He really didn't like that. He felt it was unfair. To see the same people was a phoniness to him."

Still, Dole expected to win. He had Steve Merrill behind him, didn't he? Governors were important—George Bush had locked up the governor of New Hampshire in 1988 and that helped him win the state, Dole believed. That's all it took. He didn't care what anybody said. Winning, Dole believed, was really about *process*, about knowing which strings to pull, which ducks to line up. "I came to New Hampshire [in 1988] and something happened I really didn't like," Dole told the firefighters. Then he turned to Merrill, who was standing next to him on the podium. "But this time something is going to happen I *do* like, isn't that right, Governor?"

Merrill managed a smile. Later, *The New York Times* asked Merrill what would happen if Dole actually lost in New Hampshire. "I don't think I'd have egg on my face," Merrill said. "I'd have the whole breakfast."

* * *

IT IS BREAKFAST TIME FOR STEVE MERRILL IN NEW HAMPSHIRE. BOB Dole has just lost to Pat Buchanan. Merrill watches on TV as Buchanan says in his victory speech: "Nackey Loeb is the political godmother of Pat Buchanan. Without her and Joe McQuaid, we would not be here tonight." Buchanan holds up the front page of the next morning's *Union-Leader* with the headline: NH: GO, PAT, GO! Actually, that paper does not yet exist. The *Union-Leader* has rushed a page proof to Buchanan so he can hold it up for the TV cameras.

Merrill picks up the phone and calls Dole's campaign manager, Scott Reed, and offers his resignation.

"Dole wants you on the plane tomorrow," Reed says.

Merrill catches a few hours of fitful sleep and gets up the next morning, showers, shaves, and tells Heather that Dole probably wants to fire him in person. "I've always heard about the Dark Dole," he tells her, "and now I guess I'll see it."

So he goes to the high-rise Holiday Inn downtown, where the Dole staff is, as usual, ostentatiously occupying room after room, suite after suite. (Pat Buchanan, his wife, and senior staff are crammed into two rooms in the hotel.) Merrill goes up to Dole's floor and it's like somebody had died, but worse, because the corpse is walking around and nobody knows what to say to it. Merrill goes into the living room of one of the suites and stands there, waiting. Dole walks in. They are alone.

Dole walks over to him and throws his left arm around Merrill's shoulders and says, "Are you okay?"

And Merrill says, "*I'm* okay. Are *you* okay?"

"I'm fine," Dole says. "We're going to *win* this thing." Which, he knows, is most likely true. A strange calm has settled over Dole. Even though he has lost an important contest, his moderate opponents, Steve Forbes and Lamar Alexander, have done even worse. Now, his only real opponent is Pat Buchanan, an extremist. And the Republican Party, Dole knows, is not going to nominate Pat Buchanan. Bob Dole might not understand this new generation of Americans (or any generation past 1950, for that matter), but he knows the Republican Party. And he knows in the end all he has to do is hang on, because the Republican Party is not going to nominate some nut. Stakes too high. Not going over the cliff. Nope. Gonna win it. Russell. Discipline Day. Argh.

So Dole tells Merrill, "*You* are my general chairman!"

And Merrill's heart soars like a hawk. He now knows Bob Dole *does* love him. He *really* loves him.

What Merrill does not yet know is that Bob Dole has just given him the equivalent of the Mafia's kiss of death. Steve Merrill might think he is going to continue as a major player in the Dole campaign, but from this day on Steve Merrill sleeps with the fishes. Bob Dole does not need losers to give him advice. He has enough experience of his own with losing.

But when Merrill gets on the Dole campaign plane that morning, he is as happy as a kid at the circus. Merrill has never been on a real presidential campaign plane before, and he is totally impressed, totally starstruck. There are the reporters in back, and in front of them the Secret Service agents sit with their guns strapped on, and then forward of that is first class, with little name cards on all the seats. The first row of seats on the port side is turned around to face the row behind, and Merrill finds his name card on the seat facing Bob Dole's. Can you believe it? Right across from the man himself! And on the way to Fargo, North Dakota, Dole keeps saying to Merrill, "Are you all right? Are you all right? Are you all right?" three times, real sincere.

"And it just *touched* me," Merrill said. "It just touched me."

And after that, Merrill is never heard from again.

Oh, he hangs around and they give him a desk in Washington and he attends the senior staff meetings, but a few months later Dole names Donald Rumsfeld his "national" chairman and doesn't even tell Merrill about it. So now Dole has a "national chairman" as well as a "general chairman" as well as a complete staff of high-priced talent (or at least they are getting high-priced salaries), but it doesn't really matter much because Bob Dole is not going to listen to any of them.

Which Merrill will learn later. Now Merrill thinks the loss in New Hampshire might have been a good thing, might have awakened Dole to the seriousness of what he must do in the months ahead, might have persuaded him that he really has to change his style. So Merrill starts making all these suggestions and pretty soon he finds himself on a plane, but not the same plane that Dole is on. The staff suggests to Merrill that he fly around the country on his own to sing the praises of Bob Dole. "Be sincere," they tell him. "We like that about you."

S O MERRILL IS SENT DOWN TO FLORIDA, WHERE HE LEARNS ABOUT modern campaigning. "I got up at five A.M. and flew out to Florida," he said. "I had never campaigned in a large state before. They said you're going to go to Tallahassee. I assumed I was going to speak in rooms filled with people. Like campaigning in New Hampshire. You go to a dinner with five hundred people or a church hall or a club hall or a Rotary where there's a hundred and fifty people. In Florida, we made eight stops in a day and a half. Three was the largest crowd."

Three what? I said. Three *people*?

Merrill took some grapes from the plate and tossed them into his mouth. "Three people," he said.

They stick Merrill in a four-seater plane and they fly him to Tallahassee. He lands, he gets out, he walks into some room in the airport that smells like Freon and is air-conditioned to about 10 degrees colder than New Hampshire was at 5 that February morning. There is a lectern with a Dole sign on it and a camera on a tripod facing it. "My heart stopped the first time I walked in and saw just one camera," Merrill said. "I figured there had been a tragedy in the city and everybody was somewhere else."

"No, no," a Dole aide whispered to him. "This is the ABC affiliate. This is fabulous."

"This is it?" Merrill said.

"This is it!" the aide said. "This is great!"

Then a state senator or somebody like that would come in and introduce Merrill to the camera as if there were a thousand people in the room. "I want to introduce the governor of New Hampshire, a man who has cut taxes, a man who has cut regulations, a man who has balanced the budget! Here he is, Steve Merrill!"

"It's wonderful to be here in Tallahassee," Merrill said to the camera in the empty room.

Remembering it, Merrill threw back his head and laughed. "It was *fab*-u-lous!"

Merrill gave a 15-minute speech about how great Bob Dole was. Then he got back on the plane. And went to the next stop. And did it all over again. By the third or fourth stop, he no longer mentioned the city he was in because he had no idea what city he was in. "It's wonderful to be here in . . . Florida," he said.

Sometimes there would be a print person or two sitting in the corner of the room taking notes, but this was not New Hampshire, where somebody introduces you to reporters. Afterwards, Merrill asked the aide, "Who were those people?" And the aide said, "A weekly and a daily. It's great, great."

And then back on the plane. By the fourth or fifth city, wherever it was, Merrill caught on. "I went to the person with the camera, and I said, 'I'm going to give you two fifteen-second sound bites on Bob Dole.' And he said, 'Great!' "

And that's what Merrill did for the rest of the day. "If I didn't have to use the bathroom," he said, "we'd be back on the plane in three minutes."

When it was all over and Merrill was flying on to the next state, it occurred to him that something very strange had happened. "I had spent an entire day campaigning, eight stops, and I hadn't really met a human being," he said. "I think this is the campaign of the future."

THE KISS-OFF

STEVE MERRILL FINALLY GOT THE MESSAGE WHEN BOB DOLE kicked him off his plane for good. "He put both Rumsfeld and me on the plane and took us both off because we were too candid," Merrill said, sitting straight up now, his hands on his knees. "Bob Dole doesn't want to be challenged too much. He likes to sit. He enjoys sitting." Merrill picked up his wineglass and put it back down. "He is truly naïve in a number of ways—he's lovably naïve, that's the only way I can put it, charmingly naïve, but nevertheless naïve—he doesn't want to repeat speeches; he doesn't want to do a sound bite; he doesn't want a theme to carry him from day to day. So how will he win? He figures that people will see the *goodness* within him, they will see the *goodness* in Bob Dole! Which he actually believes! Well, they won't! They *won't!*"

And so you got kicked off the plane, I said.

Merrill nodded. "People are afraid to take him on, not because he's tough, but because he is so sensitive and they believe they'll hurt his feelings somehow," Merrill said. "It's not that you'd tell him something and he'd disagree. He never disagreed. He always did exactly what we'd say. *And that is why he wouldn't let us back on the plane!* He didn't *want* to do what we said!"

But Merrill would try anyway. He did not know the magic had gone out of their relationship. He didn't *want* to know. "Senator, you can't do that," Merrill told Dole after Dole had given a particularly miserable speech. "You can't say what you did. You can't answer a welfare question by saying we need one more vote in the subcommittee."

Dole looked at him as if he had gone soft in the head. "But if we get just one more vote in the subcommittee, we would move that matter to the floor," Dole said.

"People don't know what the *floor* is," Merrill said, trying to control himself. "Let alone the *subcommittee!* They don't want to talk *process!* They want to talk *issues!* You've got to tell them what you really *believe!*"

And Dole would zone out. That vision stuff again. Spare him. He'd leave the vision stuff to Bill Clinton. Argh. That bastard.

"Do you know what Bob Dole's greatest fear was?" Merrill said. "You won't believe this, but Bob Dole said to me his greatest fear in this campaign was that somebody would make him over, that somebody would make him into something that he wasn't. Bill Clinton will become whatever it takes to succeed for the moment. And Bob Dole will not even for a moment be somebody else in order to succeed."

Which would make a great fortune cookie, I said. But how did Bob Dole expect to win with that philosophy?

"Ahh," Merrill said, leaning forward, elbows on his knees, fingers laced in front of him. "I think that Bob Dole honestly hoped the voters would say: 'Rather a stiff, honorable, honest, straightforward, plain-speaking man, than a glib, telegenic, probably dishonorable, if not downright deceitful, and dishonest man.' "

It's about a month until Election Day, I said. What does Bob Dole need to do to win?

"He needs to be more telegenic, more conversational, more malleable to change," Merrill said.

Or, in other words, everything Merrill had just accused Bill Clinton of being. In the end, in trying to explain to himself what went wrong, Steve Merrill came to believe that Bob Dole really didn't want to win the presidency. "I have this crazy theory that all he really wanted was validation by his peers in the Republican Party," Merrill said. "He wanted to get the nomination that had always been denied him."

And that was enough?

Merrill nodded. "Because when you said to him, 'Senator, this is what you've got to do to win the general election,' he always acted like winning the nomination was enough."

Either that or he just didn't get it.

"And there is a certain dignity to not getting it," Merrill said, rubbing his palms on his pants and standing up. "A certain pristine dignity to not getting it."

We walked outside to where his driver was now behind the wheel of his idling car. The exhaust sent out clouds of vapor that whipped around our legs and disappeared into the chill air.

"We stood on principle," Merrill said. "We ran a principled campaign."

I made no reply.

"And so what?" he said, reading my thoughts. "And so we are going to lose. Yes, me too. I have already lost. I have lost Joe. And Dole will lose. And we did it all for principle. And so what? So what?"

A FEW MONTHS AFTER THE NEW HAMPSHIRE PRIMARY, STEVE Merrill announced he would not run for reelection as governor. His fate was entirely tied to that of Bob Dole. A short while after Dole's loss in November, Merrill launched a very serious, well-financed campaign to become national chairman of the Republican Party. From the beginning, he was considered a front-runner.

Eleven days before the vote, the *Union-Leader* published an editorial opposing him. "True, Mr. Merrill is personable and photogenic," the editorial said, "but the party needs a leader with more substance and grit than Steve Merrill has shown in recent months."

The day before the editorial ran, Joe McQuaid called Steve Merrill to tell him it was coming.

"Well, that means I won't be Republican national chairman," Merrill said.

He was correct. His opponents made copies of the editorial and distributed them widely. Merrill lost and is now practicing law. He and Heather still live across from Joe and Signe. When they bump into each other on the street, they say hello. They do not eat Sunday dinner together. Merrill might run for governor again, but no New Hampshire governor has ever left office and then regained it.

"I think I feel badly for Steve," McQuaid said. "But he made his own bed. And now he has to sleep in it."

Which is the way it is with love affairs.

THE BEASTS ON THE BUS

★

"I have always felt that whatever the Divine Providence permitted to occur I was not too proud to report."

—Charles A. Dana, editor,
New York Sun

WHEN THE VIDEO CAMERA SMACKED JOAN EGLAND, 68, in the head, she staggered only for a moment before recovering. She had come to a Bob Dole rally in Ames, Iowa, aware that politics had become rough-and-tumble in America but unaware it had become a contact sport. "I'm *sorry*," she said to the young cameraman who had whacked her with 40 pounds of cold steel, "but that was my *head* you hit!"

The cameraman looked at her briefly, sneered, and then returned to his shot. Joan Egland was a civilian, a prop. Political campaigns assemble crowds so they can form the background for TV pictures. The props are expected to applaud; they are not expected to complain.

Joan's husband, Stanley Egland, 72, went up to the young man and tapped him on the shoulder. Camerapersons (they are officially known as "videographers," though some years ago they were nicknamed "visigoths") hate to be touched. It jiggles the camera.

The young man whirled around, and that's when Mr. Egland gave him a shove. In Iowa, good manners are taken seriously. And when you smash somebody in the head with a large piece of metal, you are expected to apologize or take the consequences.

Bob Dole was oblivious to all this. Surrounded by cameras, soundmen, still photographers, and reporters, he could barely see the audience, let alone take note of the casualties in it. The room at the Iowa State Memorial Union was a small one, and the press horde had to muscle its way through tight spaces. And while the pencil press can sometimes hang around the edges of events writing sardonic little comments in their notebooks, the TV crews must get good pictures and good sound. It is why they exist.

So the major danger from the press today is not, as press critic James Fallows argues, that journalists threaten democracy through their shallow and relentless cynicism. Nor, as Professor Kathleen Hall Jamieson argues, is the major danger that political coverage is "strategy saturated," "poll-driven," and "manipulated by artful consultants." The main danger from the press corps in America today is that they can knock your block off. The boys on the bus can be the beasts on the bus.

The number of camera crews chasing candidates during the presidential primary season has grown larger and larger with each presidential cycle. Now, nobody quite knew how to control them. "I got to an event in Iowa and found five crews *all from CBS*," one CBS producer said. "There was a crew for *60 Minutes*, a crew for a special the network was doing, a crew for *Sunday Morning*, and a crew for the news that night and a crew for the pool." Multiply that by the other major networks plus C-SPAN, add the local affiliates and independents, and the numbers begin to explode. Just a few presidential cycles ago, you would see a crew from a city like Tallahassee, Florida, or Rockford, Illinois, only if a Florida candidate like Reuben Askew or an Illinois candidate like John Anderson was running for president. Now TV crews from smaller markets travel to Iowa, New Hampshire, and other early primary states as a matter of routine. And it's not just because time on the "bird," the telecommunications satellite, is cheap and the technology is readily available. Such coverage is good marketing: "Your *Live at Five* news team covers Election '96!" It also looks good at license renewal time: Your station has helped fulfill its public service commitment. There is usually no mention at license renewal time, however, about how many citizens you have conked on the head.

There is also something deeper at work. "There is a difference in the world today, and the difference is that every local television station and tabloid show and news service and whatever is all organized for what I call Big Event television," Tom Brokaw of NBC said. "If a big event is going on, they *have* to be there. It's cheaper than going out and doing hard work or breaking original stories or investing time in doing investigative stories. They get a truck and they get a picture up and they look like a national news organization. And it's not just for politics, it's the Oklahoma City bombing, it's everywhere." TV wanted to be there for The Buzz, and it didn't matter if The Buzz was Bob Dole or the Oklahoma City bombing or O.J. Simpson or Paula Jones. It was all pictures. It was all heat. It was all news. It was all entertainment. It was all a TV show. There was no difference.

But the dynamics were changing. Fewer and fewer people—only about 48 percent of the home viewing audience—were watching network news. They could get The Buzz just as easily from their local stations, and they could get it earlier. "You have a diffusion of watchers," Brokaw said. "We now have stations in Waterloo, Iowa, competing with the *NBC Nightly News*. They can come on at five-thirty P.M. or six P.M. Central Time, a half hour or hour before I come on, and they have Washington and the video up of people running across the naval yard because the chief of naval operations has offed himself and they can tap into it. We are in the midst of trying to decide how to compete with that." One way to compete is that everybody goes after all the news all the time. Because you never know when somebody may off himself.

At a Holiday Inn in West Des Moines in February, when Steve Forbes showed up for a campaign brunch with 43 camera crews trailing him, even Brokaw was stunned. "*Summit* conferences do not get forty-three crews," said Brokaw, the only network anchor who regularly bothers to show up at news events. "The president of the *United States* does not get forty-three crews! There has *never* been a year like this."

"Please move away," Kevin McLaughlin, the Forbes chairman for Polk County, Iowa, pleaded with a press corps that insisted on standing between Forbes and the brunch audience. "We'll get started as soon as the press moves away from the podium!" The press did not move away. It couldn't; there was no "away." The press herd was so large, made up not only of cameramen but soundmen, still photographers, and reporters, that it could not help but clog all available space, even to the point of jostling people as they sat and ate. "I paid good money!" a man yelled at a camera crew planted directly between him and the candidate. The soundman turned around and mouthed an apology but did not move. They had to get the shot; they had to get the sound.

Four days later, at lunchtime in Nashua, New Hampshire, at Martha's Exchange, a restaurant and brew pub, Forbes engaged in a staple of primary campaigning: a "meet and greet" (sometimes called a "grip and grin") with diners. It is not easy under the best of circumstances—few diners actually want to be interrupted by politicians while chewing—but Forbes was still being followed by an enormous press contingent. As soon as he exited his campaign bus, he was surrounded by camera crews. Boom mikes arched overhead like brontosauruses looking for something to graze on. The reporters in the crowd were crushed belly to back like they were on the Tokyo subway at rush hour. One reporter began giggling hysterically. "This is the most sex I've had in weeks!" he shouted.

Forbes entered the restaurant and walked over to the candy counter, where he purchased some homemade fudge for $3.42, handing over a ten-dollar bill and two pennies. He then put a piece of fudge in his mouth, chewed, and turned toward the cameras. Which is when they surged forward to catch whatever gems might issue forth from his lips. And when a middle-aged woman waiting for a table got hit in the head by a camera.

"Could you please watch out?" she asked the cameraman.

"Shut up!" he screamed at her.

She froze. In Nashua, New Hampshire, the expected response for hitting someone in the head is something like "Sorry. Excuse me. I apologize." Choose one.

"What did you say?" the woman asked the cameraman.

"Shut up, shut up, shut up!" he screamed at her. Didn't the prop understand that she was ruining his sound? How stupid could she be?

America's TV news viewers have come to expect perfection when it comes to sound and video. The pictures must be in focus and steady, no bounces, no jiggles. And the sound must be interference-free. People are listening in stereo now. So it is absolutely essential for props to stay out of the way and keep quiet.

"These crushes do get big, but it's what we *do*," said Susan Zirinsky, executive producer for "Campaign '96" at CBS News (and upon whom the Holly Hunter character in *Broadcast News* was based). "Very infrequently do you miss a major shot if you're a network crew. It doesn't happen." And it doesn't happen because you have camera crews who will do just about anything to make sure it doesn't happen. They don't miss the sound either. "Sound becomes *so* critical," Zirinsky said. "If a whole news story is one comment, you don't want to miss it."

So you don't miss it. And so you would scream at your own grandmother to shut her up if it meant you might miss a sound bite from Steve Forbes.

Forbes swallowed the fudge. "Good," he said.

Then he strode through the press crush, knowing it would part for him. ("The toughest part for a cameraman is when you are in a press crush and the candidate is walking forward and you have to walk backward," Zirinsky said. "You need somebody to physically guide you backward. It can be the soundman or the producer or the correspondent.")

Because Martha's Exchange is an ordinary restaurant, with the ordinary space between tables and booths, the press herd was momentarily frustrated. The aisles couldn't accommodate all the cameramen and photographers who wanted the good angle on Forbes. So the herd got inventive: One cameraman leaped upon a table as astonished diners looked up at him. And when Forbes plunged into the kitchen—a very bad idea—the camera crews plunged after him. "Guys, guys, we have *food* here!" a waitress wailed as one camera crew dragged its cable through a tray of cheeseburgers.

"It was nuts," Brokaw said. "I did a video essay on it from New Hampshire. It was mindless and it got in the way of the process. And so much of it is done in a thoughtless fashion. I was in some of the main street restaurants in Manchester, and the thundering herd goes by and you could not *see* the candidate. There are no small exchanges between candidates and people anymore. There are just more crews out there and they have to get that picture and they are worried that something might happen and they will miss it. There might be Pat Buchanan berating Japanese reporters in a grove of trees and you missed it. So you shoot everything. It is mindless. Today the rule is: If it moves, shoot it."

The camera and sound people have a different perspective. They talk about demanding producers who, when the competition comes up with a picture or sound bite you missed, don't want to hear excuses about how you didn't want to trample some old lady. "I've never been so mean," a network soundman said. "I've never been so mean as this year."

Neither the Federal Communications Commission nor the Federal Elections Commission keeps track of injuries to civilians by the press. All evidence is anecdotal. But any number of anecdotes showed up in print: Jeff Greenfield, writing in *Time* on March 4, told of barely escaping with his life when he got in front of a stampeding press herd in New Hampshire and how at a Lamar Alexander rally in Des Moines he saw a cameraman accidentally slam a tripod into the head of young woman "knocking her into semiconsciousness." The *Union-Leader* ran on its front page an Associated Press story that at a campaign event in Center Barnstead, a tiny village in central New Hampshire, Pat Buchanan was unable to talk to any workers or supporters because of all the media around him, and that at one point a staffer had to rescue Buchanan's nephew from an onrushing camera crew by yelling, "Stop it! You're squashing the kid!" And the *Nashua Telegraph* reported on jostling within the press herd that led to a fight, after which "one cameraman was left lying in the snow."

On the day before the New Hampshire primary, Pat Buchanan mysteriously canceled what was to be his biggest event of the entire contest: a bus trip through the state. Signe McQuaid, his chief New Hampshire scheduler, later revealed why the trip was canceled. "The truth?" she said. "We couldn't handle the media. We were swamped. It has never been like this. It is not just five crews showing up from New York. It is five crews showing up from New York and *they are all Fox stations.* And they all want credentials and access and hotel rooms and space on the bus. And then you get all the other crews from all the other stations from all the other states. It became impossible. So we just canceled."

The campaigns could control it if they wanted to. They could put up rope lines to keep the press back. They could insist upon many more pooled events in which one or two camera crews share their product with all the others. But in the primaries, the candidates don't really want to control it. The press herd makes them look important; it makes them look legitimate. "I know these lights and cameras are a little distracting," Lamar Alexander told a crowd in an overcrowded church basement in Londonderry, New Hampshire, "but I'm *really* glad to see them."

Sure, *he* was glad. But candidates rarely get bopped in the head. The day after Forbes's visit to Martha's Exchange, he went north to Sunapee, New Hampshire, where his campaign searched out the quaintest general store it could find to demonstrate how Forbes, unlike Lamar Alexander, knew the price of milk. Quaint general stores have quaint narrow aisles, however, and the few shoppers inside were quickly run over by a press corps packing heavy metal.

While I was interviewing a shopper, I got slammed in the head and shoved to the side by a cameraman. As I struggled to stay on my feet, I looked at the side of his camera and saw a C-SPAN decal. I couldn't believe it. Getting whacked in the head by C-SPAN was like getting kneed in the groin by Mother Teresa. It was not so much the pain as the surprise.

"The cameras will be smaller in the future," Zirinsky predicted. "We'll be digital by 2000. We're going from tape to digital and then to disk. The nature of the beast will change." Or at least the wound marks will get smaller.

Phyllis Keeney can't wait. A small woman in her sixties, she drove twelve miles from Unity, New Hampshire, to Sunapee to see Steve Forbes in the flesh, but found herself shoved aside and unable to catch even a glimpse of him because of the beast we call the press.

"You might as well just stay home and watch it on television," she said.

THE JOB OF THE PRINT REPORTER WAS TO PROVIDE THE PUBLIC with something they couldn't get on television. Which was not all that hard. Television used pictures and sound magnificently, but it had difficulty with stories where the pictures and sound were not a key element. Watergate and Whitewater were lousy TV stories for this reason. Scandal was one thing the print press did better than TV. And one rule for what was a scandal was fairly simple: Just about anything involving a lie by a presidential candidate was scandalous.

Perhaps it is because they are the ones usually lied to that reporters are unforgiving when it comes to prevarication. Over the years, the line between a candidate's personal life and public life has become blurred to the point where it is now largely invisible, and this is especially true if any incident reflects on a candidate's veracity. A candidate can be adulterous and survive, but he cannot be adulterous and lie about it. "I have acknowledged causing pain in my marriage," Bill Clinton said on *60 Minutes* in January 1992. And even though his confession was spoken in code, it went a long way toward defusing the issue. Gary Hart might have survived the press stakeout of his house when Donna Rice was inside if he had just come out in his bathrobe with his hands up. So before running for president, candidates now researched themselves to find if there was anything in their past that they might have to fess up to. Sometimes they had even forgotten their sins, they were so long ago. But just what was a sin by 1996? What was fair game and what was off-limits? What was public and what was private? What the candidates really hated about those questions is that the press got to decide the answers.

In February 1995, Susan Feeney, a very talented and highly respected political reporter in the Washington bureau of *The Dallas Morning News*, profiled Phil Gramm, Republican senator from Texas and candidate for president. Feeney began her piece this way:

"Senator Phil Gramm of Texas describes his childhood growing up poor in the Deep South as something akin to *Ozzie and Harriet.* . . . It's an only-in-America, up-from-the-bootstraps story, Mr. Gramm says. But a look back on those years finds they were far less romantic and considerably more complicated."

These three sentences provided Feeney with the journalistic cover for what was to come: an excruciatingly personal, highly embarrassing account not just of Phil Gramm's early life but of the lives of his mother, father, and half brother. What was the justification for writing it? It was about truth and lying. Gramm had characterized his childhood one way ("something akin to *Ozzie and Harriet*"), but the truth showed something less "romantic" and "more complicated."

As it turned out, Gramm had failed to mention the more embarrassing parts of his early life (some of which he might not have known about) and he put a kinder and gentler gloss on other parts, which is a very human trait. But Phil Gramm was not allowed to be human. Phil Gramm was running for president. And the least lapse of truth-telling, by omission or commission, now made him fair game for full exposure.

The first thing Feeney revealed is that Phil Gramm had been conceived out of wedlock.

Feeney spent weeks driving around in a rental car through rural Georgia and Alabama, going from small town to small town, from courthouse to courthouse, to find the wedding and birth records. Tenacity is an admirable trait in bulldogs and reporters. And Feeney was not acting out of prurient interest. She believed that Gramm had made his mother a public figure by constantly talking about her in his speeches. Now Feeney was trying to find out what was myth and what was reality. Feeney was on a search for the truth. The chips and the reputations would fall where they might.

Eventually, Feeney found the goods: a marriage certificate that proved, as she later wrote, that when Gramm's mother married Gramm's father it was on the "eve of Japan's surprise attack on Pearl Harbor in 1941." And their child, Phil, "was born on July 8, 1942."

So let's see: If they got married on December 6, 1941, and baby Phil was born on July 8, then that's . . . *just seven months*!

Which didn't necessarily mean that Phil Gramm would make a lousy president. But why didn't he ever *talk* about it? He talked about his "maw-ma" all the time. It became a joke among reporters, who would try to imitate his slow Southern drawl. "The first economic lesson I ever learned was sitting around my maw-ma's kitchen table, watching my maw-ma and my big brother go back and forth, trying to figure out how we were going to make ends meet," Gramm would say in speech after speech.

Feeney also discovered that the marriage between Phil's mother and father was the third for both of them. They then divorced and later remarried each other. After Gramm's father died, his mother married for a fifth time.

And why didn't Phil Gramm ever put *that* in his speeches? There was more. Feeney talked to Gramm's half brother, Don White, and wrote: "The brothers' youthful talks are without mention of Charles, the oldest son from Mrs. Gramm's first marriage. In those days, one relative said, he was developmentally 'slow' and spent time away from home. Today, he lives in Columbus, a retired laborer."

Feeney dug up even more family history, which began to read like a Tennessee Williams play: Phil Gramm goes off to military school, and when he comes back home on his first Christmas break, he finds that his mother and a man named James L. Neese have filed "dueling lawsuits seeking restraining orders against each other." Neese, court records show, had served time "for killing someone and armed robbery." Neese and Gramm's mother have had some kind of "social" relationship that has gone sour.

According to a suit later filed by Mrs. Gramm, young Phil got on the phone with Neese and demanded that he "let his mother alone. . . ." The 210-pound Neese offered to meet Gramm somewhere and "beat his brains out." Gramm showed up at the appointed spot, but Neese did not. Which may be why Phil Gramm is alive today to run for president.

Feeney did not find all this information in some clipping file or electronic database. She found it through an incredible amount of leg-work and door knocking, including going to the home of Gramm's mystery "slow" half brother. His truck was in the driveway, but he did not answer when Feeney knocked on the door. Which did not save him from public exposure. It was necessary for Feeney later to reveal the identity of this man, because his brother had never done so and his brother was now running for president. Reporters gather information for the same reason sharks move through water: It is how they live, how they breathe.

Only when Feeney gathered all the information she could on Phil Gramm did she go to Gramm to get his response. This is standard pro-cedure. You never start at the top. You never alert the subject of the profile about the dirt until you have dug it up. If you alert him too early, he may make phone calls and urge people to refuse to talk to you. Or documents might suddenly become unavailable. Or if the reve-lations are really bad, he might hold a news conference and give his response before you have a chance to get your story into print.

So Feeney calls Gramm's Senate press secretary and arranges a meet-ing with Gramm. It takes place in Gramm's large, imposing office in the Russell Office Building. The office has a huge fireplace and the usual Texas memorabilia scattered around. Gramm sits behind an imposingly large desk and Feeney sits on a chair in front of it. A Gramm aide sits next to Feeney, taking notes. Feeney has a notepad and a tape recorder.

She asks Gramm her easy questions first, which is also standard procedure. If you ask the tough questions first and the person gets angry and walks out, you may be left without much of a story. If you save the tough questions for last, at least you may have half a story if an explosion comes. Also, reporters require a little time to build up their own nerve.

Eventually, Feeney asks her first tough question.

"Do you know when your parents were married?" Feeney asks Gramm.

Gramm does his usual turtle-like slow blink. "I don't know," he says.

"Do you want to know?" Feeney asks.

Blink. "I don't know," Gramm says.

"When you were small, your parents split up, divorced, and remar-ried," Feeney says. "Why was this?"

"I don't know," Gramm says.

"You know they did though, right?"

"I know."

"Have you looked this all up?" she asks.

"No, I haven't looked this all up," he says. "I know that my parents were separated. I don't remember how long a period it was when I was young."

"Do you know what day they were married?" Feeney asks.

"No."

"Do you know how long it was before you were born?"

"Nope."

"Do you *want* to know?" Feeney asks.

"I don't know," Gramm says. "I mean, if I . . ." And he doesn't finish the sentence. There is a long silence.

"One of the things they teach you in journalism school," Feeney tells me later, "is that when you arrive at a long silence in an interview, *keep your mouth shut.* But I broke that rule."

"This is the chance for you to say you were born premature," Feeney tells Gramm.

"Oh, come on!" Gramm says disgustedly.

Feeney explains that she has looked up the records, that she knows he was born seven months after his parents were married, that she thinks this is a fair question and she wants his reaction.

In doing this, Feeney has adopted what Tom Wolfe calls the "Victorian gentleman" role of the press. In this role, reporters consciously or unconsciously adopt an accusatory tone regarding activities that they might well engage in themselves. Phil Gramm's parents had sex without benefit of wedlock? John Tower wants to become defense secretary even though he once drank? Zoe Baird hired an illegal alien as her nanny and didn't pay her Social Security? The horror! The horror! Reporters point out that the difference, however, is that these people are all seeking public office, all watering at the public trough, and other people engaging in such behavior, including themselves, are not.

"Obviously, I don't . . ." Gramm begins and stops. "Things that happened before I was born, I don't know anything about. Let me also say that my mother's not running for president. I am."

"I know that," Feeney responds. "Do you know how many times your mother has been married?"

"No," Gramm says. "I might be able to go back and piece it together. But what relevance is that to me?"

"Well, you'd like to be president of the United States, correct?" Feeney says.

"Uhm-hmm," Gramm says and nods.

"Americans want to know *who* it is in the office and *where* they came from," Feeney says. "I think we certainly learned that in every race in history. Let's go back to Kennedy . . ."

"Well, I guess my point is this . . ." Gramm starts to say.

"People want to know who you are!" Feeney says.

"Look, I think anything about me is fair game," Gramm says in a steely voice. "But my mother is not running for president. I love my mother. I'm proud of my mother. But I think she has the right to privacy."

Feeney thinks Gramm has not been caught off-guard by her questions, however. She thinks he has done the same research she has done. Some months earlier she noticed a tiny item in a news story about Gramm having found out that he had been spelling his name wrong for more than 50 years. He always spelled his first name Philip, with one l. "But then, for some reason, I was looking at my birth certificate and I noticed it was two l's," Gramm said in the story.

Feeney was suspicious. Why was Phil Gramm looking up his birth certificate before getting ready to run for president? Was he checking into the same things Feeney later checked into? Both Feeney and Gramm apparently shared the same belief: That even though Gramm was a well-known, much-profiled figure who had been written about for 20 years, nobody really goes over your background with a fine-tooth comb until you run for president. Nobody found out that Gary Hart had changed his name, age, and religion until Hart first ran for president. Nobody found out that Pat Robertson fathered his first child out of wedlock and then altered his wedding date in his biographies to cover up the fact until he ran for president. Running for president means getting scrutiny you never got before. And Gramm, she believes, started checking out his own past in preparation.

"Do you remember James Neese?" Feeney asks Gramm.

"Yeah," Gramm replies.

"Do you remember grabbing the phone and you told him to leave your momma alone?" Feeney asks.

"I don't like people messing with . . ." Gramm begins. Then he tells Feeney the story about his mother and the man he calls "the stalker." But Feeney has seen the suit and countersuit and believes it is unclear that Neese was really a stalker. According to Neese's tale, Gramm's mother had agreed to marry him if he left his wife. But when he left his wife, he alleges, Gramm's mother reneged on the deal.

And this is relevant to Phil Gramm becoming president because . . . well, because Phil Gramm has never brought it up (a lie of omission) and has portrayed his childhood as something out of *Ozzie and Harriet* (a lie of commission), when really his childhood appears to be closer to something out of *Homicide.*

"Did you know he killed a man?" Feeney asks Gramm.

"I knew that," Gramm says. "I didn't know it at the time. I didn't know it until recently. Fools rush in where angels fear to tread." (Which, to Feeney, confirms her belief that Gramm had been checking into his own background in order to get his story straight when reporters like her eventually dug up the truth.)

Feeney writes her profile of Gramm, but when it appears there is one editing change that upsets her. In her original story she writes that Gramm's father and mother "were married on the eve of Pearl Harbor" and Gramm was born "on July 8, 1942, seven months later." But an editor takes out the "seven months later" because he feels it is redundant. "So plenty of people read the story and *never got it,*" Feeney complains.

After the story runs, Feeney gets a lot of compliments from reporters who never knew all this stuff about Gramm, but no real reaction from readers. Readers are jaded; everybody's life is talk show material these days.

"I didn't mean to imply that any of this made him a bad person or a bad candidate," Feeney said afterwards. But Feeney also remembered one thing about a candidate she covered in 1992, a candidate who played the "family thing" perfectly, not just defusing it, but using it.

Virginia Kelley, Bill Clinton's mother, had, just like Phil Gramm's mother, been married five times, twice to the same man. But Bill knew how to handle it. He knew that the American people wanted you to *talk* about it. Politics *was* a talk show. It was about self-revelation and selling a story and making people like you. Americans will forgive you anything if you just tell them about it. Bill Clinton was sure of that.

"When you spoke with Clinton in '92 and asked him about his mother," Feeney said, "Clinton would say, 'Ohhhhh! Virginia, my momma, sure has an *active,* big ol' *interesting* life!' He'd talk forever about his mother's husbands and it was very much part of his life, in a bighearted way. Gramm's answers were completely different. Clinton's answers suggested a comfort level with who he was. Clinton couldn't be more comfortable."

And Phil Gramm was uncomfortable. Phil Gramm had odd notions about privacy and relevance and about how he was running for president and not his momma. Bill Clinton knew better. He knew that when you ran for president, your whole family ran. And the more interesting the stories they had, the better. His half brother was sent to prison for dealing drugs? That's what motivates Bill's own hatred for drugs. His mother was attacked by his stepfather? That's what motivates Bill's deep sympathy for battered women. Bill, perhaps on several occasions, had caused "pain" in his marriage? Well, that makes him understand human imperfection all the better.

The Bob Dole campaign was endlessly frustrated by all this. Bill Clinton wasn't interesting and engaging, they kept saying, he was slippery and slick. "I think I saw on TV this thing about the religion of the two candidates," Steve Merrill, Dole's general chairman, said. "*Goodness* is important to Methodists like Dole, and *forgiveness* is important to Baptists like Clinton. Clinton has said, 'I believe in the God of second chances.' "

Merrill was disgusted by this, but isn't America the country of second chances? Isn't that why people came here from other countries? Americans will forgive you anything as long as you fess up and ask them for a second chance. As long as you humble yourself before them. As long as you talk to them.

Nine months after her first profile of Gramm, Feeney writes another, and again she has found something intriguing. Gramm once owned two St. Bernard dogs named Wolfgang and Circe. "One of the dogs," Feeney writes, "figures in an incident that critics contend shows a man who puts principle ahead of compassion." Several former neighbors of Gramm, all of whom Feeney has tracked down, say that one of the St. Bernards died and Gramm called the city to have the carcass hauled away. The city informed Gramm that they did not pick up dead animals. Gramm insisted. But the city remained firm.

"While the dispute continued, the story goes, the dead dog lay in plain view at the end of the driveway until the neighbors buried it," Feeney writes.

Ten weeks after her story appears, Phil Gramm drops out of the race for president. Perhaps the two events are unrelated. Or perhaps a new political standard has been created: Any politician who won't bury a dead dog and won't even go on Oprah to talk about it doesn't *deserve* to be president.

BULLSHIP
ARTISTS

★

"I used to be accused of trying to manage my own campaign. Well, as I look back on some of the things that happened in the last year, maybe I should have."

—Bob Dole to author,
July 23, 1996

NEITHER SCOTT REED, BOB DOLE'S CAMPAIGN MANager, nor Nelson Warfield, his press secretary, knew Bob Dole very well. They were both 36, exactly half Dole's age. Reed was a former windsurfing instructor from Delaware, whose highest political position had been chief of staff to the chairman of the Republican National Committee. Reed had never been a campaign manager before. Warfield had been the press secretary in the losing New York mayoral campaign of cosmetics heir Ron Lauder. Warfield had never worked in a presidential campaign before.

Reed took Warfield up to the U.S. Capitol to meet Dole in March 1995. Warfield had already been promised the press secretary job, but Reed thought it would be nice for Dole to actually meet the man who would present his thoughts, feelings, opinions, and positions to the media for the next 20 months. Reed took Warfield to the "Tadpole," an oval room across from Dole's majority leader's office in the Senate. Dole walked in and Reed made the introductions. Dole shook Warfield's hand and exchanged a few pleasantries. "Well, good luck!" Dole said. And then he left.

"I did not feel I bonded a lot with the principal during the interview," Warfield later said dryly. Warfield respected Dole as a person, but, like others on the campaign, was more conservative than Dole. "I had respect for Dole the man," Warfield said. "The war hero." Warfield had no idea what it would be like to work for Bob Dole, so he went to Dole's personal aide, Mike Glassner, who had worked for Dole for 11 years. "How do you deal with Bob Dole?" Warfield asked him.

"Speak only when spoken to," Glassner replied.

Which was not exactly what Warfield wanted to hear. In order to speak for Dole, Warfield had to know how Dole felt about everything. Warfield had to know Bob Dole so well that he could think like Bob Dole. But given Dole's love of long silences, if Warfield spoke only when spoken to, he might never speak again. ("Did you see his eye twitch?" attorney Bob Bennett once joked about how to read Bob Dole's body language. "That means he liked it.")

"Don't bullshit him," Glassner told Warfield. " 'I don't know' is an acceptable answer. 'I'll find out' is a better answer. If Dole catches you in a lie, he'll remember it forever. When Dole is quiet, he is thinking. Avoid any desire to make small talk. If you have an opinion, give it, but only if he asks for it."

Which was a pretty chilling list. But Warfield found out it was all true. Warfield and Dole would get on a Gulfstream jet in Washington and fly to Des Moines, and Dole would not say a word for the entire flight. Dole would sit there and look out the window and Warfield would wonder when it was going to be okay to speak to him. Eventually, Warfield summoned up enough nerve to do his job. He would brief Dole on the event he was about to attend, tell him what questions he might be asked, and go over talking points with him, points Dole should make in his speech. "And Dole would retain it like a tape recorder," Warfield said. "And he'd use it . . . or not."

Mostly not. But what was Warfield supposed to do? Upbraid Bob Dole? Correct him? Criticize him? "He'd been in Congress since the year I was born," Warfield said. "He'd seen staffers like me come and go longer than there had been color TV." Warfield lacked presidential campaign experience, but he was no dummy. And he asked himself why Dole would hire a guy like Reed and a guy like him. There was one inescapable conclusion: Bob Dole wanted an inexperienced staff so he could run the campaign himself. He wanted people so junior to him in age and experience because he did not want anybody telling him what to do. "When he quit the Senate," a senior Dole staff person said, "I said he quit the wrong job. He should have quit as campaign manager."

"Dole was in complete control," Warfield said. "There was nobody in charge below him. There would be multiple meetings going on and Dole would wander from meeting to meeting, spending a few minutes in each one. The different staff people didn't *know* what authority they had." Which is the way Dole wanted it. The easiest way to avoid being blamed for a bad decision is to avoid making any decision. And, over a lifetime, Dole had learned that decision-making was highly overrated. If you just left things alone, very often they would work themselves out. Or the blame would shift to somebody else. Which is one reason Dole was so sparse with his conversation. Dole used words as if they were rationed. If you didn't say much, it was hard to be blamed for much.

And after nearly 30 years in the Senate, Dole spoke the private language of that body. In the Senate, you didn't tip your hand, you didn't take absolute positions, you didn't close doors. If somebody came to you and asked for your vote and you didn't want to give it, you didn't say no. You said: "I'd love to be with you on that." Which meant no. Such code was second nature to Bob Dole.

"You've got to listen to his every word," Warfield said. "When Dole uses a word, it's a piece of art." Which his staff learned the hard way over the issue of what abortion language should be in the Republican platform. In the real world, nobody cares about party platforms. In the real world, platforms are meaningless documents full of sound and fury, signifying nothing. But the world of party activism is often divorced from the real world. And right-wing party activists were prepared to shatter the Republican Party over the abortion plank. Dole was pro-life, but he was, at heart, a moderate. If one listened carefully to his speeches, keeping in mind the code he spoke, one could glean the essential Bob Dole. In many of his speeches, he would throw in an anecdote about having to get a hat before he went to college, because a local banker felt all college men should wear hats. Jack Torry, who had covered Dole in Congress for the *Pittsburgh Post-Gazette* before covering his presidential campaign, was one of the few reporters who bothered to record the anecdote in print. He knew it was more than meaningless nostalgia. It explained Dole's politics and character. In code, of course.

"I went off to college," Dole would say. "I remember when the local banker loaned me $300. He said, 'You ought to have a hat if you're going to college.' And I said, 'Well, if I've got to get a hat to get the $300, I'll get a hat.' I got a hat. I never wore it. But he was happy, I was happy, and I got the $300."

The banker wanted something, Bob Dole wanted something, and they found common ground. Even though Bob Dole didn't like hats, he got one to get what he wanted. The banker was happy, Bob Dole was happy. That's what life was: You gave a little to get a little. You didn't draw a line in the sand and say, "I will never wear a hat!" You got the frigging hat. You didn't want to wear it? Fine.

Bob Dole knew that abortion was more important than hats. But he also knew that if you wanted something done on the issue, you often had to compromise. You didn't start shouting about "principle" and "ideology." Getting something done was more important than being "pure." You went out and bought the hat. Because Bob Dole didn't want to split the party even further over abortion, he wanted "tolerance" language in the abortion plank that would recognize that Republicans of goodwill could disagree over the issue. Which threw the right wing of the party into a tizzy. And tizzies were what Dole's staff had to deal with. Scott Reed and others tried to argue Dole into a tougher stance. The tolerance language should go into the *preamble* to the platform, they argued, and not the abortion *plank* itself. (That the entire matter did not affect the life of a single ordinary American did not matter. So much of politics was that way, after all.) Reed desperately wanted a yes from Dole in order to avoid controversy at the Republican Convention.

"I want it in the *plank*," Dole said. "It needs to be in the *plank*."

"It's a problem," Reed said and he made his point again about how the Christian Coalition would be insulted if it was in the plank, though they might find it acceptable if was in the preamble.

"It's a problem?" Dole said. "I guess we could move it. Why don't we see what we can do on that?"

But that was *not* a yes. Not in Dole-speak it wasn't. "Why don't we see what we can do on that?" was code for "Why don't you leave me the hell alone for a while?" Which Nelson Warfield, who had been at Dole's side for more than a year by then, recognized. But the headquarters staff, who saw Dole much less often, was not as familiar with his code. They thought Dole had agreed to put the tolerance language in the preamble. Which somebody promptly leaked to the press.

Dole was furious. "Dole *hated* the staff speaking for him," Warfield said. And to show the staff how much he hated them speaking for him, Dole went on TV and repudiated the staff and said maybe the language would appear in the plank after all. (In the end, it appeared in an appendix and the issue died down. But Dole later said publicly he had not bothered to read the Republican platform and didn't intend to. In other words, Bob Dole had bought the hat but he would not wear the hat.)

Dole did not change his ways. He continued to speak in code and continued to keep his own counsel. Some people play their cards close to the vest; Dole held his cards so tightly they might as well have been tattoos. "Maybe it was a product of the Senate, where you don't want to telegraph your punches," Warfield said. "Or maybe it was because there was no verbosity in the Dole household as he was growing up." In any case, the Dole campaign had a candidate who communicated (if that's what you wanted to call it) only in code, who believed in silence as a management tool, and who hated anybody speaking for him. In addition, you had a staff that didn't trust the candidate to speak for himself and, having been publicly humiliated, felt less and less loyalty and more and more hostility to the person they were trying to put in the White House.

Eventually, however, everyone on the campaign learned to recognize Dole's personal code for no, because they heard it a lot. "I'm not certain," Dole would say. And that meant *no*. Which was a perfect example of the political benefits of Dole-speak. If you kept saying you weren't certain about everything, it was hard to blame you for anything.

The staff, which recognized that reporters liked Bob Dole on a personal level, felt that the staff was being unfairly blamed for the Dole campaign rather than the candidate. Normally, a staff would welcome such stories. Staffs are supposed to take blame and give candidates credit. The object, after all, is to get the candidate elected. But while Dole did evoke fierce loyalty and even love from some of his staffers, others felt that Dole's silences and refusal to cooperate in the campaign process did not deserve loyalty.

Dole could also be brutally frank, even with the staff members he liked. During the preparation period for the first presidential debate, Dole read a newspaper account of how the entire senior White House and Clinton campaign staff were in Chautauqua, New York, helping the president prepare. Dole turned to his own debate prep team—pollster Tony Fabrizio, Senate chief of staff Sheila Burke, and Warfield—and said, "Bill Clinton is up there with a hundred of the most experienced people in politics. And I'm here with *you* three."

E ARLY ON, REPORTERS BEGAN NOTICING THERE WAS SOMETHING missing from the Dole campaign: Dole. Bob Dole was in the box. He was being kept away from reporters. "Perhaps the oddest thing in this odd primary season is Bob Dole's string of no-shows on television in the aftermath of caucuses or primaries," columnist and historian Garry Wills wrote. "Whether he loses or wins, he refuses to go on the specials and interviews where other candidates talk about the race." Which was exactly what Dole's handlers wanted.

In 1988, Roger Ailes, a media wizard whose string of credits stretched all the way back to Richard Nixon, told *Advertising Age* that the difference between selling a candidate and selling cookies is that "cookies don't get off the shelf and hold news conferences or make gaffes or go on *Meet the Press*." In other words, the perfect candidate was one who was as passive and obedient as a box of cookies. The perfect candidate was a product. Which perfect candidates understood. Upon walking into his first meeting with his reelection team in 1984, Ronald Reagan said: "Hi, guys; I'm a bar of soap." Now *there* was a candidate.

Bob Dole, on the other hand, worried his staff greatly. Even those who liked him did not trust him as a campaigner. And like generals fighting the last war, they addressed the big problem of his last national campaigns, the ones in which he had been "mean." Maybe it was because they felt Dole was mean to them that Dole staffers labored under the extreme fear that his meanness would be revealed to the public. Dole had, after all, said things like "get back in your cage" and "stop lying about my record" and made a crack about "Democrat wars." So the Dole staff decided that the only way Dole could be protected from committing further public acts of meanness was to put him under wraps. They decided as much as possible to keep Dole away from TV, radio, newspapers, and press conferences. All Bob Dole's public utterances would have to be tightly controlled. "We didn't want Bob Dole delivering heavy blows," Warfield said. "So I was the sharp-tongued one." Ironically, Dole often upbraided Warfield for being *too* sharp-tongued during the primaries about his Republican opponents, some of whom were his friends. This should have told the staff something: Bob Dole really wasn't very mean at all, not unusually so for a professional politician, anyway. The real Bob Dole was considerably more complex and more likable than the mean cartoon of Bob Dole, but the Dole campaign had no way to show it, having cut him off from the news media.

The staff figured that the way they were going to create an image for Bob Dole, the way they were going to let the public "get to know him," was through political commercials. But they badly overestimated the power of these commercials and underestimated the power of The Buzz that emanated from the news (or so-called "free") media. The Buzz came not just from news stories in the papers and on TV and radio. News stories just kicked things off. The Buzz was what Letterman and Leno joked about. It was e-mail and faxes and talk radio and the cover of *People* magazine and what was in the gossip columns and *New Yorker* cartoons. It was what people talked about at the water cooler and over dinner and in the chat rooms of America Online. Commercials couldn't create The Buzz. They could help, when done in coordination with other aspects of campaigning, but no political commercial or series of commercials had ever won a presidential campaign.

As the Dole adman could have told them. Don Sipple, who was hired and later fired by the Dole campaign, was somewhat of an oddity in the Dole camp, in that he had a string of successes to his credit. He had worked in the winning gubernatorial campaigns of Pete Wilson of California, George W. Bush of Texas, Jim Edgar of Illinois, Kit Bond and John Ashcroft of Missouri, and the Senate campaigns of John Chafee of Rhode Island, Bob Packwood of Oregon, and Pete Domenici of New Mexico. "There was a discussion about whether to try to control press access or let Dole be Dole," Sipple said. "There was an unhealthy disrespect for Dole's ability to survive." Even though Sipple made ads for a living, he realized that ads occupy only one place in a campaign. "You have to forge your theme in the *free* media," Sipple said. "The public gets sixteen hundred sales pitches per day. That's ads, billboards, magazine articles, everything." So people have a high resistance to ads. People channel-surf to escape ads. And except for the Willie Horton ad of 1988, which was publicized relentlessly by the free media, when was the last time anybody could even remember a political ad?

"Forget ads," Sipple said. "The candidate is the salesperson. *It doesn't work without the salesperson.* It's stage management. The Dole campaign underestimated the importance of the *candidate.*" It was Sipple's theory that you go with the pitch, you play the cards you are dealt. Dole was not a particularly articulate campaigner? Fine. So you make that a plus. You say he's a plain-spoken guy. You say he's out of Norman Rockwell's America. You say he's decent, honest, funny, and plain-speaking. And then you let people *see* and *hear* that. You don't hide Dole away from the media. If you hide him, how are people ever going to learn anything about him?

"Press conferences could have *helped* Dole as much as hurt him," Sipple said. "His staff ran the campaign as if Dole were an incumbent, fifteen points ahead, rather than a challenger, fifteen points back. I always detected in the media a respect, a fondness for Dole. He reminded them of their fathers." Besides, Dole was far better at press conferences and TV shows that resembled press conferences than he was at giving speeches. Dole hadn't appeared more times than any other guest on both *Meet the Press* and *Larry King Live* for nothing. He thrived on a give-and-take format. But the top echelon of the Dole staff was terrified of press conferences and even grew terrified of the Sunday talk shows and Larry King. You put Dole in front of reporters or people calling in with questions, and he might make a slip, a gaffe, he might get down off the shelf and *say* something. So they put him in the box and kept him there.

Which did not go unnoticed. In July 1995—more than six months before the traditional start of the campaign, the Iowa caucuses and the New Hampshire primary—Chris Matthews, a nationally syndicated columnist, wrote: "Petrified that their candidate might make a mistake, [the Dole campaign has] chosen to petrify the candidate. Instead of juicing him up for the tough fight ahead, Dole's handlers have chosen to wrap him in bandages, extract his guts and inject him with formaldehyde. They have prepared him not for campaign-ing, but for burial. They have given the country a mummy to vote for."

But even though all their testing indicated that the American peo-ple had no clear understanding of who Bob Dole was or why he wanted to be president, the Dole campaign felt vindicated on July 2, when Dole went on *Today* and reacted angrily to Katie Couric's relentless questioning about his defense of the tobacco industry. "I mean, you should, you know, you may be violating the regulations by always, you know, sticking up for the Democrats and advertising their line on your show!" Dole snapped at her.

Okay, not a great moment. But you go with the pitch. And maybe the next day you put Bob Dole on Letterman, and Dole pretends to smoke a cigarette and says he isn't inhaling or makes some wisecrack like that. (One of the most masterly recoveries in political history was when Bill Clinton went on Johnny Carson and made fun of himself after delivering a disastrous—and endless—speech nominating Michael Dukakis at the Democratic Convention in 1988.) Or maybe Dole could send Katie Couric roses and an apology. Or a box of bubble gum cigars. Or he offers to go on again. Whatever. It's not the end of the world. Bill Clinton had a terrible temper; he was a real screamer. And he had been captured on videotape screaming both about his political opponents and at his staff. But his staff did not put him in the box because of it (nor would he have let them). Yet Dole's staff felt the Couric appear-ance was exactly the justification they needed. It proved, they felt, it was safer to keep Dole away from the press and let him reach the out-side world through speeches he could not deliver and through ads that nobody would remember.

THE VICE PRESIDENT OF THE UNITED STATES STANDS IN THE doorway of his West Wing office shaking each reporter's hand as we enter, pleasantly pretending that he knows who on earth we are. No news organization has reporters assigned exclusively to cover the vice president. In modern times the chief duty of the office has been to at-tend the funerals of foreign leaders. ("You die; I fly," was George Bush's joke.) But Al Gore is different. Rarely, if ever, has a vice president been treated with such importance and respect by a president. Clinton and Gore dine together every week. Gore attends all major campaign meet-ings and contributes advice on all major decisions. Gore even gets on the phone and personally urges Democratic donors to contribute big money. And now he is engaged in something even more odious.

The schmoozing of the press. Hide from the press? What on earth for? Go with the pitch! If Al Gore is wooden, Al Gore will joke about it. ("How do you tell me from my Secret Service agents?" Al Gore asks. "I'm the stiff one.") And Al Gore invites journalists into his White House office. *Any* journalists. On this day, the collection could not be more, well, odd. The attendees include the editors of *Men's Health* and *Men's Fitness* magazines and a guy from New Paltz, New York, who wants to start a magazine called *For Fathers,* and me. Not exactly the journalistic A-list. But Al Gore does not care. He could not be more polite, he could not be more gracious, if he were ushering David Broder, Cokie Roberts, and Tom Brokaw into his office. Besides, these new men's magazines are reaching exactly the audience the Clinton campaign wants. White House polling has identified the importance of the married vote, especially married voters with children. No Democratic presidential candidate has carried a majority of married voters since 1964, but now the Clinton campaign is emphasizing school uniforms and V-chips and teen curfews. "If the White House can break even with married people, then they win the election, no problem," Martin P. Wattenberg, a political scientist at the University of California at Irvine, says in June. (As it turns out, the White House will fall just one percentage point short of that and will consider it a major achievement.)

Gore's office is large, with brown walls and beige carpeting, antique couches and armchairs, and a fine big desk, behind which stands a tall bookshelf. On the marble mantelpiece over the fireplace is an Eskimo carving. There are landscapes and portraits on the walls. Dominating the room is a huge photographic enlargement taken from outer space of Earth, looking like a giant blue pearl. Gore walks over to a plush brown armchair under an oil painting of John Adams, the first vice president. "I'm sittin' here," Gore says. There is a can of Diet Coke on a table next to him and a bowl of M&Ms. "You sit anywhere you want. You need a pen? I've got another one. Well, thank you all very much for comin' over." (Gore often drops his g's to show he is just a kid from Tennessee, though, since his father was a U.S. senator, he was a kid from Tennessee who grew up in the salons of Washington.)

Gore launches into a very smooth, highly organized talk on the American father. He uses no notes, and as he talks, he moves his gaze from journalist to journalist, looking each in the eye in turn. "Our society has undervalued the role of father and tended in the past to define families as mothers and children to a shocking degree," Gore says, occasionally sipping from the Diet Coke. "You can see the reasons why.

Mothers are usually the primary care-givers, and we have tended to downplay and undervalue the *nurturing* role, the *teaching* role, the *spiritual* role of the father." Gore goes on and on. The editors from the men's magazines scribble like mad. Gore is wonderful for their audience. "In everything government does, we ask 'What is the impact on the role of fathers?' " Gore says. The editors almost swoon. They are thinking cover story here. If they could just humanize it a little. Which is when Gore effortlessly segues into the perfect anecdote: Gore says he wants fathers to be able to tell their employers that sometimes they need to take a day off work to meet their children's teachers or take care of their kid's needs. "I have a personal example that's probably a little embarrassing," Gore says, and chuckles.

The editors lean forward.

"Last fall, I had a meeting [scheduled] with a visiting head of state in this office," Gore says, "and one of my daughters had a soccer game. And my wife was out of town making a speech on mental health. And I arranged my schedule so I could go to the game and be back in time for the meeting with the president of [the] country. Two problems came up: [The soccer game] went into overtime! And it was my turn to give the snacks out!" The editors are helpless with mirth. Overtime! Snacks! Foreign presidents!

"Then it went into *double* overtime!" Gore says, and the journalists roar with laughter. "True story! Double overtime!" Stiff? Who says this guy is stiff? This guy is *great*! "Well, to make a long story short," Gore continues, "you know, I'm thinking: Diplomatic incident!" And Gore makes this dopey face and the editors practically fall off the couch. Wait until they get this into print! "The interpreter got a little workout," Gore says, "but [the foreign president] had children and was very courteous, and I just leveled with him."

The point being that Al Gore makes the president of a foreign country wait while his daughter plays soccer because *that is what the president of the United States wants.* "I felt I had the flexibility to take that risk with my work because I know how the president feels about it," Gore says with the utmost seriousness.

Gore now hands the M&Ms around and takes questions and schmoozes and jokes until an aide walks in with a slip of folded paper and hands it to him. Gore unfolds it, reads it, and chuckles. "Another head of state just arrived," he says. "This [meeting] isn't as good an excuse." We all laugh. "It's the president of Botswana," Gore says. And we start to get up and thank Gore, but he waves us back to our seats. "Anyway, let me take a couple of more questions," Gore says. And he does! The president of Botswana is waiting, but Al Gore is not going to stiff us. (That the sending in of the note and Gore reading it aloud and then continuing on with us may be a practiced bit of stagecraft occurs to us. But so what? We are flattered he would make the effort.) After a few minutes, the conversation somehow turns to bike riding, and Gore turns to his aide and says, "That's another conference! Let's do *bicycles* next week. I *love* bicycles." And we laugh and Gore rises and shakes our hands and ushers us out. And as we exit, we see Ketumile Masire, the president of Botswana, waiting in the large anteroom of the West Wing. (Near the end of his interview with Gore, Masire may be told the president of Hungary is waiting, but that Gore will stay and chat nonetheless.)

A few days later each editor gets a 314-page booklet printed on heavy, slick paper from Gore's office. Each booklet is accompanied by a card bearing the vice presidential seal. ("One of the best things about being vice president is the seal," Gore has said. "If you close your left eye and squint a little, it says president.") The booklet is called: "A Workable Balance: Report to Congress on Family and Medical Leave Policies." Gore wants them to have it with his compliments. If they would like any more information on fathers or families or bicycles, they should not hesitate to call. The Clinton-Gore campaign does not believe in keeping journalists at arm's length. The Clinton-Gore campaign would rather smother them.

"I WAS DICKED AROUND BY THE DOLE CAMPAIGN, AND I MEAN *dicked*," Ellen Warren, a tough-as-nails reporter for the *Chicago Tribune,* was saying. "I was reduced to a new level of groveling."

Ellen Warren was not alone. Relations between the reporters covering Dole and the Dole press staff reached rock bottom early on . . . and then plunged. "Are they incompetent or do they hate us?" asked Ceci Connolly of the *St. Petersburg Times.* "A little of both. All of the above."

Dole's top press aides were equally charmed with the press. "I don't think enough of them have had editors kick back their stories and say, 'This isn't news,'" Nelson Warfield said. John Buckley, the campaign's communication director, added: "I think that there is a little bit of *whining* that has taken place with some news organizations as compared to other news organizations that is a phenomenon I have not dealt with previously." How bad did it get? So bad that when one reporter was asked if her anger toward the Dole staff was affecting her reporting, she did not issue the obligatory denial. "I'd like to think it isn't," Jill Zuckman of *The Boston Globe* said, "but it's hard to know.

I'd like to think I'm not taking it out on the candidate, but it's hard to know. I don't know if I would write a different story if I were feeling well-treated."

It all began with the phone calls. Or rather the lack thereof. A reporter who cannot get his calls returned has two choices: Leave the business or become an editor. Yet in the early days of the Dole campaign, calls made to Warfield often were not returned for days or forever. What made the problem even worse was that these were the months when newspapers were profiling the candidates for president. And just about all major and many minor newspapers wanted and expected interview time with Dole. But actually sitting down and talking to Bob Dole became a very tough ticket.

"It was late '95 and I was writing the *Tribune*'s major profile on Dole," Ellen Warren said. "After weeks of phone calls, I was desperate for an interview, but I was not getting anywhere. So I flew to Washington and I sat in the lobby of their damn offices and I said, 'Look, the *Chicago Tribune* is one of the few papers in the *universe* that endorsed a Republican for president in 1992. Illinois is a place you guys need bad. All those electoral votes? This is win-win for you guys."

The Dole campaign was not impressed. Or at least not impressed enough to grant Warren an interview. But she was not a Chicago reporter for nothing. So on New Year's Eve, she flew to New Hampshire, rented a car, and drove to Concord, where Dole was shaking hands in a bridal shop. "I went up to Warfield and I said, 'Nelson, look at me. I'm here. I don't have warts. Put me in his car to Portsmouth. I can get forty-five minutes with him and it will be perfect,' " Warren said.

"We'd like to help you, but we can't," Warfield told her, which was Dole-speak for hit the road, toad.

So Warren drove to Portsmouth on her own, went to a Dole event, and shouted a couple of questions at him from the press pen. "And that was the extent of my two-month effort to interview Bob Dole," Warren said. "I can't think of any time when I tried so valiantly or failed so miserably. Their policy was clearly to not allow access. Period. The end."

But while Warren saw this as a great failure, Warfield saw it as a great success. His policy of stiffing the press had succeeded wonderfully. "Ellen Warren wrote a great profile of Dole," Warfield said. "It couldn't have been better. Did we frustrate her by not giving her Dole? Yes. But *we got what we wanted* from her. We got a great profile." In other words, Ellen Warren had been too ethical to let her wounded pride affect her news judgment. And the Dole campaign exploited that. "If we had given her an interview with Dole, we would have inserted an element of *risk*," Warfield said. "Our objective and the media's objective were not congruent. Ellen might have decided to use that profile to make *news*. It was not always productive to make the candidate available for interviews."

Which, in theory, sounded fine. Warfield's job was to protect Bob Dole. Which was the old "fall on the ball" strategy that many front-runners used. Don't take any risks, just wait for Election Day and victory. But Dole was *not* a front-runner. He was a challenger. And the problem wasn't just that the public did not know him. It was worse than that. Some the public felt it *did* know him and didn't *like* what they knew. They felt Dole was a Washington insider, the ultimate pol, the ultimate member of Congress, an institution the public hated. The Dole campaign should have been aggressively working to *change* that image. They should have been aggressively working to get Dole profiled. Which they would have done if they had trusted their own candidate. Which they did not.

"It was a big mistake hiding Dole from the media," Don Sipple said. "So what if he makes a mistake or two? We could have made his lack of polish a *plus*. Let America get to know him! The problem was that his campaign staff had no respect for Dole. I'm telling you, Bob Dole could have *won*." (In August 1997, *Mother Jones* magazine published an article containing allegations that Sipple had beaten both of his ex-wives and that senior Dole staffers had known about the allegations but had raised no objections. Sipple denied the allegations and threatened to sue for libel, but the report had immediate effects: Sipple was forced to resign from a New York congressional campaign and George W. Bush, who was running for a second term as governor of Texas and was already being talked about as a leading contender for the Republican presidential nomination in 2000, said he was reconsidering hiring Sipple.)

Steve Merrill agreed the "keep away" tactic was a mistake. "The campaign decided we will not permit the campaign press corps to define Bob Dole with his own quotes. We will make them define him with *our* press releases. It was a theory, a hypothesis destined to failure. The staff had a vision of presidential campaigning that they thought was *reflective* of the candidate and actually did a *disservice* to the candidate." Merrill believed Dole's staff constantly underrated Dole, interpreting his long silences as a wish to be kept from people. Merrill saw it differently. "This is a generation hungry for information," he said. "Rather than believe that *snippets* of Bob Dole are enough, we needed to produce *volumes* about Bob Dole that constantly provided information to fill in the taciturn statements of policy he would make on the campaign trail." To Merrill, the print press could have helped repair the damage that Dole did to himself in his speeches.

But to Warfield, everything was a risk/benefit assessment. "Was it helpful for us to make Bob Dole available to Norman Mailer for a profile in *George* magazine?" he said. "Not likely." Dole was not kept away from the press entirely. Even Ellen Warren would be the first to admit that. "He did speak to Kit Seelye of *The New York Times* briefly in his office for *her* profile," Warren said. "And I was absolutely *fried.*"

Which was one of the other problems reporters had with the Dole campaign: While just about all campaigns give favored treatment to papers like *The New York Times* and *The Washington Post*, even if they are not fond of the coverage the papers give them, the Dole campaign made a religion of it. Witness the problem of the plane. No problem so occupied the press staff or led to such bitterness between staff and reporters.

When the Dole campaign went big-time, when it was about to get its federal matching funds and become a general election campaign, the press staff knew many more reporters would want to cover Dole. So the staff split the press into two groups: a group that would fly on the candidate's plane, which was officially known as the *Citizen Ship*, and a group that would fly on a backup plane, unofficially known as the Bullship.

This was standard operating procedure. In almost all challenger campaigns, the candidate's plane is reserved for the major press and the news organizations that traveled with the candidate during the primaries (and paid huge sums of money to do so). The backup plane was for occasional press, TV crews, foreign press, or very small news outfits. (President Clinton traveled on *Air Force One* with only a small, rotating press pool accompanying him. All other reporters traveled on a press plane.)

The Dole campaign decided to depart radically from tradition, however. Which is always dangerous when you are dealing with reporters. Reporters love order. They take the chaos of daily life and present it in supremely orderly stories. Reporters do not like chaos in their own professional lives. They like assigned seats on the airplane that they can depend on every day. They like telephones, preferably with their names taped on them, at each filing center. And they virtually insist on a regulated, orderly, impartial system for sharing information when the candidate can take only a small pool of reporters with him. This is what reporters received when they traveled with Bill Clinton. When they traveled with Bob Dole, however, what most of them received was a kick in the teeth.

Shortly before Dole left for Russell, Kansas, in August to announce his choice for vice president, an order came down from Nelson Warfield to "put the majors on the candidate's plane, where he could keep them close, and kick everyone else off" to the Bullship, according to one Dole staff member. Warfield later denied he was the one who gave the order, but what was undeniable was that *The New York Times*, *The Washington Post*, the *Los Angeles Times*, *The Wall Street Journal*, *USA Today*, and *The Washington Times* were all assigned permanent seats on Dole's plane, while the other print reporters were exiled to the Bullship.

What was the difference between the two planes? Not much in terms of creature comforts (all of which the reporters paid for). But Dole, other newsmakers, and all important staff flew on the candidate's plane. That's where news might be committed. That's where Warfield would occasionally wander back and talk to the press. That's where Dole sometimes wandered back. And since the two planes landed at events at different times, being on Dole's plane also meant the possibility of talking to him on the tarmac. Reporters on the Bullship could go for days or weeks without ever seeing Dole except at his speeches. And access to Dole was the primary concern of the Dole press corps. Though now that the time for profiles was over Dole did sometimes allow reporters to come up one by one and interview him for 20 minutes or so, in one important respect Dole was less accessible than the president of the United States: During his entire campaign Dole held only two press conferences (or three, if you count the seven questions he took from four reporters at the National Association of Black Journalists convention in August). Bill Clinton had stood at a lectern and taken questions, plus follow-ups, from reporters seventeen times in that period.

So if Dole was not going to hold press conferences, being on his plane where a pearl or two might fall from his lips was not a small matter. Besides, being on the candidate's plane carried status, a status the Dole campaign had now given to only six reporters. So Washington bureau chiefs representing four of the exiled news organizations quickly sent a stinging letter of complaint to Scott Reed. "This is totally without precedent in any presidential campaign or at the White House," the letter said. "Never has a tiny group of newspapers been given such [a] huge competitive advantage over other newspapers. . . ."

And a competitive advantage did exist. "One of the reporters with a permanent seat [on Dole's plane] was able to get a friendly chat with Jack Kemp on a day that I was not able to get within 100 yards of Jack Kemp," Ceci Connolly said. "The Dole campaign was making it hard for me to do my job." At first, the favored six reporters had no responsibilities to pool their information with the rest of the press. But the howl over this grew so loud that the Dole press staff instituted a rule that all stories had to be pooled, with two exceptions: Interviews with Dole, a reasonable exception, and one that was not reasonable at all. According to Warfield, "On occasion a reporter will grab somebody and say 'I want to speak to you not as member of the pool, I want to speak to you exclusively.' And that could happen." Which made the pool system useless. The whole point of a pool is that everything must be shared. If you can opt out of the pool, the pool system becomes a sham. Which made some of the reporters who rode on the Bullship suspicious of the quality of the information they were getting from the pool. "I read a story in one newspaper filed by one of the [favored] reporters that was about how Jack Kemp was greeted on the tarmac by his former teammates on the Buffalo Bills," said Susan Feeney of *The Dallas Morning News*. "It was wonderful, evocative, full of detail. But the pool report for that event said: 'Jack Kemp was met by former teammates.' All this is unprecedented. I covered Dukakis in 1988 and Clinton in 1992, and they put the core of the national press corps on one plane. The White House rotates all reporters on *Air Force One* on a completely fair basis. The Dole campaign can't manage to do either."

The complaints eventually grew so loud and so numerous that the Dole campaign jury-rigged a solution: Five more news organizations, Copley, *The Dallas Morning News*, *The Boston Globe*, the *Houston Chronicle*, and the *St. Petersburg Times*, would rotate into two seats on Dole's plane every day, while all the other newspapers in America could rotate into three seats. But this merely added a new level of humiliation to the lives of the reporters. Every day the Bullshippers would have to line up and be told by a Dole staffer which plane they were on that day. It was like being told if you were worthy of first class or being dumped into steerage. Jill Zuckman kept an actual file marked "Indignities" so that she would never forget how she and her newspaper had been treated. Reporters so bitterly resented their treatment that they developed deep grudges against Warfield and other members of the Dole press staff. Some reporters wanted to tell Warfield off to his face. But they had trouble finding the guy.

*   *   *

W E ARE IN NASHVILLE AT THE TENNESSEE PERFORMING ARTS Center, where Bill and Hillary Clinton and Al and Tipper Gore are all onstage talking about the American family. Backstage, the White House has, as always, set up a Press Filing Center, an area where there are tables and telephones, electrical outlets and TV monitors. Most reporters sit at the tables and watch the monitors. The reporters are free to leave the filing center and go out to the theater and actually see the first and second families in person, but few bother. At event after event, the reporters see the president and his entourage only on closed-circuit TV. The old joke is true: Covering the president means never having to say you saw him.

Why do reporters stay in the filing center? Because life is good there. The White House staff makes sure of it. In the filing center, order reigns. A dozen White House staffers are on hand to service the press. At each table there is a telephone labeled with the name of the reporter's publication. Mike McCurry is available at all times, and reporters can ask him anything they want. Many reporters are on tight deadlines, and having a place to work where there is a phone and an electrical outlet for their laptop computers is far more important to what they do than seeing the president in the flesh. This means they almost never get to see audiences or talk to real voters, but so what? What do voters have to do with elections?

While there is no advance copy of the president's speech for this event, an elaborate 12-page briefing book is handed out to reporters. Then a briefer gives a long, on-the-record explanation of the details in the briefing book. Then he stays around to take questions from reporters. Throughout the day, White House press releases are constantly being handed out. Some will make news: Hillary Clinton's response to Bob Woodward's report that she visited with a "psychic" in the White House. And some will not: announcements about developments in the rail freight industry and in telecommunications policy. But no matter what the subject, someone is always available to provide an official comment and answer questions.

The next day, I travel to Philadelphia with Bob Dole, who will deliver a major speech on foreign policy. The reporters covering him charge off the press bus at the Philadelphia Marriott and race into the Press Filing Center. Entering a Dole filing center always has a certain air of suspense to it: Will there be telephones today? Will there be tables? Chairs? Electrical outlets? This, it turns out, is a semi-good day. There are tables, chairs, electrical outlets, *and* telephones, and our spirits soar until somebody tries to make a call. And finds out the telephones are not hooked up! Wires dangle uselessly from the phones. "Where do we plug these in?" a reporters asks. The Dole press staff is stumped. Who was supposed to be in charge of the phones? As the staff is trying to figure out what to do, more and more reporters come into the filing center, pick up phones, and invariably say, "Hey, the phones don't work!" Finally, the Dole staff decides it is easier just to get a bunch of hotel rooms and let the reporters make their calls from there.

Because this is a major speech, both an advanced text has been prepared for the press and a briefer has been provided. This is extremely rare on the Dole campaign. What is not rare, however, is how things go immediately wrong. The briefer—the reporters are told they cannot use his name—has assumed that the press has read Dole's speech and the briefer will be answering their questions on the finer points. In fact, however, the advanced text is not yet available to reporters, so the briefer cannot really brief. Instead, he merely tells the press what is in the speech, a useless exercise because Dole will be delivering the speech in a few moments.

Dole's speech does turn out to be a major one, but it is also very complicated. For instance, Dole once again advocates building an antimissile defense system so the United States can protect itself against the "accidental launch" of nuclear missiles by foreign countries. Dole then says he will "engage the Russians about the mutual benefits of missile defense and urge them to cooperate with us on this very critical issue." Does this mean the United States will develop an antimissile system and then give it to the Russians so they, too, can be protected from accidental missile attack? A good question, but there is nobody around to answer it. Dole takes no questions after his speeches. The briefer is gone. Nelson Warfield, the press secretary, has never shown his face in the filing center. And nobody is available to answer this question or any other.

Which is the Dole's campaign theory of dealing with the press: If you don't answer questions, reporters will be forced to print just what Dole says in his speech. Answer questions, and who knows what they will end up writing about?

Warfield feels the perfect example of this occurred in Chicago in late May. Dole, attempting to show his concern both for minorities and women, went to an elementary school on the city's largely black West Side for a roundtable discussion on battered women and abused children.

Dole recounted how he used to deal with domestic violence when he had been a county prosecutor more than 50 years earlier, but the problem now was "magnified, multiplied, whatever the word is."

Then a reporter asks him why he thought things were worse.

"I frankly think a lot of it has been the failure of the welfare system, which was apparently designed to fail," Dole says.

Asked by another reporter what welfare has to do with domestic violence, Dole replies, "Oh, it has a lot to do with domestic violence."

Which causes Berta Hinojosa, who runs a neighborhood center on family violence, to angrily reply: "You make it sound like only people who are on welfare are victims of domestic violence."

Dole is taken aback. "Well, I didn't suggest that," he begins. "I just think that is one way we can . . ."

Hinojosa interrupts him, saying, "Let me tell you I don't think that domestic violence discriminates. The only color violence knows is the color purple, the purple color that I see on my clients. I don't think that welfare is domestic violence or domestic violence is welfare."

"That's one way to address it for some people," Dole replies. "But you're right, all economic classes, whether you're white, black, whatever."

The press focused on the confrontation, but did not play the story very high. On page 14, *The Washington Post* carried the headline: DOLE SCOLDED AT CHICAGO FORUM. On page 20, *The New York Times* went with: DOLE IS CONFRONTED ON HIS VIEW OF WELFARE.

It was not a terrible event for Dole, but to Warfield and others it just proved their theory correct: You could *not* let this guy out in public. You could not let reporters ask him questions. Bob Dole had to be put in the box, and the lid had to be nailed down tight.

WHEN "BRUNO" RAN DOWN THE HALLWAY AFTER KAREN Hosler of the *Baltimore Sun* because she had gone to the bathroom by herself, even the Dole campaign knew things had gotten out of hand. The Dole filing center at the Republican National Convention was set up on the fourth floor of the Hyatt Hotel. Unfortunately, the fourth floor was also the site of some Republican National Committee staff offices. The RNC people had little love for the Dole staff and even less for his press corps. The Democratic National Committee functioned as an arm of the Clinton campaign; the White House made sure of that. But the Republican National Committee operated independently of the Dole campaign, often frustrating it and being frustrated by it. And now the Dole people had put reporters on the

RNC's floor! Why didn't they just let *homeless* people in while they were at it?

The fourth-floor filing center was only a few yards from the fourth-floor elevators. But in order to get from one to the other, reporters would have to pass through an RNC lounge, where staffers sat sprawled on couches watching TV. And this could not be allowed. Let reporters get that close to the staff, and who knows what could happen? Intermarriage, maybe. So reporters were told that they had to get off the elevators on the *fifth* floor, walk through a maze of service corridors, and use a back staircase to get down to the service entrance for the *fourth* floor. By going through the service entrance, they could get to the filing center without going through the RNC staff lounge.

To ensure that the press would actually do this, the RNC posted guards. The problem came, however, with the washrooms. The washrooms that serviced the press filing center were in the territory declared off-limits by the RNC. And the RNC insisted that every reporter who wanted to go to the bathroom had to be escorted by a guard. The guards were volunteers, many of them elderly residents of San Diego, who thought they were going to get a chance to see Bob Dole or Jack Kemp or the convention floor. Instead, all they got to see was a bunch of reporters who wanted to go potty.

Karen Hosler was not pleased with the arrangements. "There was nothing to protect! It was absurd," she said. "I was always drinking coffee and Diet Coke and had the general nervousness of deadline tension and could easily have to go to the washroom once an hour. And each time, I would have to be escorted. So you had these white-haired Republican ladies escorting me to the ladies room or these galoot photographers to the men's room. They didn't go in, but they had to wait outside and escort us back. It was absurd and demeaning." And the escorts didn't like waiting outside the washrooms. And some would pound on the doors and shout at the reporters inside, "Can you hurry *up*?"

By the second day, Hosler was well into nonviolent civil disobedience. So she just strode past the guards and went to the bathroom *by herself*. The guards could not believe it. This was lawlessness! This was anarchy! So the next day the RNC stationed a bruiser of a security guard between the press and the washrooms. He was in his late twenties, about six feet five, and weighed 250 pounds. The press nicknamed him "Bruno."

"We were tired, cranky, and sleep-deprived, and we were being treated like children," Hosler said. "We'd complain, complain, complain, and the Dole campaign's attitude was, 'Well, just try to live with this.' " After several Diet Cokes, Hosler and a confederate waited for Bruno to turn his head and then ran past him to the washrooms. "Stop!" Bruno shouted after them. "You can't run!"

Hosler ran into the ladies room before Bruno could grab her. When she was done, she poked her head out and tried to run back. But Bruno blocked her. "I am ejecting you from the hotel!" he yelled at her.

"You're a bully and a thug!" Hosler yelled back and then side-stepped him and ran back toward the filing center. (Hosler was a marathon runner; Bruno looked like he thought chocolate doughnuts were a health food.) But Bruno lumbered after her. Hosler ran into the inner press room, where Jenny Rider, one of the few members of the Dole staff that the press liked, was sitting. "Help, Jenny!" Hosler screamed. "This guy is after me."

Rider jumped up, slammed the door shut, and threw her body against it as Bruno tried to force his way in. "She has to be ejected!" Bruno kept thundering. "She has to be ejected from the hotel!"

Eventually, Rider went out and calmed Bruno down. Hosler filed her story, peeked around the door to make sure Bruno wasn't looking, and then ran for the service exit to escape. In the lobby, Hosler saw an old source of hers, who had some clout in the Republican Party. She told him her tale of bathroom terror. He went upstairs to check things out for himself, and the next day Bruno was gone. The reporters were told they could now go to the washrooms without an escort. Hosler later talked to a Dole aide who told her he had heard that the issue was resolved only after a meeting between Dole campaign manager Scott Reed and Paul Manafort, the convention chairman. Scott Reed and Paul Manafort were supposed to be worrying about how to make Bob Dole the president of the United States. Instead, they had to worry about whether they could let Karen Hosler go pee-pee on her own.

"I wouldn't even call it hostility," Hosler said about the whole affair. "They just had a certain *cluelessness.*"

WHAT THE DOLE PRESS STAFF NEVER SEEMED FULLY TO REALIZE was that they existed for a purpose. Even if they had contempt for the press (and they did) and even if the press had contempt for them (and they did), they both had a job to do. The press existed to do stories. And the Dole press staff should have existed to get the Dole message into those stories. But they didn't. While the Clinton campaign was selling its message on a daily basis, making calls to reporters, offering information and interviews, the Dole campaign simply was not available. An information gap soon developed.

"I remember it was a big week for Dole," said Rick Berke of *The New York Times*. "He was announcing his economic plan, and I was set to have the lead story in the paper that Sunday." Berke wanted to have something newsy in his Dole story, something nobody else had. So he called the Dole campaign and told them he had the lead story on the front page that Sunday and he wanted something to put in it. "Tell me what's in the economic plan," Berke said. "Tell me *something*." Reed, Buckley, and Warfield said they could not help him. Berke did his best, but admitted that he ended up with a fairly routine story.

"Now jump to a month or two later," Berke said. "It's the Sunday before the Democratic Convention and I had the same situation. I knew I had the lead story in the Sunday paper to begin Clinton's big week." So Berke called George Stephanopoulos at the White House and told him exactly what he had told the Dole people: Give me something newsy for the front page of *The New York Times*. Stephanopoulos said he would see what he could do, hung up, and called back in five minutes.

"How about if the president calls you?" Stephanopoulos said.

And five minutes after that, the President of the United States called Rick Berke and gave him an interview.

"The Dole campaign could have done the same thing," Berke said. "The Dole campaign could have delivered Dole to me. But the Dole campaign didn't even *try*."

At least Berke was lucky in one respect. The Dole campaign returned his phone calls. Many reporters were not so lucky. "Nelson is impossible [to get hold of]," Ceci Connolly said in August 1996. "On the trips, I don't lay eyes on the guy. I don't even try to call him anymore." Reporters don't like to have their calls go unreturned; it wounds their pride. But that was not the real problem for the Dole staff. The real problem was that the Dole press staff was not getting its message out. It was not doing what it existed to do.

"When I did a gender gap story in June, I called Christina Martin [the deputy press secretary] regularly for three weeks to find out what the Dole campaign was planning to do to appeal to women voters," Jodi Enda of *The Philadelphia Inquirer* said. "In that time, she faxed me a *one-paragraph* statement and a list of Republican women who were supporting Bob Dole. I printed the statement in full because I had nothing else to use from the Dole campaign, and I interviewed a number of the women. But when I called the Clinton campaign, they made five senior staff people immediately available to me who were directly involved in the gender issue."

The irony was that the gender issue was a *Dole* problem, not a *Clinton* one. But which campaign was making the greater effort to show what it was doing about it? "It was in their [Dole's] self interest to show what they were doing about the problem," Enda said. "But they didn't." And so Enda wrote: "Dole, while voicing concern about the gender gap, still seems to be grappling with how to approach it. Despite repeated requests for interviews over a period of weeks, his campaign provided no information on any plan to close the gap." The point was not that Enda zinged the Dole staff. The point was that the Dole campaign needed to communicate to voters what it was doing to address the concerns and needs of women. While Dole was running ahead of Clinton among male voters, he was far behind among female voters. And in 1992, while 53.3 million men had voted, 60.6 million women had voted. It was hard to imagine a more pressing problem for Dole or a more depressing response when a reporter called and wanted to know what Dole was doing about it. (Bill Clinton would be elected by women in 1996. While Clinton lost the male vote to Dole 44–43, he won the female vote by 54–38.)

The Dole press staff always complained that they were short of resources, and that they couldn't compete with the Clinton campaign, which had the entire resources of the White House to call upon. But that was only partly true. The Dole campaign made a botch of the resources it had. The press staff acted in old, conventional ways. While the staff took care of the "usual suspects," like *The Washington Post* and *The New York Times*, it overlooked the vast reach of newspaper chains like Knight-Ridder, which Enda represented. Knight-Ridder was the second-largest newspaper chain in the nation (after Gannett) and owned four regional powerhouse papers: *The Philadelphia Inquirer*, *The Miami Herald*, the *Detroit Free Press*, and the *San Jose Mercury News*, all of which happened to be in states important for Dole's election chances. (Dole ended up losing all of them.) The Knight-Ridder wire goes to an additional 350 to 400 newspapers. But nobody in the Dole campaign treated the calls from Knight-Ridder reporters as if they were particularly important.

On the week of July 8, Enda tried again. She began assembling a story on the effect of character on the campaign. She called the Clinton campaign, where one might expect the staff to be defensive and uncooperative on the issue. But Enda was able to get interviews with Ann Lewis, the deputy campaign manager, George Stephanopoulos, and Joe Lockhart. Enda then called Dole headquarters and was told by Christina Martin there was nobody who could really comment on the character issue but she would try to put something together. Once again, the response made no sense. Nobody at Dole headquarters could comment on the character issue? Some thought character should be Dole's *chief* issue, the one upon which Bill Clinton was the most vulnerable. Five days later, a few minutes before Enda's completed story moved on the Knight-Ridder wires, a low-level staffer at Dole headquarters called Enda and said, "Do you need somebody to talk about character?"

"I need it immediately!" Enda said. "I needed it five days ago!"

"Well," the staffer said, "you can't quote me about it, but I'll try to get you someone."

"The Clinton campaign got me Lewis, Lockhart, and Stephanopoulos!" Enda told him.

"Gosh," the staffer said.

Three days later, after Enda's story had already appeared in papers around the country, the Dole staffer called back. "Nobody will be available to comment," he said.

Enda was more disgusted than angry. "I've got news for them," she told me, "voters aren't getting their message. By treating the press badly the Dole campaign is depriving voters of important information they should have before they cast their ballots. It's not about whether I get a comfortable seat or use of a nice bathroom. It's about whether readers get enough information about the man who wants to lead them into the next century."

N ELSON WARFIELD HAD BIGGER PROBLEMS THAN REPORTERS. "When you look back on the campaign and if you had to pick the greatest frustration, the greatest anger, it is easy," he said after the election. "The remarkable lack of respect that the Dole staff had for Bob Dole. There were really disloyal comments."

It was unprecedented in modern political campaigning. In story after story, unidentified Dole staffers sniped at Dole. On September 15, Elizabeth Kolbert and Adam Nagourney of *The New York Times* wrote a story on Dole's administrative abilities. Almost all the negative comments in the piece came from Dole staff members.

"He is someone who finds it very difficult to express appreciation and whose answers to both jobs well done and jobs poorly done is usually the same: He ignores you," said a "current adviser who has daily contact" with Dole.

"He gives you a conclusion but no insight," a "campaign aide" said. "You can't guess from a prior decision how he might make a future decision."

"Mr. Dole unexpectedly delivered an attack on the popular Family

Leave and Medical Act, astonishing his aides and immediately undermining their efforts to raise his stock with female voters," the story went on. "One aide declared in a moment of frustration after this incident, 'The campaign can't predict what he is going to do. How can the American people?' "

That Dole astonished his aides was perhaps not the worst sin a candidate could commit. Dole was a man with more than five decades of political and governmental experience. His aides had little or no experience. Perhaps Dole didn't think the Family Leave and Medical Act was a good idea. Perhaps he was taking a principled, though unpopular, stand. His position was certainly subject to analysis and criticism. But Dole began to be analyzed and criticized not for his positions but for how much he pleased or displeased his staff. It was the world turned upside down. The staff existed to serve the candidate, not the other way around. And for an aide to say that the American people could not trust Bob Dole because the staff could not trust Bob Dole might be admirable candor, but it made one wonder why the aide continued to take a paycheck.

The *Times* story also stated, "Mr. Dole's campaign this year is notable for being run by political professionals who have not worked for him before, and whose fealty is not necessarily to the candidate first." No kidding. The disloyalty of the staff was staggering. And it was not coming just from low-level staffers, as Warfield and Buckley sometimes claimed in print, but from the top echelon. "We were complained to [about Dole] by a senior staff member," Nagourney said after the election. "Dole was not reading the speeches as written and, yes, [the staff member] was hoping Dole would read the story and get the message."

"Some of the people on the campaign never knew Dole or understood Dole," Warfield said. "That alienation made it easy for them to take a shot at him." Even when stories were favorable, the staff sometimes undercut them. In a *New York Times* story about Dole's appearance before the Republican National Committee on June 1, Nagourney wrote that Dole had delivered "a crisp and energetic performance, reading from a prompter, drifting only occasionally. . . ." (It was emblematic of the 1996 campaign that political stories now routinely reviewed the speaking ability of the candidates, as if political reporters were movie or drama critics.) But, Nagourney noted, Dole did wander away from his speech in an attack on Judge Harold Baer of New York, which Dole ended up bobbling. "Mr. Dole's aides, who had worked with him on the speech through this morning, shook their heads in a moment of frustration from the side of the room," Nagourney wrote.

Dole would grow justifiably angry when he read this kind of stuff.

"You ought to spend less time worrying about what I've got to say and more time worrying about the leaks from headquarters!" he would tell Nelson Warfield.

But the most extraordinary example of an aide undercutting the candidate, one that surprised both press and staff, came when a *New Yorker* reporter interviewed Scott Reed, the Dole campaign manager. Though the *New Yorker* issue was dated November 11 on its cover, it hit the newsstands *before* Election Day, a fact any experienced politico would have known. In the interview, Reed admits that Bob Dole would probably lose. "I give him the polling numbers every morning, and I give him the electoral strategy every morning," he said. "And I have told him—I tell him every morning—I say, 'It looks like we may not win.' And he says, 'You're right.' " Reed shook his head and went on. "The truth is, nothing has changed for a long time. Four or five months. We were never able to jolt the race. . . . And it's hard to jolt a race against those guys. They're very, very good."

Yes, they were very, very good. Or at least good enough to know that you don't admit defeat before a single citizen has cast a vote.

"SOME WILL SAY DOLE WAS TO BLAME FOR NOT BEING AN EF- fective executive," Warfield said. "But he was extremely ill served by those who invested his resources and didn't mount an effective campaign." Which brought up the central question: Who was to blame? Dole or his staff?

"The Dole campaign was the worst campaign in modern times," Nagourney said. "Nobody ever knew how to win the election. Nobody ever knew what was going on. And they couldn't get the *little* things right. It was symbolic. The balloons would drop in the middle of the speech. The sound system was always terrible—the last thing you want with a candidate that age is not having the sound system work." And the Dole campaign lacked what the Clinton campaign had: a maniac. Harold Ickes would plant himself one inch off your nose and scream into your face that you were a dirty rotten fucking son of a bitch if the sound system did not work. And pretty soon you made sure the sound system worked. Dole had nobody like that. Dole's people wanted to plot strategy. Nobody wanted to worry about the crappy sound system.

"Our advance team thought they were dealing with Ronald Reagan," Warfield said. "Some used to work for Reagan. And they said, 'After the speech, Dole will turn left, wave and leave.' No, he *won't.* After the speech, Dole will go right, break through the barrier, do whatever he wants, shake the hands of the people in the wheelchairs, and exit to the right. He *is* what he *is*. And if you want him to exit to the left, then you put the wheelchair people to the left, because that is where he will go." But who worried about that? Nobody. Warfield, like all those staffers who grew to genuinely like Bob Dole, faced a contradiction: The lousy campaign was not Dole's fault, but it was Dole's fault. The staff should have served him better, but Dole made it extremely difficult to be served by the staff. Communication with the candidate should have been better, but Dole was extremely difficult to communicate with.

"Dole is from the old school," Warfield said. "He would go to a town meeting in Kansas and talk to the people there. Dole was locked into that model of addressing an audience and the media that followed him back then. He thought it was an insult to treat the audience as props and talk over their heads to the camera. He thought the media would be bored if he repeated the same speech. It is hard to criticize that. What are you supposed to say? That people *are* props? It is hard to sing out in praise of cynicism."

But in the end, it was not the staff work that doomed Bob Dole. Staffs don't lose elections and they don't win them. Candidates do that. When Bill Clinton finished a speech and was done working the rope line, he would always turn to Harold Ickes or Mike McCurry and say, "Did that speech work? Did it make sense? How was the *logic*? Do you think the audience understood?" Bill Clinton sweated over the speeches. And because *he* sweated over the speeches, the staff knew *they* had to sweat over them.

Dole did not ask his staff about the speeches. He would read them or not read them and just move on. He would get on the phone and start calling people to find out what was happening in the Senate or he would ask his staff when they were flying back to Washington. The campaign reflects the candidate. If Bob Dole had cared about good advance work as much as he cared about getting home on time, the advance work would have gotten better.

Warfield would go through what many Dole staffers would go through: On important speeches, Warfield would attach a cover memo explaining to Dole the critical importance of making certain points in this speech, of delivering them as written. And Dole would tear off the cover memo and throw it away.

"If you like the speech so much, *you* give it," Dole would say.

"He was conscious of the prerogatives he had earned," Warfield said. "He had no peers. Was he really going to take the advice of people who had never been elected to anything?" Warfield could find a dozen reasons for Dole's loss: bad advance work, a shifting message, a staff that didn't get along, a bad strategy . . . whatever. "We saw what was wrong, but we couldn't fix it," Warfield said.

They could not. Nobody could fix it because nobody could fix the candidate.

"I used to be accused of trying to manage my own campaign," Dole told me aboard his campaign plane one day. "Well, as I look back on some of the things that happened in the last year, maybe I should have."

Which missed the point by a mile. Bob Dole was exactly the kind of campaigner he wanted to be and had hired exactly the kind of staff that he wanted to hire. He didn't want to change and he didn't want anybody to tell him to change. He wanted to be himself more than he wanted to be president. And in the end, he got his wish.

MR. MICROPHONE

★

"How you doin', man? Nice doggie!"
—Bill Clinton, forty-second president of the United States,
August 27, 1996

ATT STOP AFTER STOP, SPEECH AFTER SPEECH, AS THE train pulls slowly out of town, the people stand in the weeds beside the railroad tracks and wave. For mile after mile they line the broken and gullied ground. They hold up their babies and their dogs and shout their good-byes to their president. On board the train we look out at them. Behind them we see cornfields and baseball diamonds. We see back porches in need of paint, cars on cinderblocks in need of tires, worn-out neighborhoods in need of hope. All pass by like moving pictures on a screen. In one farm field, a white-haired man wearing overalls sits on his tractor and lifts his cap to the president's train. A little girl stands on the hood of a car and waves an American flag. Three young men, in shorts and tank tops, stand on a back porch around a barbecue grill and lift their beer cans to their president. And at rail crossing after rail crossing, citizens stand and applaud as the train rolls by.

The White House staff is surprised. The staff has arranged to have crowds in and near the towns—virtually all crowds are "advanced" in presidential campaigns, and great effort is expended making sure people show up for speeches—but nobody expected this. Nobody expected people to stand beside the railroad tracks for mile after mile far away from the towns. Nobody expected ordinary citizens to stand at crossroads and bridges, at overpasses and tunnels, for a chance to see a silver train carrying their golden boy.

Bill Clinton stands on an open-air platform on the back of the last train car. He speaks into a microphone that is connected to four loudspeakers on the roof. And he says, "Bye! Bye! Thank you! Thank you!" Though, because he is in full-campaign mode now, and therefore lapsing back into his soft Arkansas drawl, it comes out, "Bah! Bah! Thang-kyew! Thang-kyew!" He waves and waves at the people until the light fades and the last person is a shadow in the twilight and the train picks up speed and his staff asks him to come inside and work on the speech he will deliver at the Democratic Convention.

But Bill Clinton will not go inside. No, not even after it is dark and he can no longer see the people will he abandon his post. There are lights above him under the overhang of the train car, and he knows the people can still see him. And so he waves to the darkness because he knows somebody might be there, somebody with a baby, who will tell that baby in the years ahead how the president came to Chillicothe or Lime City or Wyandotte in the summer of 1996, and how their poppa or mama held them up to see that man. Perhaps the child will not care. But Bill Clinton cares. And so he stands and says "thang-kyew, thang-kyew" until the sound of his voice is swallowed up by the quickening *snickety-snack* of the train, and he reluctantly turns to go inside.

"We love you!"

Did he hear that? Was that someone in the darkness? They have been shouting it to him at stop after stop. Men and women both have shouted it out. It started in Huntington, West Virginia, where he began this whistle-stop campaign trip, and a man yelled out: "We love you, Bill! We love you!" The press says people are cynical, and disgusted and bored with politics. And perhaps the mass of them are. But not the people who come out to his speeches. Not the people who call out their love for him in the night. Or maybe he just imagined it. But now he can go inside. He turns for the door, but before he opens it, he reaches above him and pulls on a cord, and the long, mournful *toot-toot* of Bill Clinton's last campaign hurtles through the night.

B ILL DALEY SITS IN A TOWER AT 190 SOUTH LA SALLE IN Chicago's financial district. The reception area of the law offices of Mayer Brown & Platt, where he works, has marble floors, wood-paneled walls, and Roman arches over the doorways. It is meant to feel like a monastery library, where monks are painstakingly illuminating holy books. A sign warns all visitors this day: FRIDAY—CASUAL DAY.

In his corner office, Daley sits in a dark suit with a monogrammed white shirt with French cuffs, small gold cuff links, and a tightly knotted tie.

This is Casual Day? I say. What do you wear on Formal Day?

He shrugs. "It's easier to dress boring," he says.

Daley, the youngest son of the late mayor and brother of the current mayor of Chicago, is the cochair of the host committee of the Democratic National Convention. Which means it's his job to raise the money to pay for it. "Rich [Richard M. Daley, his brother] bid $32 million to get the convention and said, 'We are not going to spend any city money,' " Bill says, and then his heavy black eyebrows bounce. "And I said, 'Ooooo-kay.' The DNC [Democratic National Committee] came down to $26 million. And then there is state money, a little city money, corporate and in-kind donations. But the truth is, a lot of the costs are buried. It's a *very* expensive operation." Daley figures the whole thing will cost about $50 million, an amount he considers a foolish waste. "For four days!" he says. "As civic boosters, we say this is great. But why don't we just go someplace and build a *permanent* stage and stick the conventions there. We can change the podium and the colors for the Democrats and Republicans."

A nice idea, but much too practical. Conventions are not about being practical. They are extravaganzas, shows, parties. "It's all about raising dollars," Daley says. The convention is now two months away. "Tuesday night Clinton will come here to raise money," Daley says. "We have seventy-two vice chairmen who paid $100,000 apiece to be cosponsors of the convention."

What do they get for that? I ask.

"An autographed picture of Hazel O'Leary and two tickets to a Sox game," Daley says sarcastically. "We said, 'Do it for civic pride.' But they assumed that for $100,000 they get a table at the reception for Clinton."

And they don't?

"They don't," Daley says. "And they have been calling. And I have to tell them that to get a table, it will cost them another $10,000."

Because the amount of money needed is so great, and because the heads of large, rich corporations tend to be Republicans rather than Democrats, 66 of the 72 vice chairmen Daley has rounded up are Republicans. That makes this the first bipartisan Democratic convention in history, Daley says.

So how do you know you haven't rounded up Republican moles trying to destroy the Democratic convention? I ask him.

"That will be our excuse if it's a disaster," Daley says.

I N THE BAD OLD DAYS OF POLITICS, NOMINATING CONVEN-tions were moments of high drama. Votes were traded in back rooms, arms were twisted, "whips" were dispatched onto the convention floor to change minds or to keep delegates in line. Most important of all, the outcome of the convention was not known in advance. That was the purpose of the convention: to select a nominee for president. Political reform ruined all this. The candidate was no longer selected by the party bosses and backroom boys, who horse-traded their delegates. Now, a candidate was awarded delegates by winning primaries months before the convention convened. There was no longer any suspense. And so the conventions became nothing more than badly staged TV shows. It was like watching an Oscar night that lasted four days and you knew all the winners before they opened the envelopes. Politician after politician would make speech after speech that nobody in the hall or at home listened to. The delegates, some of whom took to wearing large wedges of Styrofoam cheese on their heads, wandered about aimlessly, like stunned cattle looking for someone to put them out of their misery. The major TV networks abandoned their gavel-to-gavel coverage and now carried only a few hours each night.

It was a problem for the parties. The conventions were supposed to be showcases for the candidate and the platform. And the parties worked hard to make them visually entertaining, spending millions of dollars on elaborate, multilevel podiums, giant TV screens, and balloon drops. In San Diego in mid-August, the Republicans had put on a slick, highly programmed, sanitized show (the word "abortion" was banned from the podium) that was timed to the second and designed to appeal to prime-time audiences. It was so boring that Ted Koppel and his *Nightline* crew packed up in the middle of it and went home. "This convention is more of an informercial than a news event," Koppel said. "Nothing surprising has happened. Nothing surprising is anticipated." (Koppel was *expecting* a surprise? That's why he flew to San Diego in the first place? What kind of surprise? That Dole would withdraw in favor of Elizabeth? In the news business, surprises and wishful thinking should never be confused.)

The Democrats went a different way, however. They decided to scrap their convention. Oh, they would hold one, all right. They couldn't change that. Not for a few election cycles anyway. But, except for the single night during which Bill Clinton would make his acceptance speech, the White House decided to make the Democratic Convention supremely insignificant.

So the different approaches the two parties took toward their conventions in 1996 were striking. It was like two nineteenth-century inventors, both deciding how to come up with a brighter method of illumination. The Republicans came up with a 10,000-pound candle. The Democrats came up with the lightbulb.

Screw the convention, the White House decided. Conventions were boring, and if you brought Clinton to the convention and made him sit around while it was going on, it would make him look boring too. Solution? Take Clinton *out* of the convention and put him in a setting that was as different and exciting as it was warm and fuzzy.

Which is why the White House decided to put Bill Clinton on a choo-choo.

"The convention was *such* a TV show, it was a problem," presidential adviser Rahm Emanuel said. "It was a political event that we needed to *de*politicize. So we decided to put the podium in *America*. That was the idea behind the train trip."

But it was more than that. Television producer Harry Thomason (*Designing Women* and *Evening Shade*) and film producer Mort Engleberg (*Smokey and the Bandit*) conceived of the train trip. They knew Americans made an emotional connection to trains. Trains were romantic. Trains were fun. Trains were a powerful symbol of American expansion and power. "There is something about a train that seems to represent a better time in our lives," Thomason said. But the real advantage of the train, Thomason argued to an initially skeptical White House staff, was that it would manipulate the media.

Thomason understood stars. He worked with them every day. Stars, whether they were on sitcoms or the nightly news, clawed for as much screen or airtime as they could get. So Thomason figured that if Clinton was crossing the country on a train while the Democratic Convention was going on in Chicago, the networks would have to put a top reporter in each location. And the two would fight like wildcats every night to get their story on the air. "The person on the train would want the most airtime and the person in Chicago would want the most airtime," Thomason told me, "and somewhere there would be a news editor going crazy trying to make a decision. He had a star in each place. So what could he do? He had to *expand* the time of each one to satisfy them. And I figured we got at least a third more time for our story that way."

And Thomason knew a thing or two about the Clinton story. He had saved Bill Clinton from the worst performance of his life. On July 20, 1988, at the Democratic Convention in Atlanta, Clinton made the nominating speech. It was his first big national speech, and Clinton had been allotted 20 minutes. He began: "I'm honored to be here tonight to nominate my friend Michael Dukakis for President of the United States." As David Maraniss, Clinton's biographer, would later write, "That was the rhetorical high point." The speech was so awful that at the 21-minute mark, ABC cut away to a film. NBC also gave up on Clinton. And CBS showed a delegate slashing his hand across his throat and other delegates shouting, "Get the hook, get the hook!" After 32 agonizing minutes, Clinton said, "In closing" and the delegates applauded wildly. It was a disaster. Overnight Clinton became a national joke. He was mocked on the morning TV shows, and Johnny Carson said Clinton's speech went over "about as big as the Velcro condom."

(For years afterwards, Clinton hated talking about that night. He much preferred talking about his shortest speech: He was governor of

Arkansas and was dedicating a road at the end of a rice field when a cloud of mosquitoes swarmed off the field and began biting everybody in sight. Clinton's entire speech was: "Folks, if we don't get out of here, we're all going to die. If you want to speak to me, I'll go over to that fish place and wait for you. If you'll reelect me, I'll get rid of every mosquito in this county. Thank you very much." It took 29 seconds.)

Harry Thomason and his coproducer wife, Linda Bloodworth-Thomason, realized the speech in Atlanta was no joke. A modern politician might survive a bad policy or a bad defeat or even a bad scandal. But a bad TV performance? That was serious. And, after listening to Johnny Carson mock Clinton, Linda decided that the only way to save Clinton was to put him on the *Tonight Show* and have him mock himself. Harry picked up the phone and eventually got through to Fred DeCordova, Carson's producer.

DeCordova listened patiently to Thomason, but told him Johnny's policy: No politicians.

"Then I remembered that Clinton played the saxophone," Thomason said, "and I called back and said, 'Hey, this guy is a musician and he'll come on as a musician.' " DeCordova said he'd talk to Carson. A few hours later he called back and said if Clinton would play the sax, he could come on the show. But DeCordova wanted to know if they had a deal, because Johnny wanted to announce it on the air that night while Clinton was still a national joke.

"It's a deal; Clinton will be there!" Thomason practically shouted into the phone. "And he'll play the sax!"

Thomason had no idea if Clinton would be there or if he was willing to play the sax. So Linda called Little Rock and insisted on speaking with the governor. She was told he was out running, which is what Clinton does when he is upset. But Hillary got on the phone and Linda explained the deal. Hillary thought it was a great idea, and finally Bill came back from his jog and she explained it to him. He called Harry and told him it sounded good, but he wanted to think about it and consult with his staff. He couldn't make any firm commitments until then.

And that night, just as Carson was announcing on the air that Clinton was going to be on the show, the phone rang at the Thomasons' house and it was a Clinton aide saying the governor would go on Carson, but there was no way he was going to play the saxophone. He was a public servant, not an entertainer. "You guys don't *get* it!" Thomason said. "He doesn't play sax, he's not *on* the show!" They argued, they wrangled, and finally Clinton was persuaded that to be a public servant *was* to be an entertainer. So he flew to California, where Linda had written him some self-deprecating jokes. They drove to the studio, Clinton got made up, and just as he was about to pass through the curtain and go onstage, Harry handed him a big hourglass and told him to put it on Johnny's desk for a joke.

Clinton was announced and was walking toward the curtain when a Carson staffer saw the hourglass and grabbed it out of Clinton's hand. Clinton walked out onto the set, shook Johnny's hand and sat down, and Johnny took out a big hourglass and put it on the desk and got a huge laugh. And that is when Harry Thomason knew for sure that God smiled on Bill Clinton. "Because if we hadn't been stopped, we would have killed Johnny Carson's opening joke," he said.

Clinton was funny and played the sax and dazzled everybody. And many more people watched him on Carson that night than had watched him at the Democratic Convention. After his performance, the Thomasons threw a big party for Clinton and hung up a banner that said: PRESIDENT CLINTON IN '96.

"So we were off by four years," Thomason said.

PUTTING A PRESIDENT ON A TRAIN FOR FOUR DAYS WAS GOING to be a massive undertaking. When Clinton traveled on *Air Force One,* he traveled with a dazzling array of electronic and telecommunications equipment that kept him in touch not only with the White House but also with the nation's top military command in case of nuclear attack. In addition, *Air Force One* is equipped with a full surgical theater and can handle any medical emergency. But how were they going to stick all that on a train?

Then there was the security problem. How do you protect the president as he travels along more than 500 miles of train tracks from the East Coast to Chicago and passes through thousands of street crossings? The exact route that *Air Force One* will take in the air is a closely guarded secret, shared among a very few people on a need-to-know basis. But everyone knows where the railroad tracks lead in and out of town.

In order to protect the president, the Secret Service decided that three trains would be needed: A lead train to make sure there were no bombs on the tracks (as had been done for Harry Truman in 1948), a train for the president and his staff and the press, and a follow-up train to make sure nobody was going to ram him from behind. In other words, it was going to be hellishly expensive. The Clinton campaign would pick up the purely political costs of the trip. But the huge security and other logistical costs would have to be paid by the U.S. taxpayers.

There was another problem: Clinton and Gore had done a bus trip after the 1992 convention, and the crowds had been large and enthusiastic. But what if the crowds weren't as large this time? The press would jump all over that. A huge and prolonged fight broke out among the usually unified White House staff. "Those against the trip said it was too expensive, it was old hat, Harry Truman had already done it, Bob Dole was planning on doing it, it would mess up commuter trains, nobody would watch it, and there would be no crowds," Harold Ickes, Clinton's deputy chief of staff, said. "They had 101 reasons not to do it. And the Secret Service damn near killed it."

The Secret Service works for the president and not vice versa, but it can be reckless to disregard the service's advice. And a high-ranking member of the service went to see Ickes to complain that the train trip would stretch his resources—or "assets," as the service likes to call them—too thin. He said the Secret Service was going to have three major tasks all following on the heels of one another: protect the president and others on the train, protect them at the convention, and protect them on a bus trip planned to follow the convention. It simply would require too many assets. "I wouldn't mind if you'd skip the train," the official told Ickes.

"We're doing it," Ickes said.

"But . . ." the official started to say.

"Goddamnit!" Ickes yelled. "We're going to do the train trip!"

And they did. Though Ickes did bend to pressure on one point. He wanted the trip to begin in Pennsylvania, an important swing state with 44 electoral votes. But there was a problem, again with security. When the president traveled on a multilane divided highway, the Secret Service blocked all traffic going in his direction but allowed traffic to proceed normally in the opposite direction. But on train tracks, this could not be allowed because the trains traveling in the opposite direction would pass too near the president's train. So while the president was traveling, all rail traffic near him would have to be halted in both directions.

So, yes, Clinton could start his trip in Pennsylvania, Ickes was told, but it would disrupt all rail traffic on the Eastern Seaboard. And not even Ickes wanted responsibility for those headlines. Another route was drawn up: With his train traveling mostly on freight lines, Clinton would start in West Virginia on the Sunday before the convention, dip into Kentucky, travel the length of Ohio, the width of Michigan, and pop into Indiana. From there, Clinton would leave the train (rather than disrupt all the rail traffic in the Midwest) and helicopter into Chicago on Wednesday night. Thursday night he would deliver his acceptance speech.

But even the normally sunny Joe Lockhart was worried on the day before the train trip began. Since Clinton had never actually announced for the presidency, there had been no campaign kickoff and he had done no sustained campaigning. The train would be his first real campaign trip. And nobody knew how the public would react. "I was worried that nobody would show up at the speeches," Lockhart said. "Or only two people would show up. And they would be Republicans. And the sound system wouldn't work."

But he also figured the train trip was worth the risk. There would be 15,000 credentialed members of the press in Chicago, and they would be looking for something—anything—on which to report. "In the vacuum of anything real happening at the convention, tension would be generated," Lockhart said. "The press would write about [the riots of] 1968, or about welfare reform, or about something." The train trip was a way of announcing to the press in Chicago that there was going to be no substance at the convention, and so they all could kick back and relax. The real news was going to be made by the president on the train trip while the convention was going on. This, too, was tactical.

"If we didn't give the reporters on the train some substantive news, the networks would do a story on the extra security costs of the train trip or something like that," Lockhart said. "The train trip would have been on NBC's 'Fleecing of America.' " (Though he was asked about the costs virtually every day of the trip, Mike McCurry would say only that the trip would cost "way in excess" of $750,000. Since so much of the cost involved security, and since the White House never talks about security or security costs, the true cost of what Clinton's trip cost the taxpayers has never been revealed.) So to keep reporters from reporting how much this trip might be costing, Clinton would do more than just give campaign speeches. He would announce new policy initiatives every day. The train trip would be the forum for news, and the convention would be what it had been for years: a TV show. And if nobody wanted to watch the TV show? That was fine with the White House. The only day the White House cared about was the day Clinton gave his acceptance speech. People wanted to skip the rest of it? Fine. Who could blame them? The campaign staff even joked about it.

"To build interest in the convention," Ann Lewis, the deputy campaign manager, said, "we are going to have Ed McMahon go on TV and say he's giving away a million dollars to people who are actually *watching* the convention. And our motto will be: 'You've got to watch to win!' "

A T THE BUB CITY DINER ON THE NORTH SIDE OF CHICAGO, Mayor Richard M. Daley is entertaining Democratic state chairmen. The diner has been made to look like a Texas dance hall, with plastic sawdust on the floor that, for some reason, has been colored a violent pink. While many of the guests are in Western gear, Mayor Daley is wearing a tuxedo. He is red-faced and talking volubly. "There's a Grand Canyon out there," Daley says, speaking about the improper White House use of FBI files, which the press has started calling Filegate. "He [i.e., Clinton] could fall in it anytime. A Grand Canyon. I told him months ago, get *rid* of the FBI files. They're junk. They're not reliable. Save the taxpayers money."

But how did it come up *months* ago? I ask him. How did *you* know about the FBI files months ago?

Daley doesn't answer. Instead, he starts talking about how Clinton has too many strangers around him, including Secret Service agents, who could be leaking to the press. "I was with him at a Bears game," Daley says, "and he was surrounded by Secret Service." Daley thought Clinton was overdoing it. "I said to him: 'You get a guy over there and a guy over there, and that's all you need. If you get shot at a Bears game, you *deserve* it!' "

Daley does not like being surrounded by people he doesn't know. "He asks me a private question at the Bears game," Daley says, "and I say, 'Mr. President, I can't answer you. Why? These two guys sitting here [i.e., the Secret Service agents], I don't know them. A week from now if what I say shows up in gossip columns, I've got to blame them. So I'm not talking.' And you know what? After, one of them comes up to me and says: 'Thank you.' "

Rich Daley had encouraged Clinton to run for president as early as the spring of 1991. "Bush was at 80 percent in the polls and Rich was telling Clinton to run because Bush was going to lose and Rich liked Bush a *lot*; he would go to the White House with his whole family," Bill Daley said later.

But friendship was one thing and politics was another. And Rich Daley saw the economy going in the tank and George Bush with it. Which is why Clinton was spending so much time going around the country. He always trusted the political analysis of people like Daley more than that of people who lived in Washington.

"I was sitting with CEOs at a dinner and they *hate* Bush," Rich told Clinton. "They think Bush has screwed up the economy and they want him out. Bush is going to lose. You ought to run."

There was little doubt in Clinton's mind that he would run, but he thanked Rich warmly for his advice and ended up getting Bill Daley to chair his general election campaign in Illinois in 1992. But Rich Daley never warmed to Clinton as much as Bill Daley did.

"Rich doesn't get overly enamored," Bill explained. "And Rich has tremendous negative feelings toward Washington and the bureaucracy. If a department screws up in the city, Rich figures, 'Okay, I can fix it, so why can't Clinton fix things?' And I tell him, 'Because the president runs the PR operation at the White House.' "

TRAINS ARE NOISY, DIRTY, AND HAVE WASHROOMS THAT WERE last cleaned when Ulysses S. Grant was a boy. Trains rattle, rock, roll, and sway. Their windows bear the greasy imprint of a thousand bored heads, and their seats the indentations of a thousand weary butts. Train food? Train food is to food what military music is to music.

Except when the president takes a train.

The president's train, the *21st Century Express,* is a magnificent gleaming silver stream that is 1,330 feet long and weighs 1,339 tons. There are three 4,000-horsepower locomotives pulling 11 double-decker Superliner cars and two refurbished antique cars, one used by Harry Truman and the other used by Jimmy Carter. This train is a happy train. As the reporters climb aboard in Huntington, West Virginia, they find clean, spacious cars filled with plush reclining seats that have leg and foot rests. There are electrical outlets for our laptop computers and banks of telephones so we can file our stories from the moving train. The washrooms are clean and smell of lilacs and hand lotion. The windows sparkle.

A buffet car operates constantly and serves us smoked salmon in the morning, hamburgers and cold cuts in the afternoon, steak, catfish, swordfish, and roast beef in the evening. Dessert? Name the dessert you want and Amtrak will put ice cream on it for you. You eat at your seat on a nice little pull-down tray, and almost before you can consume the last forkful an Amtrak employee appears at your side and says, "May I take that dirty tray away? May I?" Some of these employees are in suits and ties. They are executives who have come on board to make sure we are happy. And we are.

We have everything aboard this train that we need. Information? You want information? The White House has taken the seats out of an entire car and filled it with tables and fax machines and photocopiers. Every word the president utters is taped and transcribed and handed out to us, the pages still warm from the copying machine. The observation car with its floor-to-ceiling windows has been set up as a press briefing room, with plush burgundy seats bolted to the floor and facing a lectern. When no news is being committed, we nap or eat. Since food is available at all times, we find ourselves eating continually. Want an ice cream sundae with crushed Oreos on top *before* your filet mignon? Want a root beer float at 8 A.M. along *with* your eggs Benedict? Fine. Who's to say no? Let the crowds outside chant, "Four more years, four more years!" On board the Happy Train, the press chants, "Four more meals! Four more meals!"

Only once does the White House make a drastic mistake. On the first night aboard the train, a reporter goes looking for the bar car and comes back with a breathless report that spreads from car to car with the speed of the Ebola virus: No alcohol of any kind will be served during the entire Clinton train trip. A stunned silence descends on the press corps. A Clinton aide tries to explain the policy. "It's not like on a *plane*," he says. "You can't fall off a *plane*. But what if we stop along the track someplace and you guys are drunk and you fall and *hurt* yourselves?" So what if we do? As long as we don't fall on the president, what does the White House care? Within seconds, we are an angry mob. We want off the train! Where is the emergency handle? And, by the way, how much is this rotten stinking train trip costing the taxpayers? How much exactly? To the penny. We need it for our stories.

An executive committee meeting of top White House and campaign staff convenes in emergency session in one of the staff cars to discuss the liquor ban. The argument grows heated. McCurry and Lockhart are on one side and some senior White House aides are on the other. "Look, this is day *one*," Lockhart argues. "Do you really want to be around reporters on day *four* if they can't get a *drink*?"

Within minutes, the bar is opened.

"DOES THE PRESIDENT RUN THE GOVERNMENT OR DOES HE run a public relations operation at the White House?" Bill Daley is saying. "That's the question."

But Bill Daley already knows the answer. Running the government *means* running a public relations operation. Because moving blocks of voters, who will in turn move their senators and representatives, is what the White House spends a great deal of time doing. And the person who understands what it takes to move people is the person who is most likely to triumph.

Bill Clinton likes people who think like that. Because this is the way he thinks. Which is why he picked Bill Daley to secure the passage of the North American Free Trade Agreement. To many, NAFTA was a complicated agreement between the United States, Canada, and Mexico that removed trade barriers and was wildly unpopular with labor unions, some liberals, and some conservatives. To Bill Daley and Bill Clinton, it was about public relations, showmanship, and moving people.

Harry Thomason summed it up best. "TV shows and movies and political events are *all the same*," he said. "They are all designed to move people. People in Washington try to make politics some sort of deep secret, like a Masonic handshake. It's not."

NAFTA was a bad issue for the Democrats. NAFTA wasn't their baby at all. NAFTA had been negotiated by the Bush administration—most Republicans like the idea of free trade—but the treaty had yet to be approved by Congress.

While he was campaigning for president in August 1992, Clinton came to Chicago and asked Bill Daley to ride with him in the back of the limousine as he traveled to an event. "What issues are bouncing?" Clinton asked Daley.

Daley mentioned that the labor unions were upset about NAFTA and were hoping Clinton would pull out of the agreement if he defeated Bush. The unions were sure that NAFTA would mean a loss of U.S. jobs.

But Clinton liked the politics of NAFTA. He told Daley that NAFTA needed some side agreements to protect American workers, but he wanted to support it because it would show voters that he was not in labor's pockets, that he was not Walter Mondale.

"He wanted to stand up to labor," Daley said later. "He wanted to be able to say, 'I differ with you.'" Supporting NAFTA would show swing voters and Reagan Democrats that Clinton was a person who could defy special interests. NAFTA was like Sister Souljah. It showed swing voters that Bill Clinton was not bought and paid for by Democratic special interest groups.

But after Clinton got elected, his first few months in office were chaotic. There was a battle over gays in the military and a battle over his budget, which abandoned his promise of a middle-class tax cut and instead raised taxes. "It was not like he was on a big roll," Daley said. Some of Clinton's advisers wanted him to abandon NAFTA, telling him he didn't need the headache, that it had little support among

Democrats in Congress, and that Clinton would probably lose if it came to a vote.

But Clinton knew what a powerful political symbol NAFTA was and didn't want to abandon it without a fight. So in the summer of 1993, Clinton asked Bill Daley to leave Chicago and become his NAFTA czar for a few months. Daley, who had expected a cabinet position from Clinton, but who had lost out to Federico Peña for transportation secretary, should have said no. Clinton had stiffed Daley for reasons of racial balance: Clinton wanted a second Hispanic in his cabinet along with Henry Cisneros, who got the Housing and Urban Development spot.

"Everybody assumed I was going to get it," Daley told me. "But they decided there was a need for an *additional* Hispanic, so Peña got it. I wasn't going to go just for a *job*."

Did they offer you any other Cabinet posts? I asked.

"Well," he said dryly, "Secretary of State was taken."

Daley, who kept an authentic 1915 sign in his office, HELP WANTED, NO IRISH NEED APPLY, was keenly aware of how his own ethnic group was once discriminated against, and he didn't feel like suffering for somebody else's ethnic group. And Rich Daley was furious. The brothers had worked hard to carry Illinois for Clinton. So now Bill Daley faced a critical decision: Should he be a good soldier and go to Washington on what many thought would be a suicide mission or tell Clinton to shove NAFTA where he had shoved Bill's Cabinet job?

Bill decided to take the NAFTA job. He had that rarest of ambitions for a child of Richard J. Daley: He wanted to be the first Daley to leave Chicago. He wanted to play in the big leagues. He wanted to be in Washington.

Bill flew to Washington in September to begin a 10-week battle to get NAFTA through Congress. The Senate looked like it would pass NAFTA, but the House was a different story. "I tried to find a desk; I tried to find a staff," Daley said. "Everybody assumed NAFTA was a dead dog." Newt Gingrich, then House minority leader, liked NAFTA. And he told Clinton and Daley that if they could deliver 100 Democratic votes, he would deliver 119 Republican votes and NAFTA would pass. There was only one problem. Bill Daley did not have 100 Democratic votes. On Labor Day, 1993, when he started the NAFTA campaign, he had exactly 10 Democratic representatives committed to NAFTA.

So every week, Daley gave Bill Clinton a list of representatives to call, along with a list of what NAFTA would mean for their districts. And during the week, Clinton would do well with his calls. But on the weekends, the representatives would go back to their districts, where the labor unions would twist their arms in the other direction.

"I won with 51 percent of the vote last time," a member of Congress told Daley. "Labor gave me $600,000. You going to give me that? And I'm supposed to buck labor? Is the business community going to give me $600,000?"

Daley didn't have a great answer. But he told the congressman that labor unions gave money to the Democrats, but union members gave their votes to Republicans. "Labor leaders can't deliver votes anymore," Daley told the waffling congressman. Besides, after NAFTA passed, Clinton would calm down the unions and the money would continue to flow from them.

But Daley recognized the problem: Clinton's team was winning votes during the week, but losing them on the weekends. "So Clinton began having dinners at the White House on *Sunday* nights to keep the congressmen in town," Daley said. Clinton played golf with them, called in local press from their home states, and wowed them with experts. Al Gore and Cabinet members talked with newspaper columnists and editorial writers. And Gore came up with the idea of going on TV and debating Ross Perot, one the leading opponents of NAFTA.

But Clinton shocked everybody by suggesting that he ask for a joint session of Congress and then stand in the well and take questions about NAFTA as if he were conducting a giant town meeting. (Clinton had absolute faith in his ability to win over any crowd, if he could just look them in the eye and talk to them.) Both Newt Gingrich and Daley talked Clinton out of it. Gingrich, a historian by profession, warned that if Clinton held a joint session and NAFTA lost, the presidency itself could be damaged. And Daley said if Clinton did it and NAFTA won, Clinton would have to do it for every big issue.

But Clinton and Daley were in agreement on one big point: They needed a big show to kick off the NAFTA campaign and build support. A big show would impress the voters at home, and those voters could pressure their representatives. So Daley came up with the idea of assembling the living ex-presidents, who would endorse NAFTA from the White House. It would be spectacular. "Carter, Ford, and Bush each came and spoke," Daley said. "And Reagan and Nixon sent letters of support. Carter whacked Perot. Clinton gave a great speech. And the Republicans really liked this. They knew we were in the boat with them."

There had been a dinner the night before and Daley had been invited to join the historic gathering. "I walked out on the Truman balcony," Daley said, "and I said to myself, 'If my dad were only here to see me.' "

He'd probably say, "Get back to Chicago," I said.

"You're right," Daley said.

Daley also called the leaders of major corporations. "I said, 'You go to your employees and you tell them why NAFTA is good for them. They think it's a scam for you to move your factories to Mexico. You get in there; the president can't do it all. And don't have your fat ass lobbyist in Washington call congressmen. Have your *employees* go see their congressmen." Clinton toured factories and talked about NAFTA with American workers. And Daley lined up 26 Nobel Prize winners who said NAFTA sounded like a swell idea to them.

In the final vote, Daley ended up with 102 Democrats, Gingrich came through with 132 Republicans, and NAFTA passed. And Bill Daley went back to Chicago with an autographed picture of himself and the president that read: "To Bill Daley, who led the Lazarus Project, raising NAFTA from the Dead. Thanks, Bill Clinton."

Bill Daley had showed Bill Clinton his stuff. He showed him that he understood politics; he understood entertainment. And now, raising money for the Democratic Convention would show Clinton he understood money. Money was always important. Bill Daley opened his desk drawer and took out a well-thumbed eight-page list with the names of congressmen and showed it to me. "When they call and ask Rich to come out for a fund-raiser, I pull out this list and see if they voted with us on NAFTA," he said.

So his dad would have been proud after all.

On December 13, 1996, five weeks after his reelection, Bill Clinton selected Bill Daley as his secretary of commerce. Surrounded by his family, Daley said in a live, nationally broadcast ceremony, "Public service is often demeaned and denigrated in these days. I come from a family in which we were taught by word and example that there is no higher calling or greater trust." Then he fainted, tumbling from the low stage and crashing into the seated reporters. Aided by the Secret Service, he climbed to his feet. Clinton came over to him, put his hand on Daley's shoulder, and guided him to a side door where he was examined by a doctor.

"Have you ever fainted before?" the doctor asked him.

"No," Daley said, "but then I've never been named secretary of commerce before either."

*   *   *

IT IS 10:46 P.M. IN DOWNTOWN TOLEDO. A FULL MOON SHINES through hazy clouds, bathing the crowd below in a soft white light. There are 20,000 people here packed into Promenade Park along the Maumee River. Most of the people have waited for more than three hours for Clinton to appear. Except for the moon and the lights illuminating the stage, the park is in darkness. Yet the large, multiethnic, multiracial crowd waits in an atmosphere of calm. People are squashed up against one another, they are tired, but they are happy.

When Bill Clinton begins his speech, he starts, as always, with his "thang-kyews" to local officials, local heroes, local volunteers, local sports figures, and so on. The list can be very long. This night he is only about halfway through it, saying, "I want to thank Lucas County Democratic Chair Keith Wilkowski for his work on this, and I want to mention two other folks . . ." when a man in the crowd can stand it no longer and shouts: "We love you, Bill!"

Clinton looks down modestly at the lectern and gives an aw-shucks grin. Of course they love him. They would have to in order to come to downtown Toledo at night. "Toledo at night surprised me," Joe Lockhart would say later. "Downtown Toledo at night is not the safest place in the world. But they came down." (Onstage with Clinton is Democratic representative Marcy Kaptur, who basks in Clinton's glow. During the battle over NAFTA, Kaptur vigorously attacked Clinton, saying of him, "I think he's the candidate of Wall Street and not Main Street." Now, with Clinton way ahead in the polls, she is happy to share a stage with him. And the next day at a local Jeep factory, Kaptur will introduce Clinton and inadvertently set off howls of laughter by saying, "I'll get on my knees to you, Mr. President.")

Clinton now begins really belting out his speech, telling the crowd that "America is on the right track, the right track!" The crowd interrupts Clinton continually with applause and cheers, but Clinton must carefully time his speech. At 11 P.M. the giant screens in the convention hall in Chicago will light up with his live picture from Toledo and he will address the convention delegates by satellite hookup. Some technical glitch almost always screws up such ambitious plans. This night, however, the glitch is not electronic, but Christopher Reeve, who is speaking to the convention and is going long. There is no way to hurry Reeve, so presidential aide Josh King, who is crouching on the ground in Toledo in front of the lectern and listening to Reeve on his earpiece, is giving Clinton hand signals. Ten fingers for 10 minutes. Then five. Then two fingers. Then King flashes Clinton one finger. And Clinton wraps up his Toledo remarks so he can break away and greet the delegates in Chicago.

"And so we're on the right track to Chicago and to the twenty-first century. The best days of this country are still before us!" Clinton says. He glances down at Josh King, who should be signaling that he has hit the mark perfectly. But King continues to hold up one finger as Reeve continues to speak.

"Our children will do things we haven't even imagined yet!" Clinton says, vamping. "These children in this crowd tonight will have lots of jobs that haven't been invented yet if we do what we know is right!" The crowd cheers madly. Clinton glares down at Josh King. But Reeve continues to talk in Chicago and King continues to hold up one finger.

"We passed the Family and Medical Leave Act!" Clinton says. "Twelve million American families got to take some time off without losing their jobs when a baby was born." Clinton looks down at King. King looks up helplessly at Clinton. Christopher Reeve continues to talk. Clinton glares. King makes stretching motions with his hands.

"I guess what I'm trying to tell you folks is, I think my wife was right," Clinton says. "It does take a village to raise a child!" The crowd applauds.

Clinton goes on like this for 11 minutes, speaking off the top of his head. Harry Thomason, who is sitting in a control booth in Chicago watching it all, thinks Clinton is at his best when he is doing this. "Bill Clinton's rhythms are that of black and white Baptist preachers and fundamentalist preachers," Thomason said. "These rhythms are born into people in that part of country, people who are storytellers by tradition."

In Toledo, Clinton thunders on. "Are you willing to stand up and keep helping us try to move this country forward?" he asks. "Not only by passing laws in Washington, but by lifting people up in Toledo!"

The crowd is loving this and nobody notices that Clinton is just saying whatever comes into his head while glaring down every 30 seconds to where Josh King morosely continues to crouch. Finally, Reeve finishes in Chicago. King flashes Clinton a frantic thumbs-up. And Clinton says smoothly to the crowd in Toledo, "Thank you and God bless you. Thank you. Thank you. Folks—hel-*lo* Chicago! Can you hear us? This is Toledo! Thank you, Christopher Reeve!" And Clinton is on the big screen in Chicago, and everybody treats it as if it were the moon landing. The president! On the screen! All the way from Toledo! "Thank you for loving America," Clinton says. "Stay with us and we'll be there. Thank you and God bless you."

In Toledo, the crowd breaks up. But getting 20,000 people out of a small space is a lot more difficult than getting them into one: They entered the park over a period of several hours, but they are all trying to leave at once. The Secret Service, controlling all exits to the park, will let nobody out until the presidential motorcade leaves. But the national press corps, which must travel in the motorcade, is trapped inside the park, engulfed by the crowd. There is no way to get the reporters out of the park and onto their buses. Every square inch of grass and sidewalk is covered by people, patiently waiting to be released from the park.

And then a twenty-something White House aide appears, earphone in place, microphone in sleeve, elbowing her way to the pack of reporters, who are frozen where they stand, paralyzed with indecision.

"OK," she says to us in the same tone of voice that Teddy Roosevelt might have used at San Juan Hill. "Follow me!"

Then she starts to bellow the same two words over and over as if they were magic: "National press! National Press! National press!"

And the sea of people parts! As if we were really important! So we run for it, before the people wake up and realize we are mortals and not gods and they can wreak a terrible vengeance upon us.

"Go, go, go, go!" the White House aide yells at us. But about 75 yards down the path, a young man jumps in our way. "Excuse *me*," he says, spreading his arms out to stop us. Who do we think we are? If *he* can't get out of the park, *we* can't get out of the park. But a woman reporter runs up to him, head fakes him to the left, moves right, and hits him with a hip check that would have made Wayne Gretzky proud. "I don't *think* so," she says. We run after her, escaping the park, clambering aboard the buses, throwing ourselves into the seats. This cannot go on. This mixing with actual voters is more trouble than it is worth. Next time, the White House must come up with a way that we can stay on the train for the entire trip.

THE 21ST CENTURY EXPRESS WAS OUTFITTED IN CHICAGO BEfore being sent on its way to West Virginia to pick up Clinton. When they finished, workers taped two signs to the train: A huge blue one with six white stars and the words PRESIDENT CLINTON. And a small sign in a corner window that said: THE GREATEST SHOW ON EARTH. Both signs were removed. But they could have kept the small one.

In Ashland, Kentucky, the train stops by the Ohio River. A railroad bridge spans the body of water, and from it an enormous American flag hangs limply in the baking August air. A huge crowd of perhaps 50,000 people has been waiting for hours. There is no shade. Medical tents with an ample supply of water have been set up on the fringes of the crowd, but people will not give up their places to go and get water. And as Clinton finally speaks, people begin to collapse. They are standing one moment, then they stagger and fall, usually onto other members of the crowd, who go down in a jumble of flailing arms and legs. Emergency crews pick their way through the crowd with stretchers, but the body count continues to climb. The hot weather continues and in Royal Oak, Michigan, the situation gets so bad that Clinton must act as medical dispatcher. In the middle of his speech he says: "You know, in—we need a doctor over here. We've got one here. We'll get somebody here in a minute. We've got a doctor with us. We need a doctor over here in the crowd. We'll be right there. Let me say—here we go. We're getting somebody there right now. There you go. Here's my medic. He'll be right there. Done." Clinton would have to summon doctors twice more before his 30-minute speech was over. He could have shortened his speeches to get people out of the sun, but he found shortening his speeches very difficult. Harold Ickes would argue with him about it. Clinton's speeches in 1994 ran about 45 minutes to 65 minutes and would include what one senior White House aide said was "a litany, a laundry list, an eye-glazing, mind-numbing repetition of his accomplishments."

Clinton would come off the podium and Ickes would say to him, "I'm the only one still awake." By 1996, Ickes had Clinton down to about 35 minutes on average and encouraged him to talk about broad themes rather than specific accomplishments. Ickes wanted to get Clinton down to 25 minutes, but Clinton resisted and when he was tired, his speeches would get longer, not shorter. Once, after coming off the stage from a speech that was particularly long, Clinton saw Ickes scowling and said, "The first ten to twelve minutes was the *introduction*. That doesn't *count*!"

Clinton did worry constantly, however, about how his speeches sounded. "After a speech, he will come off the stage and say, 'What went wrong with the speech? What went right?' " Bill Daley said. "He asks questions from logistics to the feel of it. He asks about the setup of the stage. The sound system. He'll ask, 'Was the speech too big? Too small? How was I? I didn't think I was on. I was off.' He *never* says: 'Well, that's over. Good performance, bad performance, who cares?' "

And what do you say to him when he asks you if he did a good job? I ask.

" 'Great!' " Bill Daley replies. " 'The best I've ever heard. The *best*!' It's difficult to say it was a real dog. I am sure he has friends who do that. But I'm not one of them."

At the start of Harry Truman's train trip in 1948, his vice presidential candidate, Alben Barkley, posed with him on the rear platform. "Mow 'em down, Harry," Barkley said.

"I'm going to fight hard," Truman replied. "I'm going to give 'em hell." And so a great political phrase was born.

Bill Clinton was no phrasemaker. Even his "bridge to the future" metaphor made an impression only through relentless repetition (the kind of repetition Bob Dole refused to do), and that line was uttered first not by Clinton, but by Al Gore the night before Clinton spoke at the Democratic Convention. Clinton's speeches had no great moments. "He's not a great speaker," Harold Ickes said. "And you can't find a memorable line in his speeches. But there is a plainness of speaking that is hard to describe. You come away thinking you've understood what the president has said, and you think he has spoken to you personally."

In Arlington, Ohio, Clinton works the rope line after his speech, the sweat soaking through his shirt. A woman, about age 60, seizes him by the back of the neck and plants a kiss on his lips. Then Retta Lafaun Plott, 98, grows woozy from the heat and begins to sway. Clinton puts his arms around her to steady her. "It's been a long time since I made a girl faint," he says. Clinton begins to hand out water bottles to the crowd. He hands one to a 9-year-old boy, whose mother, Carolyn Lytle, says she will write Clinton's name on it and keep it forever. Carolyn Lytle did not vote in 1992. But she has waited for hours in the sweltering heat to hear Bill Clinton speak, and now she will vote for him.

"I didn't think I was smart enough to have an opinion," she says. "But I think he's done a great job."

In East Lansing, Michigan, Bill Clinton gets about as poetic as he ever gets. It is 11:15 P.M. when he arrives, but the large crowd has remained in the darkness. Clinton tells them he is taking a train to Chicago in order "to begin the last campaign I'll ever make, by looking into the eyes, the faces, the hearts of the people of this country for whom I have worked and fought these last four years. And you have made me happy and pleased me beyond my wildest dreams. I am proud to be an American when I look out at you and I see you."

NOBODY HAD TO TELL BILL CLINTON TO USE THE MICROPHONE on the rear platform of his train car to talk to the people who lined the tracks as he passed by. "We made sure we equipped the caboose so any time he wanted to talk to the people, he could," Thomason said. "We knew he couldn't resist."

But on the third day of the trip, after his stop in Royal Oak, Michigan, the reporters go back to the cars, some to work and some to nap and there is a hiss and crackle from the train's intercom system, and the press begins to hear the voice of the president. "Good-bah, folks. Good-bah. Thang-kyew. Hello. How are you? Hey, folks, hello. Good for you. Good to see you out there." Up until now, the reporters were unaware that Clinton had been talking to people from the moving train.

"The novelty had completely worn off the train trip, so we had to put something new in," Lockhart said later, explaining why he decided to pipe Clinton's comments up to the press car. "Just the image of him up there doing that was enough."

"How you doin', man? Nice doggie! Hi, folks," Clinton says, his voice happy and buoyant. "Thang-kyew for sayin' hello. Good to see you running out there."

Snickety-snack he travels along the rails. The light begins to fade, the sky turning from blue to black, but the president remains on his little platform, commenting on the passing scene, even on TV antennas.

"That's the biggest satellite I ever saw!" Clinton calls out into the black of night on the way to East Lansing. A pause. He sees a clump of kids at a siding.

"Nice bikes!" he shouts.

Snickety-snack.

"Hi. How are you? Nice garden. I like your dog!"

NEAR THE END OF THE TRIP, SOMEBODY POINTS OUT TO JOE Lockhart that Clinton is probably unaware that his comments are being broadcast to the reporters on the train and, hence, to the world.

So Joe Lockhart goes back and tells him that the White House press corps has heard his Mr. Microphone routine.

"Oh, that's nice," the president says idly. Then he says: "Wait a second. What did I say?"

"Uh, you said, 'Nice dog, nice bike,' " Lockhart tells him.

"Oh," says the president, "Okay."

IN CHICAGO, EVERYTHING LOOKED GOOD FOR BILL CLINTON. BUT just beneath the surface, Bill Daley knew something was going terribly wrong. The money he was being asked to raise and the money others were raising were astronomical amounts.

"There's going to be a major scandal," he told me, months before any hint of scandal reached the press. "The public is going to revolt. Fund-raising has gotten out of hand. Today, they ask for $100,000 like they used to ask for $100. It's got a smell to it that it never had. When you add up all the DNC dollars for the presidential campaign, it's $120 to 130 million. And they get mad when people say no to a request for $100,000. You give $100,000 today, you barely get to say hello to the guy. A scandal is coming."

THE DEADLY
DANCE

★

*"The modern presidency is defined by
the manipulation of the news flow
twenty-four hours a day."*

—Mike McCurry, presidential spokesman,
to author, October 3, 1996

MOST PEOPLE WATCH PRESIDENTIAL DEBATES FOR the same reason most people watch the Indy 500: to see who crashes and burns. The possibility of seeing the mighty humbled, of seeing a presidential candidate burst into flames, is entertainment in its purest form. And it has been always thus. The most famous debates in American history, the Lincoln-Douglas debates of 1858 (which were for a Senate seat, not the presidency, are praised now for their flights of intricate rhetoric and their finely honed reasoning. But that is not what people liked about them back then.

"The Lincoln-Douglas encounters were popular mostly because they were excellent theater, and not because what was said was particularly wise or revealing," debate historian Joel Swerdlow has written. And when Lincoln ran for president in 1860, he not only refused to debate, he declined to campaign at all, refusing to speak about a single issue. The American people elected him anyway, perhaps out of gratitude.

Debates in America had not begun as a way to exchange ideas, but as a way to exchange body heat: James Madison and James Monroe of Virginia were running against each other for a seat in America's first congressional election. Normally, they would have campaigned separately, but the weather was very cold and the two, old friends, decided to travel together "not to better inform the public—but to keep one another warm in the coach," Swerdlow writes.

From such humble beginnings, great TV eventually is made. And from the beginning, televised debates were remembered for their disasters rather than any substantive issues. In 1960, Richard Nixon's makeup looked lousy on TV, and Nixon lost. (It looked fine to the reporters in the TV studio, who thought Nixon had won the debate. But they soon learned that how a candidate looked on TV was what counted. Nearly 90 percent of the voting public watched one of the Nixon-Kennedy debates that year.) In 1976, Gerald Ford stumbled badly when he assured the world there was "no Soviet domination of Eastern Europe." In 1988, Dan Quayle was on his way to winning his vice presidential debate against Lloyd Bentsen when he fell into a trap by comparing himself to Jack Kennedy. The same year, Michael

Dukakis doomed whatever chances he might have had for the presidency by not showing sufficient "passion" when CNN's Bernard Shaw asked him if he would favor the death penalty for his wife's imaginary rapist and killer. ("Bernie Shaw asked him the wrong question," one Democratic consultant said afterward. "He should have asked him how he would feel if his favorite regional planner was raped and murdered.") And in 1992, George Bush had been caught impatiently looking at his wristwatch during a town meeting–style debate, which reinforced the notion that he did not care about ordinary people. That incident, however, was no accident. Bill Clinton's campaign team had ambushed him.

"We laid out the (practice) stage in grid," Harry Thomason said. "We told Bill, 'Here are where the cameras will be. So if you will take ten paces to this point, Perot will be over this shoulder and Bush will be over that shoulder.' We showed him where to go. And I mean he hit the marks *exactly*. He knew exactly where to go and which mark to be behind." This was important because by agreement the cameras could not cut away to one candidate while another candidate was talking. So Bush thought he was safe looking at his watch while Clinton was talking. What he didn't realize was that the Clinton campaign had carefully choreographed Clinton's steps on the practice grid so that either Bush or Perot would always be caught in the background. The Clinton campaign hoped to catch them with bad facial expressions (Clinton was carefully coached about and practiced his own facial expressions), but the result exceeded their wildest expectations. "We were fortunate that in one shot, they caught Bush looking at his watch," Thomason said.

It was icing on the cake. But the cake had been very carefully baked by the Clinton campaign. Showing the same maniacal attention to detail that would mark the campaign four years later, the Clinton forces even worried about the stools the three debaters would sit on. "They [Clinton, Bush, and Perot] could never agree on the height of stools," Thomason said. "But we had been rehearsing in a bar in Williamsburg [Virginia] and Rahm [Emanuel] and Harold [Ickes] had been using these stools, so I had a truck go get one and I covered it in blue upholstery and I said, 'Hey, how about these stools?' And everybody agreed." What Thomason did not reveal, however, was that the stools were oversized and that when Ross Perot sat on his, his feet would not touch the floor. "It was designed to make Perot look like a kid," a Clinton aide said. "And it worked."

By 1996 there was no pretense that debates were anything but pure theater. It was one of the few moments in modern politicking when the campaigns pulled back the curtain and told everybody they could take a look at the man back there pulling the levers and flipping the switches. The public seemed to enjoy it immensely.

Though the candidates for president had spent their lifetimes shaping and addressing issues, the public found it quite natural that these men should have to spend days or even weeks rehearsing before they could go out on stage and talk about the same issues. The candidates memorized questions and answers from huge briefing books, the better to regurgitate the answers when debate time came. And friends of the candidates would act the part of the debate opponents. (Former Maine Senator George Mitchell played Dole for Clinton and Senator Fred Thompson of Tennessee played Clinton for Dole.) The public knew in advance, in other words, that the debates were soley about performance, and that debates had nothing to do with finding out how a candidate would react as president. (Presidents don't make decisions with 30-second stopwatches running or with cameras in their faces.) And debate performance had little or nothing to do with how well a candidate actually grasped an issue. What a debate really measured is how well a candidate could demonstrate (rather than actually possess) knowledge, passion, and concern.

The public not only went along with this, the public insisted on it. There really had been nothing wrong with Michael Dukakis's reply to Bernie Shaw's question. Dukakis gave a principled response (he was against the death penalty), reflecting a long-held position that could be defended rationally. Yet the public found Dukakis's response hopelessly lacking. It wasn't emotional. It wasn't passionate. It wasn't good theater.

And no candidate could afford to make that mistake again.

THE WHITE HOUSE PRESS BRIEFING ROOM, WHICH LOOKS SO SPAcious on TV, is actually a narrow, cramped, and joyless rectangle stuffed with broadcasting equipment and sitting atop Franklin Roosevelt's old swimming pool. When a gunman sprayed the north facade of the White House with semiautomatic rifle fire in 1994, the bullets hitting the residence windows were stopped by the special glass. But the round that hit the press room window passed through easily. No president had ever seen the need for bulletproofing the press room windows.

The press room floor is covered in industrial-strength carpeting and is often strewn with old newspapers, soda cans, and bits of dried food. Rows of movie theater seats take up most of the space. Each has a folding lap table and a brass plate with the name of the reporter's news organization. On many days, some of the seats remain empty because the regular press briefing, conducted by White House spokesman Mike McCurry, is transcribed and distributed electronically. There is often little need to be there.

But any reporter with White House credentials may attend the briefings, and in October, five days before the first presidential debate, there is standing room only as a swarm of journalists crowds inside. "There's no place to sit, there's no place to *move*," Helen Thomas of UPI says. Outside, the North Lawn, which is known as the "Hair and Teeth Zone" because of the TV reporters who do their stand-ups there, is teeming with crews. Inside, a woman with a temporary pass hanging from her neck jumps up on the little stage where McCurry will soon do his briefing and stands in front of the painting of the White House that always hangs behind his head. She throws her arms out and flashes two V-for-victory signs as a man snaps her picture with a disposable camera. The regular White House reporters are aghast. It's as though a tour bus has stopped in front of the White House, let off its loony cargo, and then sped away.

Yet even on a day as frantic as this one, it is possible to wander back and poke your head in Mike McCurry's light and spacious office, one of the four offices in the White House that has a working fireplace. (The president, vice president, and chief of staff also rate one.) McCurry's door is almost always open, and the system of green, white, and red lights above his doorway that was installed during the Nixon era and was supposed to indicate whether it was safe to knock, enter, and so on, has been long abandoned (and McCurry says he doesn't know how to make them light up anyway). Such access is impossible at Dole headquarters, located in a high-rise office building across the city near Union Station, where the press most definitely is not allowed to wander into the press secretary's office.

McCurry has a healthy amount of respect for the press, but not as healthy an amount as the press has for itself. He sees the flaws in the press, especially its lack of accountability. "Wolf Blitzer can go report on the front lawn of the White House if he has a pretty good source that tells him something," McCurry says. "It may or may not be true or it may or may not be half of the story and it may be wrong five hours from now. But if it's a pretty good story and he has a pretty good source, he's free to go out and report it. Well, *I'm* not free to go out and say whatever I want to at that podium based on having one or two people sort of indicate it's a good thing. I have to take the time to line up the answer so that it's 100 percent correct. 'Cause what's fatal to a press secretary? Having only 85 percent of the answer." Some reporters would argue that McCurry often has only 85 percent of the answer (or less) but cleverly makes it seem like more. And he is extraordinarily smooth from the podium, rarely relying on notes and effortlessly moving from domestic to foreign to legislative to administrative topics.

McCurry's authoritative air comes from one chief source, however: the president. McCurry needs to be kept in the loop, needs to have direct access to the president to do his job. Which means he often has to go to Clinton and ask him about things nobody else would dare to. "I think that's why Bill Clinton considers me a necessary evil," McCurry says. "I've had to ask him about every manner of uncomfortable subject."

Can you give me some examples? I ask.

"Like medical records," he says. "There's been plenty of times I've been the one to inform him of uncomfortable information and then ask whether or not it's true." And one can imagine how difficult it was to go into the Oval Office one morning and say something like, "Mr. President, do you now have or have you ever had syphilis? Gonorrhea? Herpes? How about AIDS? And, oh, by the way, nice tie."

In August, Bob Dole had released his medical records and challenged Clinton to do the same. Clinton had already released summaries of his records after his annual physical in May, but declined to produce more than that. McCurry said releasing the full records would violate "physician-patient confidentiality" as well as "the dignity of the office of the president."

Which, to reporters, led to one inevitable question: What's he hiding?

McCurry's mistake was believing that the office of the president still *had* any dignity, or at least any dignity the press thought was worth respecting.

"Does he have a sexually transmitted disease?" Mara Liasson of National Public Radio asked McCurry.

"Good God, do you really want to raise that question?" McCurry said.

You bet she did. And so did many other reporters.

So McCurry threw together a bunch of stuff that looked more revealing than it really was. "We put together a packet that looked official," McCurry said. "People wanted to see something that said 'Medical Records' on it." So McCurry went to the president's specialists and asked them to prepare and sign a document giving the general results of their examination of the president. "And we stapled those all together with a little medical history of the president concocted by his doctor—well, not *concocted*, put *together* by his doctor to match exactly what Dole and Kemp had produced and—bingo!—we had a medical records release and that quelled the disturbance."

And now reporters had documents that said the president's medical history did not include a sexually transmitted disease, hypertension, diabetes, tuberculosis, cancer, stroke, heart disease, or AIDS.

To reporters the incident was no big deal. To McCurry it used up the president's time. (McCurry had to go and talk to him about it and get his permission to package the medical documents and have him review what was in his medical files.) The White House staff was always saying the president's time was the single most valuable asset they had and it could not be squandered. But it was also undeniable that a significant amount of the president's time was not spent on weighty matters of state, but on getting reelected. And as Election Day neared, there was often no difference between the two.

Which is why on this Tuesday, October 1, President Clinton is meeting with Israeli Prime Minister Benjamin Netanyahu, Palestinian Chairman Yassir Arafat, and Jordan's King Hussein in an attempt to defuse a dangerous situation in Israel involving the opening of an ancient tunnel in East Jerusalem that has already caused the death of 70 people.

Twenty miles outside Cleveland, Bob Dole is giving a speech at a community college.

The power of the incumbency rarely has been so clearly illuminated. Though negotiating a Mideast peace is fraught with peril, the very fact that Bill Clinton can summon the warring factions on a moment's notice to the White House is a sign of the prestige and power that go with his job. Clinton is able to look like a statesman by picking up a telephone. And Bob Dole? Bob Dole gets to do what challengers always get to do: complain.

"Photo-op foreign policy," Dole sniffs at what Clinton is attempting this day.

But when McCurry walks into the press room to brief the media on what has been occurring, it becomes apparent just how important photo ops are to this administration. They are so important that in the midst of critical and serious peace negotiations, the White House never forgets about the pictures.

Earlier Arafat and Netanyahu had gone off to the Roosevelt Room of the White House to talk privately while Clinton and King Hussein remained in the Oval Office. At some point Arafat and Netanyahu are to come to the Oval Office for a group picture, a picture of extreme importance to the White House, since no event really can be considered to have taken place unless it is captured by a camera.

But McCurry is concerned and goes up to Clinton. "Gee," McCurry says, "when the press comes in, they're going to try to get you to arrange a handshake."

Clinton recognizes the problem. If the two sworn enemies refuse the president's request for a handshake, Clinton will look powerless instead of powerful. And this cannot be allowed to happen.

So Clinton quickly dispatches Ambassador Dennis Ross, the special Mideast coordinator, to the Roosevelt Room and tells him to "take the temperature." In other words, if Netanyahu and Arafat are on opposite sides of the room glowering at each other, Clinton will know not to try to arrange a handshake for the photographers.

Ross hurries off and when he comes back he is smiling. Netanyahu and Arafat already have shaken hands like two old buddies! Ross is delighted. McCurry is delighted. Clinton is delighted.

And later the photographers are summoned to the Oval Office. McCurry waits for somebody to ask for a handshake. But, perhaps because the photojournalists actually think *history* is taking place here instead of *publicity*, nobody asks the president to arrange a grip and grin.

And so the moment is lost. But not entirely. McCurry knows many ways of getting the story he wants into the news. And so McCurry tells the handshake anecdote in great detail, ensuring its inclusion in the next day's stories.

This also encourages reporters to ask further questions about the meeting.

"What did they have for lunch?" a reporter asks McCurry.

McCurry, who can recount decades of Middle East peace negotiations without consulting a single piece of paper, must look down at his notes for this one. "Pan-roasted chicken with melange of vegetables," McCurry says. "Couscous and for dessert, carrot cake with hazelnut cream and a side of caramelized bananas."

The questions continue fast and furious until McCurry says: "One at a time. I'll stay here as long as you need me to stay." And he will. Details are what the White House wants today. They want reporters to paint word-pictures of what the Middle East leaders were doing. Such stories advance the White House agenda, bolster the president's image, and make Bob Dole look even more irrelevant by comparison. (Nobody wants to know what Bob Dole ate for lunch this day. Crow, probably.)

"What language did they all speak in?" a reporter asks.

"The king spoke in English," McCurry says. "The prime minister spoke in English. The chairman spoke in Arabic." (There are no small details, only small reporters.)

A reporter asks McCurry if the president finds it troublesome that the administration is trying to conduct an important summit while Bob Dole is sniping at it.

"No," McCurry says and then smiles. "In fact, it's probably not very much noticed."

M CCURRY DOES NOT SAY SO, BUT AT ONE POINT DURING THE delicate negotiations, Clinton excuses himself and goes to the Yellow Oval Room in the family quarters for a debate prep session. The Mideast is important; Jews and Arabs killing one another is important, but so is the debate. And one thing keeps troubling Clinton: He is sure Bob Dole is going to slice and dice him and his wife on character. Clinton has seen the polls (he sees them every day) and he knows it will be very difficult for him to lose the election this late in the campaign. But he also knows the only events that can change the outcome are the two upcoming debates. Which is why his debate negotiating team made sure all its demands were met. "As long as we agreed to Perot not being in the debates, we could get anything we wanted from Dole," George Stephanopoulos said after the campaign was over. "Format, length, everything." The single most important thing the Clinton team wanted and got was 90-minute debates rather than 60-minute debates. "In all debates there is a witching hour that comes sixty to seventy minutes into the debate," Michael Sheehan, Clinton's debate coach, said. "Every stupid mistake comes then. The Jack Kennedy line came at sixty-one minutes. Ford's line about Communist domination, the same thing. It's like the clubhouse turn where the horse falls."

The pressures on Dole were enormous. Nothing about his campaign had worked for him so far. Labor Day had come and gone and he was still way behind. The debates were his last chance. But the debates were also about performing in public, which was his weakness. "I haven't been this scared in a long time," Dole told a Connecticut radio station.

On the other hand, expectations were very low for him and high for Clinton. Dole didn't have to do great to be declared the winner of the debates, he merely had to exceed expectations.

"He is so good, if I show up, I think I win," Dole told crowds at stop after stop.

Tom Slade, chairman of the Florida Republican Party, knew showing up wouldn't quite do it, however. Dole needed to attack. "There's no such thing as political risk when you're down 15 points in the polls," Slade said. "The best chance we've got to get back in this race competitively is to step into the ring with Bill Clinton and knock him down." And even though attacks risked alienating women voters (who disliked negative campaigning much more than male voters did), a spirited Dole attack might make Bill Clinton lose his temper. One good temper tantrum by the president, the Dole camp figured, and he would not be looking so presidential anymore.

Which was exactly what the Clinton camp feared. And, once again believing Dole would do the sensible thing, the Clinton forces believed Dole would come into the debates swinging. "The preconceptions about Dole are that he's the dark, dour Darth Vader candidate," George Stephanopoulos told reporters. "In the end, when you're under the lights, you revert to form, and that's going to be what he does. He's going to come back and slash."

Bill Daley was sure of it. "The only question is how far Dole goes on character, on morality," he said.

Such as? I asked.

"Anything!" Daley said. "Some are going to Dole and saying, 'Clinton is Rosemary's baby! He's got 666 tattooed on him! I saw it in the shower! He is the Devil's baby!' And they are pushing him to use that kind of stuff in the first debate. It's that or drugs, drugs in the White House, as if the whole staff is sitting around using dope."

And Clinton believes they will go after him with this stuff?

"He believes it," Daley said firmly. "He believes they will use this stuff. About him. About Hillary. Because what else have they got?"

So Clinton was given a fine line to walk if he or Hillary were attacked. "If your integrity or the integrity of your wife is attacked, show indignation, show passion," his preppers told him. "But do *not* lose your temper."

This was so drummed into Clinton that when he got onstage for the first debate, he took out a pen and wrote on the top of his pad the advice he had been given about not letting Dole trick him into blowing his stack.

DO NOT TAKE DE-BAIT, Clinton wrote in big letters to himself. All he had to do was stay calm, and he would stay president.

THE LEAVES ARE BRIGHT RED AND GOLD AND THE AIR IS CRISP. White puffy clouds stand motionless in the blue sky, their images captured in the still water of the vast lake that borders the Chautauqua

Institution. The grounds of the 750-acre retreat look like a college campus with a grassy quadrangle and numerous halls, auditoriums, and buildings. Located in the countryside 60 miles southwest of Buffalo, the institution, its director tells the Clinton press corps, "is where people go through a personal restoration experience." Now, the senior White House, campaign, and policy staffs, plus a smattering of 1992 veterans like James Carville and Paul Begala, have come to restore the president to fighting trim. "You're not in shape for the debate," Michael Sheehan has told Clinton. "It's ninety minutes and it's not Barbara Walters and it's not a press conference and you haven't done this in four years."

About 95 reporters have also come along for the ride, even though there is almost no news. Those parts of Chautauqua where Clinton is living, eating, and rehearsing are roped off and closely guarded. News is being tightly controlled by McCurry, who is dispensing only dribs and drabs. The press is briefed every morning in a small room that contains the usual array of tables and phones. Buffet meals are served a few yards away. There is nothing to do, nothing to report. But the news beast must be fed. There is no such thing as dead air on radio or television. There is no such thing as blank space in a newspaper. When there is no real news, pseudo-news will do nicely. "He's coming in a golf cart!" somebody shouts, and the reporters scramble out the door and run to the quadrangle to see Clinton toodle by in a golf cart, driving one-handed down the narrow brick-lined street next to the quad. Earlier, a group of kids, alerted in advance to the president's route, had held up a hand-lettered sign that said, MR. PRESIDENT, WE HAVE DOUGH-NUTS. Clinton stopped, took the entire box, thanked the kids, and took off. A dozen Secret Service vans and police cars trailed him.

The reporters kicked themselves. Why hadn't they thought of doughnuts?

Mike McCurry is dressed in blue jeans and a denim shirt. This is his morning "gaggle," a term he uses for an informal briefing, which means no cameras are allowed. So McCurry doesn't care what he is dressed like. He and the rest of the staff are wearing plastic-coated credentials that say, PRESIDENT CLINTON'S DEBATE PREP STAFF. Debate prep is no longer something that must be kept in the closet.

"Can you talk a little bit about how this is working, where they are prepping, where are they doing the mock debates, what does it look like, stuff like that?" a reporter asks McCurry.

The reporters are poised, pens ready over notebooks. This is standard feed-the-beast stuff. Reporters need this to set a scene, paint a verbal picture. Usually, McCurry plays along. Not today.

"They're just up the hill at this little auditorium and they work in there," McCurry says. "He reads some briefing books and he has some Q&A and some dialogue with the people there. Nothing surprising about it."

"Is it an identical set to what was agreed to for the debate Sunday night?"

"I don't know," McCurry says, sounding irritated and bored. "It looks like a debate, you know? It's like a podium and you talk."

"Is it just like a debate with a TV set?"

"Yes. It just looks like a debate," McCurry says. "You know. Standard thing."

"Are they going to dress up in a coat and tie to, like, actually create a mood of the formal occasion, or is this casual?"

"Look," McCurry says, "this is sausage making. The sausage is Sunday. Watch it and you'll have a good idea of what it looks like."

Which is supremely unhelpful, and McCurry knows it. The reporters can't wait until Sunday. The reporters need a peek so they can do stories *for* Sunday.

The reporters start complaining. They have stories to do! Why does he think their news organizations sent them here?

"I know," McCurry says. "You want color. And I'm not giving it."

Which is the opposite of what McCurry had done for the Mideast meeting at the White House earlier in the week. So I ask him about it afterward. He provided color and background for that story, he said, because that story helped Clinton. This story does not. "Yet another story about preparing for the debate is going to get nothing done for us in terms of our political agenda or anything else," McCurry says. "So I gave them minimal details."

And you didn't want to give them details because it was useless?

"I would just prefer, you know, it's . . ." McCurry says and stops. "There is endless coverage of *process.* Endless coverage of the *mechanics* of presidential leadership or presidential campaigning. And I think, frankly, it turns Americans off. I think they're not interested in which debate coach sat where in the room and what the cameras looked like. I think they are more interested in what the overall argument is. To the degree that you build up all of the fear around this debate, you take away interest in the performance itself. You see more reported about the drama behind stage than the actual meeting of the two candidates."

Which is true, but the drama behind the stage is often so much more interesting than the debate that is held on the stage. The actual debate is so overly rehearsed and overly programmed, with the two candidates playing it as safe as possible, that all the drama has been squeezed out of it. So how the candidates prepare for the debate is often far more interesting and revealing.

But McCurry sees this as a symptom of a greater disease. "You know, it's like you want to tell the press: *it's not about us here in this room*," he says. "It's about the candidates for office. It's about their argument to the American people. It's about what the American people want to choose as a course of direction. You know, let's get over this self-*obsession*. A little more humility on the part of everybody would be much appreciated by the American people. Probably."

AT A FEW MINUTES BEFORE 10:30 A.M., BILL CLINTON STROLLS easily out of the front entrance of the stately old Athenaeum Hotel on the Chautauqua grounds and ambles down the steps. He walks down a grassy knoll, hands in pockets, and stops in front of a group of reporters. He is wearing a brown ribbed crewneck sweater over a white shirt and tie, and pleated dress pants. George Mitchell, tieless, wearing a blue V-neck sweater and chinos, stands next to him. They both bask in bright sunlight. Behind them, the white facade of the Victorian grande dame hotel glows brilliantly, the flags on its roof snapping in the breeze. To the side, the sun glints and shimmers off the lake. The timing, the light, where each man is standing, is no accident. It has been worked out to the last detail. Which is why it looks so natural. On a presidential campaign, natural doesn't just happen. Natural is planned.

"Good advance can subtly enforce things you think are true," Jim Loftus, a Clinton advance man, says. And the thing that the Clinton campaign wants us to think is true is that Bill Clinton is a man of light. Light is illuminating. Light is warm. Light is upbeat, happy, and good. Light is life. Bill Clinton is light. So Bill Clinton's silvery hair and ruddy face gleam in the sunshine this day. And at his outdoor rallies the podium is set up wherever possible so the sun will face him.

TV will carry pictures tonight of Sunny Bill at Chautauqua. TV also will carry pictures of Dark Dole in his gloomy rehearsal room in Bal Harbour, Florida. Dole is harshly illuminated by bad lighting. A shadow slashes across his face, making him look like the Phantom of the Opera. The next morning's *New York Times* will carry a truly shocking pair of pictures atop page one. In one picture Dole and Fred Thompson sit in beach chairs wearing suit jackets and deep scowls. Not a hint of sunlight illuminates their gloomy expressions. In the other picture Clinton and Mitchell are lit by bright sunshine and are smiling. They looked relaxed and happy. True, Dole has a built-in disadvantage with his dark, bushy eyebrows and deep eye sockets, but that is not the difference between the two candidates. The difference is that one candidate never worries about the picture and the other always does.

There is another difference: Though Clinton will spend parts of his days at Chautauqua golfing and strolling and holding Hillary's hand as they watch aides play touch football under the golden elms, most of the time his staff has trouble keeping him out of the debate rehearsal hall. That is where Clinton really comes alive. Various staffers will play the role of moderator Jim Lehrer in the rehearsals, until, one by one, they get tired and bored and have to be replaced. Clinton never flags. He spends hour after hour behind the lectern, practicing his technique. Bill Clinton never tires of playing Bill Clinton.

Bob Dole loathes rehearsing. Just as he would not rehearse his acceptance speech all the way through before giving it at the Republican Convention, he will not rehearse for the debate for a full 90 minutes. "I'm ready. Stop. The end," he finally says. "It's like filling up your tank with gas. It can only hold so much." And just in case his staff misses his point, he takes some pages from his briefing book and throws them over the balcony of his condo. (Dole's mood is worse than normal because of the lack of sunshine in Florida this week. He is obsessive about his dark mahogany tan, which he believes summons up the image of health. Others believe it summons up the image of melanoma.) Because Dole has complained that Clinton has him outgunned with a vast prep staff up at Chautauqua, the Dole staff makes one of its more curious decisions. To help Dole prep for his debate, they fly in George Bush. Bush jets in from Houston and goes to Dole's condo, where he sips iced tea poolside with Dole and Elizabeth. A reporter asks Bush what advice he is going to give Dole for the debate, based on Bush's own experience against Clinton in 1992.

"Well, I don't know," Bush says. "I thought I did well—but then maybe I didn't. So I don't know."

So why did the Dole campaign get George Bush? Probably because Richard Nixon was dead.

Back at Chautauqua, Clinton is joking with reporters about how well George Mitchell, playing Dole, did in the rehearsal the night before. "Senator Mitchell won last night," Clinton says, hands in pockets, rocking on his heels, head tilted back, and smiling. "Tell the truth, George. You beat me like a drum, kicked me all over the place. Tell the truth." He shakes his head, laughing. "I am badly out of shape on this, but I'm trying to get better. And I woke up this morning and sort of massaged my bruises and I'm ready to go at it again."

The reporters laugh. They assume Clinton is kidding, being modest, joshing them along. He is not. The night before, Mitchell *had* won.

MICHAEL SHEEHAN CROUCHED BY THE VIDEOTAPE MACHINE, making small notes on a pad. Bill Clinton stood on the stage, behind the lectern, beneath blazing lights, answering questions. Sometimes Sheehan noted on his pad when the president had made a good comment or a bad one, but he often made notes merely about Clinton's gestures or the expression on Clinton's face, whether his lip curled or his forehead crinkled. Or simply how Clinton stood.

George Stephanopoulos joined Sheehan at the tape machine, watching Clinton on the monitor rather than watching the live Clinton who was standing just a few yards away. How it looked on TV is what mattered, not what it looked like in real life.

Sometimes, Clinton would come down from the lectern and stand over Stephanopoulos and Sheehan and say, "Show me."

And Sheehan would roll back the tape and say, "Be careful of your reaction at the end" or "That looks good, keep that." And Clinton would nod and make a mental note.

At the second debate, which would be a town-meeting format, Clinton would be able to move around on the set a lot, and Sheehan carefully prepped Clinton to move *toward* Dole because he knew Dole would find it disconcerting, even threatening. "I wanted Dole to hear the pitter-patter of his feet," Sheehan told me later. But for the first debate, the two would remain relatively stationary. Or at least that's how Bob Dole viewed it. To Sheehan, TV presentations were almost always about movement. The movement was not always obvious to the participants, but it could have a huge effect on the viewer. "We scripted Clinton's moves in all the right places," Sheehan said. "We told him how to perch behind the lectern and how to use reaction shots."

"When he goes negative on you," Sheehan told Clinton, "have no reaction at all. None."

"Don't worry," a Clinton aide interrupted. "They can't use reaction shots. Both sides have agreed." Heads nodded around the room.

"You're all *nuts*!" Sheehan shouted. "And I'm going to *quit* if we don't practice for reaction shots *now*!" His fellow preppers were shocked. Sheehan was a mild-mannered, entertaining person. He didn't shout. But he was shouting now. Didn't they all remember how

Harry Thomason used a reaction shot to destroy George Bush in 1992? And there had been an agreement not to use reaction shots back then, too.

After they calmed Sheehan down, Clinton practiced some reaction shots for him. "You listen to Dole with a cocked ear when he attacks you," Sheehan said. "When you are attacked, just jot it down. To react to the attack is to reinforce the attack."

And even though the two men were not supposed to move about the stage, Sheehan worked out with Clinton exactly when he was to step inside the lectern and when to step outside the lectern at the first debate.

But didn't this all get very complicated? I asked Sheehan afterwards. Clinton had to worry about what he was saying, what Dole was saying, what his facial expressions should be, how to move, how to gesture. Wasn't that an awful lot to absorb?

"That's why we went through it so *much*," Sheehan said. "It was an organized, coherent, rational process. Erskine Bowles [who would later become Clinton's chief of staff] put together the meetings: There was me for style and performance. George [Stephanopoulos] and [Mark] Penn [Clinton's pollster] for substance. And then the mock debate. We'd go through it *again and again.* We'd begin late morning and early afternoon. Then he'd play golf. Then we'd do a run-through. The first night we did a full ninety-minute debate."

And, to the amazement of everyone, Clinton was not very good. Because George Mitchell turned out to be a better Bob Dole than Bob Dole ever was. "You are an embarrassment to the presidency!" Mitchell, playing Dole, thundered at Clinton. Clinton had cooked the books on Whitewater, Mitchell raged on, mishandled FBI files, and demeaned the office of president. He could not be trusted, and his wife could not be trusted.

Clinton's forehead broke out in small beads of sweat. Mitchell slammed him and slammed him and slammed him and it got so bad that Clinton broke character and turned to Sheehan. "How long are we into this?" Clinton asked, hoping the debate was almost over.

"Only forty minutes," Sheehan told him.

"You're kidding!" Clinton said. "That's all?"

After the campaign, Stephanopoulos could laugh about it. "In practice, Mitchell was Dole on steroids," he said. "He never stopped his attack. And it worked. We knew the only way for Dole to win the debates was for him to go negative. We also knew he couldn't do it." The Clinton staff felt that Dole could not possibly afford to be that venomous. It would lose him more women voters and reinforce his mean image. But the staff wanted Clinton to be prepared for the worst. And, as it turned out, they got to see Clinton at his worst.

In responding to Mitchell's attack, Clinton grew shrill and preachy and endless. He wanted to respond to every detail, wanted to explain Whitewater from day one to the present. "If you can't straighten it out in a ninety-minute press conference," Sheehan told him, "you're not going to straighten it out in sixty seconds." Clinton didn't care. He wanted vindication.

Mitchell reacted perfectly. He showed no emotion whatsoever. Which made Clinton even angrier. It was exactly what Clinton could *not* do on TV that Sunday.

After the Thursday rehearsal was all over and Clinton went back to the Athenaeum for some rest, the staff huddled. Nobody gave Clinton a win that night, which made them depressed and angry. Some had never seen Clinton fail at anything, let alone a performance. Some were genuinely afraid that if Bob Dole did the right thing, he could actually win the debate and turn the race around.

"It's Thursday night," Sheehan told them. "I don't care about Thursday night. Let's worry about *Sunday* night. Let's not rattle Clinton and give him eight hundred things to remember."

Besides, Sheehan had an ace up his sleeve. In previous debates he had helped script "zingers" for his candidates like the "You're no Jack Kennedy" line he had written for Lloyd Bentsen. Sheehan believed in zingers and sound bites. A good sound bite could win a debate. But by 1996 there had been a dramatic change in the way debates were being scored.

"Getting a good sound bite was no longer effective," Sheehan said. "And that's because the media instantly went to focus groups and asked: 'Who won?' And the people did not like negative comments. So what helped us win in '88 or '92 would lose in '96. Attacks in '96 were disdained by the audiences."

In mid-September, Sheehan had sent a memo to Clinton telling him not to go negative during the debates, to give long answers, and to be substantive, because this is what the focus groups liked. Sheehan recommended they keep the zingers to a minimum, just a few for each debate, because the interplay between candidate and the press had changed. Instead of using zingers to impress a bunch of reporters, it was now necessary to impress the focus groups that the media had assembled.

"In the deadly dance between the media and the candidate, the tempo of the song had changed," Sheehan said.

The Dole staff didn't know from tempo or dances. They knew Bob

Dole was a master of the zinger, and they decided that's how he could attack Clinton without looking mean. Dole would zing him and use a little humor to take the edge off. It would work like a charm, just like zingers had always worked in the past.

The Washington Post and NBC assembled a number of focus groups to watch the first debate, and the *Post*'s David Maraniss reported on their reaction. Maraniss concentrated on Dole's scripted zingers. In one sense, they had worked. Dole drew big laughs when, in answering a question about whether America was better off than four years ago, Dole looked at Clinton and said with a smile, "Well, *he's* better off than he was four years ago."

But Maraniss also noted that the focus groups "responded negatively almost every time Dole went on the attack, even when he was using his sarcastic form of humor to make his points."

Sheehan had been correct. The deadly dance had changed. But only one side knew the steps.

F IVE HOURS AND FIFTEEN MINUTES BEFORE THE FIRST PRESIDEN-tial debate began, Chris Dodd, cochair of the Democratic Party, walked into the press room in Hartford, Connecticut, and announced the loser.

"Dole," Dodd said. "What does he stand for?"

And so the spin began. In the vast basement of the Hartford Civic Center there were seats for 1,000 journalists. In front of the seats was a wide aisle with the professionally lettered sign SPIN ALLEY mounted above it. Spin had started out as slang, and negative slang at that. It meant a shading of the truth, a kind of personal interpretation of reality. (It may have come from the spin a good pool player can put on the cue ball or a pitcher on a baseball to achieve any kind of direction he wants.) The late Lee Atwater, a former chairman of the Republican Party, claimed to have invented spin in 1984, when after a poor performance by Ronald Reagan in a presidential debate, Atwater came out to where the reporters were sitting and told them how brilliant Reagan had been.

Since then spin had grown only in the number of practitioners, not in candor. There is nothing as utterly predictable as spin—the Democrats say the Democrat won and the Republicans say the Republican won—but spin fulfills two essential purposes: It fills stories with official "react," and it is an excuse for reporters to leave home. Consider: Reporters fly hundreds of miles, staying in expensive hotels, eating expense account meals, to watch an event on TV that they could just as easily watch from their newsrooms or at home. Reporters enjoy this—travel is fun and there is a summer camp atmosphere at these events—and the excuse to do it is spin: You can get the spin only by going to the event. Sort of. In reality, the spinners go on TV before they go into Spin Alley, and so the home audience gets the same information as the reporters and even gets it first. It is technically possible for reporters to devise questions so penetrating that they actually do get some good information from the spin, but how many reporters do so? Besides, you would have to shout it in a crowd, sharing your gem with 50 other reporters. So spin remains what it always has been: banalities disguised by bon mots, drivel masquerading as information.

While Dodd was still spinning, Haley Barbour, chairman of the Republican Party, showed up wearing industrial-strength makeup. He was asked whether Dole had to be likable during the debates. Barbour paused, as if the question had never occurred to him. "Did you know that for the last three times in a row, the employees of the Capitol voted Dole their favorite member of Congress?" Barbour said. "And I mean elevator operators, cooks, security, the little people. It would be great tonight for the American people to see him as those people do." Yes, it would. And all Dole had to do was show it to them.

A few minutes after Barbour, Mike McCurry entered Spin Alley. Unlike Dodd and Barbour, who were dressed in expensive suits, McCurry was dressed well only from the waist up because that is the only half that would show on TV. He had on a blue blazer and shirt and tie on top, but from the waist down he was in wash pants and jogging shoes.

In the debate hall, Michael Sheehan had already picked out what Clinton would wear. "He usually has two suits he's comfortable with," Sheehan said. "On the night of the debates, I'd go out on the set and hold each up against the background. The suits are both navy, but a lot of navy has gray, some has black, it's different. You have to know the difference. He would leave two or three ties out for us to pick. A little color is good. One I picked was blue with white checks. I wanted a little liveliness."

Inside the press room, McCurry, lacking a lively tie, was visibly bored. He considered spin, especially spin a few hours before the event was to take place, to be both silly and draining.

"I think he must continue to make a strong, positive case for where he wants to lead the country," McCurry said of Clinton in an almost toneless voice.

"In 1992, Bill Clinton referred to *President* Bush as *George* Bush," a reporter asked McCurry sharply. "Do you expect Bob Dole to refer to President Clinton in that manner?"

McCurry blinked slowly. "Mr. Dole will refer to Mr. Clinton however he wishes," he said.

Another reporter shoved a microphone at McCurry. "I'm from *Comedy Central*," he said.

"Then you're the only person who knows what he's doing here tonight," McCurry replied.

IN THE HOLDING ROOM BEHIND THE STAGE, BILL CLINTON WAS tense. To the three other men in the room—Sheehan, Stephanopoulos, and Mark Penn—he resembled a prizefighter who wanted to go out and begin knocking the other guy's head off.

Clinton refused to sit. The three men grouped around him.

"Let's work," Clinton said.

Sheehan began doing a light warm-up with Clinton, what Sheehan calls his "pepper drill."

"That fifteen-percent tax cut, what's wrong with it?" Sheehan asked and then he listened to Clinton's answer, watching his facial expressions, seeing how he moved.

"I just wanted a light sheen of sweat on him," Sheehan told me later.

After a few minutes, they got the signal that it was time for Clinton to go onstage.

"Let's do it," Clinton said. And then he turned and left.

As Sheehan saw his broad back receding down the hallway, once again he marveled at just how good a president, just how good a performer, Bill Clinton was.

"For me," Sheehan said, "working with Clinton is like Kazan getting to work with Brando."

IT IS 10 DAYS LATER, AND MIKE MCCURRY GETS OUT OF THE WHITE House van and walks quickly across the lush green lawns of the University of San Diego. It is the evening of the second presidential debate and McCurry is nervous. Unbeknownst to many of the reporters who joust with him daily and the millions of viewers who watch him on C-SPAN, McCurry is *always* nervous each time he must do his job in public. "I get nervous before *photo-ops*," he says. "I get nervous before *every* briefing. Margaret Tutwiler [assistant secretary for public affairs at the State Department under James Baker] once told me, 'Anytime you get ready to walk into the press briefing room and you're not scared witless, turn around and walk back, because there's something you haven't thought about. Never walk in there thinking it's going to be a piece of cake.' "

McCurry lengthens his stride, barely noticing the charming Spanish Renaissance campus of the small Catholic university. Not just cities, but now colleges, have gone nuts competing for presidential debates, believing that they will somehow yield good publicity. Some 43 universities and colleges competed for what was supposed to be the three presidential debates of 1996. Washington University at St. Louis was supposed to host the first one, having proven what lengths it would go to in 1992, when the university hosted the first presidential debate between Clinton, Bush, and Perot. Prior to the debate, Perot's campaign team complained that Perot had not been provided with a private bathroom, and the university tore up a floor to provide the necessary plumbing and quickly threw up some walls. Perot never used it. (He's the kind of guy who *always* goes before he leaves the house.) As a reward, Washington University had been granted the first debate in 1996, but the Clinton forces had no intention of allowing three debates, so St. Louis got stiffed. The university had already gone to the expense of putting together "goody" bags filled with local products to hand out to reporters. And after the debate was canceled, the university spent thousands of extra dollars to *mail* the goody bags to the press, proving this was a university that *really* understood how to get good publicity.

The press centers at each debate were paid for by Philip Morris, one of the corporate sponsors of the debates. Philip Morris dispensed meals to the reporters free of charge, plus goodies. In the past it has been gold Cross pens, calculators, lighters, and, of course, cigarettes. This year it was free disposable cameras, Oscar Meyer wiener whistles, and Toblerone chocolates. And, of course, cigarettes. Virtually every news organization in America forbids its reporters to accept anything of value as a gift, but hundreds of reporters took these goodies—deciding, apparently, they were valueless.

The University of San Diego is so pleased at being selected to host the second and final presidential debate that it has spent $1.7 million of its own money to spruce up its debate hall for the 90-minute show. That is a lot of money for an institution with only 6,380 students, but the university cannot resist the status of hosting a presidential debate. "The competition for students is so intense, you need name recognition," USD spokesperson Kate Callen says, "and we're going to get it: big time." What the hell, it's cheaper than buying a football team.

McCurry ducks through a building on the way to the press center, and Jesse Jackson steps into his path. "Can I see you, buddy?" Jackson asks softly. Jackson wants McCurry to pass along some last-minute debate tips for Clinton. Like most people, Jackson expects Dole to attack Clinton on what is loosely called "character," which includes everything from womanizing to firing the White House travel staff. Ever since the first debate, Dole has been promising to do this.

"He talks about an ethical administration," Dole had said in Kansas City on his way to San Diego for the second debate. "He does not have an ethical administration. And we're going to go after that in the debate on Wednesday night!" The crowd cheered and Dole decided to take an instant poll. "You think I was too easy on him the last time?" he asked. The crowd roared. "That's what I thought!" Dole said.

(Upon arriving in San Diego, Dole said to the crowd that greeted him: "We're very honored to be back in San Francisco." The crowd moaned. "Oh. San Diego," Dole said. "Sure.")

But Sheehan has studied Dole and doesn't think he has the heart for an all-out attack on Clinton. "He can go negative in front of a crowd of 2,000, when they are yelling for you," Sheehan says. "But up close? With just a few people? And Clinton very close to him? That is very hard." And Sheehan has made sure Clinton will be on *top* of Dole. This second debate is a town-meeting format, with Dole and Clinton on stage with 110 "nonpartisan" citizens selected by the Gallup Organization. (The Secret Service checked out the first Gallup list and found 14 nonpartisan convicted felons, heavy drug users, and serious misdemeanants, all of whom were rejected.) Clinton is a master of the town-hall format, having used it throughout his political career. And Sheehan has choreographed Clinton's moves around the stage so that he will be looming over Dole every chance he gets. Sheehan thinks Dole will not be able to keep up a sustained attack on a man who is almost on top of him.

Dole was aware of Clinton's tactics—his aides had watched tapes of Clinton in previous debates. And Dole aides said they wanted a white line painted down the middle of the stage that neither candidate would be allowed to step over. The producers of the debate pointed out to them that this would make the stage look like a tennis court. Dole aides said in that case they could forget about the white line as long as Jim Lehrer, the moderator, would interrupt the debate and admonish Clinton if he stepped too close to Dole. Lehrer refused to act as playground monitor and the Dole campaign dropped the issue.

Though the Dole aides were constantly trying to get Dole to relax, the debates had put them in a state of near panic. They were so worried about Dole's ability to deliver a memorized statement that in the debate negotiations they had demanded that opening statements be dropped.

"But the opening statements are only two minutes long," somebody pointed out to them.

"That's two minutes less that Dole has to answer questions," a Dole aide replied.

The Clinton negotiators refused to drop the opening statement, and once again the Dole side gave in.

Clinton's negotiators were far more concerned with the stage setting at the second debate, constantly calling from Albuquerque, where Clinton was doing his debate prep, and demanding the exact measurements of the stage so they could draw their practice grid and program Clinton's every step.

The only thing the Dole team really insisted on was that Elizabeth Dole be in Dole's line of sight for the entire debate in order to help Dole "relax." (Her real job was to smile, so that Dole would remember to smile.) To that end, the Dole negotiators first insisted that Elizabeth sit among the 110 questioners. They were told this was ridiculous, that the questioners had to be nonpartisan. The Dole people said their demand was "nonnegotiable." In the end, a special stand was built for Elizabeth so Dole could watch her smile throughout the debate. (A duplicate stand was built for Hillary, just to keep things even.)

The two candidates were allowed into the debate hall separately before the debate so they could get comfortable with it. Dole did a whirlwind tour and left. Clinton spent an hour walking all over the place, going into the audience seats to check sight lines and talking to the technicians. He stopped to chat with Bob Goodwin, who had been a debate negotiator for George Bush in 1988 and 1992 and was now working for the Commission on Presidential Debates.

"I really like your tie," Clinton said to Goodwin.

"You can have it," Goodwin said.

"Naw," Clinton said. "They wouldn't let me wear a really sharp tie like that."

Goodwin didn't tell him that the tie came from the Rush Limbaugh Collection.

Now it is a few minutes before airtime and Jesse Jackson wants to make sure Clinton is ready. "If they come hard on the moral issue, define what is character," Jackson tells McCurry. "Jesus says you measure character by how you treat the least of these. So you begin to measure character not by who came to the White House and got fired, but how you treat defenseless citizens. How you treat children, how you treat the poor." Jackson goes on and on. McCurry nods, listens, nods some more, says a few words, and they part. There is no way McCurry is going to pass any of this on to Clinton. But the care and feeding of Jackson is something McCurry takes seriously. "My politics are not in the same place as his in terms of the Democratic Party," McCurry says, "but my heart is where his is. He wants his concerns addressed and those of his supporters addressed."

McCurry emerges from the building and starts approaching the press building, outside of which reporters are enjoying the fine Southern California weather.

"This is CNN!" McCurry says in a basso profundo voice as he passes Wolf Blitzer.

Camera crews rush over to McCurry and soon he is surrounded. Someone sticks a boom mike with a gray furry wind-cover on it in his face. McCurry pretends to bite it. Then he pets it. "Nice microphone," he says. "Nice microphone."

"Ken Khachigian [a Dole adviser] says that the president is going down the hill on skis without ski poles," a reporter says to McCurry. "What would you say to that?"

McCurry laughs. "I have not a clue as to what that means," he says and then laughs again. "I would say Ken Khachigian is lost in the desert without water!"

"But what would you *say* to that?" the reporter persists.

"It's either true or untrue and we'll know in 21 days," McCurry says.

More and more reporters gather around him, forming a clot.

"What happened to your idea of not coming out here and spinning us?" one asks.

"That's what I'm doing," McCurry says. "I'm out here not spinning you. I really don't have anything to contribute."

"Will the president counterattack by bringing up Dole's peccadilloes?" a reporter asks.

"We'll known soon enough, won't we?" McCurry says. "Okay, see you all later, bye!"

Hurrying over to the private spin room where he will watch the debate with the other Clinton spinners, McCurry begins talking about how the press has been goading Dole into attacking.

"They want something to cover! They're bored," McCurry says. "Boredom defines the press coverage of this campaign. In politics we, of course, are judged by every word we utter every day, and it goes into the perpetual memory bank of some electronic database somewhere. The press can be entirely capricious. They can say today we *want* you to be negative and tomorrow, well now, we'll criticize you for *being* negative."

Leslie Goodman, an aide to Pete Wilson, stops McCurry in mid-stride. "All right, little known fact," she says. "Forty percent of Californians think that your president is *against* affirmative action and forty percent think he is *for* affirmative action."

"Perfect," McCurry says.

IN THE CLINTON SPIN ROOM, THERE ARE NUMEROUS ROWS OF chairs and six TV sets on rolling stands. The inevitable buffet with its cheese slices beginning to curl sits along one wall. Along with a bevy of elected officials, there is Democratic Party cochair Chris Dodd, Secretary of the Interior Bruce Babbitt, Secretary of Health and Human Services Donna Shalala, and various Clinton campaign operatives, such as Ann Lewis and Joe Lockhart.

McCurry sits in a chair against the back wall, with a phone at his side. Lockhart sits in front of him.

Even though the sixth game of the National League play-offs is on Fox, all the TV sets in the room are tuned to CNN, where Bill Schneider is saying, "Bob Dole must convince people that the election is about Bob Dole."

"Yada, yada, yada," McCurry says.

Charley Black, a former Phil Gramm adviser, now a Dole adviser, is interviewed next. "This is a battle for the undecided voters," he says. The Clinton spinners begin to laugh. *What* undecided voters? What poll is he reading? The undecided voters have *decided.*

In a few minutes the debate begins with Jim Lehrer introducing Dole for his opening statement.

"Thank you very much, Jim," Dole says. "Let me first give you a sports update. The Braves one, Cardinals nothing. Early on."

"A million television sets just changed stations, click, click, click," McCurry says, slouching in his chair. (Actually, the viewership of the debate will trounce the baseball game by better than 2–1.)

On the screen a woman named Cecily Kelly, one of the average voters selected by Gallup, asks Clinton if he is willing to send American troops to Israel or the West Bank as peacekeepers.

Clinton answers smoothly and says, "We have never been asked to send troops to the West Bank."

McCurry snaps upright in his chair. He picks up the phone. "Give me Sandy Berger," he says. Sandy Berger is Clinton's deputy national security adviser.

He waits a few moments. "It's McCurry," McCurry says into the phone. "We've never been asked to send troops? Unilaterally? Okay."

Lockhart turns around. "We okay on that?"

McCurry nods. "We can handle it." If Dole makes a mistake during the debate, it's just another mistake. If Clinton makes a mistake, it's a president who doesn't understand his own foreign policy.

The debate drones on. "Can we turn to the game?" Lockhart asks.

"Yes!" McCurry says.

The camera takes a two-shot of Dole talking and Clinton looming behind him as if he were ready to pounce on Dole and sink his teeth into his neck. The *Los Angeles Times* will run a photo the next day in full color with Dole in the foreground, a strained look on his face, gesturing with his left hand, his right hand gripping that black pen. A few feet from him is Clinton, who, having walked around his lectern, is leaning up against it, gazing at Dole with a bland and slightly bemused expression on his face. It is exactly the expression that Michael Sheehan has rehearsed with him.

McCurry toys with a bottle of Evian water, turning the cap back and forth, making scritchee-scritchee noises. "Jesus," he says, "there can't be a television set still turned to this. It takes every ounce of strength not to get up and turn the channel." He starts beating the water bottle against his chair, disturbing the hell out of people, but nobody, not even the cabinet secretaries, is going to tell Mike McCurry to knock it off. He spends a lot more time with the president than they do.

Just past the 60-minute mark and just as Sheehan had predicted, Dole makes a mistake. "We have the worst economy in a century," Dole says.

The Clinton room erupts. The worst in a century? What about the Great Depression? "That's the line!" Lockhart shouts. "That's the line!"

In response, Clinton says, "No attack ever created a job or educated a child or helped a family make ends meet. No insult ever cleaned up a toxic waste dump or helped an elderly person."

In the press room, the reporters groan. What bilge! What an obviously scripted line that Clinton has rehearsed for days. But that is the reaction of reporters. And reporters are not real people. Real people, the focus groups show, love stuff like this. They are flattered that anyone would fake so much sincerity for them.

"Baseball game!" McCurry shouts.

The debate begins to enter its last 10 minutes, and Lockhart turns his chair around and says to McCurry, "Okay, what's the spin?"

Dole and Clinton are still talking on the TV, but the spin team ignores them.

"I don't know what the fuck to say," McCurry says. "What do you say? It was a great debate? We ought to say we're proud of the president. There were good questions. It was a good debate."

"Why did Dole pull his punches?" a spinner asks, imitating a reporter.

"It wasn't working," McCurry says. "Here. Here's the line: 'The stars tonight were the audience. There were good questions.' Then, boom, we're outta here."

Lockhart is a little less eager to wrap things up so quickly. "Two points," he says. "Senator Dole clearly is disconnected when he said this was the worst economy in the century. And the most lively exchange was on the family leave bill and Medicare, and those are our issues."

"Let's be a little humble," somebody warns.

"Humility is one thing," Lockhart says. "But we've got to say we're very happy. Humility is good. But let's not be defensive."

"We ought to say Dole had some good moments," McCurry says. "He did. Let's not be overly heavy."

Behind them on the TV screen, the president of the United States is giving his closing statement, but most of the people in the room have heard it before . . . too many times.

"I just want to get *out* of here," McCurry says. "That was a snooze."

An aide comes into the room with a boxful of small plastic tops. Spinners, get it? These will be handed out to the press to show that the Clinton campaign people are so with it, so *above* it, they can make fun of spinning.

"I'm trying to think of a one-liner," McCurry says. "I don't have a one-liner."

"He tried to go negative, the president didn't take the bait, he kept it about the future. Period," Lockhart says.

"That's it," McCurry says.

Now McCurry must brief the senators, governors, cabinet secretaries, and others who will do most of the actual spinning to the press.

"Just like last time, no gloating," he tells them. "We don't want to overly brag about the president's performance. Clearly we're very proud of him, and it was a very strong night. Dole tried his negative attack and it didn't work. It was a very good night for us, but let's be a little bit humble."

Then McCurry tells them to take some of the spin tops and make fun of spin to the reporters. Not even humor is left to chance in the Clinton campaign. "Everybody agrees that spin is overdone," McCurry tells the spinners. "We thank you all; the stuff you do, especially with regional press, is very, very helpful. The national press, talk to them, but as quickly as you can, get to regional press—that's where you are likely to get more coverage."

McCurry then exits the spin room, walks a few yards outside, and plunges into the madness of the press room. Spin Alley is packed with reporters, TV crews, and spinners from both sides. It is hot, sweaty, and noisy.

"It was a very good night for both candidates, but especially for the audience," McCurry tells the reporters standing around him. "Senator Dole tried to go negative and it just didn't work. Senator Dole forgot about the Great Depression. The president clearly made strong arguments." McCurry pauses. "That's our position and we're sticking to it."

The reporters laugh.

"And I imagine the viewership on the baseball game will be real good," McCurry says.

As some reporters break away to grab other spinners, new reporters take their place. McCurry gives his spiel again and again to anyone who wants to listen: national press, regional press, underground press, Swedish radio, Italian TV.

"Who won the debate?" asks Susan Baer of the *Baltimore Sun.*

"The American people," McCurry says in a singsong voice.

"I've never heard *that* one before," Baer says with a laugh.

"I suggest we all adjourn and have some soda water," McCurry says. "Or maybe even a beer. Let's just get *out* of here."

Backstage, Bob Dole is trying to get out of here too, and go to a post-debate rally. But Clinton is still in the debate hall, talking to people, shaking their hands, and signing autographs. By the toss of a coin, Clinton had won the right to leave first, and the Secret Service had set up the two candidates' motorcades that way. So Dole was trapped. (While he stewed, Elizabeth stayed in the hall, chatting with the audience.)

On TV the three networks announce the results of their instant polls: ABC has Clinton winning 56–27, CBS has Clinton 54–26, and CNN-Gallup have Clinton winning 59–29.

The polls make no sense. In reality, Dole has given one of the better performances of his political career. He made a goof or two, but still he did well. He was loose and easy when he needed to be and forceful and direct when the situation required it. He also moved around the stage pretty well. Even if he did not win the debate, he certainly did not lose it as badly as the polls reflect.

What the polls are really showing is that Americans have already given their hearts away. Bill Clinton is warm and caring and likable. Bob Dole? Well, it was like the joke said: Maybe George Bush reminded every woman of her first husband, but Bob Dole reminded every woman of her first husband's divorce lawyer.

Eventually, Dole is allowed to leave the debate site and go to his rally.

"Did you win?" a reporter asks him there.

"No. I don't know," Dole says. "We showed up."

FINALLY, BILL CLINTON WOUND DOWN. HE STOPPED GRIPPING the hands of the audience members. He stopped signing autographs and listening to the stories. The people in the audience wanted to go home. It was getting late. And so the president let them. His aides are noticing a wistful quality to him in these last weeks. He knows that if elected he will make history—the first Democrat since Franklin Roosevelt to be reelected to the presidency. But one terrible thing will be lost to him: He will never get to run again.

As he leaves the building and heads toward the limousine, he stops for a moment. "Well," he says, "that was my last debate."

AFTER THE ELECTION WAS OVER, GEORGE STEPHANOPOULOS WAS asked why the Clinton campaign had insisted on holding the debates so late in the year, especially on the same night as an important baseball game, when millions of people would not be watching.

"We didn't *want* people watching the debates," Stephanopoulos said. "We wanted the debates to be a metaphor for the campaign. And we didn't want people to concentrate on the campaign."

In Character

★

Gingrich, Dole, and Clinton find
themselves in Oz. They go to the
Emerald City and meet the great
Wizard, who grants each a wish.
"I want a brain," says Gingrich.
"I want a heart," says Dole.
"That young lady and her dog still
around?" says Clinton.

—Popular joke, 1996

BILL CLINTON LOVED TALKING TO PEOPLE, IMPRESSING them, winning them over. He loved being the center of attention. He wanted to be the groom at every wedding and the corpse at every funeral. In 1992 his staff often could not pry him out of the back of his campaign plane where the reporters sat. He'd amble back there and talk about politics, government, sports, and history late into the night. Some reporters would actually pull blankets over their heads in an attempt to escape his chatter. He would chuckle, assuming (wrongly) that they were just joshing him.

And Clinton was friendly not just with reporters that year. He was pretty friendly with his flight attendants too. Which his aides tried to control the only way they could, since they could not control him all that much. According to Christy Zercher, a flight attendant on Clinton's plane in 1992, Clinton aide and troubleshooter Bruce Lindsey told her and the other attendants not to appear on the tarmac with Clinton when cameras were around and not to accept Clinton's invitations to work out with him at the Little Rock YMCA. (Lindsey told *The Washington Post* he does not remember this.)

Clinton once startled Zercher by hugging her and saying, "Oh, I could get lost in those blue eyes" and "You don't know what that outfit does to me." A few months after Clinton's inaugural in 1993, Lindsey called Zercher to find out if reporters had been checking into Clinton's mile-high behavior. According to Zercher, Lindsey asked, "Did you say anything to anybody? What did they want to know? Did they want to know if Clinton was flirting on the airplane?" Then, Zercher says, Lindsey told her to say "all positive things."

Clinton's aides worried that his "flirting" would get exposure in the press, but they probably didn't need to. Clinton's image had a certain element of roguishness to it. Clinton had already admitted, even if only in code, that he had committed adultery. Appearing on *60 Minutes* in January 1992, Clinton had said, "You know, I have acknowledged wrongdoing. I have acknowledged causing pain in my marriage." But unlike many in public life (Bob Dole, Phil Gramm, and Newt Gingrich, to name but a few) Clinton had stayed in his marriage. (Or, to view it another way, Hillary had not kicked him out of the marriage.)

He stayed and helped raise his kid. He had not run off and picked up some trophy wife. And in America in the nineties, he got points for that.

But once Clinton became president, nobody knew how the public would judge his flirtations. He was the president now, and a certain dignity went along with the office. Harold Ickes would talk about how Clinton's physical posture had changed when he became president, how he carried himself much more upright and had abandoned years of slouching. "He was the president now," Ickes said. "And he knew a lot of eyes were on him and a different image was expected of him."

Which made even more startling a paragraph that appeared in a story by Laura Blumenfeld in *The Washington Post* just twenty-four hours before Election Day, 1996. Blumenfeld has one of the best eyes in journalism and is known for her revealing personality profiles. And she wrote in the middle of a long story about a Clinton road trip that he was sitting onstage at Ohio State University, where "Clinton was conducting his own one-on-one campaign event with Jenny Nelson, a student representative. He nudged his right shoulder up against her left shoulder and smiled into her eyes. 'So,' he said. 'Where are you from?' "

Harmless enough. If it were Dwight Eisenhower doing the nudging. But Bill Clinton? What was *that* all about?

Then there was the story about Clinton and the gorgeous makeup woman who worked for a national TV show. She was powdering him one day before he was about to go on the air, and he looked up at her and said, "Whenever I go out of town, I get a different makeup person and people say I always look different. Say, could you travel with me? When you leave, give me your card. But give it only to *me*."

Then there was the time Clinton was chatting with Larry King about King's love life. King was almost as well known for his many romantic partners as he was for his suspenders.

"So who are you dating now?" Clinton asked King.

"Cyndy Garvey," King said.

"I admire your flexibility," said the president of the United States.

Clinton's aides did not like such behavior or such stories, but there was little they could do. They knew their president. If you spent most of your life seducing crowds, how could you not seduce an individual or two?

THOMAS JEFFERSON WAS A SEDUCER OF WOMEN, AS WAS WARREN Harding, who carried out his affairs both inside and outside the

White House. Franklin Roosevelt had a mistress while president. Eisenhower allegedly slept with his military driver, Kay Summersby. John Kennedy would crawl into the beds of female staffers, saying, "Move over, this is your president." Clinton's conduct, real or imagined, was treated in a unique fashion, however. Clinton's alleged sexual behavior was not the subject of rumor, gossip, or innuendo. It was the subject of late-night TV.

According to one poll, 40 percent of people under 30 years of age said they got information about presidential politics from late-night comedy. If that is true, then this is what they learned about Bill Clinton:

"Clinton has this race sewed up unless there is a big scandal by November," David Letterman said. "Like if he's caught in bed with his wife."

"If the election were held today between Bob Dole and Bill Clinton, it would be a dead heat," said Jay Leno. "That's because Dole acts like he's dead and Clinton acts like he's in heat."

When Bob Dole made his Citizen Dole transition and campaigned with an open shirt, Letterman said Clinton "campaigns with, what? An open fly?"

Leno said that when *Air Force One* hit an air pocket, Clinton had to return his flight attendant "to her full upright and locked position."

Listing the "Top Ten Signs President Clinton Is Well Rested," Letterman included "Feels ready to ask Paula Jones for sex again" and "Gets his pants down twice as fast."

Such jokes would have been unimaginable on TV even a few election cycles before. So why did comics feel free to make them now? Bill Maher, host of *Politically Incorrect,* blamed public taste. "If you do a joke about Clinton being fat or horny, or if you do a joke about Dole being old, people find that funny," he said. "As a comic, you have to go with that."

Well, you didn't *have* to. Tom Brokaw remembered that as a boy in South Dakota he watched his father tip his hat to Franklin D. Roosevelt when the president visited the state. Brokaw's father, a conservative Republican, told his son: "I'm not doing it for Roosevelt. I'm doing it for the office."

"You'd never see anybody doing that anymore," Brokaw said today. "I don't mean to raise politicians to sainthood level, but we're kind of all in this together. If we just constantly demean people who come into public service in the most base possible way, I don't think that's such a great idea."

On March 21, 1996, Don Imus, the radio shock jock, told milder jokes about Bill and Hillary than the ones Letterman and Leno routinely told, but Imus told his at a banquet with the Clintons sitting a few feet from him on the dais. Imus was not only widely condemned, but Mike McCurry called C-SPAN, which had broadcast the banquet live, and asked the network not to rebroadcast it. (C-SPAN refused and showed it twice more.)

In the electronic age, it was bad taste to do jokes to a president's face, but hilariously funny to broadcast them to millions of people.

But were such jokes taking a toll? On June 15, 1996, the Associated Press put out a story about a new poll on presidential character. "When respondents were asked to name the best aspect of Clinton's character, the most frequent response was that he did not have one," the AP said.

And Clinton often seemed determined to keep it that way. It has long been known that power is an aphrodisiac (how else could Henry Kissinger ever have gotten a date?) and Clinton not only had power, but he was an attractive and vigorous man. And though it was anybody's guess if Clinton was curtailing his actions after becoming president, he saw no reason to curtail his speech. In May 1996, at a fund-raiser in Connecticut, Clinton began joking about the Ice Maiden, the frozen remains of a 13-year-old girl discovered at the summit of a volcano in Peru.

"I don't know if you've seen that mummy," Clinton said. "But, you know, if I were a single man, I might ask that mummy out. That's a good-looking mummy. That mummy looks better than I do on my worst days, I'm telling you. You need to go see her." The audience laughed. "I'll hear about that before it's over," Clinton said. ("In high school, she dated Bob Dole," Senator Joseph Lieberman added. The fund-raiser, attended by 800 people, brought in $2.3 million to the Democratic Party.)

Some couldn't decide if Clinton was the Teflon president (nothing stuck to him) or the Velcro president (everything stuck to him, but it didn't seem to matter). By his own admission, however, he was the Astroturf president. In February 1994 Clinton was speaking to a group of auto workers in Shreveport, Louisiana, and began talking about the El Camino pickup truck he had in the seventies, which he called his Cowboy Cadillac.

"It was a real sort of Southern deal," Clinton said. "I had Astroturf in the back. You don't want to know why, but I did."

Clinton later appeared on Don Imus's radio show, where Imus asked him: "The bed in that old El Camino wasn't large enough to play football on, so, Mr. President, what was that Astroturf for?"

"If you wanted to put—that's the only car I had then," Clinton said. "I carried my luggage back there. It wasn't for what everybody thought it was for when I made the comment, I'll tell you that. I'm guilty of a lot of things, but I didn't ever do that. But I don't think I should disclaim it, really—just leave it out there."

"That's like saying you didn't inhale, Mr. President," Imus said. "Come on, here."

"No," Clinton said. "It's just that I didn't inhale in the back of the pickup."

Very funny stuff. Though not to Team Clinton. "I could have done without the Astroturf talk; he ain't paid to be funny," a senior White House aide told a reporter. "But it does show that while he can be as intellectual as anyone, he still can talk to Bubba or Joe Six-pack."

Clinton's sexual behavior, past, present, and future, became an inside joke. On September 14, 1996, Clinton hosted an ethnic day event at the White House, an off-the-record session with 100 leaders from various ethnic communities. When Al Gore introduced Clinton, he told a story about how the founder of a college came back to give the commencement speech, collapsed, and died.

"So I cannot be considered the stiffest speaker ever," Gore joked.

Then Clinton got up and said, "For obvious reasons, I don't think I could have gotten away with that joke."

The crowd hesitated and then roared.

ACCORDING TO PRESIDENTIAL HISTORIAN GIL TROY, "SINCE THE turn of the century, politicians and journalists had shied away from publicly discussing candidates' private lives." But that changed when presidential candidates became "personalities" and people wanted to know much more about them. The rise in popularity of Freudian psychology, Troy argues, also caused a change because now people "scrutinized candidates more carefully, assuming that everything counted, that the smallest of incidents could reveal the man."

After Watergate and the ignominious resignation of Richard Nixon, the press decided it had been too easy on presidential candidates, and news organizations decided they should pay far more attention to the character of the people running and holding high office, which meant closely examining their personal as well as their public lives. The paradox was, however, that Nixon's personal life contained no real scandals. He was honest at home, but dishonest in the Oval Office. There were never rumors about Jimmy Carter fooling around (except in his heart), but such rectitude did not make him a particularly effective president. Yet, with the rise of personality journalism, magazines like

People, and tabloid TV shows, the concentration on the personal life of presidential candidates increased. (The public had always been interested in the personal lives of entertainers, and weren't presidential candidates just entertainers in bad suits?) When Jesse Jackson ran for president in 1988, his wife dealt with rumors of his sexual escapades in a unique way. "I don't believe in examining the sheets," she told reporters. "If my husband has committed adultery, he better not tell me. And you better not go digging into it, because I'm trying to raise a family and won't let you be the one to destroy my family."

The role of the spouse became paramount if infidelity surfaced in the candidate's background. If the spouse accepted what the wayward partner had done, then to many Americans there was, to use a basketball term, "no harm, no foul." (Gary Hart's wife was conspicuously absent at his press conference in 1988 following revelations about his infidelity. Had she been there, reporters might have been too intimidated to ask Hart if he had ever committed adultery.) Further, in the last years of the 20th century, adultery was no longer the third rail it once was. Like divorce, adultery was now survivable for a presidential candidate. If there was anything Americans liked better than a good story about corruption, it was a good story about redemption. Candidates who sinned, admitted weakness, and begged the public for forgiveness could be more popular than their sinless opponents. Some voters liked the sinner *more* than the saint. They could identify with the sinner, while they wondered what the saint was hiding.

And when a tabloid story accusing Bill Clinton of having had a long-term love affair with Gennifer Flowers broke during the New Hampshire primary in 1992, Clinton and his staff knew exactly what to do. Harry Thomason remembers getting a call late one night. Thomason was in California, and Mickey Kantor, the Clinton campaign chairman, was calling from New Hampshire. "Bill is in trouble," Kantor said. That's all Thomason needed to hear. He put down the phone, picked it up again, called the airport, and told them to gas up his private jet.

"And at eleven at night we climbed into a plane, and flew to Manchester [New Hampshire]," Thomason said. "It was zero and snowing. It was the first time I had ever met Harold [Ickes]. His hair was askew and his blue eyes were flashing and I said to myself, 'This is a crazy man.' "

But Ickes was a crazy man who understood sin and redemption. And he, Thomason, Kantor, Rahm Emanuel, and a few others sat down and worked out the strategy. Thomason, an Arkansan, struck the perfect note. "It's not just Bill," he said. "The pride of the whole state is on the line." So he made some calls, and busloads of "Arkansas Travelers" started heading north to New Hampshire, where Bill Clinton's friends would literally go door to door telling voters what a fine person Bill was.

And then, inevitably, came what Bill did best: the performance. The group decided Clinton should use his strongest format, the town meeting. "Frank Greer [a Clinton media adviser] and I went searching and found a PBS station out in middle of the wilderness," Thomason said. "It looked pretty horrible. So I went out and bought some carpet and some staplers, and we went onto the set and started stapling." The idea was to stick Clinton down in the middle of the carpeting, surround him with New Hampshire voters, and let them ask anything they wanted on live TV. Not everybody in the campaign was wild about the idea. There was no way to control the event. But that was the point. When Clinton got near the people in the audience and eye-locked them and answered their questions and made their hostility and their hearts melt, then the hostility and hearts of the people watching would melt, too. "He got a couple of tough questions," Thomason said. "But Frank and I were *praying* for tough questions. He did so well, we were ecstatic." Clinton adopted a simple line, one that New Hampshire voters found refreshing. "If you want a perfect candidate," he said, "vote for somebody else."

But now in 1996 Clinton was president. And after more than three years in office, rumors about his infidelity had not diminished, they had grown. There were accusations that he had used Arkansas state troopers to provide him with women, and Paula Jones was accusing him of exposing himself to her in a hotel room. Yet the public did not seem overly concerned.

"At some fundamental level, the race *was* about character," Mike McCurry told me after the election. "The American voters decided to put aside doubts about Clinton personally because of the job he had done: The economy was good, he had managed the nation's affairs well, and there was peace and prosperity. And so he had his contract renewed."

Though nobody was really sure that would happen until after June 1996. June was the nightmare month for Clinton. He was forced to apologize for improperly obtaining FBI files on prominent Republicans. The Republican majority on Al D'Amato's Senate Whitewater committee concluded that the Clintons had "committed misdeeds and—in some cases—possible crimes of grave proportions." Bruce Lindsey was named an unindicted coconspirator in the trial of two Arkansas bankers. Paula Jones's accusations were revived on the nation's front pages when the Supreme Court delayed her suit until after the election. Ex-FBI agent Gary Aldrich published a book alleging that Clinton left the White House regularly under a blanket in the backseat of a dark sedan driven by Lindsey and was taken to the J.W. Marriott Hotel, where he had trysts with an unidentified woman, possibly a "celebrity."

At the end of the month, the Clinton team looked carefully at their popularity polls. And were delighted. "We came out of the month *with no change*," Stephanopoulos said. "We *won* the month."

It was not as if people were endorsing immorality. Undoubtedly, some did not believe the accusations against Clinton, and Aldrich admitted he had no proof for the Marriott story. Others felt that *all* politicians were immoral and Clinton was no worse than the rest of them. And others felt that as long as Clinton was doing a good job in his public life, who cared what he did in his personal life? A Pew Research Center poll asked people to choose words to describe Clinton's personal image. The results were: "Good, wishy-washy, okay, dishonest, liar, fair, trying, intelligent, slick, great, honest, crook, leader, two-faced."

In other words, Clinton was whatever you wanted him to be.

The late Mayor Richard J. Daley of Chicago was famous for demanding marital fidelity from his underlings. Fooling around with a few ballot boxes here and there was one thing, but fooling around on your spouse was another. His youngest son, Bill Daley, was now Clinton's golf partner and pal, and was putting together the Democratic Convention for him. "My mother will soon be ninety," Bill Daley said and knocked on his wooden desk, "and is in good health. Older people are not as tolerant as younger people, but she thinks all this stuff about Clinton is all a smear. 'They did this to Kennedy,' she says. Her support for Clinton never wavered, never, even through Gennifer Flowers. She feels if you're married twenty-five years, you have your ups and downs. They're still together and raising a wonderful daughter. And people are saying, 'Okay, just give it a break.' "

The Dole camp recognized the problem: Clinton was not going to lose the election; they were going to have to win it. "If character had been a driving issue in the campaign, we would have been twenty points ahead," Tony Fabrizio, Dole's pollster, said. "People were picking issues over character two-to-one."

It was even worse than that for Dole. *The Washington Post* and ABC News took a poll that showed 77 percent of the voters thought it was more important to have a president "who understands the problems of people like you" while just 22 percent said it was more important to have a president of "the highest moral character."

And if there ever was a "people like you" president, it was Bill Clinton.

DOLE WAS BLINDED BY HIS OWN ASSESSMENT OF CLINTON AS an immoral, inadequate, political playboy, someone who had not come up the hard way like Dole had but had led a privileged life leading to overly swift advancement (Georgetown, Yale, Oxford, Arkansas attorney general, Arkansas governor, president of the United States.)

Dole (in his public life, anyway) lived by trust. When you gave your word to a colleague, you honored it or risked condemnation and ostracism by the other members of the private club known as the U.S. Senate. Clinton? He'd say one thing about the draft one day, one thing about smoking pot, one thing about womanizing, and then change it. The man had no foundation. He was a chameleon who would turn plaid if you put him down on a plaid rock.

Which is why Dole could not understand how anybody could like or trust the guy. So when Dole was addressing about 400 people on April 15 in Havertown, Pennsylvania, a suburb of Philadelphia, he decided to try out one more reason why people should vote for him over Clinton.

"If something happened along the route and you had to leave your children with Bob Dole or Bill Clinton, I think you'd probably leave your children with Bob Dole," Dole said. (Right. You'd leave your kids with a 73-year-old guy who would be dozing on the couch by 10 P.M. while your kids were setting the house on fire.)

But there was a subtext to Dole's statement. He was trying to imply something. Why wouldn't you leave your kids with Bill Clinton? Would Clinton abuse them? Smoke pot with them? Teach them to be draft resisters? What was Dole really trying to say?

Dole's comment, which he made off the cuff, was reported but did not cause a stir until Dan Balz of *The Washington Post* picked up the challenge. "Not since Gary Hart encouraged reporters to follow him around has a presidential candidate thrown out such an inviting idea," Balz wrote. The *Post* did a survey of 1,011 adults and found that 52 percent said they preferred to leave their children with Clinton and 27 percent said they'd leave them with Dole.

When Dole was asked where he got the notion that people actually wanted to entrust their kids to him, he said, "It's what a couple of people have told me who had focus groups. I'm just repeating what focus groups said—liberals, men, women, Democrats, Republicans, conservatives."

As usual, Dole's staff immediately sold him out. Unidentified

"Dole campaign officials" told Balz "the focus group findings didn't come from them," and the findings, such as they were, had been passed on to Dole "in a casual conversation."

"I don't think he was ever encouraged to talk about it," a Dole official said.

Translation: The old coot strayed out of the box and screwed up once again.

But now Dole's baby-sitting challenge became a big national story and it was hurting Dole, not Clinton. Stories recounted how Dole saw so little of his daughter, Robin, when she was growing up that when Robin wanted to get her ears pierced she put the request to her father in writing. "I wrote him a note because he wasn't around much," Robin told Dole's biographer, Jake Thompson. She also told Thompson she later studied psychology in college to help her make sense of her parents' divorce. Other stories pointed out how Dole walked out on his wife and daughter after having had dinner with them only two times in the preceding year.

Jay Leno summed it up for the nation: "See, people trust Clinton *as* the baby-sitter. They wouldn't trust him *with* the baby-sitter."

At the end of that month, Clinton reached his highest approval rating in over two years: 56 percent. And in the horse race matchup against Clinton, Dole reached his lowest level ever: 37 percent.

About a week later, appearing at the White House Correspondents Dinner, Clinton did his own riff on the issue.

"But this baby-sitter debate raised only one of many pertinent questions the voters have to ask themselves before they choose the next president," Clinton said. "I mean, for example, let's say that you were going on vacation for a couple of weeks: Who do you trust to water your plants? Bob Dole or Bill Clinton?"

The audience burst into laughter.

"And suppose you were too busy shaking hands tonight and you didn't get to eat, and you go home tonight and you decide to order a pizza? Who do you trust to select the topping? Bob Dole or Bill Clinton?"

Laughter and applause.

"Now if you don't think these questions are relevant or they may not seem relevant, I ask you: Who are we to question the wisdom of Senator Dole's focus groups?" the president concluded.

The reporters, editors, publishers, elected officials, and power brokers in the audience were convulsed with mirth. Some dabbed away tears of laughter from their faces with their dinner napkins. In just a few brief moments, Bill Clinton had done what nobody had ever done to Bob Dole in his more than 35 years in Congress: He had made Bob Dole look like a buffoon.

Michael Kinsley, writing in *Time* on April 29, said: "In every presidential election from 1968 to 1988, the Democrats nominated a goody-goody (Hubert Humphrey, George McGovern, Jimmy Carter, Walter Mondale, Michael Dukakis). And they lost every election during those decades except 1976, when the Republicans also nominated a goody-goody (Gerald Ford)." But in 1992, Kinsley wrote, the Democrats nominated a "slippery politician" who "is also morally flawed."

Bill Clinton had never wanted to be a goody-goody. All he ever wanted was to be a winner.

ON OCTOBER 21, 1996, APPEARING ON MICHAEL JACKSON'S TALK radio show on KABC in Los Angeles, Hillary Clinton was asked to identify her husband's character flaws. She didn't even have to think about it.

"Hogging the remote control," she said. "And chewing ice."

JUGGERNAUT

★

*"Becoming president is an utterly
personal business; the candidate must feel
the beat of the people he hopes to lead;
their heart is his target."*
—Theodore White, 1960

ABOARD *AIR FORCE ONE* THE MOVIE *FARGO* HAS REACHED cult status by the end of the campaign. The film, which is both funny and violent—one of the bad guys feeds the other bad guy into a wood chipper at the end—appeals to the reporters, who are often accused of grinding up others but more often feel ground up themselves.

Air Force One is not configured like an ordinary plane, nor like the plane in the Harrison Ford movie. The interior does not look like a long tube with an aisle running down it and seats on each side. Instead, the plane is divided into a series of rectangular rooms, some with airplane seats and some with conference tables and chairs. A few couches and lamps are scattered about to give it a homey feel, but essentially *Air Force One* looks like a flying insurance office.

One of the rectangles toward the rear of the plane on the starboard side is the press cabin and here, as in other parts of the plane, movies are shown on television monitors. Unlike aboard a regular aircraft, however, the occupants of each cabin phone the technicians in the front of the plane and tell them what movie they would like to see. (Unlike regular airplane movies, these are uncut, uncensored, and often first run. Of the 15 films available on *Air Force One* in the last month of the campaign, four are PG-13 and the rest are R-rated. They include: *The American President, Braveheart, Crimson Tide, Diabolique, Goldeneye, Rumble in the Bronx, Waiting to Exhale,* and *Fargo.*)

About a week before Election Day, the journalists keep requesting *Fargo.* It has become the *Rocky Horror Picture Show* of the press corps, in that many of the reporters and photographers dispense with the headphones and shout the dialogue at the screen. As soon as the movie is finished, the technicians start it again, so after a week of travel, it is possible to see *Fargo* 20 times. Some reporters are more enamored of this than others.

(Very early on Election Day, Hillary Rodham Clinton will come back to the press cabin at 2 A.M. and, as one of her staff records everything with a video camera, Hillary pretends she is a reporter, throwing out questions to the press about the "Fargo Cult." What kind of socially redeeming values does *Fargo* bring and how does it help the country? she asks. The reporters joke around with her and ask her if she has seen the movie. "Yes," the first lady replies, "and there is room for a wood-chipper in my neighborhood.")

Ron Fournier, an Associated Press reporter covering Clinton, is a fan of *Fargo*, requesting it time and again. Claire Shipman of CNN is not and is more than a little sick of it. Mike McCurry could intervene and ban *Fargo* from the press cabin, but McCurry has his own keen sense of the absurd. After Clinton finishes speaking at Ohio State University in the last week of the campaign, McCurry walks through the press filing center singing "Onward Christian Soldiers" at the top of his lungs. And a press pool report records that as McCurry returned to *Air Force One*, he "pranced back on board like a demented over-age leprechaun . . . shrieking, 'Wake up, America!' " Needless to say, McCurry finds the Fargo Cult to be fitting and proper—and exactly what the press deserves. So the movie continues to run hour after hour, day after day.

On the Sunday morning before Election Day, the reporters who will be flying on *Air Force One* line up in front of their hotel to have their hand-carried bags checked for weapons by military personnel. This is standard operating procedure. Tape recorders are turned on and off, as are laptop computers and cell phones. But on this day, whoever has checked Ron Fournier's bag has forgotten to turn off his cellular telephone. Fournier does not know this.

And when Fournier climbs aboard the "Wire One" van, reserved for wire service reporters and photographers, in the presidential motorcade, he puts down his bag and somehow this activates the redial button on his phone. Unbeknownst to him, the phone automatically dials the last number called, which happens to be Fournier's wife, Lori.

The phone rings, she picks it up and hears the burble of voices from the van, one of which she recognizes as her husband's. There is some laughing and horsing around and a general locker room atmosphere seems to prevail. And Lori hears her husband trying to get Claire Shipman to come over to the van so he can persuade her to stop fighting the showing of *Fargo*.

"Get over here!" Ron says. "Come over here!"

Shipman good-naturedly refuses and walks back to her own van.

"That's the last time I sleep with you!" Ron yells out after her.

The motorcade takes off and proceeds to a church where Clinton is going to speak. As the reporters file inside, Fournier's pager goes off, instructing him to call home. Alarmed, he heads to a stairwell to call.

"Who in the hell is Claire Shipman and why won't you sleep with her anymore?" Lori asks, laughing.

Fournier, though baffled, delivers a hasty explanation: *Air Force One, Fargo,* cult movie, absolutely harmless, just having fun, and so forth.

Lori accepts his explanation.

But word about the incident spreads throughout the press corps. (Reporters are great gossips, and besides, what else are they going to talk about? How Clinton wants every 8-year-old to be able to read, every 12-year-old to be able to log on to the Internet, and every 18-year-old to vote Democratic?) And later that day, when *Air Force One* is airborne, Fournier looks up from his seat in the press cabin to see the president of the United States standing over him.

"I hear you have a story to tell me," Clinton says.

"No way," Fournier says.

But the president insists and Fournier, with a considerable degree of embarrassment, tells the tale.

The president laughs. "I'm going to have to call your wife and say I haven't seen you since we were in Little Rock," Clinton says. They had been in Little Rock a few days before. "Gimme your home phone number."

Fournier had covered Clinton when he was the governor of Arkansas and knows that he is not a practical joker. Assuming the president is just kidding about calling his wife, Fournier gives him his home phone number.

After a few more stops, *Air Force One* lands in Florida. On a whim, Fournier calls home and asks his wife if she has heard from the president.

"I can't talk to you now," Lori says. "Cher's at the door. And I'm having tea with Lady Di." Then she asks: "Who was that woman who called and said, 'Can you hold for the president?' "

Fournier can't believe it. It really *was* the president, he tells his wife.

Clinton had, indeed, called Fournier's wife and had said, "Hi, this is Bill Clinton."

"Yeah, right," Lori said.

"I'm kind of worried about Ron," Clinton said. "I haven't seen him since Little Rock."

"That's all right," Lori replied, goofing around, assuming she was talking to some reporter imitating the president. "He *loves* Little Rock."

"Don't worry," the president said. "He'll be home soon." He chatted a little while longer and then finally wrapped it up.

"One of my aides told me this whole campaign is like a dinner party that has gone on for an hour too long," Clinton said.

* * *

BOB DOLE WOULD AGREE. HE HAS BEEN RUNNING FOR 19 MONTHS, and by now he completely hates it. He hates the travel, he hates the speeches, he hates reading about his daily "performance" in the press as if reporters were theater reviewers and he were an actor. But most of all he hates how little any of it seems to matter. The magic bullet he has hoped for from the very beginning—a major scandal dirtying up Clinton—has been fired from what looks like a still-smoking gun. Illegal Indonesian money has poured into Democratic coffers and an Indonesian syndicate's top U.S. representative was given a job in the Clinton administration. A twice-convicted drug dealer was invited to the White House to meet with the president and first lady, as was a reputed Mafia associate and a Chinese weapons dealer. Al Gore went to a fund-raiser in a Buddhist temple, where the Democrats raised $140,000 from monks who had taken a vow of poverty and then Gore denied knowing it was a fund-raiser.

But what has happened since these revelations? Nothing. Yawns from the public. A couple of dismissive lines from the president. And where's the press? That's what Bob Dole wants to know. Does anybody remember Watergate? Bob Dole does. He was chairman of the Republican Party then, and the press was on him like stink on a skunk. He couldn't breathe because of all their questions and investigations and accusations. But now the press is filled with negative stories about him and glowing stories about Clinton. Read *The New York Times* if you don't believe there is a liberal press in this country, he tells the crowds at stop after stop. Dole is disgusted and angry, though he has started carrying a religious medallion around with him that says, THY WILL BE DONE.

If he loses, it is God's will, he tells people. (It is *The New York Times's fault*, but it is God's *will*.) "Maybe there's another plan," he says. Maybe there is another plan that won't take him to the presidency, but will take him . . . where? Not back to Kansas, that's for sure. Elizabeth would have his guts for garters.

The strain is beginning to show. And he arrives at that state of mind not uncommon in politicians who are resigned to defeat: He is saying whatever comes into his head.

On October 26, campaigning in the Central Valley of California by bus, Dole introduces Bo Derek, who is making appearances with him, by saying: "Bo Derek. I've been trying to get on her bus all day." Then, at another stop: "We are going to borrow that Red Cross truck, just me and Bo, and get out of here. Don't tell Elizabeth."

No longer trusting his staff, Dole has taken over the daily scheduling of the campaign. Only he knows where he will head the next day. His aides make sure this is leaked to reporters because the aides don't want to be blamed for having Dole campaign day after day in California, a state he cannot possibly win. (He will end up losing it by a staggering 13 percentage points.) Since the staff does not know where Dole is going to go, they have difficulty making hotel reservations, a little nuts-and-bolts matter that never occurs to Dole. On Monday, October 28, some 200 hotel rooms for staff and press in Denver must be canceled when Dole decides not to overnight there, deciding to stay in California instead. The Clinton campaign, meanwhile, has announced a highly detailed, highly programmed, carefully selected 43-city final push for Clinton and Gore and their wives.

The low point for Dole, however, comes exactly a week before Election Day. Dole starts out the day in Irvine, California, speaking to the World Affairs Council of Orange County, but it doesn't matter where he is because all he can think about—and talk about—is going home.

"I am gonna try to get to Denver yet today and back into National Airport before 10:20 before they send us to Dulles," Dole tells the baffled crowd. National Airport, which is just across the Potomac River and a little down from Dole's Watergate condo, closes early at night because of noise restrictions. After it closes, planes must land at Dulles Airport in Virginia, which adds about 25 minutes to Dole's limousine ride home.

But who, especially among the members of the World Affairs Council of Orange County, knows this? Or cares? And isn't a breakfast speech at 8:18 A.M. a little early in the day to begin worrying about going home? And, say, now that you mention it, isn't Dole supposed to be running for *president*? And doesn't that require a little heavy lifting? At least in the last week of the campaign?

Dole flails on. "In any event, that's a small matter," Dole tells the World Affairs people. "The press thinks I only have one suit. So I want to go back. And I think they only have one suit." The crowd titters nervously. "The TelePrompTer doesn't work, by the way," Dole adds, though the audience had probably guessed that already. Dole goes through his now usual attack on Clinton's ethics, bringing up a donor named Yogesh Gandhi, whom Dole usually refers to as a relative of "the Mahatma Gandhi." But this day he inexplicably refers to him as a relative of "the Mahoover Gandhi." Dole also praises Strom Thurmond, the 93-year-old Republican senator from South Carolina. "I used to follow him around," Dole says. "When he ate a banana, I ate a banana." Dole then tells the crowd that getting elected president in a week's time should be a "piece o'cake."

"You're electing a president, not a talk show host," Dole says, as if anybody needed reminding.

Dole concludes, motorcades to the airport, and takes off for Denver, where he will make his second and last speech of the day. Once airborne, Dole wanders back a few rows short of the press section in the rear of his plane and stops.

"National or Dulles?" he calls out to the press.

"National!" Tamala Edwards of *Time* magazine shouts back at him.

"File fast," Dole urges the press and then retreats to his seat.

In Denver, Dole fails to deliver prepared remarks on his economic plan, instead saying, "If I had a dollar for every time Bill Clinton kept his word, I'd keep one and give the other to Elizabeth, but I can't think of two times when he did." Dole then hurries through the rest of his remarks, thanks the audience, and rushes out of the building, shouting, "National, here we come!"

He lands at National Airport at 9:25 P.M., happy as a clam. He has made it.

The next day press accounts of his behavior contain the words "discombobulated," "rambling," "baffled," "frantic," and "a campaign gone awry." Nelson Warfield had called this part of the campaign Dole's "final push," but Dole seems barely willing to make it a final nudge. And Dole now realizes that what he considered some harmless joking around about getting back to National Airport has made him look old and tired and doddering.

And he decides to show the press and the public and his own staff that he is none of these things. Now, in his mind, the campaign is no longer about winning. It is about showing people that Bob Dole is no quitter.

BILL CLINTON LEANS BACK AGAINST HIS DESK ON *AIR FORCE ONE* and pulls a knee toward his chest. If the office were oval, you could call this the Flying Oval Office, but like everything else on board the plane, it is a rectangle. The room is relentlessly beige. The walls are beige, the carpeting is beige, Clinton's desk chair is beige. The only splash of color is a blue golf jacket with Clinton's name and the presidential seal on it draped over his chair. The emperors of Rome did not have as many visible symbols of their office as a president flying on *Air Force One.* Just about everything has the presidential seal on it: the glasses, the plates, the paper napkins, the pillows, and the little boxes of M&Ms (which replaced packs of cigarettes during the Reagan administration). And, just in case the president forgets what office he holds, there is a seal of office bolted to the wall at eye level right next to his desk. (About the only thing I could find on board that did not have a presidential seal on it was a plastic motion sickness bag.) The daily menus, printed up on heavy cream-colored paper bordered in gold, have the presidential seal engraved in gold at the top and "Air Force One" in gold at the bottom. The day before, the lunch menu had read: "Sloppy Joe on Hamburger Roll. Fritos. Cole Slaw. Apple-Filled Oatmeal Cookies. Choice of Beverage." The food is military food. The president may be a man of large appetites, but they are simple ones, and he thinks the food on *Air Force One* is mighty fine.

When, in the spring at the White House Correspondents Dinner, an officer of the organization promised from the lectern to try to get better food for reporters on *Air Force One,* Clinton turned to McCurry on the dais and said, "We've got to do something about that. I thought reporters got the same food we did."

"They do," McCurry replied.

Now, Clinton perches on his desk, whose wood grain is slightly scratched. (While presidents lead a life of luxury compared to most Americans, it is government-issue luxury. The paint on one of his presidential limousines is also scratched, the backseat is said to be grungy, and anyone who has gone through the press office in the White House is struck by how old the fax machines and other office equipment are. And just outside the lower press office in the West Wing, hanging on a wall, may be one of the last rotary phones in America.) Across from Clinton is a couch that is piled with clothing, toys, and presents.

"I see you have all your booty," McCurry says to the president. This is the stuff that people in the crowds hand Clinton. In Royal Oak, Michigan, during Clinton's train trip, history was made when a woman handed Clinton a brand-new Yves St. Laurent suit, size 46 long, which he accepted with thanks. (Asked later if 46 long is really the president's size, McCurry said, "It is a reasonably good guess.") The same day, Clinton was also given a two-foot-high pink Energizer Bunny. Now, Clinton points out the spoils of his latest campaigning.

"I got my running clothes," Clinton says brightly, gesturing to a gray sweat suit with an Ohio State University seal on it. "I'm getting some good winter running clothes." There is real enthusiasm in his voice. Though he makes a pretty good salary ($200,000 a year plus a very hefty expense account), he is millions of dollars in debt from legal bills, and he and Hillary do not even own a home anywhere. Until he became president, Clinton had never earned more than $35,000 a year. A free set of winter running clothes looks like a pretty good deal to him. Besides, when does he get time to shop?

"Hey," he says to me, walking over to the couch and picking up a beer stein, "look at this: an Elvis stein." And there is, indeed, a nice likeness of Elvis Presley painted on the side of the stein.

"A guy in Chicago makes these," Clinton says, examining it as if it were by Vermeer or Holbein. "He gave me a plate with Elvis on it. I have it in the Music Room at the White House." (Jackie Kennedy would have been so proud.)

Clinton's mother, Virginia Clinton Kelley, was an Elvis fan, writing in her frank and delightful autobiography that she owned a "pukashell necklace" that Elvis once wore "and sometimes I can still smell Elvis's Brut cologne coming from the porous shells" and "I've even got a bust of Elvis in the corner of my dining room. But I ask you: Does any of that make me an Elvis nut?"

I know your mother once saw Elvis perform live, I say to Clinton. Did you ever see him?

At the mention of his mother, a cloud seems to pass over his face. "I never saw Elvis perform," he says quietly. "My mother went to see him in Pine Bluff once in the seventies." Then he brightens and points to a T-shirt a woman has given him this day.

"She said, 'God has chosen you,' " Clinton says. "Wow."

Clinton is always doing this, telling anybody and everybody the nice stuff people say to him after his speeches. He does this without any embarrassment whatsoever, even though people tend to say extremely nice things to him.

This morning he had given a speech at St. John's Arena at Ohio State University, and on the rope line afterward he shook the hand of David Mitchell, the Coast Guard veteran. "I've been to more Coast Guard stations than any other president," Clinton said to him. Which was enough for Mitchell. "I was a Dole supporter, but I've changed my mind," he replied to Clinton.

(Clinton often claims to have done more, seen more, accomplished more than any president in history. Campaigning in Ypsilanti, Michigan, Clinton went to a Greek restaurant named Abe's Coney Island Restaurant and ordered gyros for everyone in his entourage. Leon Panetta, his chief of staff, asked him what gyros were. "I have more Greek friends than any president in history and you don't know what gyros are?" Clinton said to him.)

After talking to the Coast Guard vet, Clinton turned to Wendy Smith, who works in the White House political affairs office, and said:

"Did you hear that guy? He said, 'When I came here I was voting for Dole, but I changed my mind.' Did you hear him say it? Did you hear him?"

After the Ohio State speech, Clinton heads for the airport but suddenly stops his motorcade in front of the Immaculate Conception Elementary School when he sees a bunch of little kids assembled outside. He exits his limousine and spends a considerable amount of time shaking the hands of the kids, sometimes grabbing two or three of their small hands in his big one. The kids squeal with delight. Clinton walks down the line of kids, his long motorcade creeping down the street behind him. When Clinton has shaken every student's hand and has crossed the street to shake some adults' hands and then recrossed it to shake some kids' hands a second time, he finally says, "Have I missed anybody?" One of his Secret Service agents rolls his eyes.

But before Clinton can be persuaded to get back into his limousine, a little boy tells him, "You're on my spelling test!"

Now, a few minutes later on board *Air Force One*, even though Clinton is preparing for his next speech, running the country, thinking about global affairs, and worrying about a stock market plunge the day before, he turns to me and says, "Did you hear what that kid said to me? 'You're on my spelling test.' I *love* those little kids."

There was another comment from a kid that Clinton did not hear, though it probably would please him also. A few days earlier the kids at Immaculate Conception had voted in a straw poll and Clinton had beaten Dole handily. Guidance counselor Barbara Thompson asked a second-grader why he voted for Clinton.

The second-grader thought for a moment. "Dole is like the grandfather you want to get away from," he said.

Clinton takes one last look at his booty on the couch. "I got a fruit basket," he says. Then he pushes aside a fake Wheaties box with a mirror on the front that is supposed to make whoever looks at it a "champion" and sits down on the edge of the couch. "My eyes popped open at 7:30," he says. " 'A week from today'—that's what I thought."

Although he has been more nervous about Election Day than his staff, he is no longer worried that he will lose. His polls indicate he will have a landslide victory in the Electoral College. But Clinton fears that the campaign financing stories are going to cause some independents to shy away from him. "And he very, very, *very* much wanted to get at least 50.1 percent of the vote," a senior aide told me later. Though this wasn't, as many thought, because Clinton wanted a mandate, a sign that the public wanted him to carry out new initiatives in his second term. "Getting more than 50 percent was going to be his *vindication*," the aide said. "It was supposed to vindicate him for Whitewater and all the other stuff."

Air Force One starts to roll down the runway and McCurry tries to get Clinton to stop talking so McCurry and I can leave and buckle in some place. But Clinton keeps chatting. "I had mixed feelings about it," Clinton says, speaking of his realization that this is his last week of campaigning. "I'm trying every day now to do something that people never do in campaigns. I'm trying to have one serious talk a day to get people to think about things."

The warning system is going "bong-bong" from the ceiling and the plane is picking up speed. McCurry is edging toward the office door, but Clinton keeps talking. "I think it's important at the end of the campaign that we keep talking about things that will affect people's lives that may not come to political rallies," he says.

Bong-bong.

"We're trying to generate high turnout among people," Clinton says.

An aide sticks his head in the door, probably to make sure Clinton is buckled in his seat, and is shocked to see us standing there and Clinton still perched on the edge of the couch. The plane is roaring down the runway.

"You *must* be seated," the aide says to us. He can't really tell the president to be seated in his chair and buckle in, but the aide hopes Clinton will take the hint.

"I think it's important to talk about the issues that should make all citizens vote that really affect their lives and shape the future," Clinton goes on.

The four gigantic engines on the Boeing 747-200B are roaring so loudly now that it is hard to hear Clinton, and the forward motion is beginning to press McCurry and me backward.

"That's the other thing I did this morning after I got ready," Clinton says. "I sat there and went over the speech three times, trying to work it around some more. I wanted it to be *good*."

The plane is hurtling with such speed that McCurry and I start looking for something to grab on to as Clinton gets up slowly and begins to walk over to his chair.

He stops and shakes my hand on the way.

"This is nice of you to do this," Clinton says.

And he laser-locks me with eyes so deep and so blue that looking into them is like falling into a swimming pool.

As the nose of the plane lifts from the ground, McCurry and I stagger out into the hall and fall into seats, grabbing for the seat belts.

As we thunder skyward, it takes me a few moment to realize the president has just thanked *me* for interviewing *him.*

B OB DOLE COMES UP WITH THE PERFECT IDEA FOR THE CAMpaign that never really started: In its last four days, it will never stop. He will campaign around the clock for the last 96 hours, skipping hotels at night, giving speech after speech. The geezer will become a geyser.

The White House staff is unimpressed. Dole is going to start working hard at the very end of the campaign? Big deal. Clinton has been working hard for weeks, sometimes giving five or six speeches a day. (Some of the speeches are at fund-raisers, which are closed to the press. When, in Southern California, the press has nothing to do for seven hours while Clinton raises money, the campaign gives reporters free tickets to the Universal Studio tour.)

But the White House misses the point of what Dole is doing. Dole has not had a really good publicity stunt during the entire campaign. And now he has a great one, especially in that it involves the press. The reporters will have to stay up for 96 hours, too. Which guarantees colorful, saturation news coverage.

"The last time I fought around the clock for my country was in Italy in 1945," Dole tells a crowd in Florida. "I will give it all I've got for 96 hours." Bob Dole will begin his own Longest Day. But it is three in the afternoon and the Florida speech is only his second speech that day, which is laughably light scheduling for a presidential race. And he already looks exhausted. A reporter asks him why he is doing the 96-hour marathon.

"I couldn't think of anything else," Dole says. "It's my last option."

While some reporters rush to telephone home asking that extra underwear be Federal Expressed to them, others are complaining that even when the Dole campaign is announcing a publicity stunt, the Dole press staff still doesn't understand how to get publicity. Though Dole gives a rare briefing to reporters aboard his plane to announce his plans for the final 96 hours, the radio pool reporter is excluded, told there is "no room."

"No room for one microphone!" Elizabeth Arnold of National Public Radio tells me, outraged. "These guys have *never* understood radio. Do you know how many people we reach?" Arnold explains that CNN, which has gotten several one-on-one interviews with Dole, reaches about 400,000 people on average, while CBS radio, for example, reaches about 2 million people during morning drive time. "I have been traveling with Dole since Iowa, and I have never gotten an interview," Arnold says. "*No* radio reporter has. Clinton understands radio. The Dole people don't *care.*"

Dole knows his staff has done a second-rate job, but he also knows who is going to get the blame. "I have been around long enough to know it is going to be the candidate's fault," he says. "If I lose, the rest of them are going to be home free, but it will be the candidate's fault." His analysis skips over, however, who it was who assembled the staff.

Dole will visit 20 states in four days, making 29 stops and traveling 10,534 miles, while stopping to sleep in a hotel for only six hours. But his voice gives out quickly, and by the time he gets to Phoenix on the day before Election Day, his stump speech is down to two minutes.

"While I still have my voice," he croaks, "I want you to know, I'll keep my word." After bouncing from issue to issue during the campaign, Dole has finally settled on one for the last four days: character. At some stops, "unofficial" leaflets are handed out showing a picture of Hillary Clinton with Jorge Cabrera at a White House Christmas party in 1995. Cabrera is one of a number of thugs, hoodlums, and lowlifes who were able to gain access to the president and first lady after making large contributions to the Democratic National Committee. Cabrera did time in 1983 for conspiracy to bribe a grand jury witness, and again in 1988 for tax evasion, both convictions related to narcotics trafficking. But he gave $20,000 to the DNC in 1995, and a month later he got invited to the White House. Cabrera would miss the 1996 Christmas party, however. He was sent to prison on a 19-year sentence for transporting 6,000 pounds of cocaine into the country.

Eric Wynn was an ex-con who spent nearly two and a half years in prison on a 1989 guilty plea for theft and tax evasion. According to published reports, he was also an associate of the Mafia's Bonanno crime family. Wynn attended a White House coffee on December 21, 1995, where he was able to chat with the president for 45 minutes. Just five months earlier, Wynn had been convicted on 13 counts of conspiracy, securities fraud, and wire fraud and was sentenced to 52 months in prison. At the time he was sipping java with Clinton, Wynn was out on bail and seeking a pardon. Two days before his audience with Clinton, a Florida firm that Wynn reportedly had partial control of donated $25,000 to the Democratic National Committee. (After his name surfaced, a newspaper did a simple electronic database search on Wynn—something nobody at the White House bothered to do—and found a story in *Forbes* magazine from 1989 that said: "Federal documents say Bonanno family capo Frank Coppa, his associate Eric Wynn, and other friends paid a visit" to a stock promoter and "bashed him on the side of the head with a telephone." So, in a sense, Clinton was lucky. He emerged from his meeting with Wynn uninjured.)

The list went on and on. Roger Tamraz drank coffee with Clinton in April 1995, his U.S.-based oil company having given $72,000 to the DNC in 1995 and 1996. At the time, Tamraz, a former banker from Lebanon, had been sought for eight years on an Interpol arrest warrant for embezzlement charges. Wang Jun had coffee with Clinton in February 1996. He was a Chinese arms dealer, whose company, according to *The New York Times*, "was the focus of a federal undercover operation that ultimately snared $4 million in semiautomatic weapons headed for West Coast street gangs."

Clinton remains sanguine about all this until his daily tracking polls show a disturbing shift of independent voters away from him and toward Ross Perot, who had been yammering about campaign finance reform for years. Clinton knows he cannot lose, but he does not want to become the first president in history to be elected twice without a majority of the vote. So on November 1, in Santa Barbara, California, Clinton says: "Everybody knows the problems of campaign money today. There's too much of it, it takes too much time to raise, and it raises too many questions." Which was what Bill Daley had been warning people about for months. But the Clinton campaign had indulged in an orgy of fund-raising very early in the process, both to keep potential primary opponents out of the race and to put a series of campaign commercials on the air accusing Republicans of wanting to destroy Medicare and Medicaid. "I don't think any president has ever raised money so fast," Harold Ickes had told me. "It surprised us." Now, the surprise was where some of the money came from: foreign nationals, foreign countries, fugitives, drug dealers, arms dealers, mobsters, and people who wanted to spend a night in the Lincoln Bedroom.

After the campaign Daley told me: "When you raise that much money, everybody is just vulnerable. You can't raise that much without making mistakes. The Republicans raised $400 million (compared to the Democrats' $200 million or so) and they were *out* of power. What do you think they would have raised if they were *in* power? You don't get that kind of money by sending out letters. The money is just too dominant and too constant."

"We have played by the rules," Clinton tells the crowd in Santa

Barbara at a picture-perfect rally, the Pacific Ocean crashing onto rocks below him. "But I know, and you know, we need to change the rules."

After the election, that is.

Bob Dole, his face drawn and haggard, speaking in Loma Linda, California, his sixteenth stop in three days, struggles to find a reason for people to vote for him.

"Character *does* count," he says. "Character *does* count."

He looks out at the silent crowd and blinks.

"Does character count?" he asks.

IN THE PRE-DAWN DARKNESS, *AIR FORCE ONE* HEADS FOR LITTLE Rock on Election Day. On the ground, hundreds of people have gathered along the streets. Some hold up a WELCOME HOME sign and others wave sparklers. On board the plane there is a certain "end of the road" giddiness. Staffers produce a tape recording of the macarena, and while Hillary demurs, Bill goes through the motions for a couple of minutes while everybody laughs. Clinton has made 20 stops in 15 states in the last six days.

Two days earlier in Tampa, the Clinton motorcade had passed a small clump of people, who had gathered to wave at his limousine. To their amazement, the limousine abruptly stopped, the door opened, and Clinton got out (as the rest of the motorcade screeched to a halt, the cars and vans nearly piling up onto one another). Clinton walked over and shook their hands. One of the startled spectators invited him to come home and stay.

Clinton seemed to hesitate for just a second before shaking his head. "Take a rain check," he said.

At noon on Election Day, Bob Dole returns to Russell, Kansas, to vote at the First Christian Church.

"My name's Bob Dole," he tells the clerks.

They ask him to spell it.

"They run a clean outfit here," Dole says. "This is not Chicago. You can only vote once."

No crowd has been assembled in Russell, because Dole does not want to give a speech. He wants to vote and head home to Washington to watch the election returns. But as he heads out of Russell down brick-lined Main Street, the street that ran past his father's grain elevator and past the drugstore that a young Bob Dole worked in and where the famous shoebox sat where people could contribute to his hospital bills, he sees that the schoolchildren of Russell have been let out to greet him, and scores of his hometown friends have come out to wave.

Dole's motorcade does not stop.

IN WASHINGTON THERE IS VICTORY AND THERE IS THE LIVING death known as losing. There is no in-between. There is no honored place for those who have struggled. So on election night, Bob Dole goes to a basement in a hotel on the edge of Chinatown to concede defeat. The networks had announced his loss two hours earlier, but he has waited for the polls to close in California.

The ballroom is long and narrow, and the crowd is compressed by the press riser to make it look larger. Dole has few friends in the crowd. The people here tonight are mostly young staffers and volunteers who have been handed tickets and told to fill up the ballroom for the TV cameras. They have been drinking for several hours and many are now drunk. Some smoke large cigars and send up clouds of smoke past the sweltering TV lights. They mill aimlessly, barely watching the large TV screens as Clinton's numbers mount up: He will win 31 states and the District of Columbia and 379 electoral votes to Bob Dole's 19 states and 159 electoral votes. But Clinton will be denied his "vindication." He will get only 49.2 percent of the vote. Bob Dole will get 40.7, and Ross Perot will get 8.4 percent.

When Bob Dole walks into the ballroom at 11:23 P.M. Eastern Standard Time the band strikes up the theme from *Top Gun* and Dole pumps his left fist into the air. For the last few weeks he has stopped dying his hair, and now the silver shows along his temples. His suit gapes at the neck, emphasizing the weight he has lost during his 96-hour marathon.

After quieting the raucous crowd and before going into his prepared remarks, he makes one of the most poignant statements of his entire campaign.

"I was just thinking on the way down," he says, "tomorrow will be the first time in my life I don't have anything to do."

THE DAY AFTER THE ELECTION, THE LEAD EDITORIAL IN *THE NEW York Times* makes two bare-knuckle points: If Bill Clinton "wants to avoid being remembered simply as the most-investigated president in the modern era, Mr. Clinton must first do something dramatic about ethics."

Of Bob Dole, the editorial says that he was "a man who might have been a good president had he been a better campaigner."

What were you able to teach Bob Dole? I ask Don Sipple, Dole's adman and adviser, after the campaign is over.

"Virtually nothing," Sipple says. "The cosmetics of modern campaigning is something Dole thinks should not make a difference. The appreciation for the picture, the asthetics of the road show, the lighting, the sound. He didn't think it should *count*."

THE DAY AFTER THE ELECTION, CLINTON WALKS INTO THE WHITE House press briefing room for a small party with reporters. Not many are here. Many are home with families they have not seen in a while or are sleeping or are working on analysis stories for their Sunday editions. A beer cooler has been brought out and sits in front of the lectern where McCurry usually conducts the briefing.

Though it is very difficult for reporters to relax around Clinton, he seems very relaxed around them, joking and laughing and telling them that he really needs a vacation. They remind him he is a young man, only 50.

"I'm the oldest man for my age in America," Clinton says. "The last two weeks were so tough, I asked myself what could I say to blow this? I get my full pay as my pension right away, right?"

What was the funniest moment of the campaign? a reporter asks.

"The train!" Mike McCurry answers. "The back of the train."

" 'Nice doggie,' " Clinton says, quoting himself. " 'Biggest satellite I ever saw.' " He shakes his head and laughs.

Clinton chats, promising more press conferences, something McCurry has been working hard on. McCurry wants Clinton to have better relations with the press in his second term. McCurry, who had previously worked in the presidential campaigns of John Glenn, Bruce Babbitt, and Bob Kerrey, is no longer a jinx.

"I finally gave McCurry a winner," Clinton says. "I broke his string."

After a few more minutes of this, McCurry tries to get Clinton to go, but he remains for another 10 minutes, chatting and shaking hands.

"We're going to have a raffle at the White House for the press corps," Clinton promises before he leaves. "An all-expense-paid trip to Indonesia!"

TWO MONTHS AFTER CLINTON'S INAUGURATION, THE GALLUP Organization asks 1,009 adults: Is Clinton honest and trustworthy?

Only 44 percent say yes, while 51 percent say no.

Then the pollsters ask: Is Clinton honest and trustworthy enough *to be president?*

This time, Clinton wins. Fifty-five percent say yes and 41 percent say no.

In March 1997 Clinton justifies his fund-raising excesses by saying "I don't regret the fact that we worked like crazy to raise enough money to keep from being rolled over by the biggest juggernaut this country had seen in a very long time." Juggernaut? When did the Bob Dole campaign reach that status exactly? After Dole embraced assault weapons or after he said smoking might not be any worse than drinking milk or after he fell off that stage in Chico, California?

Harold Ickes had been right when he complained that the Clinton campaign was spending vast sums of money on commercials that "nobody will remember by Election Day." Nobody did. Bill Clinton didn't win because of commercials. He won in part because of a Republican Congress that overreached and because of a government shutdown that people blamed on the Republicans. But he won mainly because of his own uncanny ability to connect with voters both in person and on television, and a set of issues that positioned him as moderate, caring, and likable, especially to women. A campaign team that was obsessive, energetic, imaginative, and talented didn't hurt.

Bill Clinton did not need to raise millions in funny money to put campaign commercials on the air to defeat Bob Dole. Bob Dole himself did an effective job of beating Bob Dole. As one of his staff members suggested after the campaign, their motto should have been: "We came. We saw. We kicked our ass."

When you got right down to it, not since the Nixon White House tried to sabotage George McGovern had more time, energy, and money been spent to combat a more hapless foe.

"It's strange," Dole adviser Alex Castellanos said after the election, "but Bill Clinton wasn't president before this campaign. He never became president by governing. He only became president by pretending to be president in the campaign."

Which misses the point. Campaigning for president, performing for crowds and for television, projecting the image of the president, is not a pretense. As historian Gil Troy has written, modern campaigns function "as elaborate auditions for the rhetorical themes and central policies" that shape the coming presidency. Performing, articulating a message, selling yourself by making the hearts of the people your target, as Theodore White once put it, and bringing about consensus is not an act. It is the presidency.

In October a poll conducted for Knight-Ridder revealed that nearly two-thirds of the respondents would *not* want their child to become president. They would prefer that their children become college professors, doctors, ministers, carpenters, athletes, lawyers, governors, or mayors rather than become leader of the free world.

Significantly, the people ranked only one career lower than president: movie star.

Perhaps they realized they were almost the same.

AFTER THE ELECTION, BOB DOLE APPEARS ON LETTERMAN AND Leno, *Saturday Night Live* and *Suddenly Susan*. He does a Visa commercial that runs during the Super Bowl and is in a newspaper ad for Air France. He is warm, funny, engaging, and relaxed.

In December, Dole signs on with legendary superagent Mark McCormack, whose IMG agency was a model for the fictitious SMI agency in the movie *Jerry Maguire*. McCormack represents Tiger Woods, Andre Agassi, Itzhak Perlman, and a number of supermodels. McCormack says he will represent Dole in deals for books, international speaking, commercial endorsements, and broadcasting.

After 45 years in politics, Bob Dole finally gets it.

He has decided to become an entertainer.

EPILOGUE

THE CURTAIN FALLS

H E HAD BEEN RUNNING FOR OFFICE FOR SO LONG THAT he had almost forgotten how to stop. In the twenty-two years from 1974 to 1996, Bill Clinton had run for public office ten times and had lost only twice, once in his first race when he was just 28 years old and thought he wanted to be in the Congress and once for governor of Arkansas, a job he ended up getting elected to five times. Though he had never given a really memorable speech, the kind that people went around quoting afterward, he was nonetheless a dazzling campaigner. His "people" skills were almost scary. In September 1996, working a rope line in Longview, Texas, he came across Annette Robinson of Arkansas, who proudly told Clinton that he had spoken at her school twenty years before. Immediately Clinton not only recalled the speech and details about the school but also the name of Robinson's teacher.

(So it was with some amusement that people who knew Clinton heard him state publicly some months later that he could not remember if he personally had made calls from the White House soliciting huge contributions from wealthy corporate executives and others. George Stephanopoulos used to marvel at Clinton's ability to retain political minutiae. "He always knows how many times he's been to a city since he's been president," Stephanopoulos said. "It just always blows me away." But as to whether he dialed for dollars from the White House, Clinton's memory grew inexplicably cloudy. "I don't want to flat out say I never did something that I might in fact have done just because I don't remember it," Clinton said at a press conference on March 7, 1997. He could remember a schoolteacher's name from twenty years before, but how could he be expected to remember sixteen months after the fact whether he called August Busch IV in November 1995 to ask for $100,000? Though Busch seems to have gotten a tickle from somebody: two weeks later Anheuser-Busch contributed $100,000 to the Democratic National Committee.)

But now his last campaign was over. And watching Clinton in the final days had been like watching some splendid clockwork machine begin to wind down. "I will never seek office again," Clinton said, though, characteristically, he left himself an out. "Unless I go home and run for the school board some day." It was unlikely. Voters take school board elections very seriously.

Running was so much part of him that he had almost forgotten how to make policy decisions based solely on their merits rather than on the political impact they would have on his next election. But now he faced something much more frightening than the judgment of voters: He faced the judgment of history. Presidential history was his hobby. He loved to impress everyone from staff members to visiting dignitaries with his knowledge of America's previous presidents. He knew what accomplishments made their stamp on people's memories and what was swept away by the tides of the moment.

So shortly after his 1996 victory, he gathered his inner circle in the Oval Office and started talking about how he wanted to be remembered: It would not be for any of the "bite-sized" policies that got him reelected. It was hard to imagine that in fifty years many people would care about school uniforms or V-chips. No, now was the time for more imposing plans. He wanted to be remembered as the president who tackled the nation's oldest, most dramatic, and fractious social problem: race. Bill Clinton would begin the healing of America.

There was an added benefit, of course: If he really was remembered for the progress he made on race relations, Whitewater and Paula Jones and campaign fund-raising would be largely forgotten. He was always considering what the next generation would think of him, which made it easier for him to deal with what the current generation thought of him. A voracious reader of newspapers and magazines, he simply skipped those stories that mentioned subjects he found embarrassing. (Which meant on some days he skipped several pages.) But he had learned the trick long ago. "I put it in the smallest possible box in my brain," he told his staff. "Otherwise I couldn't get my work done."

"He is totally disconnected," Mike McCurry said several months into Clinton's second term. "He deliberately is not following it. That is one way to deal with Whitewater and the contributions matter. He is more content and more at peace with his job than I have seen him in the last two and a half years. It is almost like a *spiritual* thing. You go in to prep him for the mean, nasty things he will be asked and he smiles and shakes his head and wags his finger and says, 'No, they won't get me to talk on that.' "

And why is he so at peace, why is he so spiritual? I asked.

"His political life is over," McCurry said.

Which meant he could turn his attention to his legacy. He knew what people remembered about presidents (if they remembered anything at all). How many people remembered the scandals of Harry Truman's presidency? How many today could tell you what a "Five Percenter" was? Most people could during Truman's second term. But who now could remember the procurement scandal that dominated those headlines or the attorney general Truman had to fire? What they remembered was that Harry Truman was plainspoken and gave 'em hell and said the buck stops here and that he integrated the military and dropped the bomb on Japan. In other words they remembered a lot of his show and some of his substance. And when it came time for people to remember Bill Clinton, Clinton was sure they would not remember Flowers or Jones or Huang or Lippo or Riady. They would remember, he vowed, that he tried to build a bridge to the twenty-first century, where America's racial and ethnic differences were causes for pride rather than division.

Not everyone listening to his spiel in the Oval Office that day was persuaded. What policies about race could they come up with? What legislation could they get through Congress? And wasn't Clinton raising expectations awfully high? The press was going to be very, very skeptical about this one. Clinton, sitting behind his desk, the same desk John Kennedy had sat at, waved away their doubts. That was small thinking. He invited them to ask him the real importance of racial healing in America, and when they did, he said simply: "Foreign policy." Then he just watched the baffled expressions play across their faces as he leaned forward and explained: Empowering American minorities would ensure that America would continue to be the leading economic power in the world. American blacks who were in business in America could relate better to the African blacks wanting to do business with America. Asian Americans empowered in this country could be more competitive and do better deals with Asians in Asian countries. "That is the value of a diverse workforce," Clinton said, "making sure enterprises are globally connected. It is not just 'let's all live together in harmony.' It's about enhancing our economic power in the twenty-first century."

He loved talking about stuff like this (McCurry called it his "professor" mode), and he grew even more excited as he talked about how race dovetailed with one of the other big initiatives of his second term: balancing the budget. If the economy continued to be strong, Clinton said, white Americans would not feel threatened by the rising prosperity of minorities. By 2050, white Americans were no longer going to be in the majority in America, but if they felt economically secure they would have a much easier time getting their minds around that fact.

The press will think it is just about race, Clinton told his people, but it is about foreign policy and economic policy and America's leadership role in the world.

"And that is slightly over the heads of reporters," McCurry added later.

Not that reporters would be allowed to miss the high points, high points that would be both substantive and, of course, a good show. There would be a kick-off speech by Clinton on race and the creation of a race advisory board, made up of distinguished black, Asian, Hispanic, and white Americans, whose meetings would be held in public. (The first meeting, held on July 14, 1997, was so dull that most of the reporters who showed up for the morning session failed to come back after the lunch break.) And to the surprise of almost nobody, Clinton also decided he wanted to do a series of national town meetings on race. Town meetings had never failed his political career and he was sure they would not fail him when it came to his spiritual one.

Before all such presidential initiatives, McCurry would write a memo to the president explaining the "roll-out," how the White House press office would present the story, how it would "amplify" the message and catch the attention of what it perceived to be a bored, cynical, and often dim-witted press corps. Such memos usually ran three to four pages. McCurry's memo to the president on the race initiative ran twenty-seven. "Listed below," it began, "please find the press strategy developed for the upcoming speech and initiative on race relations. The strategy is to essentially tell two stories over the next two weeks: 1. Your life-long commitment to seeking solutions concerning race relations and 2. The national dialogue you and your newly announced advisory board will lead over the next year." McCurry also asked Clinton to make a "significant time commitment" for interviews with the press.

McCurry listed the reporters and news organizations by name and how many minutes each would be allotted. "Women's, men's, children's and parenting magazines" would be handled by others in the administration. The editorial boards of *The Washington Post, The New*

York Times, USA Today, and the *Los Angeles Times* would be contacted by high-ranking members of the administration and McCurry promised his office would find "creative ways to use the Internet to distribute the President's message."

The memo was the result of months of careful planning. This was going to be a really big show by a really big showman and the entire White House was mobilized for it. Nobody would talk about it publicly until the time came to carefully leak those elements that the White House wanted leaked. It was a perfect plan except for one thing: Nobody counted on Bill Clinton getting carried away. But it turned out that he was so gosh darn eager to get this show on the road, he just couldn't contain himself.

IN A SENSE IT WAS MCCURRY'S OWN FAULT. AT THE BEGINNING OF the second term, he had persuaded Clinton to have regular Friday "schmooze" sessions with reporters in order to make a stab at better relations. Mutual distrust between the press and president was to be expected, but mutual contempt did neither side any good.

"To him [Clinton] the press is a gaggle beyond the klieg lights that asks obnoxious questions," McCurry told me. Nor, he went on, did the press truly understand Clinton. "They never see him struggle and try to shape policy, to set aside bad arguments, to see him struggle with hard calls. They have no measure of the man himself."

And while McCurry was certainly one of the more popular press secretaries in modern history, his credibility was now under attack. On November 20, 1996, just two weeks after the election, *The New York Times* lead editorial about Oval Office meetings between Clinton and Indonesian billionaire James Riady was headlined AN INSTINCT TO DECEIVE and began: "What will it take to persuade the White House to tell the truth simply and promptly once a scandal is brewing?" It went on to say that McCurry "was left with his reliability in tatters" and that he had become part of the "personal wreckage" of the growing scandal.

After reading it, McCurry called Howell Raines, the editor of *The New York Times* editorial page, but the conversation did not go well. "He's psychotic," McCurry told me afterwards. This was the first hint I got that McCurry was planning to leave the White House. Press secretaries who are planning to stay at the White House do not go around calling *New York Times* editorial page editors psychotic (whether they are or not). "It's the first serious shot I took in two years of being here," McCurry said. "For a whole day I was grumpy and bemoaning my fate.

But I thought about it. Bill Clinton has woken up to this every day. It made me understand his bitterness."

Bitter or not, however, McCurry wanted Clinton to spend more time in informal sessions with reporters. It just made sense. McCurry didn't expect reporters to swoon over Clinton the same way some voters did, but he knew that few people were completely invulnerable to Clinton's personal charm. So McCurry got Clinton to agree to schmooze sessions, where he could talk to small groups of reporters on "deep background," a term generally accepted to mean that the president could not be quoted, nor could any information be used except as a starting point for future story ideas.

So on Valentine's Day, 1997, Clinton found himself standing in the doorway of the Oval Office, greeting five new White House reporters, giving them firm handshakes and telling them how nice it was for them to drop by. Clinton knew they would be a little bit awed (he also knew, for example, how proud it made reporters feel when he called on them by their first names during televised press conferences and how much it impressed their bosses) and how an Oval Office interview was the highest level of access to Clinton that a reporter could expect. Many reporters had spent years on the White House beat without getting one.

Clinton ushered them into the room and then sat down in a gold upholstered armchair. There was a coffee table in front of him and a couch and chairs on each side of the coffee table. The reporters took seats on the couches and chairs. They had been told that note-taking was allowed, but that Clinton would be more candid if they didn't do so. Jodi Enda of Knight-Ridder decided to take notes anyway. "I wanted to get something substantive," she said later.

Clinton settled back in his chair. "What do you all want to talk about today?" he asked.

There was a little small talk, which Enda interrupted with: "I know that race relations has been an issue that you've worked on for much of your career. Are you planning on making race relations a key part of your second term?" It was a shot in the dark; Clinton's race initiative was still a secret. "But it seemed odd to me that he would go through eight years and not take on something so important to him and the nation," Enda said.

Clinton should have ducked the question, something he was good at, but instead his eyes lit up. Yes, yes, he said, he'd been asking himself whether there was some sort of larger effort he could make other than just speeches and using the bully pulpit of his office. "I was wondering whether there was some *structured* response" that he could make, Clinton said, and he mentioned the possibility of a race commission.

All of which was a long way from being finalized, but Clinton was getting excited. He leaned forward in his chair, the enthusiasm growing in his voice, motioning with his hands, and, as always, lasering, lasering, lasering. "He stared right into my eyes while he was answering," Enda remembered.

Clinton said he was trying to decide his "mission" and whether he could take the discussion to a higher plane. He said his "legacy" would be improving race relations and "changing the culture."

"There will be a new major effort you haven't seen yet," Clinton promised, and went on: "The way I envision how this would work out—this country would be exceedingly well positioned for the world we're going to live in. If we pull it off we will enormously revitalize America and it will be quite wonderful."

Which was quite a wonderful little declaration, except the White House was months away from any announcement on race. McCurry's memo had not even been drafted. There were scores of people to get on board and in line and a lot of polling to be done before anything could be revealed to the press. Besides, the rule of the modern presidency was supposed to be well understood by Bill Clinton: The president of the United States never makes news himself. It is made for him long before he speaks.

"The president has *never* made an announcement," McCurry told me months later with a laugh. "We've already leaked it or gotten it out somehow. The press is already doing the *analysis* story by the time he *announces* it."

The schmooze session went on to other subjects, but when it was over, Enda knew she had a good story. So she went to McCurry and asked if she could quote Clinton directly. McCurry refused, but gave her the names of some of the administration officials who were working on the race initiative. (McCurry later gave Enda permission to quote the president from her notes for this book, though she was not allowed to do so in her newspaper story.) It took Enda two weeks of digging and interviewing to piece the story together, but on March 4 she wrote: "Eager to leave an enduring legacy, President Clinton privately is nurturing a grandiose ambition to help remedy one of the nation's most intractable and explosive problems: race relations."

The official roll-out eventually geared up and reached its peak during the two weeks before Clinton's race speech. "Through the television interviews, you will reach millions of viewers including soccer moms and targeted white males," McCurry promised Clinton in his memo. McCurry also listed twenty-five "surrogates/validators" who would swear to reporters about Clinton's lifelong interest in good race relations and provide fascinating anecdotes. The first three names on the list were old Hot Springs friends of Clinton: David Leopoulos, who Clinton had known since the fourth grade, his wife, Linda, and Carolyn Staley, Clinton's next-door neighbor, classmate, and close friend for decades.

Staley could tell reporters of those days in 1968 after Martin Luther King, Jr., had been assassinated, and Clinton, a student at Georgetown University who had earlier memorized King's "I Have a Dream" speech, picked the visiting Staley up at National Airport in his white convertible. "Hi," a somber Bill Clinton said, "I've signed up to do volunteer work." And then he drove Staley into the still-smoking riot areas of Washington with food and first-aid supplies in his trunk. There were few white faces on those streets in normal times, but now Clinton and Staley stood out for a mile. "We were scared to death," Staley would tell reporters, "but Bill needed to step into history. He felt personally that he wanted to be part of King's team and Kennedy's vision."

This was wonderful stuff, exactly what "surrogate/validators" were supposed to provide and exactly what carefully staged roll-outs were all about. Lacking something exciting like new riots to write about, the press needed some way to make race seem interesting. And the White House was there to help.

David Leopoulos told reporters how Clinton and Staley and he had all grown up in a Hot Springs of segregated schools and segregated swimming pools, and how they were 11 years old when Governor Orville Faubus defied a federal order to admit black children to Little Rock Central High. (Clinton would fly to Little Rock on September 25, 1997, to commemorate the fortieth anniversary of the day the nine black students were escorted inside Central High by federal troops.) Leopoulos told reporters how his mother had sat Clinton down and explained to him there were no gray areas when it came to racism and how Clinton had told him years later, "You know, your mother had a lot to do with how I feel about race. She was the only person who ever pulled me aside and told me how wrong prejudice was."

(This implied that nobody in Clinton's own family had done so. And in 1966, a 19-year-old Bill Clinton had sent his maternal grandmother, whom he called Mammaw, a postcard of a grinning black child eating a watermelon. "Dear Mammaw," Clinton wrote from Georgetown, where he was a freshman, "Thought I should send you one of your cards just to prove I'm using them!" Thirty years later, when

President Clinton was running for reelection, a cousin auctioned off the card for $4,125. There was no criticism from black voters. When the auctioneer showed the postcard to black teachers at the Brooklyn school where he taught, one teacher said, "It will take more than a postcard to make me vote for Bob Dole.")

Clinton gave his major race speech in San Diego on June 14, 1997, and afterward sat down for six back-to-back media interviews, as McCurry had requested. Clinton had slept little the previous night, however, because he was constantly reworking the speech, and Joe Lockhart, who was now in the White House press office and was in charge of the event, figured Clinton would never sit still for six interviews at the end of a grueling day. The presidency has its perks, and one of them is canceling interviews at the last moment.

But after his speech, Clinton told Lockhart he was ready for all six. He had given his main performance and now was eager to deliver a few encores. The interviews were conducted in a holding room at the Birch Aquarium of the Scripps Institute of Oceanography, and as the reporters waited their turn they wandered around looking at the incredible array of marine life. And when each was finally ushered into Clinton's presence, they would invariably say to him, "Have you had a chance to see the *aquarium*, yet, Mr. President? It's *great.*"

Clinton got through his last interview and Lockhart felt like cheering. The staff was exhausted and the press corps was eager to get back home. But Clinton was in a bubbly mood. He had liked the interviews and had thought that while the reporters showed their usual skepticism, they had taken his race initiative seriously. His legacy had made a good debut.

"Okay," Clinton said, getting up from the table and turning to a worn-out Joe Lockhart, "when do I get to see the fish?"

The press got back to Washington at 2:30 A.M.

DURING THE CAMPAIGN, THE WEEKLY WHITE HOUSE RESIDENCE meetings had become famous. They were called that because they took place in the Yellow Oval Room located in the family quarters, or residence, of the White House. Upper-echelon staff, pollsters, and media consultants would sit around an ornate Louis XVI–style furniture and talk political hardball. A portable screen would be set up and Clinton would be shown slides of his latest polls as well as the latest TV commercials. The mood was always electric, and the subjects practical: What was working, how the money was being spent, how they were stomping the life out of Bob Dole's campaign. After

Clinton's reelection victory, however, the meetings lost much of their purpose. But Clinton insisted on keeping them going.

"The purpose is psychological now," one participant said. "The president enjoys them. It gives him a certain comfort level. But there is no feeling of energy or impact anymore. They are very diminished." The room was still set up in the same way, as if to give Clinton the illusion that there was still a campaign out there, still something to be run for and won. Four wingback chairs were set up in front of the room and were occupied by Clinton, Gore, and chief of staff Erskine Bowles, with the fourth one often left empty. Hillary did not attend, nor did she attend during the campaign. The publication of Bob Woodward's book *The Choice* in the summer of 1996, in which he revealed that Hillary had imaginary conversations with Eleanor Roosevelt and Mahatma Gandhi, profoundly affected the way she operated. "Hillary no longer trusted people within the White House," a White House staffer told me. "She stopped coming to meetings. And Gore operated much the same way. There was a cone of silence around them. They only talked to people in a very small circle of those they felt they could really trust." A similar change was noticed in Clinton, even in the residence meetings, which were supposed to be candid and freewheeling. "The president is much more circumspect even in private and even in front of his staff," an aide said. "He has to figure that one-third of his staff people are negotiating book contracts at any given moment."

The residence meetings focused on what the president was doing now, while the real political operatives on the staff were much more interested in what was going to happen in 2000. They expected a large field of candidates on both sides, with Al Gore being the presumptive front-runner for the Democratic nomination but by no means a sure thing.

"We are on the brink of a new, a profoundly new era," said Doug Sosnik, who was now a presidential counselor as he made preparations to leave the White House. "It's like whether you graduated from college in 1963 or 1965. In 1963, there were still proms, you wore a tuxedo, you listened to Sinatra, and you drank martinis. In 1965, you wore jeans and smoked pot and listened to the Beatles."

In 2000, Sosnik believed, the role of money would be different. Huge fund-raisers, once bragged about by candidates, would be avoided. This would mean that freezing out primary opponents by locking up the big money, as Clinton did in 1996, would be far more difficult. Extensive grassroots field operations raising dollars from small donors would replace the giant fund-raisers. "But money will be less important," Sosnik said. "Message will beat dollars." He saw candidates stressing broad, inspirational themes. "In 2000 it will be slick versus down to earth," Sosnik said. "Slick is out and authenticity is in." In other words, candidates would have to become more adept at looking less adept.

The Republicans in 2000 would face the same dilemma the Democrats faced at the end of 1988: The candidate who wins the primaries by appealing to party activists can't win the general election. The place to be is not near the edges where the activists are, but near the middle where the voters are. The Democrats had headed toward the middle with Bill Clinton. Could the Republicans swallow their pride and their ideology and do the same?

And TV commercials would play even less of a role. "Increasingly people are cynical about paid political messages and are increasingly looking to peer groups, friends, and neighbors for information," Sosnik said. So in 2000 if you could control The Buzz, you might be able to control the election. But how did you do it? Ads and consultants and high-priced staffs were clearly not enough. Bob Dole had all those things. What Bob Dole lacked was an understanding of what moved ordinary voters and an ability to connect with them.

And when I sat down with Dole after the election and asked him why he lost, he used the same excuse he used in 1988, when he had lost a crucial New Hampshire primary to George Bush: It was his bad arm.

"I think I'm a pretty good speaker," Dole said with utter seriousness. "I always felt kind of bad, you know . . . and I don't want to fall back on this but I only have *one hand*. So when he [Clinton] goes down a rope line like this" —Dole made hand-over-hand motions— "I said, boy, I'd like to do that too, but *I can't do it*. So I gotta go *slowly* and I've got to pull my arm *back*. Like I've still got a swollen knuckle from the campaign."

At least Dole correctly recognized that Clinton's rope-line work was important, even if he incorrectly believed his own disability was what was wrong with his campaign. In fact, it had nothing to do with the arm. Dole didn't have to shake with both hands on the rope line, or even with one hand. He could have worked the rope line with his hands in his pockets and just *talked* to people. They would have understood. The fact is, Dole looked upon the rope line as a necessary evil and gave it scant time or attention while Bill Clinton lived for it.

"I think my political instincts are pretty good," Dole said, "but obviously I'm not as deeply into it as Clinton. My view is that there wasn't anything--I don't mean it to be totally critical—but there wasn't much they *wouldn't* do to be elected. And I think there has to be certain limits on ambition."

There are. It's called defeat.

B Y THE SUMMER OF 1997, MIKE MCCURRY WAS SURE HE WAS going to leave the White House. "I am figuring out a way to get off the stage with the audience still applauding," he said. "By the end of 1997, the applause may be diminished." He had few illusions left, not even about why his boss was still doing well in the polls. The booming economy, he admitted, had made things easy for Clinton. "Reagan enjoyed the same type of confidence on the economy," McCurry said, "and he had a relatively easy time because he had a pleasant, pleasing personality. Clinton is more complicated. There was genuine affection for Reagan. There is not the same affection for Clinton." Though McCurry did add that the public had an "appreciation" for what Clinton had done. "And no president will ever again have the affection Reagan had," he added.

Why not? I asked.

"There is not the tendency in the media to regard elected leaders with anything approaching esteem," McCurry said. "There seems to be a campaign to see who can sneer the loudest. It contributes to the sense of 'Where have all the statesmen gone?' This led to the false expectations for Colin Powell, the 'savior' we have been looking for. But Powell will get churned up in 2000 in the meat grinder like everyone else. There will be a huge disappointment."

And Clinton is confident his name will be remembered not for his scandals but for his accomplishments? I asked.

"He is confident because he has done nothing to besmirch his office in a major way," McCurry said. "There will be ethical potholes, but all presidents have that."

And what about the stagecraft? The optics and theatrics? Working the rope line? How do you persuade people that what Clinton did was not just an act?

"Because what he did was *real*," McCurry said. "Interacting with Americans for their vote is *real*. Responding in a human, individual way to people is *real*. These are precious moments in our democracy. The real question is how do we preserve them?"

McCurry said that one of his big frustrations during the campaign was that the press didn't treat the rope line seriously enough. "I actually marketed the rope line," McCurry said. "I asked reporters if they wanted to go along and see him work the rope line. Only two did: Judy Woodruff and Ron Fournier. The others said, 'Oh, the rope line. Who cares?' But on the rope line they would have heard what people were talking about. They weren't talking about Huang and Riady, they were asking, 'What can I do to raise my family?' There were wrenching personal moments on the rope line. You had people saying, 'Look, I've got a mother in a nursing home and I'm real worried.' You've got to have a candidate who can look into someone's heart and soul. The people looked at Dole and they looked at Clinton and they said, 'Who understands me?' And they made their decision."

And they are happy with that decision? I asked.

"The people feel they know what Clinton is about," he said. "He may disappoint them—how could they not have doubts with so many stories? But despite all that, they feel he's trying to take care of people like them."

O N ONE OF THE WORST DAYS OF HIS LIFE, THE DAY HIS MOTHER died, Bill Clinton found he could still think about the stagecraft. It was 2 A.M. and he was talking on the phone to Carolyn Staley, his childhood friend, who was in Russia on a singing tour. "I need to know what Mother would want sung at the service," Clinton said. Staley offered her condolences and her ideas: "Amazing Grace" and "His Eyes on the Sparrow."

"I was struck by how quickly he was into the *planning*," Staley said. " 'Let's plan the music,' he said. And then he started naming singers and who should perform."

Clinton had been president for just under a year and no church in Hot Springs was large enough to hold all those who wanted to attend the service. His mother's pastor, Reverend John Miles, suggested holding the service at the racetrack, his mother's favorite place. ("I am a preacher's kid and he's a gambling woman's son," Staley told me, "but the president is a very spiritually grounded man.") Clinton opted for the Hot Springs Civic Center next to the Hilton Hotel instead. Three thousand people attended.

It was a lovely service. And though few in attendance knew it, Clinton had already planned his own funeral service. Carolyn Staley had given him the idea without even realizing it. Years before, in January 1978, she had watched Hubert Humphrey's funeral service on TV. "I was very drawn to it," she said. "It was a very staid funeral in an Anglican-looking church, everybody behaving very proper and sad and grieving. Then a black choir started singing and it was almost an assault on the senses. They infused the funeral with soul and warmth and realness. Before that, nothing had pulled at my heartstrings, but this made me tear up."

The song the choir sang was "Goin' Up Yonder," a rip-roaring gospel hymn. "It was these black faces saying, 'Let us tell you how *we* face death and how *we* feel,' " Staley said. " 'We want to give our brother Hubert, who died after doing so much for us, a send-off *our* way.' "

Staley told Clinton all about it. Years later, when Clinton was governor, Staley was over at the mansion for dinner one night and, as usual, a few guests gathered around the piano afterward, where Staley played and Clinton sang songs by Peter, Paul, and Mary or "The Green, Green Grass of Home." But this night, Clinton asked Staley to sing "Goin' Up Yonder" for him. She did it from memory in the same style the black chorus had done it for Hubert Humphrey and when she was done, Clinton turned to the other guests and said, "She's going to sing that at my funeral."

Staley was stunned. How could this young, vibrant man with his whole life ahead of him be planning his funeral? Or maybe he was just joking. "Oh, Billy," she said to him with a laugh, "you'll never die."

The years passed and Staley forgot the whole incident. Billy became the forty-second president of the United States and moved to Washington, but he still loved having his old pals come to his house and sit around and talk and play the piano and sing. But after one such White House visit, when Staley was about to go, an aide took her to one side. The president had made his wishes known on the matter of his death. "You're the one we will call," the aide said, "if it should come to that."

Staley still remembered the words and she later sang them for me:

> *If you want to know*
> *Where I'm going*
> *Where I'm going soon*
> *If anybody asks you where I'm going soon*
>
> *I'm going up yonder*
> *I'm going up yonder*
> *I'm going up yonder*
> *To meet with my Lord*

I can take the pain, the
heartache life brings.
The comfort comes in
knowin' I'll soon be there.

Bill Clinton had planned his last performance.

ACKNOWLEDGMENTS

I MADE MY FIRST TRIP FOR THIS BOOK ON AUGUST 10, 1995, TO A Ross Perot rally in Dallas, Texas, and made my last trip nearly two years later on July 17, 1997, to Pittsburgh and Chicago, where Bill Clinton gave back-to-back speeches to the NAACP and the National Association of Black Journalists. In between those trips, I came across some of the most generous people in America.

These were people who were willing to share with me their time, their thoughts, their insights, their friendship, and in some cases even their notes and interviews. I owe them a special debt of gratitude. Along with the candidates for president themselves, I would like to thank: Dan Balz, Jodi Enda, Mike Tackett, Susan Baer, Jack Torry, G. Robert Hillman, Debra Rosenberg, Susan Feeney, Michael McCurry, Stephen Merrill, Joe McQuaid, Joe Lockhart, Doug Sosnik, Signe McQuaid, Nackey Loeb, Michael Sheehan, Nelson Warfield, Josh King, Larry King, Juli Mortz and the staff of *Larry King Live*, Bill Daley, Richard M. Daley, Harold Ickes, Janice Enright, George Stephanopoulos, Harry Thomason, Rahm Emanuel, Julie Mason, Michelle Crisci, Ann Lewis, Carolyn Staley, David Leopoulos, Rick Berke, Adam Nagourney, Ceci Connolly, Bruce Morrison, Elizabeth Arnold, Mark Z. Barabak, Don Sipple, Ben Roth, Mark Starr, Angus King, Lisa Anderson, Harvey Benenson, Joel Benenson, Steve Duchesne, Dick Polman, Steve Thomma, James Warren, Tom Hardy, Flynn McRoberts, Ellen Warren, Joe Kirby, Ron Fournier, Mike Briggs, Nancy Balz, Chuck Raasch, Cragg Hines, Ariane DeVogue, Terry Michael, Greg Mueller, Richard Cohen, Karen Koshner, Brian Kelly, Pat Wingert, Rick Kogan, Collette Rhoney, David Axelrod, Michelle Apostolos, Maralee Schwartz, Kerry Digrazia, Paul Galloway, Paul Risley, Peter Moore, Joan Gartlan, Eleanor Randolph, Bob Reeder, April Ryan, George

Condon, John Harris, Scott Reed, Laura Blumenfeld, Gwen Ifill, Carl Cannon, Mark Meritt, Heidi Kukis, Terence Samuel, Dan Solomon, Tim Poor, Debra Cohn, Mike Abramowitz, Amy Bayer, Lori Anderson, Tom Brokaw, Tim Russert, Tammy Haddad, Kate Kelly, Max Kelly, Karen Hosler, John King, Jim Loftus, John Harwood, Terry Holt, Steve Hirsh, Carl Leubsdorf, Jill Zuckman, Jake Thompson, Basil Talbott Jr., Lynn Sweet, John Buckley, Jenny Rider, Brigid Schulte, Bob Goodwin, Susan Swain, Michael Kinsley and *Slate* magazine, Mike Kelly and *The New Republic*, Carl Cameron, Janet Clinton, Virgil Spurlin, Edith Irons, Marty Walker, Karla Clinton Searcy, Betty Kate Carney, George Frazier, the Institute of Politics at Harvard University's Kennedy School of Government, and Group Nine of the National Issues Convention in Austin, Texas.

I also found the following books both excellent reading and very helpful: *See How They Ran* by Gil Troy, *First in His Class* by David Maraniss, *Unlimited Partners* by Bob and Elizabeth Dole, *The Choice* by Bob Woodward, *Leading with My Heart* by Virginia Clinton Kelley, and Daniel Boorstin's *The Image*. The special post-election issues of *Newsweek* and *Time* were also especially well done in 1996.

At Times Books I am very grateful to Harold Evans, Peter Bernstein, Luke Mitchell, Nancy Inglis, and Geoff Shandler. And to my longtime friends and colleagues at Creators Syndicate, Rick Newcombe, Anita Tobias, Mike Santiago, and Katherine Searcy, I send my thanks. I am also grateful to Westlaw for access to its invaluable database.

Two people were absolutely indispensable to this book: Bob Barnett, my agent and friend, without whom this book never would have been published; and Marcia Kramer, my wife, editor, and best friend, without whom I wouldn't have wanted to write it.

INDEX

ABOUT THE AUTHOR

ROGER SIMON is a nationally syndicated columnist. He was formerly a staff columnist at *The Baltimore Sun* and an investigative reporter and columnist at the *Chicago Sun-Times*. He lives in Bethesda, Maryland.